SPIRIT OF PLACE

Lawrence Durrell

SPIRIT OF PLACE

Letters and Essays on Travel

Edited by Alan G. Thomas

LEETE'S ISLAND BOOKS
New Haven, Connecticut

Published by Leete's Island Books, Inc.
Box 1131, New Haven, Ct. 06505

ISBN 0-918172-17-9

Library of Congress Catalog Card Number:
84-081240

Contents

SPIRIT OF PLACE

Preface

Lawrence Durrell has achieved success in many forms of literature—
nullum tetigit quod non ornavit—and one of his most striking qualities as
a writer lies in his ability to render scenery and the feel of places. His
early years were spent in India, and since 1935 his total residence in
England can hardly add up to more than a year or so. In the meantime
he has lived in Corfu, Greece, Paris, Egypt, Rhodes, the Argentine,
Yugoslavia, Cyprus and the Midi. Before the publication of *The
Alexandria Quartet*, in which the city itself looms almost larger than the
human characters, Durrell was most widely known for his books about
Greek islands; these are not so much travel books, 'it would be far more
accurate', as Richard Aldington remarked, 'to describe them as "foreign-
residence" books.'

In addition to Durrell's books, a number of articles describing
scenery, generally Aegean or Mediterranean, have appeared in magazines, small privately printed pamphlets, and so forth. These essays
and sketches are now gathered for the first time in book form. To
provide something of the setting in which they were written I have
collected passages from letters which Durrell has written to his friends
over the last thirty years and linked them together with some brief
biographical notes and a few memories of my own.

One of the difficulties which confronts any editor of Durrell's letters
is the fact that he almost never dates them. T. S. Eliot, with a kindly
eye on future scholars, had the admirable habit of noting the date of
receipt; in some cases postmarked envelopes have survived, in others
there are internal clues, while Durrell's frequent movements from one
country to another provide a general framework into which most
letters can be fitted. I know that some of my conjectures may well prove
inaccurate, but hope that almost all the letters have been dated within
a year of their having been written.

I have had one advantage not generally available to literary editors.

[11]

When work on this book was well advanced Durrell came to stay with me, here in Chelsea, for a month, and I was able to consult him regarding the queries which had accumulated; indecipherable words, mistakes in typing, obscure references etc. For example, a hand-written letter from Cyprus contains the sentence: '. . . Rose Macaulay? She adopted us and whizzed us off to bxxxe in her old car.' I scanned the map of Cyprus and read through a guide trying to find a place-name beginning with b (Durrell often fails to capitalize) and ending with e, but in vain. I asked Durrell to read the passage: '. . . whizzed us off to bathe.' In an account of shooting in Corfu, in 1936, one typewriter key had failed to strike home: 'So far I've prohibited herons. They're such heraldic creatures, and when they're wounded they use their great razor bill like a tailor. I shot a couple and one chased Leslie and nea ly, nipped him in the arse.' Was this word nearly or neatly I asked. 'How can I remember what I meant to say more than thirty years ago? Put "neatly nipped him in the arse", that will annoy Les if he ever reads it.' My friend John Bradley, the editor of Ruskin's letters, was also staying in the house at the time, and this unfair advantage almost drove him round the bend. When *he* gets stuck he can't run downstairs and ask Ruskin. Just as well perhaps as he has a very attractive young daughter.

No attempt has been made to identify all persons and places mentioned, thus loading down every page with notes, or, worse still, putting them at the end. This is intended to be a readable book; not a definitive edition. Besides, time is too pressing; I am not in the position of one scholar I know who gained a Guggenheim which enabled him to spend two years in Rome working on *one* Milton letter.

Several of Durrell's friends have helped with suggestions and elucidations, and in particular Dr. Theodore Stephanides has placed his knowledge of Greece, the Middle East and the Greek language at my disposal. But consulting Theodore is a rich pleasure in itself, for some small question about dating or a reference to mythology unlocks a flood of erudite or amusing memories, and it seems as if he carries the whole of Greece in his mind. I would also like to thank my secretary, Shirley Ossipoff, for her stalwart help in copying the letters and for her enthusiastic devotion to the book in general; Mrs. Rose Briggs, who read both typescript and proofs, has made a valiant attempt at coping with my inability to spell.

But especially I am indebted to those of Durrell's friends who, having kept his letters over the years, have now placed them at my disposal. Catha Aldington and Alister Kershaw for letters to Richard Aldington, Mrs. T. S. Eliot for letters to her husband, John Gawsworth, Diana Gould (Mrs. Menuhin), Mary Hadkinson, Alfred Perlès, Hugh Gordon Porteus, Lawrence Clark Powell, Anne Ridler, Patricia Rodda, Lady Smart for letters to Sir Walter Smart, Freya Stark, Theodore Stephanides, Buffie and Gerald Sykes, Mrs. George Wilkinson for letters to her husband, and Gwyn Williams.

The debt of future literary scholars to Hugh Gordon Porteus might well have been greater, for he received many letters from fellow poets and accumulated a good deal of material when writing his excellent life of Wyndham Lewis. He sorted all this original material into two groups, important and less important. Unfortunately he placed the former in a paper bag similar to the kind he used for the disposal of garbage. He returned home one evening to find that his charlady had given this to the dustmen.

Many of Durrell's letters already repose in the rare book rooms of American University Libraries; and it is a pleasure to thank the librarians concerned for their courtesy and kindness in allowing me to print the letters which they have preserved. Especially those of The University of California at Los Angeles, for letters written to John Gawsworth, Lawrence Clark Powell and Theodore Stephanides, of The Academic Center Library of The University of Texas, at Austin, for letters to Patricia Rodda and Alfred Perlès, and to Mr. Frank Paluka, of The University of Iowa, for letters to George Wilkinson. Some of the pieces now printed for the first time in book form were originally published in journals, and I am grateful to their editors, especially to the editor of *Holiday Magazine*, who have kindly allowed them to appear here; more detailed acknowledgements appear at the head of each essay. In a few places the texts have been revised slightly. I would also like to thank Lawrence Clark Powell and F.-J. Temple who produced the original, privately printed, editions of *A Landmark Gone*, *Beccafico* and *Down the Styx*.

Early Days

Lawrence Durrell was born in India, at Jalunda, in the United Provinces, on the 27th of February 1912: the families of both his parents having been long established in that country. He is sometimes described as an 'Irish Poet', but, although his mother's family is of Irish extraction, he has never set foot in Ireland itself. His father was an engineer of uncommon ability whose magnum opus *was the building of the Tata Iron and Steel Works. When his eldest son was still quite a small boy, Mr. Durrell, senior, moved his family to Kurseong where he had a three-year contract for engineering work on the mountain railway that snakes its way up to Darjeeling through the lower slopes over the Himalayas. The immense snow-covered peaks which filled the northern horizon during his childhood made a deep impression that has lasted with Durrell all his life.*

In early boyhood he attended the Jesuit College at Darjeeling, and it was here that he received his first encouragement in literature from Father Joseph De Guylder, a Belgian schoolmaster of unusual perception and sympathy.

At the age of twelve Durrell was sent 'home', together with his younger brother Leslie, 'to get the hall-mark' as his father used to say, by going to a public school. The two boys were lodged, in somewhat Spartan conditions, at Dulwich, and during his first year in England Durrell attended St. Olave's and St. Saviour's Grammar School. This is situated in Southwark, more or less on the site of the early theatres; in the lunch hour the young boy used to spend much of his time in Southwark Cathedral, which contains the tomb of Gower; and it was here that he first fell in love with the Elizabethans. He next proceeded to his public school, St. Edmund's, Canterbury. Here he was bored and fairly unhappy at school; but his ability as a boxer, promoted during the holidays by the training and expertise of Stone, the family manservant, preserved him from the bullying that all too often constitutes the lot of sensitive boys who do not conform to tribal conventions.

After the early death of his father Durrell inherited a small income, left school, and went to live in Bloomsbury with the ambition of becoming a writer. It was the Bloomsbury of John Gawsworth, King of Redonda, Count Cedric

Potocki of Montalk,* the Polish Royalist, Mulk Raj Anand and other characters.

Having an ability to do many things with dash and brio *Durrell augmented his income by a number of jobs; as a self-taught pianist he worked for some time in the Blue Peter Night Club, and many of the jazz songs which he played were of his own composition. He met Nancy Myers, then a student at the Slade, who was to become his first wife, and for some time they ran a photographic studio together.*

Durrell, himself, gives a lively picture of his Bloomsbury days in the following essay contributed to an, as yet unpublished, volume celebrating the fiftieth birthday of John Gawsworth.

* Now of Draguignan and Lovelace's Copse, Plush Bottom, Dorset. See: *The Private Library*, Spring 1967.

Some Notes on My Friend
John Gawsworth
1962

Some notes on my friend John Gawsworth may not be out of place in this compilation as I have been a friend of his for nearly thirty years, during which we both have been through a number of ups and downs. I first met him when I was about nineteen I suppose; he was my first Real Writer—a professional, living by his books. I say 'living', but the word should have some qualification, for he barely existed on his work, inhabiting an old attic in Denmark Street, with a huge dormer window and a rotting wooden floor through which seeped the noise of jazz being played by Percival Mackay's band rehearsing downstairs. I was a complete literary novice and a provincial and the meeting was an important one for me, for in John I found someone who burned with a hard gem-like flame—the very thing I wished to do myself; moreover his gem-like burnings then were sufficiently good to merit the attention of real publishers, while my post-Imagist maunderings and occasional derivative sonnets did not.

I had moved to London at the behest of my mother who, tired of my antics, said one day: 'You can be as Bohemian as you like but *not in the house*. I think you had better go somewhere where it doesn't show so much.' So I left Bournemouth to study Bohemianism at first hand. I had some help in my researches from a young and beautiful student of the Slade School whom I married; but while we weren't actually starving money was short, so she went on the stage as a temporary measure and I played the piano very inexpertly in the Blue Peter Night Club in St. Martin's Lane. My engagement was a brief one as the police closed the club down, though fortunately the raid took place while I was near an upstairs window, or I might have started my professional studies with a prison sentence. This explains why John and I met at about three in the morning in the Windmill Café, drinking coffee, for it was here that I first ran into John. He was correcting the galley-proofs of a book with a heavy self-commiserating air and drinking black coffee. I watched him fascinated; I had never seen galleys. Soon he borrowed a match and we got into conversation. I soon began to congratulate myself as I heard him talk, for it seemed that he knew everybody of importance. He had actually met Yeats and Hardy; he had corresponded with poets like de la Mare and Drinkwater; he knew Wyndham Lewis on whom he was doing an essay. He had *seen* Eliot! I was agog. I was in the presence of a Real Writer, someone who could tell me something about literary life in the capital. We got very friendly right off, though I remember wondering what a Real Writer could see in a callow youth of nineteen—though a pretty wife is quite a help in moments like these. We walked back, the three of us, to his little attic and there by the light of a flickering gas-jet he showed me an enviable collection of treasures in the way of first editions, manuscripts and letters of famous poets, and also a number of literary curiosities which he had picked up in the sale rooms which he regularly frequented; he had a skull-cap of Dickens', a pen of Thackeray's and so on. . . . He even had a ring belonging to Emma Hamilton which afterwards I unfortunately lost for him, but he was a very good-natured person and didn't blame me. Nor did he ask me to pay for it.

At this time John was just staking his claim as a poet, bibliographer and essayist and had big plans for the future, but he did not seem to have many friends of his own age. His literary admirers and acquaintances were for the most part elderly, and while they were always glad to see him they were not the sort of people to enjoy squatting on the floor and drinking beer: few of them existed, as we mostly did, on Smith's Potato Crisps. This is probably why he allowed me to hang about, drinking in through every pore the thrilling literary information which he disbursed so liberally.

In physique he was of medium height and somewhat pale and lean; he had a broken nose which gave his face a touch of Villonesque foxiness. His eyes were brown and bright, and his sense of humour unimpaired by his literary privations. At that time he was an ardent student of the nineties, and looked forward rather hopefully to a Dowsonesque death by alcohol or the dagger. In fact as a poet he was proud to proclaim himself a post-nineties man rather than a modern poet; but the death by alcohol evaded him. He was relatively abstemious as poets go, and enjoyed good health too much to take absinthe. He had just published a sequence of love-lyrics called *Kingcup* which I admired extravagantly, and which had won him both a prize and election to the Royal Society of Literature. He must have been by far the youngest Fellow for in those days one had to be a hundred before achieving such an apotheosis. But this honour was more valuable to others than to himself for it gave him a leverage on his elders which few young writers then possessed; and apart from the hard gem-like flame John burned with a passionate ardour for literature itself. The faintest whisper that told of a writer in straits alerted him like a foxhound; he had a very special look at such times. A mixture of ferocity and brute determination irradiated his features. He would drop everything and work night and day until he found some help for the writer in question. 'I think', he would mutter, 'I'll just pop round and see Abercrombie or Masefield' (I am inventing the names at random). At any rate he was always 'popping' somewhere to 'fix' something. He was one of nature's lobbyers—a tireless and relentless fellow. I am sure that on many occasions the Royal Society groaned as they saw him coming down the street; they probably locked the front door and got under sofas. Lobby, lobby, lobby. He would not rest until petitions had been devised, signed and distributed; moreover he was cunning and knew how to use the press. I can think of several writers who owe him thanks for a pension in their old age. He literally wore out his elders with his assiduities, and bent them into reasonable attitudes by force of will.

His royalism also chimed with his literary attitude; even when he was very poor he would rise at dawn and pad down to Covent Garden to buy a large white rose to place upon the statue of Charles I; this, of course, on the anniversary of the King's execution. He was full of little gestures like these, though he seldom spoke of them to others. A real Romantic. I thought this was splendid, and still do. But the romantic side was offset by a brain as sharp as an awl when it came to any matter which touched on publishers or publishing. He knew the whole business backwards. I do not think he would have been able to avoid having to take a job otherwise. But while he never spoke of poverty, and was always neatly dressed and properly shined of shoe, he was often in great straits. At such times he would depend on his gift for bibliography to provide his breakfast. This was a truly remarkable side to his character. He literally picked up a few pounds in a matter of moments from the threepenny boxes outside the bookshops in the Charing Cross Road. This was a feat I never tired of watching, and I suppose I must have watched him at it about a dozen times; more than once when I was broke I shared his bibliographic breakfast. This was what he did. He would stand for a moment over a threepenny box of throw-outs, barely touching them with his fingers. His hands became all sensitive like a pianist's. Then he would give an expert riffle here and there like a cardsharper. Finally he would pick out a book and mutter. 'Edward Carpenter. Hum . . . Carpenter. . . . That must be the 1915. Christ! that is the mispaginated edition surely.' If it was he would add quietly: 'About thirty bob I should say.' He would take a twenty minute patrol down Charing Cross Road and on his return sell the books to Foyle's Rare Book Department. His memory for bibliography was simply amazing, and had he cared to be a bookseller he would now be the greatest one in England. Of course, his haul varied each day, but I should say on an average this breakfast patrol never brought him in less than a pound; yet I myself was with him on two occasions when he made finds which earned him very much larger sums. One was Mary Shelley's *Frankenstein* in three volumes (a first), and the other a rare edition of *Dracula*. This was a fine and flexible way to start off the day, and the proceeds would provide bacon and eggs and coffee at the Windmill Café.

John helped me to print my first wretched fascicules which are now fetching ridiculous sums among collectors; I don't believe either of us have any copies ourselves today, and the stock was mercifully blitzed during the war. He also got a few of my poems into youthful anthologies. Even though he knew my work was weak he was always kind and considerate to me at a time when he need not really have bothered. Certainly I did not merit any sort of attention then. But he was also valuable to me in another way for he was a walking literary calendar of London, and seemed to have a gigantic mental file of anniversaries tucked away in his brain. Thus we would drink to Dr. Johnson on appropriate days in Lambs Conduit Street, or eat a chop in the memory of Sheridan or Goldsmith whenever the requisite moment dawned. I can hardly think of London even today without remembering these walks, those visits to remote chop houses or pubs; he always knew where to knock up a glass of Burgundy ('Machen came here every day') in Fleet Street, or a glass of Canary ('Try this: Ouida's favourite tipple') in Cheapside. He was as much of a Londoner as Lamb or Leigh Hunt or Hazlitt—and indeed he never tired of talking about them and their London, and comparing it to the rushing and grubby city in whose rainswept streets he walked, determined to carry on the great tradition they had left us.

His activities at that time were multiform and the pace at which he lived was astonishing; part of his day was spent on research of the nineties, and the rest in literary pursuits. He was responsible for the reissue of work by a number of good poets of his chosen period—like Canon Gray and Richard Middleton, as well as a number of discoveries of little-known texts and stories which, but for him, would have perished completely. But he was also keeping a hawk-like eye on a number of his elders, just to make sure that they were not starving. I remember him disappearing for a week-end to visit Arthur Machen in Buckinghamshire whom he suspected of being too proud to ask for help at a time when he (John) knew full well that the old writer was in grave financial difficulties. He just wanted to make quite sure before going down to terrorize those people at the Royal Society of Literature.

In matters of literary theory we had our differences though these made no difference to our friendship and generated no heat whatsoever; it was impossible to quarrel with someone so good-natured. John's passion for the nineties had made him something like an anachronism poetically; I mean it was odd for a youth of twenty to be copying Dowson at that time as he was and ignoring Eliot, Yeats, Lawrence. But the only time when I saw him really incensed was when *New Signatures* was published containing the work of university poets unknown, like Auden, Spender etc. He felt then that the very head-springs of poesy were being polluted by this sort of stuff and that some sort of answering broadside should come from those stern traditionalists who stood for English unmashed, unsquashed, pure! His own favourite poets then were not bad poets as poets go, but when he assembled them the result was rather weak and wishy-washy. It was, to say the least of it, a queer idea to hit Mr. Auden with John Freeman and Mr. Spender with Harold Monro. But despite these sometimes wrong-headed ploys his essential good nature and his passion for literature remained undamaged. One day when he was being rather tedious about the university poets I told him that I had recently heard that both Mr. Auden and Mr. Spender were in great straits, in fact virtually starving in adjoining garrets in Wapping. At once his expression changed. 'Are you sure?' he asked hoarsely. 'Positive,' I replied solemnly. His face took on the look I knew so well. Matters of literary principle were one thing, but starvation among writers quite another. 'I think', he said *sotto voce*, 'that I'll just pop round and see Masefield and Abercrombie. . . .' Of course, I confessed that I was lying before he did so.

Among the odder romantic histories of that epoch none was more beguiling than the story of the island of Redonda, of which John is now King—in exile of course. The father of M. P. Shiel the novelist had seized an island of this name in the Caribbean. He had declared himself a sovereign King. But when phosphates were discovered on the place the British Government took the island away from him. Shiel refused to relinquish his kingdom and a furious debate with the Colonial Office began which doubtless continues to this day; on the death of the old man, M P. Shiel declared himself rightful King of Redonda, and created a number of dukes to help him carry on the battle. John came across Shiel in the course of his nineties researches and vastly admired his work, which later he edited for the press. When I first met John he was in close touch with the exiled King who, as far as I understood the matter, was then living on fruit and nuts in a tree near Horsham. John frequently visited him to discuss literary matters—though whether he climbed the tree or whether Shiel came down to earth to talk to him I forgot to ask. . . . At any rate Shiel must have seen the makings of a wise King in my friend for on his death he left the throne to John on condition that the battle over Redonda continued. To this end John now began to create dukes whose duties consisted of bombarding the Colonial Office with memoranda about this wicked injustice. As the prevailing temper of his mind was largely literary it was natural that for the most part he showered these honours upon writers he admired. We are a motley lot, we dukes of Redonda. Unfortunately, just after he had honoured me with the title of Duke of Cervantes Pequeña he ran into financial difficulties which prevented him from engrossing the titles on parchment, as was apparently customary; thus to this day I am still lacking armorial bearings, and do not know what the devices on my shield should be. A duke without benefit of heraldry feels rather naked. But perhaps this is just as well. I could see even then some rather acrimonious passage-at-arms with the College of Heralds over these dukedoms.

Our ways separated after this period and we met rarely, usually when I was back in England on leave from some foreign posting or other. John turned up in Cairo briefly during the war and we met once or twice; but these were glancing blows, so to speak, as he was in the RAF and being moved about like a pawn. In the post-war period he hit a long patch of ill-health and wretched luck which is probably why he published so little work. My last glimpse of him was about six years ago. I saw my King walking down Shaftesbury Avenue wheeling a pram—a large Victorian pram. I thought to myself: 'Ah, my dear John; life has caught up with you as well. Like the rest of us you have shackled yourself with children, three lots of twins I'll be bound, and have been forced to walk them in the Park instead of writing the sonnet you had in mind.' But judge my relief when I caught up with him, for the pram contained nothing more sinister than a mountain of beer bottles—empties which he was on his way to sell. We were delighted to see each other, and of course repaired to a pub to celebrate. It happened to be someone's anniversary, so we drank several glasses of wine to the shade of . . . was it Gibbon? I forget. Yet despite this long period of bad health and bad luck John was still very much his old self, still gay and amusing and full of typical quirky ideas. There were a few dukedoms still going, and he solemnly created my brother a duke as we stood at the bar.

At closing time, much refreshed, we parted. John's pram had been liberally re-stocked with a vital, life-giving stout; he wheeled it off into the dusk at a leisurely pace, stopping at the corner to wave a royal hand.

Floreat!

At length, having had their fill of English bohemian life Durrell and Nancy cut loose and spent a year with their friends George and Pam Wilkinson in a cottage at Loxwood in Sussex. Here Durrell wrote the greater part of his first novel, Pied Piper of Lovers; *and, in collaboration with Wilkinson and the Bloomsbury bookseller J. A. Allen, founded The Caduceus Press which issued two slim volumes of his early poems:* Ten Poems, *1932, and* Transition, *1934.*

Shortly after the death of her husband Mrs. Durrell (Mother) had left India and brought her family home to England; settling, after one or two hesitations, in Bournemouth. Meanwhile, at the end of a year, the foursome at Loxwood broke up, George and Pam Wilkinson emigrating to Corfu while Durrell and Nancy joined the family.

H. G. Commin, where I was then working, is an old-fashioned bookshop, with a nineteenth-century atmosphere; tens of thousands of books filling the whole of five floors. Customers were free to wander at will, so little molested by pressure to buy that we occasionally locked them in when we went home at night. Working hours were long in those days, but a good deal of our time was spent in congenial conversation with fellow spirits. Once he had discovered the shop Durrell, generally accompanied by Nancy, came in almost every day; and in a short time I was spending almost every evening and week-end with the family.

There never was more generous hospitality. Whatever Dr. F. R. Leavis may think about Durrell's writing, nobody who has known the family at all well could deny that their company is 'life-enhancing'. All six members of the family were remarkable in themselves, but in lively reaction to each other the whole was greater than the sum of the parts. Amid the gales of Rabelaisian laughter, the wit, Larry's songs accompanied by piano or guitar, the furious arguments and animated conversations going on far into the night, I felt that life had taken on a new dimension. Larry was writing, Nancy painting, Leslie crooning, like a devoted mother, over his collection of unlicensed firearms. One day he borrowed, from the shop, a book called Tombstone *which described life in an American western town, and I remember his delight on discovering that the most infamous bad man in those parts was known as 'two-gun Leslie'. Every basin in the house was unusable because Gerry, then only a little boy, but already an animal collector, had filled them with newts, tadpoles and such-like; he roped me in to serve as a giant in the circus which he organised in the garage. Margaret, realizing that book-learning was no part of her world, was rebelling about returning to school, and soon succeeded, backed by the rest of the family, in staying put.*

While one could hardly say that Mrs. Durrell was in control of her family, it was her warm-hearted character, her amused but loving tolerance that held them together; even during the occasional flare-ups of Irish temper. I remember Gerry, furious with Larry who, wanting to wash, had pulled the plug out of a basin full of marine life. Spluttering with ungovernable rage, almost incoherent, searching for the most damaging insult in his vocabulary: 'You, you (pause), you AUTHOR, YOU'.

Nancy was a striking and beautiful girl, very tall and slim, with a clear white complexion and light blonde hair; more than once I have heard people in the street call out as we passed: 'Look—Garbo.' While in Bournemouth, Durrell and Nancy were married. It seems rather absurd, now, looking back, that they insisted on a secret wedding. Children, then as now, were in revolt against their elders, but nobody could feel themselves in opposition to so humanely tolerant a woman as Mrs. Durrell—who would have rejoiced in the wedding anyway. I was sworn to secrecy and asked to act as a witness. Then there was some perturbation because Nancy and I were both a good deal taller than Durrell; none of us knew anything about the marriage ceremony; we might find, at the end of all the uncomprehended rigmarole, that the registrar had joined Nancy and me by mistake, without our realizing it. With a view to avoiding any such contingency we approached a couple of midgets, then appearing in a freak-show at the local fun-fair, and asked them to act as witnesses; but their employer refused to allow such valuable assets out of his sight.

Passionately interested in mediaeval architecture, I introduced Durrell to Christchurch Priory, the Norman parts of which were built by Ranulph Flambard as a trial run for Durham Cathedral. We used to get permission from the Vicar to go up through the cavernous space between the vaulting and the roof timbers and then out onto the leads, clambering over walls and buttresses. From this height a wide view extends over the little town, the water-meadows, the marshes and Christchurch harbour. Often, on those autumnal Saturday afternoons, we stayed aloft until it was almost dark, descending by spiral staircases into the great church as a few scattered worshippers gathered for evensong. It is this picture of England that Durrell recalls in his letter to me in The Black Book. And it was from this point of departure that we each set out in different directions, he into the future, I back into the past.

Corfu and England

*There were no ties binding the Durrell family to England; none of them had been born here, and Larry, having put down no roots, was feeling restless. From time to time a letter would arrive from George Wilkinson describing their idyllic life in Corfu, and the island began to sound more and more evocative. Naturally I was very loath to lose the most brilliant and exciting friends it had ever been my good fortune to make, and I attempted to counter their plans with a few feeble arguments. 'Alan,' retorted Durrell, 'think of the times in England when every-*body that you know *has got a cold.' Wilkinson's latest letter had described the orange groves surrounding his villa. I was silenced.*

Early in 1935 Durrell and Nancy set out as an advance guard, travelling by sea to Brindisi, where they were held up for some time by the revolution then taking place in Greece. The rest of the family followed a few weeks later. Durrell's first novel, Pied Piper of Lovers, *was still under consideration by Cassell's when he left, but their offer to publish came through shortly afterwards, in time for me to send a message which caught up with the family,* en route, *at Naples; this enabled them to announce the good news on their arrival in Corfu.*

It is difficult to believe that any place in the world today can rival Corfu, as it was then, as an elysium for a young writer and a young painter. It was not only warmer and sunnier than Bournemouth, it was cheaper. Durrell had a private income of about £150 a year, Nancy an allowance of £50; on the combined sum of £4 a week they lived in comfort and at ease in their own villa, and their outgoings covered a maidservant and a sailing-boat—the Van Norden.

Corfu is greener and more fertile than the sunburned islands of the Aegean, and the higher economic level, together with certain residual advantages left over from the Venetian and British occupations, provided a greater degree of amenity than was then to be found in the starker islands farther south. Skilled medical attention, for example, was afforded by the presence of Doctor Theodore Stephanides. But, for the Durrells, Theodore became much more than a physician; for one would be hard pressed to find a more erudite, civilized and charming man;

a mine of every kind of knowledge relating to the island, he became the perfect friend and mentor of their new world.

But it was not only the lyrical beauty of Corfu and the prismatic clarity of Greek light that appealed to Durrell; nor even the eternal legends handed down from classical times but intimately wedded to the landscape of today; there were qualities in the character of the modern Greeks themselves which struck deep chords with his own nature; so that Greece and the Greeks have formed one of the major influences in Durrell's life and writing. His own feeling for Corfu has been expressed in the most poetic and least troubled of his island books: Prospero's Cell; *but the day-to-day life of the family has been vividly described in Gerald Durrell's* My Family and Other Animals, *the continued success of which is partly due to the fact that it provides the perfect 'escape book'. Most people set out with high hopes in their youth—they will not be caged in the rat race; but all too often disillusion sets in, they marry, produce a family, give hostages to fortune, and ultimately face the realization that they are going to live out their lives as strap-hanging commuters. And here is this fantastic family living an uproarious life in magical surroundings; so long as the book lasts the reader, too, can live in Arcadia. Again and again, people who came into my bookshop would ask me: 'Is it true? Was it really like that?' From my own brief experience of life on the island I can certainly affirm that the book is true in essence; but Theodore Stephanides, who was in Corfu for the whole time, confirms that virtually every incident described really took place. Not necessarily in the same order, of course, not in one uninterrupted series, but it all actually happened.*

Cassell's published Pied Piper of Lovers *in 1935 (the dust-jacket bearing a design by Nancy); it received little notice and only a few copies were sold. As the greater part of the edition was destroyed when Cassell's warehouse went up in the London blitz, it has become a rare book, sought after by libraries and collectors, and therefore valuable. In later years, in the hope of supplying one or two of the requests which so frequently reached me as an antiquarian bookseller, I wrote round to those friends who had bought copies of the book when it came out. Their replies might well form the basis of a short essay on how books become rare: '. . . unfortunately I left it in a train'; '. . . when we were divorced my wife took the fiction and I kept the non-fiction'; 'All my possessions were destroyed when a furniture repository in Jersey was burned to the ground.' (Lord Jersey's great Rubens went in the same holocaust). Meanwhile Durrell was at work on a second novel, the landscape and general ambience of which were largely influenced by Corfu. The provisional title went through a variety of forms, Phoenix and the Nightingale, Music in Limbo, but it was finally published, by Faber's in 1937, as* Panic Spring. *Early books by young writers are generally derivative to a greater or lesser extent, and Durrell's second novel owes a good deal to Aldous Huxley and Norman Douglas; but the original quality which does begin to emerge is a remarkable capacity for rendering scenery. As this is also a scarce book, and as Durrell does not intend to reprint either of his early novels, a number of selected passages, mainly those describing landscape, are reprinted here.*

But life on Corfu had one more gift for Durrell. He had the good fortune to live at leisure, free from all outside pressures, free from the need to write for money or work to a date-line, while he matured and finished his first important book, written under a number of provisional titles, Lover Anubis, Anubis, Anabasis, until it emerged as The Black Book. *As John Unterecker was to say:* 'The writing of it was in an odd way both a consequence of spiritual agony and a labour of love. For Durrell had no expectation that any publisher would risk bringing out a book so savage in spirit and so uncompromising in language. It was, in this sense at least, the purest work that Durrell was ever to do; it was a demonstration, principally for Lawrence Durrell's private benefit, that he had the potential of becoming a major writer.'

Durrell sent the only typescript to Henry Miller in Paris, telling him to pitch it into the Seine if he did not approve. Miller was enthusiastic, he urged upon Durrell the importance of retaining his integrity, of not compromising, of not allowing an expurgated edition. He put aside the writing of his own Tropic of Capricorn, *and, helped by Anaïs Nin, typed out three copies, one each for Herbert Read, T. S. Eliot and Jack Kahane. Kahane was persuaded to publish* The Black Book *in Paris, and Miller saw it through the press himself. In due course copies 'in plain wrappers' began to filter into England and America where Cyril Connolly and T. S. Eliot buttressed Miller's high opinion with their own tributes: Eliot writing:* '[it] is the first piece of work by a new English writer to give me any hope for the future of prose fiction.'

When The Black Book *was reprinted in Paris after the war Durrell wrote in the new preface:* 'This novel—after twenty-odd years—still has a special importance for me and may yet leave its mark upon the reader who can recognize it for what it is: a two fisted-attack on literature by an angry young man of the 'thirties. . . . With all its imperfections lying heavy on its head, I can't help being attached to it because in the writing of it I first heard the sound of my own voice, lame and halting perhaps, but nevertheless my very own. This is an experience no artist ever forgets—the birth-cry of a newly born baby of letters, the genuine article.'

[28]

To George Wilkinson.   [Bournemouth 1934 ?]

. . . Anent ourselves: Corfu is the ideal place to use as a base for Mediterranean exploration: Nancy is rabid to examine the traces of early Byzantine painting down that coast of Greece, while I am mad to get to Knossos and examine the traces of a Minoan civilization, of which by this time I'm quite sure, my ancestors were a part. Do you know that the average height of the race was five four? Think it over. They were sturdy and lustful, and had a vital art of their own, which owes practically nothing to the huge contemporary civilizations around it. Only one more discovery will complete my certainty & happiness: did they wear silver candle-snuffers upon their most wholesome privities? I pray hourly that they did.

I'm doing my level best to assemble a huge small library to bring out, so that we'll have food for study & delight. I'm planning a specialized essay on Elizabethan writers, not because I hanker for the scholarly life, or a scholarly reputation, but because I've been reading so much lately that it helps to pour it into some sort of mould. It is also teaching me to concentrate, which is a valuable thing, hitherto neglected. I've got a great number of valuable reprints by scurrying round, and a *huge facsimile* Shakespeare fourteen ins. high by nine wide by nearly three thick . . . which ought to sink the boat . . . lots of poetry, too, some philosophy, some art-books (Nancy's), but very little modern reading. For about the last three months I've not read a single contemporary thing: as the rich Yank art-collector said when he was showing Epstein round his collection: 'My taste stops after 1633.'

Gong.

Having sealed up your letter and forgotten to post it, I gave way to an ungovernable impulse, dearies, and wipped it cwudely open. The days are so dun and gloomy that we pant for the tropics: as much too, to see your faces again. My mother has gotten herself into a really good financial mess and has decided to cut and run for it. Being too timid to tackle foreign landscapes herself, she wants to be shown around the Mediterranean by us. She wants to scout Corfu, largely because your letters have stimulated her so. If she likes it I have no doubt but that she'll buy the place. For my own part I'm a leetle worried by its proximity to Albania. Have you read about the marriage of George & Marina? The papers deny any state of motive, but it occurred to me that we are more and more afraid of being unable to guard trade routes through Suez, and Greece will be the ideal base of operations against any southern country: more than that, if you look at the map you will observe how wonderful a base Corfu makes if Balkan trouble happens: Ideal . . . What I want to know is, will you, Wilkinson, give your life for gallant little Greece, our gallant little ally? I thought not. Then move a few islands south. Personally the intentions of us are (strictly dishonourable as ever) to have a glance round for a good base of operations with a cheap exchange and pit out our existence for a year or two until our stock as artists goes up. . . .

Love and love. Send us a snap or two sumtime.

To Alan G. Thomas   Hotel Internazionale
                                                    Brindisi, Italy [1935]

Dear Alan,

You will see from this that we have arrived so far—at a certain cost. The whole town has been alive with rumours of the Greek revolt—and the services have been disorganized. The place swarms with people who are held up. But by some special dispensation we have discovered a boat which will drop us off at Corfu sometime in the middle of to-night. I hope you can read this scrawl. I can get you a copy of the infamous Lady Chatterly for 14 liras—about 5/-.

If the English are a nation of shop keepers, then the Italians are a nation of waiters. Positively they radiate a sort of charming servility. I have never been as waited on in any country—or, I might add, so badly. All the service is done from the wrong side.

I feel most disinclined to write. It's very wearying kicking one's heels in this military and naval port.

I've got quite a lot of amusement parading the slums and attending funerals. Most impressive. But the excitement of Greek civil war—and Italian importunity consumes me. However we leave tonight. God knows what time we reach the island. Dawn, I imagine. We have met a charming Greek boy who speaks Italian and has taken us round the town; the only night-haunt—apart from the more obvious houses of Venus for the soldiers—is a vacuous café with a very bad amateur band. In order to give what Pat would call 'body' to their music they accompany an exceedingly improbable and tinny gramophone. As the instruments are tuned from a piano which is several tones flat you can imagine the resulting noise.

Still I bear up very well under the stacks of local vino I am forced to consume. I'm developing a paunch like a channel buoy.

. . . For the rest—I'm too bored and the pen is too bad to write more. If I perish in the revolution you might save this letter as an example of what Italy can do to a gallant Englishman.

P'fui
Larry.

To Alan G. Thomas   Pension Suisse, Corfu [1935]
Dear Alan,

A line to tell you we're alive, but held up owing to the non arrival of the bloody baggage. We hope it'll come on tomorrow's Greek boat from Trieste. Not another word from either Mr. Curtis or Mr. Brown: there must be some mistake about the novel: certainly they spelt my name Durnell: perhaps someone wrote a novel called 'Pied Piper of Buggers' and that, being fashionable, was chosen! Today, tired of inactivity, I went into a shop to buy some exercise books to do some notes for the next novel. After a hell of a search (the amount people here know about their stock would give Baker the shudders) I ran a couple of dust-heavy books to earth and asked the price. Believe it or not they *weighed them!* On a great swivelling baggage weigher—like they have in the customs—with brass weights—and said, with uncertainty—24 dracs—1/-.

Enclosed are a few rotten scraps. More soon.

Love to everyone
Larry

To Alan G. Thomas   Pension Suisse, Corfu [1935]
Dear Alan,

What a smile on the face of the tiger! The family crawled ashore today and took us in bed so to speak, and wrung my withers with the

[31]

news. We dashed straight off to the consul and seized the joyous letters. Of course accept. Positively accept. I feel like a sort of pontifical Lawrence this morning—I suppose the bloom will wear off in time. In a few days time my address will be Villa Agazini, Perama, Corfu. The scenic tricks of this paragon of places are highly improbable, and I don't quite believe my eyes as yet. Let me digest—But *I hate the Italians.*

. . . Cheerio and a million thanks—my love to Cooper—Pat—and anyone else who needs it.

Lawrence Durrell

To Alan G. Thomas   Villa Agazini or Bumtrinket
                                     Perama, Corfu   [1935]

Dear Alan,

As you will see, we have more or less moved in. The paint is still drying on our furniture however, and there are a hundred and one things to be done yet. I've told you how unique it is up here, stuck on the hillside, haven't I? Well, multiply that by four. Today we rose to a gorgeous sunlight and breakfasted in it. Our breakfast table looks out plumb over the sea, and the fishing boats go swirling past the window. There's a faint mist over Albania today but here the heat is paralysing. Bees and lizards and tortoises (yesterday I caught a tortoise eavesdropping on us) are making hay; and the peasants together with those animals who cannot make hay are making water beautifully and indiscriminately. Soon I'll send you some photographs—but even they can't do justice to it all. Sometimes I almost suspect the whole thing; I don't think I can yet really believe in it.

George has bought a cool white sailing-boat and we bathe from it every day: in really deep blue water: fathoms of it. Of course, like all Edens the place has its drawbacks—and I don't mean the donkeys' foreskins. The peasants are incorrigible thieves and liars, but make up for it by having the dandiest arse-action when they walk. This is due to always carrying huge weights on their heads. They're very saucy and can be persuaded to do almost anything within reason. Food is cheap: but the wines are not as brilliant as in Italy—and the milk is poor stuff: also the butter. But local stuff is good and cheap. For instance there is a good peasant wine which tastes and looks like iced blood. It costs 6 dracks—3ᵈ per bottle. What more does one want? In England I couldn't buy a bottle of horse-piss for 3ᵈ. Yesterday we dined very royally on red mullet—as you know a most epicurean dish—it cost 10ᵈ. But prices will bore you stiff. The revolution has rocked the drachma up to 517: we hope it'll go to six hundred, and it may.

Peter Bull, the actor, of whom you wot, is coming out next month for a week or so, to stay with George. He's going to have a long way round from N.Y. The island is littered with writers of all degrees, sizes, shapes, religious denominations, nationalities, and capabilities. George is the sort of grand old man of Corfu: his charm and his whiskers make him much sought after. I'm too much of a sans-culotte and bellicose gamin ever to be popular in society. However people are very charming and decent. The luggage hasn't arrived yet. I'm praying for it daily. Leslie is in his element rowing boats all over the place and has nearly been wrecked once: blown down to Benitza and been forced to paddle back.

I am in pod again and am pupping a novel: but it's too upsidedown here as yet to really work. God but the Sun. I've written a lovely poem which I transcribe for you on the back of this.

Give my love to everyone. Mrs. Penry, Pat, Watts, etc., and tell them to come out here. Also a chunk of greeting to the giant intellects of the Municipal College.

Adio

Larry.

The other day Professor Dawkins blew in to see George at A. J. Symonds' request. You may remember him in Corvo's *Desire and Pursuit of the Whole*, as Macpawkins, the 'blubber-lipped professor of Greek'. A nice little man. Going to Mt. Athos to write a book about it. Laughs like a penny whistle.

A LYRIC OF BODIES

What sweet white meat our bodies are
Who have no canon but delight:
Such pretty devil's food—
O! daintier by far
(We triflers in a foreign night)

[33]

Than all those delicately-tended meats
That weight the tables of the rich.

Angels have little meat in them
But vague and evanescent shapes
Declare the wise
Who hoard their comforts up for paradise.
Are we then brutes, my dear, or hinds
Who for refreshment can devise
A sport so rich, a food so able
That soul, a gracious wedding-guest
Waits at the body's table?

Corfu 1935

Sometime when you have it to spare, will you send me the Turner satire? Like a B.F. I lost it.

Sorry

Larry

To Alan G. Thomas

Villa Agabumtrinket
Perama, Corfu   [1935]

Dear Alan,

. . . I'd like to tell you how many million smells and sounds and colours this place is, but my stock of superlatives would give out. As I sit, for instance. Window. Light. Blue grey. Two baby cypress lulling very slightly in the sirocco. Pointed and perky like girls' breasts. The sea all crawling round in a bend as the coast curves away to Lefkimo with one sailing-boat on it. In the road, which I can't see since the lower sill of window hides it, the peasants are passing on donkeys. Raving, swearing crashing colours, scarves and headdresses. To the north nothing. Ahead Epirus and Albania with a snuggle of creamy cloud clotted on them. South mists and the mystery of the other islands lying out there, invisible, in the water.

In this quiet room above the sea I've just played the fourth* again. I know it now—every stich of it—more intimately than I know Nancy. I've got it in my bowels. Sort of empathy. I've *been* it. I act it, sleep it,

* Beethoven Piano Concerto.

[34]

shit it, sleep with it—everything. And I can tell you that compared to it, the Emperor is a collection of musical platitudes written for a lavatory-paper musical box by a deaf mute. So There!

Can you arrange my paper reviews for me with the slip I sent you? Let me know how much money you want and I'll send it you. And for god's sake only send me good reviews if there are any. The least bit of discouragement and my present novel will go farting off the rails into the blue. Wait till I've finished it and then I can face the superior sneer of the reviewer runtlings. . . .

My God! talking of epics. Have you read a book called *Tropic of Cancer* by Henry Miller? Published by the Obelisk Press, Paris. I implore you either to order the shop a copy and read it, or buy one yourself. There isn't a word with which to express its excellence. Of course, like all works of genius it's strong fruit and you'd have to be careful about getting it into England. If you know anyone who is going to Paris make him get it for you. You won't regret it.

Everyone champs for the Lawrence here. I'm eager to read it as hell. Lucky swine you are being in the trade. *BUT GET THE MILLER.* It's of another pedigree but as large as anything as yet written in the novel line.

And don't feel guilty about not writing me long letters very often. I understand perfectly.

Hail!
Larry

EZRA
Ci-git Ezra
Who knew ten languages
  But could not choose
When writing English poetry
  Which to use.

W. H. DAVIES: 'COUNTRY NEWS'
A bed I have
  So white and straight.
All night I lie
  And copulate.

A mirror on
  The mantel-shelf,

So I can lie
   And watch myself
While I am warming
   To my task.
What more can any
   Poet ask?

To Alan G. Thomas   c/o The Ionian Bank, Corfu
Dear Alan,   [1935]
    . . . We've just spent a week or so with the Hudsons at the north
of the island, in a little bay where their house is [Mangkephali]. It's
much more bristly and rocky and male country up there. Cliffs and
promontories. We're thinking of taking a house up there for the
winter, which would be a daring and lonely thing to do. It's built on a
great rock over the water. In winter they say the sea fairly licks up at
the drawing room windows.
    Yes, the Lawrence is a great book.* I've just finished it. But man
what a disgusting little thing he was. His own personality decreased
as the saga grew. I've lost every shred of interest I had in him. What a
little neuter, ripping and goring his body because he loathed it so.
There's no touch of healthy sperm anywhere in the book, and as for all
that talk of the men degrading him by talking about their wives, ill-
nessess, food etc., well Pfui to him. He seemed to be nothing but a
tedious adolescent applying the thumbscrews of denial and torture to
himself. Yes, a sort of nasty child. There's not one healthy straight-
forward emotion or conviction in the whole thing. Yet the thing is epic
somehow. Poor little fellow.
    Sometime when you have the money you might buy Henry Miller's
Tropic of Cancer, pub. at 50 francs by the Obelisk Press. 338 Rue St.-
Honoré. Paris. This is the book for our generation. Of course it may
shake you a bit on the physical side, because you don't really know
every inch of physical passion, and your experience in the world of the
body is limited as yet. But when you do manage to explore this exquisite dimension of sense you will find your experience bearing out
all he has to say, and the book will really grow on to you. In the mean-

* *The Seven Pillars of Wisdom.*

time read it for what you can get out of it, and really salt yourself to it.
Keep it on the shelf. As we grow we'll realise more and more what it's
about. I am convinced that it's the greatest thing written in our life-
times. Roughly it's idea is this. Where all the other people like Joyce
and Lewis got stuck in the morass and dirt of modern life, Miller comes
out on the other side with a grin, whole, hard and undamaged. He's
the first man really to cross the modern bog safely. The rest—all those
tedious Ulysses and Chatterlies got stuck and choked up to the eyes:
or else, like R. Aldington, stayed on safe romantic ground and spent
their time moaning about the bog without ever going near it. For your
own sake you must understand the book. It's a manifesto. A world,
says Miller, in which there must be no hope, *but no despair*. There is the
different angle. Everyone else has been only too successful painting the
despair, but no one has rejected it, and really jumped headlong into
the dirt *with guts*. For Godsake Alan read this book. Get someone to
bring it back from Paris for you. Even if you don't like it the first edition value is going to be enormous. Even George dimly likes it! . . .

Love and Love,

Larry

CARD-PLAYERS: STILL-LIFE

Observe then with my eyes what I have seen.
Remark the small inn asleep among olive-boughs:
The curtain of scavenging flies,
Like hanging bead, in the doorway: and men
Snoozing against an olive-bole or playing
Slow, greasy cards. Thumbed colours of conquest.

At their backs, stacked up under the wall,
Long rows of formal melons in sunlight,
Melodious pippins, bright as lighted butter,
Crushed full of juice in crazy sizes
Between black shadow and shadow.

If you could see my scene, would you believe
That men can slough the creeping pale-skinned north
And become one with the afternoon silences,

With the loungers,
The gnomic card-players in a dead tavern
Out of all time and circumstance?

There's no regret here, nor circumspection.
The sun devours these morsels strip by strip
Until we are one among the brown men,
The respectful snoozers in hats of straw.

Nothing, nothing is vocal now, nothing's to say—
Unless the melons burst their heavy cheeks
And dither in the dust, in uproar,
Haunting the incandescence of the sun!

Perama. Corfu

Now when are you coming out to see us?

To Alan G. Thomas   Corfu Greece [1936]
Dear Alan,

Sorry I haven't written for some time but I've been busy getting this novel off my chest. Soon you'll have the last batch of paper. What horrid fruity stuff. The discussion on Walsh, however, is a good bit of work—different to the rest. I think someone might want to print it—the ghost story too is good literary journalism. I sent it off last night. Did you get the first batch? I think *Music in Limbo* is a better title. Short and quite as expressive. The book *means* nothing. I've tried—just for an exercise in writing to create characters on two continuous planes of life—the present—meaning the island and their various pasts. It does not progress as an ordinary novel progresses. The tentacles push out sideways while the main body is almost static. Whether I've managed to create the two planes successfully, or whether the total result is interesting I can't tell. But I do know that there's some interesting writing in it. I am beginning to feel that my pencil is almost sharpened. Soon I'll be ready to begin on a BOOK.

As soon as this goes off to you I begin preparing myself for writing. I'm starting at Vol. 1 of the *Encyclopaedia Brit.* and reading through all the big subjects. History. Biology. Surgery. Philosophy. And anything else that interests me. It will take me an age. . . .

There was a young girl of Balboa
Who had lots of fun with a boa,
She found she could get it
All in if she wet it
In oceans of spermatozoa.

Old Noah had a wife on the ark
Who sleep-walked a bit after dark.
But the rhino, the camel,
The mandrills en famille,
Soon gave way to the nose of the shark.

Not very good: except for the felicitous middle rhyme.

Old Noah developed a grouch,
He was sick of this floating whore—houch,
He was fed up of leavin'
His Biblical semen
To rot in the kangaroos' pouch.
                        Love

                              Larry

Rain again: hot damp sirocco and the sea piling up under the window
in great tufts: an absolute doomed feeling, trapped here with the olives
going it and purple buds falling off. It seems to affect even the peasants.
During dinner in our huge stone-floored dungeon of a dining-room we
heard our landlord go pleasantly mad with his mandolin. Playing a
haunting tune in slow skips and quartertones: I asked him what it was:
The Fishermen: I ask you? It would take a Greek to write a tune which
would do royally as incidental music to *Hamlet*, and then christen it
'The Fishermen'. Ask him if there's any love-song he knows, but no,
he's too shy. Says he doesn't know any Erotica. Meanwhile our gigantic Olga sniggers and opens her legs wide wide wide and sniggers.
She's deputizing for Helene who is slender and silk-skinned as an angel
or an Indian. Poor H is pupping in town.

I hope to god you got the other bits of the novel. I sent off two bits
already. I've no copy. Two more bits go tomorrow. It'll be about
100,000 all told. Get it prettily typed, will you, dear Alan, and edit it.

[39]

It's full of mistakes which I can't notice I know it so well. It's good in a poor way. Particularly Walsh. That, my man, is more than just fiction: it's literature. Reuben and Francis show fire but a paucity of conception. What I didn't make clear was the fact that it's silly of her to mind him going off to fuck one of his madonnas and get money for them: it's the wretched possession of love that I should have stamped on hard. Not used their pain as a cheap emotional pivot for a scene. I'd like to rewrite the whole book and create the people, but it's no good. I've no patience with myself. I can't go back any more. What's past is past. Vale. My next will be better, and the next better until people recognize me. *Aut Caesar aut nihil.* A pretty thought. But one has to be so many nihils before the Caesar if any emerges. And now I no longer care: really care I mean down inside whether tomorrow all my poems are scrapped, or whether I'm scrapped myself. A new phase I spoze. Literature as such is slipping away like turds. Tell me what you get from Miller, I'm keen to know. Sometime I'll send you a few rough notes I made on Tropic. Sorry the copies came here. I've told Curtis Brown to send you another. When you've typed *Music in Limbo* will you send it on to him? I never want to see it again. Tell me what you think of the writing. God I'm so despondent to write a BOOK. Something with contours and blood and stuff in it: not just romantic viscera that quiver at the sight of any rainbow, and a precious turduous STYLE à la Strachey. The Walsh bit is a good omen, do you think? What do you think? You see I've changed my tripe swinger's ribbon? That signifies a change of heart. Adio. Adio. Adio. But I'm despondent until I see what new abortion I'm going to bring forth.

. . .

Kali nikta sas,
Larry

To Alan G. Thomas   c/o The Ionian Bank
                                           Corfu Greece [1936]

Dear Alan,

    Yes, we got them all, after a considerable delay, and all in the wrong order. However, thanks lots for the typist etc. Is she an Oxford Grouper because my manuscript is dotted here and yon with occasional fucks. Really I've got so that I can hardly tell what is pretty or not as far as literary morals go. We've got so lax, what with Leslie farting at meals, and us naked nearly all day on the point, bathing.

Les came for the week-end with his 16 bore and yesterday we shoved some food in the boat plus the gun and rowed north, past St. Stephano to the huge sweep in the channel where the big tides from the open sea come crashing up along the coast all britted and pitted with heat and the sun. Sun-blind, with the scurfy Albanian coast only a few miles away, knolls dotted with white Turkish-Byzantine towns and fortresses. The wind! With the gravel-boats scooting by us with their coloured sails wagging and groaning. On a hard stone beach, facing into the sheer tide and wind we dragged up the boat and unloaded. If you want to get the feeling, look at some of the buccaneer prints of boats on the Cuban beaches. And the sun! Shades of Esquemeling. The country is patched and blank with sun: rising in great hard breasts, with flinty rocks jutting from the hot dry covering of bushes. You can see a man miles away from the top of a hill. Dour, dour, with the flint hot as hell under your feet. Not much Celtic numen, here: only a sort of grasping hate for the land, dry and bone-hot. A hell. Occasional patches of ripe cypress: and the interminable little olives, powdery with heat and dust. But I love it, really, because it's so savage and unapproachable. You can never feel inside like you can a northern landscape. You're always a stranger, in rather a frightening position, among a savage people. You know? At any moment the undergrowth might push a viper out on you. However, we were cursing this bare north coast—rather Les was, because there was nothing to shoot, when I suggested a promenade. Patrol to you. He'd only brought 4 rounds with him, and was in a bad humour about the lack of game. We walked ten or twenty metres and nearly fell into a natural lake, complete with reeds, and SOMETHING. What? 7 or 8 specks on the further water, lolling quietly, at ease, I clapped the glasses to my rolling optics and saw a whole flight of wild duck, sitting there as if from the minute of creation, completely calm. They'd never been shot at; nor seen any men except an occasional fisherman. Les began to foam quietly at the mouth and curse himself. Only 4 rounds. Then things happened. Wild pigeon whoomed over. Two big water birds. Les nearly went off his head. He winged the pigeon, which fell, but in the deep undergrowth at the hill-top. We beat for hours but couldn't find it. He killed a duck on the lake, but it took a long dive, and tho' he crawled about in the chest-high mud for ages he couldn't pick it up. Sod's luck this.

One of the duck got up along the surface and I missed a jammy shot. Sum total: two kills and nothing to show.

Of course Les is transfigured. He loves the north now. On the way home in the boat we discovered two other lakes, as perfect as unshot, and with game on them. Only four miles or so from Albania, the richest shoot in the world. The big tasty duck come over to these nooks and hide out. No one seems to know except my landlord who fishes the lake once a year for eel. So next week Leslie is coming with two guns and a whole stack of cartridges to shoot the piss out of the lakes. Dear me, does Henry Miller jar? . . .

Larry

To John Gawsworth   c/o The Ionian Bank, Corfu [1936]
. . . Yes this war is worrying. Of course we're scared shitless because if there's any place Benito wants more than Ethiopia it's Corfu. He smashed up the town with bombs in 1925, and had to be chased out by the British: and everyone here is afraid he'll do it again. Great excitement in the town yesterday coz an Italian bomber came over, reconnoitring, I thought our number was up when I saw this aluminium giant fart overhead. *Grace à Dieu* we're living in the extreme north of the island, and if there's trouble we'll have to get a fisherman to row us over to Epirus, and escape thence to Athens. What with brigands on the main-land and Italians here I should probably lose my honour all the way to Athens. However, what can one do?

When things quieten up a bit why not come out for a holiday with Barbara and stay with us? It's cheap living. The drachma has crashed and we get good money for the pound. Rent 2 quid a month, for a big house over the water. Sea dashed up under our drawing room windows, and the dolphins slink by all day as I sit and write this. I'm so glad you're full of work and plenty, and have got over your rutty bit. Hope the Shiel novel goes well. I must go and bathe now. Naked, by God, with nothing in sight except Lefkas on the horizon.

Our regards to you both,

Larry.

To Alan G. Thomas   c/o The Ionian Bank, Corfu   [Spring 1936]
Dear Alan,

I've been very down in the jaw lately over this fucking book [*The Black Book*] which won't go as it should. It's difficult. If I ever finish it to my satisfaction I shall feel that virtue has gone out of me. Real virtue. It's like fine crochet, done at one dead level of emotion. Very queer and difficult for an up and down chap like me. I feel a bit cross-eyed even after thirty thousand or so. Also a lot of new theories and principles which will be the death of me. I find that half our trouble is bad emotion. By that I mean romantic indulgence: vide Limbo. This comes from shallow sexual experience I feel sure. What I am after is the real feeling for things uncomplicated any more by our pal J.C. or ethic or code or whatnot. You will see what I mean in Villon. In Lawrence. In Miller. The *Ballad of the Dead Ladies* for instance is purer, more sharply pure and concentrated like a blow-flame, than, for instance Aldington's Dream. One is the result of experience: the other a romantic indulgence. I don't say I rend it and reject it: but I accept it henceforth as an indulgence, as man might eat another iced cake although he knew his diabetes would suffer. What I am for from now on is the essential male and female relationship uncomplicated by mirages and falsities and wish fulfilments. By which you will see that I am getting a very old man. I was twenty-four a month or so ago. But believe me Alan, this is a point worth looking at. I see now what Lawrence means, what Miller is at, and I corroborate it, not just intellectually, but with my own feeling and experiences and bowels. And it's a very depressing thought. It means that 99 people out of a hundred never grow up emotionally. Never. Which is dismal. But pah! all this may come to nothing. I simply have no belief in my ability to follow a plotted path. I was inconsistent even in the womb my mother tells me, so there's no hope of a change. Meanwhile the book, whose title changes daily, has got its head in its mouth and won't budge. It started as Lover Anubis, then Anubis, then Anabasis, then *The Black Book*. Tomorrow it might be anything or nothing. Just Opus One. Quick, quick, a tabernacle to precocity and preciousness. But I am grateful having you in the van with a bloody standard. Also for the practical side of really quizzing books. I can't bring myself hardly to look at a thing when it's done, or not properly done even. It's so much inert meat. . . .

[43]

Well the north is flowering under the rain. This poor shot and dropping stone countryside has flowered in soft grass the height of ankle-boots. The iris and the flag stare at one like stone carved and coloured delicately everywhere. And the asphodel are going through their Victorian aspidistra stage. Moderate fishing. Ten miles south the family brawls and caterwauls and screams in the cavernous new Ypso villa. George and Pam are buying land and building a house. Why I don't know. When the good weather comes we start our explorations of the virgin north end, with a donkey & a tent. I send you the voting slips from the recent elections. Le roi is the phoenix rising again. Poor devil he'll burn right enough if he's not careful. He's a good man, but the people are hopeless. Politically hopeless as a nomadic tribe. I'll type out a poem on the back I've just done. My landlord is sweetly learning English under my tuition, and I Greek incidentally. Here's his first parrot memory feat.

I have a little garden and every summer day
I dig it and I rake it and I pull the weeds away . . .

He declaims this to the people in the wine-shop thus:

Ai hef an leetle gungdung end effery zummer die
I deeg it end I rack it end I pule the veeds awaye.

I happened to hear him impressing a chum who came to help him grind the olives up. You should just HEAR him end up, fortissimo with a gesture: and O the wed wed woses that bloom so sveetly there! Laugh? I fair shat meself.

I liked your limerick much. You're getting a real hand at these affairs. We'll do an immense heroic satire one day entirely in limericks. As soon as I feel free of this book. It oppresses me, like a sort of malignant constipation. It will not get out. Ah well. Asta mañana and all that sort of crap.

A hail and a Hail.

Larry.

To Alan G. Thomas   KOULOURA [1936]
Dear Alan,

Thank you so much for your long letter. I'm so glad that the news Pat mentioned is really news: hurrah for your good luck, and the horse-sense of Cooper to keep you on.* No, my dear man, none of the stigmata, watch-chain, season-ticket, etc., really apply. It's a question of temperament, not status. The most cultured people I have met, the most gentlemanly, the most proper, in my sense of the word, have been tied by a willing leg here there and everywhere. But a bookshop of your own is wonderful. I'm almost tempted to come back and join you. Only the English weather po po po as they say here, shaking their rueful heads. Too awful. Which reminds me that we've had some lovely weather. Ringing blue days, smelling of ice, but with bright bright sunshine. Today we climbed to the cliff-top and lay for hours in it, out of action. Irises studded everywhere, lemons ripe and oranges. Olives picked and crushed already. Summer is icumen in already. Soon we shall bathe. We are planning trips everywhere when we get our tent made. To Signès, the surprising crater under the very chin of old man Panto, where there flourishes a sudden torrent of holm-oak. So queer, like a green wound in the middle of the stone and rubble and shot and smashed metamorphic rock. There is a drunken papas who rides a mule, is dirty, lascivious and 84 who will make a good photo. Our land-lord welcomes us with a kiss on the wrist when we arrive from our sojourn in the lowlands with my people. Altogether hurrah and that kind of thing.

The day before we left Margaret picked up a couple of jongleurs in Kerkyra and brought them to the family villa in the car. They sat on the porch and played turgid Greek jazz with a guitar, a mandolin, and their strong voices in unison. *Tha geiresis*—I think it means I will come back. One was a sharp featured boy with black eyes and a corrugated forehead, and one a queer humpy man in a cloth cap, with a strong, absolutely flawless voice. He was blind. I was reminded of them putting out birds' eyes to make them sing. Very queer melodies under the olives, with the old plectrum smacking away at the mandolin, and their right toes tapping in time. Afterwards we took them back into town, and went by car, royally, with music along the roads by the sea. But how can I express this queer place to you. Sometime you must come and share it for yourself. . . .

HAIL AND HAIL AND HAIL.

Larry

* My employer, Ernest Cooper, was retiring and had offered me the opportunity of buying his bookshop.

To Alan G. Thomas   Corfu [1936 ?]

Dear Alan,

. . . We have taken some amusing photos of the island which are being enlarged in Athens, when I get them I'll post them to you and you can submit them with a letter to the *Geographical Magazine* if you will. A week or 2 ago we went up to a death-swamp lake in the north, Les and Nan and me for a shoot. Tropical. Huge slime covered tracts, bubbled in hot marsh-gas and the roots of trees. Snakes and tortoises swimming quietly above and big toads. A rim of emerald slime thick with scarlet dragon-flies and mosquitoes. It's called: ANTINIOTISSA* (enemy of youth). I shot my first big duck in flight, and we got a couple of herons each. I've bought a gun. And tomorrow we get our boat, a lovely 20 foot cutter, which we are going to haul out and scrape and paint ourselves. Send you a snap. It's a bride of a boat. We are fitting it out and next summer or the next we'll set off to the Aegean in it alone, with enough food, a gun, a reel. Live virtually on what we shoot and fish and land oktim. When we start I am going to begin a series of letters, long ones to you, which we can print in a book afterwards. A travel book.

My poems are at the printers being quoted. We've started the Dugong series. Pat [Evans] will do his poems too. And afterwards I'll do the *Prurient Duck*, satires, and Pat an essay on varieties of religious experience. Will you weigh in with a Provençal diary or an open letter to the anti-birth control league. I'll send you a copy, but much as I love you I'm not going to ask you to hawk me around and incur the wrath of the council. You're a respectable householder now so just you sit tight and cheer from the stalls. The poems are good. There's no question of doubt. I know what they're worth myself. And I don't care if anyone buys them or not. A little bored with writing these days. I'm going to retire soon, not write except occasionally when I have something to say. At peace a little with *The Black Book*. It's not as good as I thought I was. Well, I don't care. I'll do the trick yet. Great strength will return the mite. But it must come in its own time. May not publish it. When it's done I'll send it to you. What you'll think will be valuable, because although you're a bit of a hermit, you really have got the philosopher's stone hidden somewhere in your dirty rags. O by the

* So called because this lagoon was once very malarious and people who contracted the disease in youth looked older than their years.

way, Pat says you don't like Miller. Let me buy the copy back will you? I was afraid you wouldn't, because it's a book which moves in terribly rare air. I couldn't read it in England myself. But it's the book of a great exile, and I'm one myself (minus the great to quite that degree). A greater exile even than Villon is old Miller. I love the red naked personalities of prophets appearing suddenly in the decorous circus of literary literature. It shows up the conscious craftsmen like hell, and makes them see what maggots they are. Away with these old buggers who want art to be a superior cabinet-making. Real art is life. And Miller is a real live Miller all through, not a literary sempstress. As for CHARLES MORGAN 'THAT Giant bluebell of Observer literature', what a thin smell of urine and fag-ends goes up from *Sparkenbroke.* IS THERE NO ONE WRITING AT ALL IN ENG-LAND NOW? What do you read when you spend a wet Monday alone? Myself I read one of the sciences. The most exact one to date is demonology. It is fun to follow the growth of science out of magic and demonology, and see it declining again in our time back to magic, its parent. WE SHALL NEVER KNOW ANYTHING. The Victorians tried to destroy our psyche by their cheap watch-chain certainty, their half-hunter universe. Thanks God someone had the sense to break it wide open and uncage the real mysteries for us to feed on.

Adio.

Larry.

To Alan G. Thomas   Corfu [1936 ?]
Dear Al,

. . . Well we have a blazing sun again after a few weeks of rain. Just a slight nip from the mountains. I'm a little sunblind these days. I don't know what poetry or prose I'm writing really. It's all happening through a dark velvet curtain. But the great thing is, it doesn't matter any more. If I write I write. . . .

You wouldn't recognize Leslie I swear. His personality is really amazingly strong now, and he can chatter away in company like Doctor Johnson himself. It's done him a world of good, strutting about with a gun under each arm and one behind his ear, shooting peasants

[47]

right and left. Did I tell you about Antiniotissa? Enemy of youth? We're going up soon after duck. And as soon as *Van Norden* can hoist the binnacle and splice a nifty poop we're off to try for deer and wild boar. I'm queer about shooting. So far I've prohibited herons. They're such heraldic creatures, and when they're wounded they use their great razor bill like a tailor. I shot a couple and one chased Leslie, and neatly nipped him in the arse. But duck is a different matter. Just a personified motor-horn, flying ham with a honk. No personality, nothing. And to bring them down is the most glorious feeling. THUD. Like breaking glass balls at a range. And the meat is delicious. I could slaughter hundreds without a qualm. They've no meaning, no real life. It's like shooting flying motor-horns honestly. Delightful.

Have you ever seen an octopus killed? Last night we got a big one. A stick with its hook hidden in a few bits of greenery. They're very gullible. Tease them and they come skating out of their holes and spread like a cobra. Then's your time. You lunge out, hook, and drag them up. Behold, you have a pink deadly gesticulating umbrella trying to get at you.

The big one coughed up a huge spout of water plumb in our faces, panting heaving and writhing. Their suckers are terrifying. They wrap themselves round your wrists, heaving and squirting and pulping. Altogether filthy. Or walk up and down the wood with a continuous syrupy, sucking noise. Utterly foul. We put it on shore and watched it trying to get back to the sea. Curious, because it travels along the ground, throwing its tentacles out, but not in the air. It moves like lava, with a dull squelch. But funniest of all. When you stab it with a knife, huge electric tremors run through, it lights up for a second like a light, and then changes colour. When you sever the chords above the right eye, half of it dies and goes deep green blue, then over the other eye, and the other half dies. But very very filthy. I'll send you one in an envelope.

Well, see you on paper soon. And do I send a grand salute of five guns to the terrible cyprian on whom you dote, and whose talons are hooked in your vest? Madam I do. If I'm not one of the bloody family, then what am I? Eh?

Cheers chaps. Larry.

To Alan G. Thomas   Sotiriotissa [Corfu 1936]
Dear Alan,

Broadside of a hundred guns.* I'm delirious with the news. Hurrah. June is usually a ringing month. We shall have the *Van Norden* in the sea and can make several amusing trips for you: to Mourto, a Turkish port opposite us here. To the little islands at the north etc. Such fun, and champagne and sand. Well that's grand. I was wondering where the cash was coming from to make the Venice trip. Now I have a respite. Perhaps when you've been here a little while you'll forget where you come from and who you are. Lose your memory I mean. Then we'll chain you by the leg and make you live on the beach until September, just giving you enough fruit to eat, and reading Miller to you all day.

I'm glad you ignore *Tropic of Cancer*. It means that the backlash that is waiting for you from this writer will be even greater. All great men are fifty years ahead of their time, and H.M. is no exception to the rule. It's largely a question of experience I think. When I first read Tropic I was delighted with it, not as a new bible, but because it bore out a few theories about writing that I had been trying to formulate. The art of non-art. You remember us in Bournemouth on this theme. Real art being absolutely devoid of 'artifice', in the literary sense. The experience proper which is in the core of the book I was rather afraid of: the reason was this. When I read it first, my repulsion from it was the reflection, NOT OF ANYTHING INHERENTLY REPULSIVE IN ITS CONTENT, but of my own habit-pattern, my own upbringing. I was reading into it an unpleasantness which was my own mind. Getting to know Miller a little I see that the medal has an obverse side which very few people will grasp unless they are spiritually adult. Even Zarian in his obscure way is still fighting this bogy. I NOW REALIZE TO THE FULL THE PARADOX WHICH SUCH A BOOK, SUCH A MAN HOLDS IN STORE FOR US. It is this: TROPIC OF CANCER IS THE PUREST BOOK WRITTEN IN OUR TIME: by reducing everything to a common denominator of phenomenon, it achieves a P U R I T Y of soul and cleanliness of spirit, against which people like Joyce and Lawrence in their most abandoned moments seem a little grubby: a little hand-soiled by the great northern mantrap (our disease, our death) THE GUILTY

* I had accepted his invitation to come and stay in Corfu.

[49]

CONSCIENCE. I italicise this coz I want you to read it over and meditate on it. The paradox is there, and sooner or later you will grasp it, reciprocate it with your own conscience and soul. When I say that this is at once the greatest piece of writing in our time, and also the most religious book, IT IS THIS PARADOX WITH ITS LIVID IDEOLOGICAL EDGES WHICH BURSTS OUT OF THE MUMMY WRAPPINGS AND CONFRONTS ONE. You will get it in time: but the toll a great work takes is not a light one. To confront a nakedness so dazzling it is necessary first to achieve a reciprocal nakedness. My dear Alan, I have no fear in saying this to you, because it is the simple and inevitable truth. I was never so poor a critic that I could be lead astray on anything as open and obvious as this. . . .

As to *The Black Book*, you might like it. But you will notice the slight contamination of conscience here and there infecting the sentiment—a peculiarly English disease. I hope to outgrow it. The sails are set. I'm starting out now in a more splendid curve than you would ever have imagined possible of me, with all your infectious faith and gaiety and loyalty. Don't be worried by my touches of megalomania here and there, my saying that I'm the best writer in England etc. What I mean is this: I HAVE BEGUN TO BE A REAL WRITER. There is no one else on the horizon in England who seems to be developing into the same kind of faun. At the best, brilliant literary practitioners, which is on a level with cabinet-making—any poor fool can learn it at the polytechnik. So when I Durrealize, please understand: I am not comparing myself to the Walpoles, the Morgans, the Aldingtons of the world. I do not compete. By degree I may be lesser: by genus I belong to another race. It is a qualitative difference in which I blow the Lawrentian trumpet. I my own kind, I haven't begun. Beside Lawrence, beside Miller, beside Blake. Yes, I am humble, I have hardly started. BUT I AM ON THE SAME TRAM. As for the Morgans and Eliots and Co. Why, they do not wear the first eleven cap. You will understand all this better when you see my writing on the heraldic universe. You will exclaim with delight in time, my dear, as certainly as Monday. You will exclaim.

MORE ANON. LOVE LARRY.

To Alan G. Thomas   c/o Ionian Bank, Corfu [1937]
Dear Alan,

Just been out to Paleocastrizza, where we are having our meeting this spring to arrange about the house. Lovely weather—the fields are crushed hip-high in asphodels and spring flags and millions of wild flowers whose names I don't know. I am lolling a bit, resting really for the 1st time in my writing life, content and at ease with myself. There is nothing I want to write just now. We walk about the fields with the dogs, are out to callers, and lie in the sun. I want to tell you about Paleocastrizza, so you will expect neither more nor less than you get. We are going round the island to it in the boat, and will anchor in the little bay. Here Koster is living in a little peasant house, and as his girl is leaving him soon, here he has offered us a room—a guest room. It is about as big as your old room in B'mth. I am putting a comfy bed in it, a few pictures on the wall, a table. Very bare. Ourselves we will be camped in the glade near the house under canvas. We will eat together —god knows what I don't. Bread and cheese and Greek champagne: you might find the diet a bit wild. Figs and grapes if they're in. Anyway—very rough eats. But from the bay itself we will excurt every day in the *Van Norden*—to the islands at the north where we will try and find Calypso's grotto. This is Homer's country pure. A few 100 yards from us is where Ulysses landed. The women still wash their clothes in the stream. To the big sand-beaches at the south also, Myrtiotissa, Synaradès etc. When the time comes for you to leave, WE WILL MAKE THE JOINT TRIP BACK ROUND THE ISLAND TO THE CORFU SIDE TOGETHER, stopping off to look at the Greek theatre in Butrinto, and at Cassiope the old Roman summer villa of Tiberius or some such. Enclose a map of our plans. You will move from one, to two, and from two to three, as marked. I am not, of course, making anything cast-iron—you may feel like a week's sun-bathing and nowt else when you come. O.K. But the islands are there, and we'll see them. Nothing to stop us. We have a fine little black boat, tent, blankets etc. And the good talk we'll have! I myself want you to arrive on June 1st. Because the moon begins then and on the 8th is full. If the weather is fine we can sail all night, drowsing in the moonlight, among the islands. You'd love that. It should be just nice, not too hot. A boiling English summer. July is the stinker. Take note please of the clothes you must bring:

A LOIN CLOTH???

ONE PAIR OF VERY LIGHT LONG TROUSERS made of any lightweight linen. (You may find the sun a bit burny).
A pair or two of shorts.
A couple of old shirts.
A PAIR OF SANDALS OR BEACH-SHOES.

Nothing else. Now you won't get a bath until we get back to Sotiriotissa: and the food may be bread and cheese and beer and figs. But in compensation you'll have the finest bathing and scenery in the world—and ISLANDS!

I'm looking forward to your trip, and I hope you won't stint yourself about time. You need the sun to get strong and ruddy again after killing yourself over the business. Remember it's an investment in its way—health gives you more fuel to run on. Don't work too hard and let me know what you think.

The *Van Norden* is all black and brown, with white bowsprit and sails. A dream, my good friend, a black devil. Wait till you see her!

Enclose a map of your travels to give you some idea of the topography of the island. The names must muddle you up no end.

Athens day after tomorrow. More anon.

Love.

Larry.

To Alan G. Thomas   c/o Ionian Bank, Kepkypa,* Greece
[1938]

Dear Alan:

Just a line to apologize for my neglect of you. We have been moving about again this summer and allowing mail to accumulate without bothering even to deal with it: living off the grape-country by the big sand-beach of Aghios Gordios. Also, I have been in Athens three and four times, as people came to stay and I couldn't work at home.

News of the island? The same idiocy prevails—the afternoon silence broken by nothing but the crack of the Belgian consul's rifle, as he wings pigeons from his office, safely guarded by a national flag and

* A joke. The actual spelling of Corfu, KERKYRA, in Greek letters.

diplomatic papers. Spiro flourishes greatly. His English has become simply horrible this year, as Leslie is teaching him to swear.

Theodore, to everyone's sorrow, is probably leaving the island to take up a job on Cyprus; Koster left for Paris last Friday, nearly mad with inaction and blue. I expect he will have to have a plate put in his skull. He hasn't painted a stroke since you were here: not a bloody *nature-morte* even; and when he admits it he looks rather *nature-morte* himself. It reminds me of the Creswell epigram

> Master John Blank, the poet, has cut his *throat*
> The only perfect line he ever wrote!

As for me I am in the middle of a book called the Aquarians. *The Black Book* should be out by the time you get this letter. I am also embarking on a verse play; a certain amount of stuff got printed in magazines this year but nothing so very good. I feel a little estranged in writing about my work to you, because I feel that I am quickly taking up a stance which you don't understand, and consequently don't subscribe to. Differences in experience are always tedious things. So I am content always to let time do the dove-tailing again. There is no hurry. I have suddenly discovered what it is I want to say: and you are one of the people I want to say it for!

Alors be of good cheer, father patience. The future is never too far away.

My God sorry about this scrawl. I am down with grippe and hate typing on my stomach. Pen a bit costive too, needs a laxative.

I think we are possibly coming to England in a month or two to live for a little while there. Serious financial troubles! I am keen to see how you are getting along with the bookshop; no less than with your Gauguin woman or your beard. . . .

Miller coming down here he says to stay and Perlès. All the Best. I hope to look you two up soon: and smell the bindings: so Ella and Alan, Salut—

Larry

To Anne Ridler   [London ? 1939]
Thursday as I live on the eve of the cataclysm:
Posting from Stratford I find the poem I promised you, good Mistress

Anne, lying on my desk, unposted owing to the thin and nauseating web of procrastination woven around me by the charwoman daily. I have discovered, if not Shakespeare, Arden, Avon, Snitterfield, and the delectable county of Warwick. I am a little drunk but in good repair. (This is to apologize for the delay). But I must tell you about the journey.

As you drop over the Oxon border by Long Compton there is an air of another territory; the country arches and curves, and behaves in an entirely new way. The trees behave with a propriety and decency altogether fantastic. The air goes all sour-sweet with the bells from the little minsters, and you feel you have reached common land at last, a kind of green limbo between territories which breeds fantasy, medievalism, wrack, ullage and Pentavalon her shining and tainted pavilions. From this point until you reach the swan that lulls so soft under the Trinity spires, you hold your breath. In Stratford even the petrol pumps were gaudy and in keeping; and the river runs like sound through steel tubes—a little icy tinkle by the weir. It is so still in the afternoons that you could breathe on a mirror and not find it so still. And the swan does little cobbles with her horny black foot on the absolute water. Lie on your back in Shottery with a good pipe going, the noise of mowing, the tourists passing, and you begin to see the edges of this huge industrial myth Shakespeare; you begin to bless the arm-in-arm girls and boys maundering on the greens, waiting for the shows to start, with their texts pocketed and their labours lost in love. Shakespeare is not a text but a festival, a rite, and there's no clue to give you the meaning of it. After all, one cannot be a disciple, merely a devotee. There is no order and no rule; merely this pilgrimage to this particular town where the records are so scant that they make you jump for joy. The visitors' books are swollen with weird and ghastly names; and him in his niche by the altar is full of a kind of indecent pride; not for literary benefits or the shabby flourishes of the critics, BUT SIMPLY BECAUSE HE GOT SO MANY OF HIS FAMILY BURIED IN AN HONOURABLE PLACE INSIDE THE ALTAR RAILS. Lashings of them. No, his is the burgess-pride, the small-town pride of the local boy who has made better than good. And that is why the Americans love him, god bless the reverent slinkers in holy places; they rejoice in the trouble he took to buy his arms and set up prosperously in New Place with the river running silver under his elbow, and a fig for Momus* as exemplified by London or the muse.

I had a long and fruitful meditation in New Place, the little trim garden where the house stood from which he was carried down by water (I would hope) to Trinity when he popped off. I thought of the will he left; reading it, you intrude, because this is not Shakespeare as we think we know him, but a small cloth-weaver, or bailiff's butt, or a parish choir-master. The simplicity of purpose dazzles one; it is so self-possessed and enclosed in its private items that you see at once that there was no writer left by this time; only man. Then, knowing his writing, and reading his will, you begin to understand how self-possessed this great artist must have been in order to outgrow his art and enter his manhood. The subtilty and purity of this conclusion moves me almost more than this most tragic tragedy. Indeed, I like the five-year silence the best in his life; because across this silence I seem to hear the quiet lucid notes of musical LIVING fall at last. From the fluent and profuse Folio subtract the formal will, the epitaph, the little memoranda of his lawsuits, quarrels, barterings and swappings. You get a kind of precipitate—a tiny residue of meaning which is harder than a diamond and so obvious, so beautifully obvious, like a mathematical conclusion. This is the kind of thing that tells you all you need to know; the other falsifies. Have you ever read the list of books in Greco's library? Or the list of works in Newton's library? Half a page of them and you nod and begin to see the style of the soul shining through. All the factual details, the problems of the man in the cloak, or the duke who wore a feather, or the dark nobody—these are simply the husk of things, contaminated by passing through the wringer of time. There is a message, of course; not an absolute commandment, but a hint, a riding-post on a hill. It is Prospero's last epilogue over the Venetian water; the secret is embedded there for all who want it. It is the gesture of a chap who stuck close to the mystery, mastered it, and learned a kind of inner service to events. Otherwise he would have left us a suitcase of notes about his love-life like poor Johnny Gawsworth; or would have thrown his biographers off the track like dear artless and great simple Henry Miller. Or he would have hopped like a flea and piped my kind of indecency from every tuffet.

I wonder if I can express what haunts me about the Silence, more

* Greek God of ridicule.

[55]

than anything the Silence? I think immediately of Lao Tzu going over the hills to the land of Dragons on his patient water-buffalo. Don't laugh; the analogy is close. I think quickly of the Pythagorean silence in Barbary. A peasant in the Ionian. A shop-girl who lives in Gloucester Terrace. Four kinds of the very same mystery; a kind of buoyancy in the event, non-attachment, the inward patience, the inner substance taut and yet resilient. In these people, all of them, I get the same silence = and from them a kind of parable of the good life spent in the service of infinitesimal seconds. I can't make it any clearer; the mere metaphysics of the thing doesn't stand up formally. But I mean realizing how PATIENT every second is as it passes through the heart and causes its tick; and the trick of dwelling on that patience, resting on it until the mirage clears, and the world becomes, FOR THE FIRST TIME, REALITY. I mean becoming the living signature of the paradox; not merely making one and passing on. It is really so simple, and yet these quiet smiling gentlemen in their graves leave us limping at it, and gnawing the edges of fear and restraint.

Really, I haven't strayed from Avon; I am closer to Shakespeare than ever. Because this is the X you will find written all over his town and grave and monuments; and this is the lack which you see in his worshippers—the empty place inside which they cannot fill, and so come to Stratford drawn by a dim tribal necessity for ritual and learning.

It's getting late and my hammering disturbs Nancy; but I could write more and shall about this X which I need to anchor-pin my own self. I looked back from the last Warwick hill and gloated. I suppose it is too ridiculous. Love to Vivian.

Lawrence

Greece

When the clouds of war loomed up Mrs. Durrell brought the younger members of her family back to England. In 1939 Durrell, accompanied by Nancy, moved to Athens working first for the Embassy as an unestablished press officer, and then for the British Council who subsequently posted him to Kalamata in the Peloponnese where he taught at the Institute of English Studies. While in Athens he met two Greeks, strikingly different in character, who were to remain close friends for life. The gentle and sensitive George Seferiades is the leading Greek poet of our time, an able diplomat who, in 1957, was to be accredited as Ambassador to the Court of St. James's. He writes under the name of Seferis and some of his poems have been translated into English by Durrell. In direct contrast, George Katsimbalis is a larger-than-life Rabelaisian figure with huge gusto, whose character suggested to Henry Miller the title of his book of Greek experiences, The Colossus of Maroussi. *During the First World War Katsimbalis and Theodore Stephanides served together in the same battery in the Greek artillery.*

From time to time Theodore reminisces about his days as a gunner. No man, it seems, could be commissioned as an artillery officer unless he had directed the fire of a gun at least once. At that time the allied armies were cooped up within a narrow territory, each unit almost on top of another. Theodore was given the relative data the night before the test, and, determined to succeed, worked out the bearings over and over again with his habitual scientific accuracy. The great moment came, the gun fired, and the projectile landed upon a tent, belonging to the medical corps, in which a surgical operation was in progress. Absolutely certain that his calculations were correct, Theodore insisted that they be investigated; he was proved right, the data being based on true north, while the gun had been 'laid' by magnetic north. 'I am probably the only doctor', Theodore is accustomed to recall with a smile, 'who has dropped a shell into an operating theatre.' Considering that his book Climax in Crete *is one of the best individual accounts of a campaign written from the human point of view, it is to be hoped that one day he will publish his experiences in the first war.*

For several years Durrell had been trying, in vain, to persuade Henry Miller to come on a visit to Corfu. But now at last he came to Athens, and then, together with Durrell and Nancy, made the journey through the Peloponnese in a small borrowed car, which he describes in his book.

In 1941 the Nazis invaded Greece, and the ensuing blitzkrieg *swept through the country in a few weeks. At this time Durrell and Nancy were living in Kalamata, and they managed to escape from Navarino, carrying their three-month-old daughter Penelope (Pinkie) in a pannier basket, 'like a loaf of bread'. Refugees of all kinds crowded onto an old caique; fortunately the seas were calm, for the ship had a heavy list and was dangerously overloaded. By day, in order to avoid being dive-bombed by the German planes which seemed to fill the skies, they anchored close up against cliffs. When darkness fell the caique chugged out to sea, the engine emitting a constant trail of sparks, an almost perfect target. However, after a number of incidents, some of them rather picaresque in retrospect, they reached Crete.*

The Embassy in Cairo sent a ship to rescue the King of Greece, the British diplomats accredited to him, and various Greek worthies who, having fled from Athens, were gathered in Crete. There was a slightly Wodehousian touch, for when the ship was about to sail the King could not be found. By now it seemed that half the Middle East was in flight, as hundreds of people crowded onto a freighter which sailed about the same time, but at last the whole motley company, the Durrells among them, reached Alexandria in safety.

To Anne and Vivian Ridler   40 Anagnostopoulou, Athens [Late 1939]
Dear Anne & Vivian,

Just a note to bless you for Xmas and the new year which becomes more problematical as the days pass. We have just arrived back dog-tired from a trip to Sparta. A friend of mine lent us his little Morris and Nancy, Miller and I went on an atmospheric adventure to Mistra, via Corinth, Argos, Tripoli, Sparta. The country is so still and wild; valleys unbelievably remote and pure. A serpentine hogsback to Sparta like the nether end of Tibet: huge sailing white clouds, and snow like lies on Taegetus. I'm trying to write a little thing about it now. Miller is in a permanent delirium about Greece: left for U.S.A. yesterday in a whirl of emotions. If ever there were valleys and enchanted places where the charm still holds good, it is here. Until you have seen the lion gate at Mycenae or the huge gumps of rock where Tiryns lies in the Argive valleys, you can't get the impact of those weird Homeric phrases which always disturbed me. 'The halls of Atreus'. Nemea too: a still pure meadowland surrounded by snow-bound hills, and great soft cloudscapes. The modern villages lie in dirty straggles over these wonderful sites, with their inhabitants yawning and scratching themselves. In Corinth on Xmas eve was strange; we felt so unreal we began sending fantastic postcards everywhere—even sent Eliot one of the more crazy. Talk about *The Poet's Tongue* which I have just been reading: these people spoke of bricks and ramps of solid rock. It was funny to scratch up a finger-bone in Mycenae: quite preserved and white from the earth, but of no weight, like wood washed up by the sea. Funnier still to read the crazy folk-songs of Auden in the book. The taste of mock-naiveté is like the taste for negro sculpture: runs off the rails every now and then.

OLD GREEK FOLK-SONG

Old Aegisthus warmed his balls
In Agamemnon's marble halls,
Marble halls, marble halls.

Clytemnestra on the spot,
She said nowt but thought a lot,
On the spot, on the spot.

Put a watchman on the shore,
Just to please her paramour,
On the shore, on the shore,

One day came a puff of smoke,
From their lustful couch they woke,
Puff of smoke, puff of smoke.

'Agamemnon comes' said he,
A-counting of his rosary,
'Comes' said he, 'Comes' said she.

'Lay the table. Make it snappy!'
Thus Aegisthus, far from happy.
'Make it snappy, make it snappy!'

[59]

Clytemnestra hatched a plot,
She said nowt but thought a lot,
Thought a lot, *thought a lot.*

'Agamemnon! what a cough!
Take that soaking armour off!'
What a cough, what a cough.

In the barf-room this prosaic
Wife nailed him to the mosaic,
The mosaic, the mosaic.

Then with minds for words too full,
They sacrificed a cordial bull,
Words too full, words too full.

We know simply nothing about them; at once on our coming back
we began to hunt up the history and archaeology of the Argos plain;
sad what a muddle it is in; a tissue of conjectures and hypotheses built
upon grains of rice and traces of horse-manure. No. But the places
await their real interpreters; even bloody mud-lashed Eleusis with its
grimy petrol-stations. Somewhere we have missed the whole point, of
that I am sure. All we can do is this sort of thing, which I am sending to
the *N.E.W.*

Song in the valley of Nemea:
Quite quiet, quiet, quite quiet here.
Song of the cock pheasant in Argos,
The purr of the doves in Corinth,
Quite quiet, quite quiet.

Under the sward the sword,
Under the dolmen the man's helm:
Over Agamemnon tumulus, tumulus,
Under the stone queen cumulus.

Song in the valley of Nemea:
Quite quiet, quiet, quite quiet here.
Song of the wild bone in the ruined hall,
Song of the fox's paw on the yellow skull,
Quite quiet, quite quiet.

Which shows our limitations at a blow; but what can one do? Our spiritual expense begins and ends with good wishes. Plenty of every kind for you two in the new year. YOU MUST See Greece one day.
love. l.

To Anne Ridler   40 Anagnostopolou, Athens
                                         October late   [1939 ?]

Dear Anne,

I have been more or less tonguetied: the war is like a great severance, and your voices sound muffled across the gulf. I have written to no one, because there is not an atom of comfort to be given. It is a huge symbolic contortion in which individual lives seem to lose their significance and shape. I am cut to the heart and dumb.

We performed a masterpiece of unnecessary escape from Corfu when it came in a weather weird and autumnal; vast Japanese craters of pearl grey cloud over Albania, a dazzling thin rain like star-dust, and a black sheet of viscid water between us and Albania. Standing on our balcony over the sea it seemed like the end of the world. The whole hillside lay with its cheek in a cloud, the cypresses all stiff and priapic with dew. The children weeping in the garden. Every able-bodied man was mobilized and every horse; the town was swarming with escapists. Only one boat came so far north to disgorge Cretan infantry. It was the most mournful period of my life those dark masses of humanity murmuring by the lapping water like the Jews in Babylon; such passionate farewells, so many tears, so much language, it made one deaf. I had nothing to say goodbye to except the island, and it seemed already lost. Huge naphtha flares on the boats unloading flour and bullets. Four regiments deployed in idiotic positions over the north east of the island, sitting in the dark. I managed to go round the defences before coming away; Leslie and I always swore to defend Corfu against the Italians, and we fought the whole thing out during the winter shoots, taking into account everything, including fleet movements. Ill luck found him in England; and I could get no ratification of my naval intelligence job, so the one thing to do was to get to Athens. It was horrible leaving them to fight the wrong battles in the wrong places; the commander of the fort was in hysterics, planning to place submarine tubes outside our house and mine the straits and God knows what else. The infantry marched about with stony faces, smelling like hell, but with great morale; how the Italians are loathed! All the village was sent inland to a secret dump of arms, Nicholas the schoolmaster, horny-handed Jani with the limp, who can lift the cutter by the bowsprit, and Anastassiou our suave, cool, beautiful landlord, too feminine and hysterical to handle a cold rifle I always thought. There were only the women left to weep round the wells, and the uncomprehending black children with eyes like mulberries. I ached for them all. The voyage was terrific; all the weathers blew at once, mountainous seas off Ithaca and Santa Maura, and got us pitching and swinging in this damned smoky little steamer. From Patras we caught the automotrice and arrived in Athens at dead of night.

For the last month I have been working for the Legation here as a sort of private Godfrey Winn, checking on opinion. Now a new man has arrived from England and sacked the whole of a very efficient and necessary department. It was all very Compton Mackenzie, racing round Athens in taxis, being followed and escaping. Now good English departmentalism has triumphed over those of us who knew Greece and Greek, and liked both. His Majesty's Press Attaché rules the roost. The same inert supine attitude as the last war; the same idiotic complacence and over-confidence. Our money will save us, however, whatever the dolts do.

I am moving in Nov. to the British Council, where I am to teach Greeks so help me; will be back in Corfu by the Spring I hope, unless Italy comes in, in which case I will get back sooner in some naval unit I hope. I do not want to fight in the north; I have absolutely no confidence in the cause or the fight promoters. The whole business stinks to heaven as a bankers' war, and I hope the bankers are the first to be bombed. If England was really as great in heart as geographically great her honour would be quicker over the Czechoslovakias of the world. For me I feel our international dignity is irreparably damaged; I put my name down to fight over the Czechs. But not after this shabby let-down of Poland, and the flabby bowelless attitude of the political casuists. Only look at the faces of cabinet without reading their hogwash and you see that they are a pack of degenerates. As for the French, they are beneath contempt both as neighbours and allies; mean, grasping, cringing. If nations can't have a sense of responsibility corresponding to their size (not their 'interests') then I don't feel that any of us who are honourable or passionate should lift a finger to help them. Bang! These are the uncharitable sentiments which I have been hugging under my player's hide while I was a faithful servant of his majesty, writing wonderful articles in the Greek press, and conceiving wily schemes for the furtherance of our arms. Now as a teacher I breathe more freely.

L.

To George Wilkinson   40 Anagnostopoulou, Athens
[1940 ?]

Dear George,

It was good to hear from you again, even if your diffidence was quite alarming. I don't know where you got the hollow laughs with which you punctuated your letter; they didn't come from me. I regard weaving and raffia work and all allied crafts with the deepest reverence. And rejoice to see you making panniers for a living; it's certainly a more noble living than making puns or poems. I haven't written anything for ages; and now the war has come I am all corners and edges. Nancy should present the world with a prodigy in May or so; watch the heavens for appropriate comets. I worked here for the legation for awhile which gave me a spurious caste and quite incidentally a decent salary; then we were closed down neck and crop, Theo and I, and half a dozen other worthies all neck and neck in the desperate pot-hunting game. In the meantime official lunacy runs like a millrace. British propaganda is enough to break your heart; huge manuals of *Times* prose served up like indigestible dumpling to an avid but illiterate public. . . . In the meantime I am teaching English with abandon and circumspection at the British Institute; in May the institute closes for a holiday and I am off to the islands to hide out. What news there is is either too true to repeat or too much repeated to be true; multiply the Corfiot rumour by twelve and you get an idea of the kind of humming which keeps Athens going. Nevertheless the Acropolis is quite pure and beautiful on its plateau of white space, and the sun shows no sign of minding. In a way it's pleasant to live thus, with the future amputated and the Finnish mists gathering, and a numbness in the hands and feet.

First spring weather arrived just in time for carnival; masked figures, and huge branches of almonds being sold in the street; a performing bear answering to Turkish commands. On Sunday we gather at Wuthering Heights (Katsimbalis' home) in Amarousion, and talk Greek literary politics until my heart bleeds. The mountains are still covered with snow and air is fresh as ether and electrical. Tomorrow is Monday and I begin my classes again. Earning a living is an awful business. Love to Pamela and Nicola (who will be Nicoloula when she visits Greece). All the best. Drop me a line when you feel like it. And spare not the rod with your young prep school boys with their shining morning faces. I make not mention of perversion. But avoid it if you can. Cheerio.

Larry.

———————

To Anne Ridler   40 Anagnostopoulou, Athens
                                  [Early June 1940]

Dear Anne,

I haven't written because the silence was becoming heavier and heavier to lift; and the bombs getting easier and easier to drop. And now this damned breakdown in France! One gets so baffled. Nine months ardent boasting and preparation, and Adolf walks through like taking the baby's rattle away. And all our nice red heroes fighting like lions to what end? Then when I see the kind of mummies who have the responsible jobs here, I begin to understand and sympathize with those who start parties; there is still this mental vacuum in which the English gentleman is busy despising the Greeks too much to propagand, and trusting the willies too much to enquire whether they are pure in heart. Now the whole thing must start all over again; and tomorrow Benito speaks, and I wonder whether this will reach you. Terrific wave of pessimism about us in the Balkans; they live, you know, on the successes of the strongest, and this retreat has badly shaken them.

As for me, my dears, I am all but a master of hearts here—and a widower of arts. I did a few little poems not awfully good, but I am too distracted by what is looming up. I have been offered a council job in Cyprus now, with more money; but if the Mediterranean goes up in smoke I don't know how I'll get there. Nancy is still withholding the superman; it might have to be from island to island by fishing boats and across Turkey. O dear. The Council people here are a splendid lot, very popular and efficient; the British colony spends its time trying to get them sent to the war. The only terror about Cyprus is that they might mistake me for a mule and pop me into the muleteer corps; I'd prefer something either safer or more glorious.

I have done the whole first act of the play but am not sending it anywhere; my collected poems are coming out in newspaper form in Cyprus with my first month's pay; no review copies, just one for you and one for me and one for the dog. Miller is fighting a huge battle in USA for an edition of the B.B., and I am trying to stop him; you've no idea what a funny story the whole thing is. He is cracked about Greece, writing a book about it now, and about us all it seems.

Is Eliot coming here? Tell him to come and wash away the taste of Binyon, who bumbled and bombinated for a few weeks and then crawled away into the woodwork of the Orient Express again. If he does come here and I am not near, will he please get in touch with George Seferiades, his Greek translator, and chief foreign press censor, who is a remarkable poet and person: the most civilized man in Balkania. He is at the ministry of tourism here, and will show him Greece if he cares to see it like no other man.

I did rather despise the flavour of off-licence sherry and lilies which *Horizon* distils, but so happy that you are up and coming; if one has anything good, you know, it does no harm where it appears. . . .

Somebody just blew in and told me that four-fifths of the B.E.F. is saved; I hope it's true. It will be a triumph of a sober kind. Here the situation will be more amusing, the fighting more open if it comes, and full of funny panics and staggering advances. When you write Moore ask him to send me a bundle of copies of 7 in which I appear; I love reading my own stuff printed so far. Like talking to my own ghost. . . .

Today is a blue day, pure as a kingfisher from here to Nauplia; I wish I could cut you a slice of this bell-blue heaven and water and time. One leans forward on the toes and has the sensation of flying; and the whole town lies outside the window, polished and graven up like a shield. Anyway I send you a little poem which is quite quite inadequate.

If all goes well we shall leave for Cyprus on the 13th; write us care of the BRITISH INSTITUTE, P.O. Box 42. Nicosia. Cyprus. Otherwise if we get stuck I shall willy nilly have to be Lawrence of Albania or Corfu.

And so, my dears, all the best for the turning of the water of our tears into the wine of victory; and safety and an après la guerre when such things will be written as make the philistines to gape and the little fishes to dance.

love. larry.

To Anne Ridler   c/o British Institute.
                                       Hermes Street, Athens   [1941]
Just a swift note dear Anne and Vivian to find out if you are all right: just got permission for this to fly round in the bag, so there is some hope of you getting it. What an awful mess this war becomes: let us hope some agreement by arms can be reached short of absolute destruction. Woe on the damnable apathy that's brought us to this! Woe Chamberlain!

I feel a little guilty because here the sun's great candle etc. and the sea rolls quietly at the foot of the temple in Sunion without any interest in our scurvy wars: went to see *Agamemnon* on Sunday. The heights of the rock blazing hot, dizzy with cicadas, and the Argolis so sweet and calm like always. Bathed naked at Kinetta from a pure dazzling white shingle beach, every pebble perfectly oval as if sucked by generations of Chinese women: and twenty feet of water clear like heavy glass, slightly frosted over: later from the Corinth road saw dolphins playing like black shields in the Salamis. So remote from Heinkel and Hair-raid shelter were we. Did you know? I have a thumping daughter, with the ancestral nose and a voice like a bittern. We are supposed to be sent down to Kalamata in southern Peloponnesus in late August to start a school there. Rich wild and unvisited country again—how I adore Greece, and how lucky I am to be here really, in spite of everything. I am not writing a line needless to say except little poems; one can't somehow with the war going on. But I'm germinating a marvel-lous novel which I shall never have time to write.

Miller has written a huge book about his Greek trip with fantastic portraits of all of us in it. Very amusing.

I hear from no one in England—and no one hears from me I spose: even lost touch with my family.

I can't do better than quote Miller's last post-card to end this letter: "Bless you and keep you: we belong to the new world, remember, so keep yr head." Don't forget that Anne—and make Vivian keep his head *down*—I have a feeling we'll all come through.

Love—Larry

To Anne Ridler   Institute of English Studies
                                                  Kalamata, Greece [1941?]

Dear Anne,

Just a line to tell you that my poems have been sent off and will probably arrive before the invaders do. By now you must be feeling like Sir Thopas

'Love is a Lord of misrule
And keepeth Christmas in my corpse'

I do hope it's a boy and at least as much fun for you as Ping-Kêe [Penelope] is for us with four rabbit-teeth and a snub nose: she can now make every sound within the range of a seven and sixpenny dollie. It is strange this lovely valley: orchards and undulations and oranges: particularly unreal when the sirens go and the little children dash for the trees. Last week an Italian seaplane nearly flew into our room: no bombs, just curiosity but we all got a fright. Places round about have been plastered and we have had visitors right overhead and low several times but as yet no bombs—Just as I wrote that a terrific explosion outside. Rushed down to get Pinkie who was being walked by the sea: mystery. No planes—no damage. They say perhaps a mine has exploded against the further harbour.

By the way, will you ask Eliot if he ever received the Modern Greek translation of the Rock and Wasteland by my friend Seferiades the poet? It's the best translation into any European language and S. is the Eliot of Greece: can Eliot read Greek?

He says he sent E. a copy c/o Faber a long time ago: Miller is doing a sort of Crazy Gang book about Greece. Wish I could do something but just can't. Am still waiting on the Air Force: and of course we are waiting for the Bulgarians too.

In the meantime I am a peripatetic teacher of English in a Greek factory town. Not so Socratic or so damned rusty as might be: I have gigantic plans and bulging notebooks—but no πνεῦμα. [soul].

I enclose a topical comic anti-wop song much sung here: with all good wishes to V. and you and Alan Pringle and D.B.

After this damned war we won't half write things of value, won't we?
'εν τὸ μεταξὺ in the meantime

Love from us all

Keep yourselves safe

and hurrah for the spring-child

Larry

Egypt

The hordes of refugees that poured into Egypt were held in two camps until they had been screened; for the authorities feared, not without reason, that Nazi agents would have been infiltrated into their company. Those proved to be innocent were accommodated in requisitioned hotels while they arranged the transfer of money, found a place in which to live and generally organized their new life. Theodore Stephanides, now a medical officer in the R.A.M.C. and stationed in Egypt, went in search of his friends and found them living in Cairo at the Luna Park Hotel.

During his first months in Egypt, Durrell supported himself, to some extent, by writing a weekly funny column and a fair number of leaders for The Egyptian Gazette. *In August he was interviewed by Sir Walter Smart, Oriental Counsellor, and taken on by the British Embassy in Cairo as Foreign Press Officer. He had been chosen because he now spoke Greek fluently and had a considerable knowledge of the Greek temperament. His field of work lay in supplying the Greek press with information and generally influencing their editorial line in harmony with the Allied cause. In 1944 he was posted, as Press Attaché, to Alexandria, a city where the Greek population, numbering some three hundred thousand, supported several daily newspapers and a variety of weekly journals in their own language.*

During the war years in Egypt Durrell was, to a large extent, cut off from his friends in northern Europe, most of whom, in any case, were scattered in the services; but he was soon to form important new friendships that were to prove enduring.

Cairo was, at least nominally, neutral; the Germans did not attempt any bombing; indeed, it was one of the few large cities of the old world to escape the 'blackout', and the lights shone brightly all night. The front line at Alamein was only eighty miles away; when friends disappeared into the desert to fight and then came back for the weekend, it seemed as if they had been riding to hounds rather than taking part in a war. Brilliant people from many walks of life found themselves at the nerve centre of the Middle East and coalesced into groups bound

*by mutual interests; indeed Cairo almost took on an aspect of London, and the
social life of this somewhat seedy capital received a shot in the arm.*

*G. S. Fraser, looking back on those days, quoted the title-phrase of Hazlitt's
essay: 'This was the time of my first acquaintance with the poets.' Among the
young writers stationed in Egypt were Bernard Spencer, Keith Douglas, George
Fraser, Gwyn Williams, Patrick Leigh Fermor, Xan Fielding and Lord Kinross;
while, later in the war, the celebrated ballet dancer, Diana Gould (now Diana
Menuhin) spent some time in Alexandria. Under the stimulation of these conditions a good deal of poetry emerged, some of which first appeared in the eight
numbers of a magazine, edited by Durrell and Robin Fedden and printed in
Cairo:* Personal Landscape, A Magazine of Exile, 1942–45.

*During the general apprehension and disruption of life caused by the near
approach towards Cairo of the Germans under Rommel, Nancy moved to
Palestine, taking Pinkie with her. The marriage which was already under some
strain now broke up and Nancy did not return to Egypt. About a year later
Durrell met and fell in love with an Alexandrian girl, Eve Cohen, who was to
become his second wife.*

Thinking about 'Smartie'

Reprinted from Walter Smart by Some of His Friends. 1963.

Despite the eminence of his official rank nobody in the Cairo Embassy ever succeeded in thinking of him as anything but 'Smartie'—even down to the secretaries and typists. Where the nickname came from I do not know but it imposed itself on us all and carried with it a concrete image of this lovable, whimsical, curious and delightful man. Perhaps the most endearing of his many qualities was that he was afflicted by one of the intellectual pieties which one finds more often among Frenchmen than Englishmen: he was an 'artist-cherisher'.

This was brought home to me during my first week as a junior in the Press Department of the Cairo Embassy. I was late for the office one afternoon (I had been lunching with an Egyptian poet), and when I arrived I heard, with sinking heart, that my Oriental Councillor had been looking for me: had, indeed, actually dropped into my office. This was unheard of—for normally juniors were summoned, not *visited*. I immediately concluded that Smartie was a low-down dog who had been testing my punctuality and general efficiency by a surprise visit. (I was rather weak in both qualities.) I picked up the phone and rang his office; immediately his voice came over the wire, warm and reassuring. 'I wanted to talk to you about your new book of poems which Amy and I got yesterday,' he said. He sounded almost apologetic for troubling such a great man!

Talk we did, later that evening, in his beautiful Cairo house, with its great army of books, on a terrace overlooking a shady garden and my timidity melted almost as swiftly as the ice cubes in my glass. I had discovered (as everyone did) The Smarts. The house itself was a fitting frame for a life which might be described as one of pure intellectual curiosity—it was crammed with books, paintings, manuscripts, pamphlets in a number of languages. But it was not merely the house of a ' great collector, or an antiquary, or a patron of the arts. There was a continuous and *purposeful* life being lived there among its treasures which included several big grave thoughtful paintings by Smartie's wife Amy Nimr. And so many books! Persian, French, Arabic, Greek . . . The house of the Smarts was a hinge between a dozen cultures; their world was completely international and the house reflected it. It smelt of Paris, Damascus, Jerusalem, Istanbul, Cairo, London and New York. I became (as everyone did) a frequent visitor. If one were invited to tea one never knew whom one would meet—a soldier just back from India or Ethiopia, a parachutist-poet like Patrick Leigh Fermor or Xan Fielding, a Persian poet, a mystic, a scholar of international renown, or perhaps even a pure eccentric deeply cherished by Smartie and Amy for a wayward habit of life or a singular theory about the Holy Ghost.

Smartie's first anecdote fully illustrated this physiological predisposition towards the arts and sciences; he told me, with that delightful self-deprecating ruefulness with which he always gave point to a story against himself, just how as a junior accredited to Cairo he had committed the worst of all sins by forgetting, not only to sign the book, but even to present himself for duty for a number of days. The reason for this lapse was that someone had given him an introduction to a then completely unknown Greek poet called C. P. Cavafy who lived over a brothel in Alexandria. Smartie had been impelled to visit him and spend several days talking literature with him. It was well worth the reprimand, he added.

But if Smartie adored and cherished artists he never used them for copy, so to speak; he savoured and enjoyed them, derived amusement and self-instruction from them, but would never have dreamed of publishing anything about them. He was like a Persian monarch in his attitude to his artists. An English poet once said: 'Smartie is so refreshing because he always makes art seem worth while.' And it was something more than a *boutade* when someone else coined the phrase, 'Art for Smartie's sake'.

After the war, and after Suez, the axis shifted though not the central preoccupation; for the lovely Norman house belonging to the Smarts took over the role of the now sequestrated Cairo one. Poets, writers, painters converged on Gadencourt to gladden Smartie's heart with their banter and their theories, while for his part he delighted in building log fires and stoking the Aga against the mammoth meals which were put before them.

Physically he was very tall and thin; he had a sort of head which made sculptors feel hungry. A long wide slanting nose which gave his face sometimes (in repose) a slight resemblance to Wellington, but more often to some Norman knight of the past. There was always the suggestion of a smile—and indeed one cannot think of Smartie's smile without instantly hearing the small and wicked chuckle with which he always greeted a jest. The general impression he created was one of gentle singularity, while the lively eager flow of his questions held always a hint of ingenuousness. Something in him remained fresh and unspoiled, like a child bubbling over with youthfulness; and I cannot recall ever meeting a happier man. And, of course, happiness is infectious. With Smartie everything became a treat, even a bus ride across Paris, even walking to the corner to post a letter. The whole world held a sort of pristine freshness for him—it was always newly born, curious, variegated and utterly absorbing. And, of course, after a few moments with him one began to see it through his eyes rather than through one's own. There was inspiration to be gained this way and encouragement—as necessary to artists as oxygen.

I dare not mourn his passing—the memory of his chuckle inhibits me. Besides, he himself once told me wistfully that he would have given almost anything to have a chance of discussing poetic theory with the Sufi poet Jalaluddin Rumi—'if only one could reach the brute'. Perhaps he has. At any rate I seem to hear the quiet laughter and conversation of their shades as I write.

L.

To Theodore Stephanides   British Information Office
                                           Alexandria [Spring 1944]
Dear Theodore,

Thank you for your letter which was entertaining but rather too Pun-gent for my taste. But then, as Paul says, your bite was always worse than your Barce;* yes, I think the material you mention is excellent. One thing is important—I think you should keep the locality

* Barce, near Benghazi, where Dr. Stephanides was serving at the time.

the same all through—Greece, or Corfu, but always the same place; because as well as the facts you must also put in some colour. Paragraphs? Yes—like this—

XX–III–40

'Today Spring has moved a step nearer: the anemones in the great field below Glysoura are bright and pristine once more after a night's rain, and Marco sings in the fields at his work. He is singing a song called "Is Death a Kind of Sleep?" and as I listen to it sitting in this white sterile laboratory, I am reminded once more how deeply the limitations of science weigh on us: how impenetrable the veil is. "Is Death a kind of sleep?" Biological death, according to Purdy, is . . .'
'Flower-hunting with young David I find that he does not know that butterflies are blind:—The gorgeous stupid waste of so much colour in flowers plays no part in the biological scheme of things . . .'

Quite freely and easily bringing in your information in a given context. Invent some people, peasants and so on—and treat them quite boldly. Put them in and forget them just as you feel inclined; short sentences—no purple patches—no *Leacock*—and I think you should have a good book on your hands.

As for X words—I get too many of those from my womenfolk to know how to place them for you. When do you get some leave? Billie and Paul [Gotch, in British Council] would like to know. Come and Stay. And see the Embassy people, you silly.

[Signed with caricature self-portrait.]

To Anne Ridler   [Cairo, Egypt 1942 ?]
Well my dear Anne,

Once more the communiqué with its familiar disasters making one feel quite loquacious and talkative; I haven't felt like writing a line to anyone, being so dead to the world in this copper-pan of a blazing town with its pullulating stinking inhabitants—Middle East is Far enough east for me. But it is so nice to get your lovely letter AND marvellously well-recollected and unstrained poem for Vivian. I must dash off at eight and show it to Bernard [Spencer]—poem and letter and to Dorian Cooke.

No sooner did I get permission to use the bag than I loaded up four envelopes with poems and sent them direct to TSE. I also sent some translations of Rilke by Ruth Speirs, and have persuaded Bernard S to collect for a book which God willing will also wing its way Faberwards. There is nothing else doing—*Personal Landscape* should be in London by now—One Special copy on light paper we printed specially for TSE as an inducement to send us a poem about IT.

The photo is awfully nice and how frightfully healthy she looks—O I wish we are all in the Orkneys instead of in this terrible blinding sand-pan with its mocking hideous tombs and minarets. Such a country—cripples, deformities, opthalmia, goitre, amputations, lice, flies. In the street you see horses cut in half by careless drivers or obscene dead black men with flies hanging like a curtain over their wounds and a crowd hemming them in with ghoulish curiosity. Dust in the air carrying everything miasmic, fevers, virus, toxins,—One writes nothing but short and febrile like jets by this corrupt and slow Nile; and one feels slowly walked upon by the feet of elephants. . . .

To Diana Gould [Menuhin]   British Information Office
                                            Alexandria   March 1944

Dearest Diana,

I can't think why you haven't heard. I've written twice and sent you two little poems—the best I can do at the moment—which I am putting in the anthology for you. . . . Rainy streets; a decaying poster on a hoarding lit by a splash of light from a tobacconist's shop said DIANA GOUL   THE MER   IDOW. PEELING. And back at the office I open a copy of *Vanguard* and find you dancing from left to right with deep captions in French and your strained rather pale face looking out at the world with that curious mixture of self-possession and self-deprecation. . . . Meanwhile we sing your duck song in tragic voices Gwyn and I by Mareotis and wonder how soon we can get out of this country. Now that the press pictures of the Italian front come in I feel a little nearer to you—pictures of Vesuvius carrying away towns and trees and churches. I suppose you must have received Gwyn's charming epigram by now?

> The proof that you're in Naples, not with us,
> Is the misbehaviour of Vesuvius.

Meanwhile the ubiquitous dust and blackness; the faces of the Arabs with their weakness and cupidity.

The thin exhausted lusts of the Alexandrians running out like saw-dust out of dummies; the shrill ululations of the black women, the rending of hair and clothes in mourning—a skilled occupation—outside the whitewashed hospital. The tarbush, the dark suit, the rings, the French accent; the scrofula, the pox, the riches, the food. Even in your Italian brothel I cannot think how to write or speak to you from this flesh-pot, sink-pot, melting-pot of dullness.

I have typed out your clerihews for the anthology . . . which looks very good to me—god knows how it will read in the muddy light of an English summer; to the woollen and gaitered literary gents who are fast turning literary practice into a ministry of dehydration. A lot of variation in the material; a sense of humour; AND NO PERSONAL PUBLICITY. NO NOTES ON CONTRIBUTORS. 'Miriam Featherwight writes "at the age of twelve I was apprenticed to a glass-blower from whom I learned all about life. He urged me to write in the intervals of blowing retorts for the grammar school laboratories. This is my first published story. I can box, throw stones, and am fond of chess." '

Dearest Diana, your Bexhill Menu is a beauty. We have also collected a number of shop signs and wall-notices. For example 'THE OXFORD IRONY' (Cairo Laundry Sign).

I am meditating a section on puns too—perhaps to include Barron's revolting story of the two bugs in the mortuary. One saying to the other 'Come on, let's make love in dead earnest'. . . . My love to you.

[Signed with caricature self-portrait.]

Rhodes

Durrell did not return to Greece until 1945. The Dodecanese Islands, captured from the Italians during the war, were destined, a few years later, to be handed over to the Greeks, but in the interregnum they were governed by the British. Durrell was appointed Public Information Officer with his headquarters in Rhodes, responsible for running newspapers in three languages and other forms of publicity. He was accompanied by Eve, and they established themselves in the Villa Cleobulus, a charming little house set in a Turkish cemetery; where, for the greater part of their free time, they lived out of doors under an immense plane tree which shaded the courtyard.

It was a great joy for Durrell to be freed from the atmosphere of war, to get away from Egypt and to be back in Greece once again. But there was a sharp distinction from the 'bliss was it in that dawn to be alive' atmosphere of pre-war Corfu. Many people in the Middle East were starving or living in conditions of the most fearful poverty and hardship; on the mainland civil war was being waged with the ferocious cruelty that forms a dark side to the character of this passionate people; while the ever-present menace of Stalinist communism pressed against the very frontiers of Greece itself. But despite the dark undertones this was one of the happiest periods of Durrell's life; Greece and the Greeks meant as much to him as ever, his position as a government officer conferred considerable privileges and freedom of movement; and, even if some of his colleagues were banal, there were others such as Romilly Summers and, especially, the Quaker doctor, Ray Mills, who became good friends. But above all he was deeply in love.

From time to time it has been Durrell's custom when living in some out-of-the-way place such as Rhodes, Ischia or Nicosia, to produce privately printed editions of his own works in limited editions; small booklets which have become the delight and despair of book-collectors. In Rhodes, being in charge of a whole battery of printing presses, he issued two of these: Zero and Asylum in the Snow, *two surrealist pieces which are reprinted in this book, and* The Parthenon, *a poem, for T. S. Eliot, printed in an edition of about thirty copies as a Christmas Card for friends.*

Life on Rhodes provided the material for Durrell's second island book, Reflections on a Marine Venus, *mainly written, in retrospect, after he had left the island. The original version was a great deal longer than the published text; too long, Fabers felt, for publication. Loath to perform disagreeable surgery upon a book which embodied so much of his own life, Durrell entrusted the task of cutting to Anne Ridler, the poet and critic, and an old friend whom he had met when she was working as secretary to T. S. Eliot. She carried out the work with perceptive sympathy; and in this form the book was published in 1953.*

Durrell had been writing for over twenty five-years before his books reached the general reading public; whereas his younger brother Gerald became widely popular, almost overnight, with his first book on collecting wild animals, The Overloaded Ark. *When* Reflections on a Marine Venus *received some good reviews, an old lady telephoned my bookshop: 'I want to order a book by a Mr. Durrell, not THE Mr. Durrell, it's not about animals at all.'*

Meanwhile, in 1945, Faber's published Prospero's Cell, *followed in 1946 by* Cities, Plains and People, *the first volume of Durrell's poetry to be issued by a regular publisher; and Tambimuttu, in charge of Editions Poetry London, brought out* Cefalû, *written, so Durrell was inclined to say, to pay for his divorce from Nancy; and* Personal Landscape, An Anthology of Exile, *a reprint in book form of the magazine published in Egypt during the war.*

To Gwyn Williams

Public Information Officer, Rhodes, Dodecanese Islands [1945]
MOI. BMA. ATB. MEF.

Dear Gwyn,

How nice to get your letter together with one from Diana saying that she'd seen you and was happy. . . . We have panned out with the most extraordinary luck: of course with every wangle known to man also involved: the embassy, the army, the Quakers and the pashas. It finally, like some spool of greasy film, unwound and there was a *laisser passer,* and we found ourselves on a filthy little Norwegian tanker in Alex harbour, with the inevitable last minute policeman trying to stop us, as in a film. I can't tell you how excited it was to see that misty eggshell blue go down as we tooled away from Alex. . . . We were locked up for two days with an assortment of Norwegian cut-throat

[78]

sailors, very good fun, before being shot into the lovely island of Carpathos. . . . What followed was so like one of my Mykonos dreams that even describing it spoils it. We went ashore and were led by ten little children, very clean and polite, through the warm scented morning through the bright crazy Douanier Rousseau town: no Douanier is too harsh: Paul Klee. Rows of pastel pink blue yellow and sugar-white houses in the bowl of the harbour. The children led us deftly through a German minefield to bathe on a dazzling scorched beach where the sea was livid and nitric. Then we all went up the hill together hardly speaking, and lay under a big spreading olive in an almond-orchard and here the children sat in a circle round us like druids and sang. It was beyond words clean and pure and life-giving. Then they got us water from the mountain spring, and were indignant when we wanted to tip them. And at every door in the village wonderful old wrinkled people blessed us and asked us in for a drink. E was in tears. And so, after two days' terrific northwind to the softer rounder fatter Rhodes. . . . Food is scarce and poor here but we are living in a Cecil B. de Mille hotel and masses of fruit to eat: I have a bunch of yellow grapes by me as I write. . . . Bathe in green sea at six. Run on grass. Sunshine like the wand of Apollo. Only there are too many military here with their NAAFI and coarse sports and false moustaches. Otherwise heaven.

write soon   Larry

To Gwyn Williams   MOI. Rhodes [1945]
Gwyn,

The corner of Wales sounds absolutely lovely and we were full of envy to hop over—but the work and the weather does not permit. Instead we have been seeing this island—the three ancient cities Lindos, Camiros and Ialysos: have been to Eve's first Panagyrie in a pine-forested hollow sacred to Saint Soula—whoever she is—dispenser of miracle water. We drive about all stately in a huge captured German car which must have belonged to at least an Oberkortschfunkler-Kommandant, all very official and respected servants of the crown: and we have already discovered two little houses which I would buy if I had any money. One lies on the lovely sinuous road to Calithea, on a small headland, bare and smooth, between two fig-trees. The other stands on the wutheringest height of Monte Smith (sacred to that British tree-nymph Sir Sidney Smif), tucked into the shoulder of hill and looking down twenty miles of valley.

Ach the blueness. Lindos lies like a city built of dazzling mica around a circle of shock-blue sea. One boat, clear, a man in blue shorts, two solidified ripples; it moves with the languorous slowness of a beetle in a glass of water. Camiros Castello on a bluff over the sea. Dead silent. A huge palpitating emptiness under it, and then the sea striking like a gong. Kestrels swerve about and a sudden wind swishes in the parasol pines. A man whistles his dog in the underworld and it echoes. I am snoring among the ginger-beer bottles and the crumbs of our picnic. Greece—you can't capture what the silence keeps erasing, a permanent fluidity at the edges of the world, washing away. And the warmth of the sun on old marbles or pebbles, or drying and warming the salt on the lobes of your ears so it crisps in your fingers. I am very happy. . . .

larry

To Sir Walter Smart   MOI. Rhodes 5 December 1945
Dear Sir Walter,

I am glad you liked Prospero. Which was read under what you might call test conditions! I'm afraid though that the life it tries to depict is impossible under a military dispensation however humane and liberal. The B.M.A. is doing a very good job here, but looking round them one wonders how the Somaliland Postal Service managed to spare so many of its most experienced men to administer this area. The people are ghastly, the island lovely, and the Greeks delightful and unspoiled —troublesome of course: argumentative, of course. But there are no party politics here. A complete calm. We live however very much alone; I have a case of books and Gipsy Cohen [Eve] is working in the office; every Sunday we take a pack and walk over the hills. There are places which still lie dreaming their pre-cyclopean dreams, untouched except where the German barbed wire traces its minefields round them. Camiros is far the loveliest of them; a blinding white town tucked in a knuckle between two limestone hills covered with deep green ilex and supple bright cypresses. You look down from the central plinth across a winding main street backed by the taut hard unpaintable blue of the sea, and the smoky chunks of the Turkish mainland.

Latterly *ONE* person has been a perfect companion on these trips. Romilly Summers, round as the setting sun, ruddy with good humour, wine and food; a companion out of the old world, a great walker and chatterer.

Every curve of the coast reminded him of somewhere in the Tyrol, somewhere in Hungary: a night in Buda: an incident on a train in Slovenia: a cheese in Gottingen, a wine in Tours—until one felt that he carried the whole of Europe synthesized and digested inside himself. Poor Romilly, he is being sent back to Egypt, a victim of a departmental intrigue! One still pays, it seems, for liking the Greeks and saying so! Everyone here hates them and loves the Italians. We are going to miss him terribly—a new sensation for me.

Formerly a provincial from a remote island who did not value talk and companionship enough, I find I miss the wonderful life that Cairo built up for itself, with its exiled poets and ruffians, and its visiting secret agents with poetic talent. . . . It is your fault for making a pasha of me and letting me learn about the good things of life.

All good wishes
Sincerely,
Larry Durrell

To Diana Gould   MOI. Rhodes 15 December 1945
. . . Dear Diana, I have been wanting to write to you but simply didn't dare because I was afraid I would sound so heartlessly healthy and the country so Shangri la that you would write me a stinker calling me a peach fed sod. But honestly the whole thing is a dream—I am so ashamed of the life we are leading here; and occasionally I let it out in a letter and get a wince back, a cry of anguish. Like Miss Grenside of Faber to whom I described the wonderful trees swollen with ice-cold and brilliant yellow tangerines, scented and gravid. She replied telling me how UNKIND I was—they hadn't seen fruit for years. So finally one gets cautious—like dealing with invalids. And I took down a pomegranate as big as a piano and tried to send it to her with a friend

on python;* but he sat on it in a transit camp in Egypt and had to eat it at last so he says. And you, my poor dear, what can I do for you but make you writhe and your mouth and soul water? I wish you could get out of England. Of course the food is dull, mostly macaroni, but the island is swollen with fruit and vegetables. There is no deprivation anywhere, except in friends. The military are beyond words awful. Cohen and I are quite alone. For an all too brief time we had Romilly Summers here, but he was posted again. However we have lovely rooms in this great hotel Shepherds on Sea, with private bath-rooms, running water . . . Oh shut up . . . This week we got a tin of butter from Egypt. How we enjoyed it! We sit and play chess on the little pocket board that Roland Pym gave us and read; by God's good grace, and my experience of islands, I managed to spend some money on books; lots of Proust, Dostoievski, and poetry. So we are going to withstand the siege of the winter I feel—ah but Diana you should see the landscape of Greece—it would break your heart. It has such pure nude chastity; it doesn't ask for applause; the light seems to come off the heart of some Buddhistic blue stone or flower, always changing, but serene and pure and lotion-soft on the iris. And the islands . . . Simi built up from the water in a series of eagle's nests; Calymnos like some grey scarab, grey sandstone mixed with milky specks and dots and dashes of blue; and the spacious olive-glades below the marble town of Camiros in Rhodes: and louring Leros. . . .

Lots of love and a bit of blue broken from the sky by special messenger

Larry

To T. S. Eliot   MOI. Rhodes April 1946
Dear TSE,

Many thanks for your letter. Yes, any contract you say. I've just received copies of CITIES PLAINS AND PEOPLE and am delighted with the production. I don't know how Faber does it, but I feel most grateful.

Latterly I ran off a poem which I felt I would like to dedicate to you

* Under Python leave any soldier who had been in the Middle East for more than four years was granted one month at home with his family and then three months in some unit in Britain.

as a mark of thanks for all your kind forbearance and generousness. I intended to make it one of my very best and worked for about three months hard on it. I then printed about thirty copies on the linotype and it seemed good—but I must leave it to dry for another six months; I am not sure but what it won't seem too cloying and overcharged. I send you another copy in case you didn't get the first.

There is no news of vast importance. I have been twice to Athens to hunt a job but found it full of mondaine people also hunting jobs; I fear we have done Greece harm by all the propaganda we've done for it these years. Everyone wants to go there now, and our market value as poor teachers and beggars has sunk. Heavily endowed literary figures are now on the scene like wasps round a jam-pot. I managed however to recover most of my *Book of the Dead*, which has set me thinking; and recasting to the tune of about five thousand words. But I can't be alone with myself these days. This job is beastly. And the verse play *Adam and Evil* has gone. But no matter; I have found a tiny house in a Turkish graveyard with a very low rent, and simply do not intend to go anywhere near Egypt if I can help it. Also I MUST do this big book sooner or later if I have to starve for the bloody thing. . . .

One thing that is driving me almost cuckoo about English writing today is this terrible cult for the urbane; anything that's too hot, that disturbs at all, is not permissible. It comes out of this fervent desire on the part of Englishmen to be gents. A terrible inheritance for a writer to start with. This just after reading Charles Morgan reviewing Henry Miller, and the *Manchester Guardian* cursing him for using 'gutter-words'! Such a farce it is.

Now the only big subject left in English is sex really! I want to do a book involving the attitude of the near-Levant to sex—it's so passionate and natural and really wonderful. How am I going to do it in English? In French or Greek it would be possible to do it without overtoppling. But in England you bring the ceiling down if you talk above a whisper. And then again, I don't want to accentuate anything. I am not proselytizing with dark abdomens or anything. But the central dramas of life here come out of sex; and sex informs and warms everything. One is saturated and exhausted and bored to death with sex; consequently it is only here that one is ever *free* of it, as it were, and able to devote oneself to art or God or whatnot, and make the whole world an Eros—but an eros of contemplation and real biblical love. In

[83]

the north—ach but why go on? I am not coming anywhere near England for years yet; and I'm seriously thinking of starting to write in Greek or some tongue where one is at ease, comfy, unbuttoned, etc.

Just been to Patmos to see the heavenly cave of the Apocalypse. How the devil do you manage to stay on in the fogs and cramps of that damned island?

So many thanks for the book. I think it's awfully good. My book I mean. Which means it will get a bad press. No matter. All this *Christian-introverted-self-congratulation-God-poetry* the young write in England these days. Why don't you stop it and make them write like human beings for a change.

Enough. Is there anything that I can send you from this part of the world? If so please tell me what.

Sincerely   Lawrence Durrell

To Anne Ridler   MOI. Rhodes 15 June [1946]
Dear Anne,

Just got your letter—It was awfully nice to hear after all this time. I kept track of your growing fame and fortunes. It seemed to me that the play had an awfully good press. Congratulations. On the whole *CITIES PLAINS AND PEOPLE* had rather a rough maiden voyage. Yes; I thought it good—as usual too good. I was surprised to find that while one group of papers thought it dry and scholarly, another thought it full of 'audenesque gags' and the atmosphere of the 20's (sic.) Queer I thought. Perhaps I am rather a dated writer from being so long out of touch and so little interested in the preoccupations of the home poets. There's so much word spinning going on—I turn the pages of these terrible anthologies and journals in the hope of finding something clear and strong—nothing but apocalyptic nonsense. I'm afraid that we've had a bad influence Henry and I's books about Greece. It is becoming a cult. In the last few weeks the number of poets who are compiling anthologies called SALUTE TO GREECE has risen; I have letters from them beginning 'Sir: I would be glad if you would contribute to a strong powerful anthology dedicated to Greece. Excellent contributions have been sent in by Sheila Sniggs, Roly Besom, and John Baller.

We are expecting work from T. S. Eliot, Henry Miller, and Max Beerbohm shortly. While we cannot pay. . . .'

Well, dear Anne, here I am in Rhodes, and happy again—or as near to that precarious state as one can get in this beautiful world of ours. I have earned my money, just sent off the proofs of a novel called *CEFALU*, and hope to be divorced this summer. Three years is a long time to wait for people to pull their finger out. My immediate preoccupation is to find time and place to attack a really good book for a change. I don't know how I'll manage it but I must sometime soon. I'm bursting with material—like an old suitcase; it trickles out in my conversation, and I make Cohen's life a misery acting scenes from the book I can't find time to write. Meanwhile it is quite clear that when this job stops (how sweet the NO of Molotov sounds to this jaded ear) I shall be on the parish—so to this end I have constructed and am racing through a farcical piece of theatre called *BLACK HONEY** (the private life of Baudelaire's octoroon mistress), I think it might be actable. Can I send it to Browne—as you suggest? Later I want to do a verse play about SAPPHO on Lesbos—not what you think, though! A book about Rhodes, an autobiography, and a lot more poems. As you see I am spinning like a weathercock. MEANWHILE I AM EDITING A DAILY GREEK, DAILY ITALIAN AND WEEKLY TURKISH NEWSPAPER which is killing me!!! And I can't find time to do more than lunch with Brigadiers in all their boredom.

The people here! My God the people! The administration has certainly finished me as far as the British are concerned. No greater collection of defrocked priests, ex-jockeys, haberdashers, and ruined boxers was ever gathered together to lord it over an innocent and peaceful people; your hair would turn white to see the condescension and rudeness with which these slum c3's treat the Greeks—whose fishermen and farmers are as fine as Cornishfolk, only poorer. The police, recruited from people who have spent years arranging sprigs of parsely over the testicles of Canterbury Lambs in our shops at home, have swollen like bullfrogs in their uniforms, and would have you think that they are having a dangerous and difficult job holding down a turbulent people. My shanty-Irish blood boils in me at their manners. And their wives! It is unbelievable—unthinkable that such people should ever be

* Never printed or produced. There is a typescript in the library of Iowa State University.

[85]

allowed to leave Luton or Swindon to represent England abroad. I'm told that Cyrpus is even worse. It's depressing. So far wherever I've seen the Union Jack flying there is the same story. Obtuse, dense bureaucrats with cockney accents refusing to mix with the natives and ordering whiskies in the British Club. I won't have it. I simply will not stand it. And then they ask me—why don't I get a permanent civil service job in a colony. YOU SHOULD SEE EGYPT!

Meanwhile the weather smiles—I can't think why. It hardly gets an answering smile from the lugubrious neurasthenic who rules the roost here or his simpering comic opera staff. Still, we do our best to smile back. Specimen of conversation in a mess. Newly arrived wife: 'Of course the people are backward and dirty and life is hard, but one might do worse.' When you hear that we are living in the biggest hotel in central Europe with private bathrooms, hot water, a superb beach and all the drink we want and almost all the food, in surroundings so idyllic that NOWHERE in the world could you match them just now—the remark will have its full value. Sailing, motoring and swimming. Simply lovely. But spoiled by these horrible Marx and Spencer throwouts. There! That's off my chest. As I can't print it in my newspapers I make you a present of it. My dear Anne, England sounds so dreadful from my brother's letters that I can't face it for a year or two. I'm awfully tired, as you must be, helping everyone to prepare the next war; how about an anthology dedicated to the atom bomb, with strong powerful contributions from Tony Sniggs, Gerald Verve, Peter Piston, and Romney Botth-Gaunt? Pictures by Beaton? Let me know before next spring. . . . And while we cannot pay. . . .

Love larry

To T. S. Eliot   MOI. Rhodes 20 October 1946
Dear TSE,

I have just made up a new book of poems called *ON SEEMING TO PRESUME* and sent it off to Faber. I hope that you accept it. I think some of them are OK some so-so and some wonderful. Of course unless one is toothless in England one can expect little beyond the reviewer's lip-service; and as reviewers are this breed of prim hermaphrodite—rather like Foreign Office nominees—one can't expect much. However we live and burn? I am just off to Athens for a week; have some more poems in the workshop still but will send. My future still uncertain— I mean about a job here. Shall probably stick on for another year if I can get someone to pay me enough to do so.

By all accounts London sounds hell; I remember you telling me once how you liked best the wet weather and a blazing fire for working! Well you're right; but here we have those AND in between we get whole fortnights of ringing blue sea-days where the mind can expand. I walk about in my Turkish graveyard, or sit for hours on the tomb of poor Hascid the satiric poet and brood upon mortality—or morality whichever way you look at it. The tall eucalyptus trees shed their spines and form a dense thick nap to walk on—the tombs are plodding marble with turbans on—like a forest of huge mushrooms. An air of ineffable decay and gloom—winding gloomy paths: like a Christina Rossetti peytol trance.

In Athens I am going to see Seferis and Katsimbalis and give modern lit a bashing with them; also Rex Warner is there they say.

To Hugh Gordon Porteous   MOI. Rhodes [1946?]
Dear Hugh,
. . . In January I hope to marry my latest and greatest nymph— Gipsy Cohen: picture attached: if she looks pensive it's because she is wondering what is in store for her: address me Public Nymphomation Officer: in other picture I am brooding on ways and means after Huxley!

These islands are really heavenly when the weather allows one to get round them. Please reserve the following islands for a visit in the future—*Patmos*! Straight middle ages stuff with the strangest atmosphere of any place I've visited—*Carpathos*—pale chalky, beautiful as an anemone, clean pre-historic picked bone—one wants to undress and climb trees—*Cos* very Hipp! Hipp! Hippocrates! Green verdant and mildly lenitive—Coan wine a washout nowadays—Rhodes the great dark abdominal FEMALE PRINCIPLE!! The Italians have emasculated it and sugared it all over—and weakened its lovely undulous femininity. All these places must be seen my dear Hugh—far more important than Arundel or Corfe or Epsom—Myself I have become a complete Levantine and cannot face another English winter. Hoping very much to make Paris for a year next year and then afterwards India, China or South America, for a 5 year spell.

Write a line when you feel like it.

L.

Larry.

To Gwyn Williams   MOI. Rhodes [1946?]

Dear Gwyn,

. . . I have all but recovered from my wonderful visit to Athens, moving and melancholy as it was. What it means to be a Christian in a Christian country—however bloodthirsty! There is little enough news in the newsy sense—even the weather which has been spouting rain and even snow has suddenly balmed itself into a spring cocoon. On Sundays we take a pack, some white wine, biscuits, sandwiches, and walk over the hill, past the old stadium with its bogus pillars, out into the country, lovely and green and gashed everywhere by emplacements, trenches, OP's etc. It's an archeologist's paradise for the German sappers have made holes everywhere and pottery is hanging out of the walls. . . . I am turning about in my mind to do something about Patmos—an enchanted island by the way—and the apocalypse. . . . But another trip to Athens this Monday just to pick up my trunks and be picked up by my drunks. The passes were deep in snow and I got stuck. Athens looked so strange under snow—the Parthenon like some diseased Christmas Card by Raphael Tuck and Son! But the roaring voice of Katsimbalis filled in the four horizons . . .

Larry

[88]

South America—Yugoslavia

When the English administration of the Dodecanese came to an end in 1947 Durrell returned to England, where he had not been for ten years, and rejoined his family in Bournemouth. This was not an easy time for him. The remuneration accruing from his writing could in no way be described as an income; he had no immediate prospects, and found himself unable to settle down to writing during the frequent periods of restlessness which ensued. Indeed he spent much of his time painting vivid and colourful pictures with poster paints.

Towards the end of the year, having been engaged by the British Council, Durrell, accompanied by Eve, set out for the Argentine. This was the farthest he was ever to travel from the Mediterranean, and of all the countries in which he was ever to live, he disliked it the most. The interaction between climate and character is very much a matter of personal temperament; Gerald Durrell, in contrast to his brother, took to the Argentine with enthusiasm, enjoyed life there, and is always happy to return.

Durrell spent much of his time in the Argentine at Cordoba, a university town, dominated by the Jesuits. Here he gave a series of lectures for the British Council that were later published as Key to Modern Poetry; *but otherwise this was a sterile year in which he did no creative writing. By the end of 1948, having broken his contract with the British Council, Durrell was back in Bournemouth, where he spent the next few frustrating months with his family, pacing up and down, seldom able to relax; and it came as a relief when the Foreign Office sent him to Yugoslavia, as Press Attaché, in July 1949.*

Conditions in Belgrade were grim; Yugoslavia had been subjected to desperate suffering under German occupation, and there was a shortage, indeed an absence, of all but the barest necessities of life; while, in any case, the birth struggles of a communist state are hardly the happiest times through which to live. In 1940, when Durrell had settled in Athens, he soon made friends with 'the two Georges', Seferiades and Katsimbalis, and other kindred spirits. In Belgrade, an incipient friendship with a young Yugoslav writer was swiftly nipped in the bud when the young man was flung into prison for associating with a western imperialist. The corps diplomatique, forbidden to mix with the rest of the population, was confined within a claustrophobic social circle in which they constantly met each other in an endless round of parties where the guests never varied. At some of the more informal parties Durrell would play and sing a blues of his own composition.

Life diplomatic
Once was ecstatic,
Sweet as a serenade,
Although we keep drinking,
Our spirits keep sinking,
They're sinking like New Belgrade.

Moscow and Prague,
Belgrade and Vienna,
They *sound* so romantic
But I'll bet you a tenner,
They've got those Iron Curtain blues.

The Naval Attaché hung himself on the stairs,
We brush past his body now—nobody cares,
He's got those Iron Curtain blues.

And so on *ad lib.*

His experiences in Yugoslavia gave Durrell the raw material for a number of books which he was to write in later years after he had left the country: White Eagles over Serbia, *an adventure book for boys in the John Buchan tradition, and the Antrobus stories,* Esprit de Corps, Stiff Upper Lip *and* Sauve Qui Peut, *humorous books about life in the diplomatic service. Meanwhile, two books which he had already written were published in England:* Sappho, *a play in verse, which came from Faber's in 1950, and* Key to Modern Poetry, *published by Peter Nevill in 1952.*

Durrell saw a good deal of Yugoslavia, for his duties as Press Attaché took him up and down the country, to Sarajevo, to Zagreb, to Bled, and so forth. He managed to acquire an immense German official-entry vehicle which had once belonged to Goering. Although quite impractical for private use, Durrell could not bear to part with this car because it made Tito jealous. The Press Attaché's car was bullet-proof, the Dictator's wasn't.

There were also three holidays abroad.

In 1950 Durrell and Eve spent some weeks in Ischia, where a remarkable eccentric and friend from Corfiot days was living. This was Zarian, an Armenian writer and journalist, doughty upholder of all matters pertaining to his race, who is one of the major characters in Prospero's Cell. *While in this island Durrell produced another of his private editions,* Deus Loci, *printed in a limited edition by Mato Vito.*

Penelope Durrell, it will be remembered, had been born just as the Germans were invading Greece, and was carried into exile as a babe in arms under hazardous conditions. This was hardly an experience that any parent would care to repeat. The year 1951, when Eve was expecting a baby, was a time of apprehension in Belgrade; Stalin was hurling invective and threats at Yugoslavia, and his tanks were on the frontier. The invasion was expected from day to day. Not wishing her child to be born in the path of a blitzkrieg, Eve came to England and rented a furnished house on the outskirts of Oxford. When the baby was due, old Mrs. Durrell, Mother, planned to join Eve, and we drove her up from Bournemouth. The house was quite small, and, before entering the nursing home, Eve had engaged a room for us in a nearby hotel. When I went round to check this and deposit our luggage the proprietor denied all knowledge of the booking. Later it emerged that a friend of Durrell's had stayed there the previous week-end. This man was a strong believer in non-violence, a sentiment not shared by the hotel proprietor. The argument between them grew more and more heated until the pacifist knocked the landlord down. No friend of the Durrells was persona grata *in his hotel after that.*

The third holiday from Belgrade allowed a brief return to Greece. In those days the wide new autoput *that tunnels its way through the mountains and leaps across the valleys of Macedonia, along which thousands of tourists now speed every year, had not been built; but Durrell and Eve drove southwards over appalling Balkan roads, and set up camp in Chalcidice, the promontory which ends in Mount Athos. Not exactly a Boy Scout manner of camping, for they engaged a woman from a nearby village to cook and clean and to guard the camp while they were away during the day. It was on this occasion that Durrell wrote telling me about a Greek island which could be purchased for £60. I was fool enough to let the opportunity slip. What madness! This is among the most acute minor regrets of my life; even if I had never managed to get there, I would have had sixty pounds' worth of throw-away conversation talking about my Greek island.*

Durrell's term of service in Yugoslavia took place at the time when Tito, backed and encouraged by the West, succeeded in detaching his country from the bonds of Stalinist Russia. For those who worked at the British Embassy, who saw it all from inside, holding their breath, so to speak, while the broken bones of foreign policy, so tentatively re-set, were slowly knitting together, these were fascinating days.

The success of this important détente was celebrated and sealed by the visit to Belgrade of Anthony Eden, then Foreign Secretary. His meetings with President Tito and the official junketings were given great publicity; a time of intense activity for the Press Attaché.

Twelve long years separated Durrell's departure from Egypt and the publication of Justine; *during all that period the novel was germinating in his mind, and as the ideas grew nearer and nearer to their final form the frustration of having no time to write became almost unbearable. By 1952 he realized that his own crisis had come; if he was ever to make his break-through as a writer he must act now. Towards the end of that year Durrell wrote to Henry Miller: 'By the way, I'm quitting the service in December and we are setting off to Cyprus, I think. No prospects. A tent. A small car. I feel twenty years younger. Heaven knows how we'll keep alive, but I'm so excited I can hardly wait to begin starving.'*

To Anne Ridler   Blue Star Line
                                         Montevideo [Autumn 1947]
Anne,

Here we are in Montevideo, birthplace of poor Laforgue—a fly-blown Neapolitan town as flat as a pancake on a dirty estuary. Filthy dusty streets and no monument older than 20 years. 'Well, you *would* go abroad.' I know. I know. And Buenos Ayres is reckoned worse than this. But the object of this brief note is to tell you to put *Brazil* on your visiting list as the most fantastic country in the world. In the first place it is the size of Europe—and only 1/10th explored—but Rio! My dear Anne I have seen nothing like Rio since I was 12 and stood on Eagle's Crag in Kurseong, India. For miles you follow the dull alluvial water of a tropical coast, an occasional yellow-brown seagull with a long beak patrolling. Then you turn and enter a bay full of coral islands with thick tropical vegetation coming down to the water, bamboos, coconut-palms. Rio is dead white, rising like a dream, a mass of aerial Sky-scrapers against a chain of stupendous mountains on whose very top stands a great barbaric stone cross with a stone Christ on it, half-hidden in cloud. The whole picture is as of a gigantic organ, the hills the fluted pipes, the town the white keyboard. It is completely Rider Haggard. Laid in a glittering crescent round a marvellous bay the skyscrapers are punctuated by cones of granite which rise clear out of the ground beside the buildings—from your 20th floor you lean out and kiss a precipice. A spider web of railway takes you up to the sugar-loaf mountain. But the streets are connected by huge tunnels lit by arc lamps and lined with marble, so that to go from one end of the town to the other is like going through a series of mad looking-glasses and finding more and more skyscrapers built round more and more dazzling bays. Rio is the dream of an ant bound hand and foot and delivered over to one of its own nightmares. The main street is as wide as—say the width from Marble Arch to Oxford Street. As *wide*! You walk between these huge buildings, looking down vistas of as much as four miles, feeling as if you were wandering about the ruled table-lands of a geometrical Chirico. It's completely hallucinating. Pure blue oxygen air, and on an island in the bay a silver aeroplane per minute lands and takes off. For sheer magnitude and overpowering frenzied weight of scenery there is nothing like it. And for *modernity*! Meanwhile the jungle is lapping at the very edges of these marble palaces—you have the impression that every day they cut it back half a mile and every night it advances on them and mosses up the roads. Meanwhile the mountains keep appearing and disappearing in clouds so you can never count them, and the light changes all the time. The journey was worth it if only to see this hallucinating spectacle: Rio de Janeiro. Picture a country the *size of Europe* containing two towns more modern than New York—1/10th explored—containing also the Amazon, upper and lower, and all the theories of Darwin! After this B.A. will doubtless be very small beer.

. . . I have written some poems—good I hope. If you see Theo give him my love and tell him I'll try and materialize at his next séance with a green coconut in my hand. And Anne dear *please* ask Faber to *register* everything. I expect to go 800 miles inland to Cordoba for a month's leave and understand that the postal services consist of state dromedaries driven by gauche gauchos. Hence *register*! Meanwhile onward from Trotsky, Blavatsky, and back to Potocki via Ouspensky I have met a marvellous metaphysical Armenian who has 8 crates o hermetic writings on board and have been reading Laforgue's *Hamle* and Mallarmé's *Igitur*, both perfectly seasoned for this voyage and my state of mind.

———————————

To Mary Hadkinson · · · · · · · · · · · · · The British Council
· 190 Lavalle, Buenos Ayres
· 7 February 1948

Dear Mary,

. . .

You envy us? Argentina is a large flat melancholy and rather superb-looking country full of stale air, blue featureless sierras, and business-men drinking Coca-Cola. One eats endless beef and is so bored one could scream. It is the most lazy-making climate I have struck: not as bad as Egypt, of course: but I'd give a lifetime of Argentina for three weeks of Greece, fascist or no fascist. Here one is submerged in dull *laisser faire* and furious boredom. People quite nice in a very superficial and childish way. I think the States would be better. However I'm contracted for a year so I can't think of escape until next March. The only fun is horseback riding which we do plenty of—across the blue sierras, à la Zane Grey. But it's all very dreary really. As for the meat it's rapidly driving me vegetarian—next week I move into Cordoba, my new post, and take over amid polite bowings—I did as a matter of fact write to Katsimbalis, but one-way correspondence is inevitable with him: one is always left holding the leading strings—But we THINK on him a great deal—Tell him that *Papissa Joanna* is now in proof in a very GOOD Translation (so says Theodore who is vetting my text with the original in London). *CEFALU* should be out by the time you get this: new book of poems going into print *ON SEEMING TO PRESUME*. My verse play being considered for possible production. Next on the list a Rhodes book and another verse-play I hope—O but this country makes you feel as lame as a Peruvian bishop—Tell K. that Henry has added 1000 unprintable pages to Capricorn in USA and I hope perhaps to fly up and see him if I have the money during my next leave. There is no other news—I leave space for a beautiful description of landscape—it is quite pretty in a cow-like way, and smells of the stock-whip. I really think I would prefer England to staying here. But this may pass with the weather. Endless thunderstorms and drops of temperature—Brazil is the place to go to if you must—not here. Ach it makes me so homesick to think of you trotting about in Athens that I must stop. Love to Henry, and you—Eve is writing separately, probably with more intelligible news.

Larry

To Lawrence Clark Powell
The British Council
190 Lavalle, Buenos Ayres
[March 1948]

Dear Larry Powell,

If I may trade a Larry against a Larry. I'm sorry I faded out on you so abruptly but I've been travelling like a maniac across this blasted pampas, lecturing in one place and another, until finally I have come to rest in Cordoba, 'the Oxford of Argentina' as they call it, rather misguidedly I think. It's a variation on a small Henry Miller town in the dust belt. The people are charming but zombies. The town is pleasant compared to anywhere else in Argentina—but give me Naples any day, even any hot day when the smell from the rotting fish is enough to put a philosopher out of countenance. On the whole I dislike Argentina heartily. It is empty, noisy, progressive, money-ridden —all the sins including those by Coca-Cola Inc. and Buick. But I could stand all of that if only the climate were not like a piece of wet meat laid across the nervous system. Life goes on in a muted sort of way—as when you press your hand on the piano strings and play. No concentration, no power of holding on to things: and yet they eat meat here as the staple instead of bread. You see a picnic party all eating loaf-sized pieces of beef washed down with red wine. Never bread. There should be enough raw power you'd think to think a single great thought—but it never comes. It ends in Coca-Cola, in Studebaker, in movie. The irony of lecturing about Shakespear in this ambience is something that perhaps only Shakespear would enjoy. I don't. Meanwhile however I have a new volume of verse coming out from Fabers, and am halfway through a book about Rhodes—slow going I'm afraid. Also the Greek novel I translated. *POPE JOAN* is coming out soon in England, while *CEFALU*, another novel, has just been put out. In the U.S. it is called *The Dark Labyrinth*.

[95]

Meanwhile several poet friends find themselves in America and tell me to see it before I go home. They say that some of the smaller universities might employ me for a two year spell to lecture. Do you know if this is so? I have no academic background beyond my books. I ran away to Europe when I shd have gone up to Cambridge. But sooner or later I must get near a library and finish my account of authorship in Elizabethan times: I've been some ten years taking notes on every aspect of writing then, and had planned at the end of this part of my contract to get sent home for a six month rest to finish it off: which I'll do. But I suddenly thought when I got a letter that if I could go home via USA I might get a chance to visit Henry en route. Do you ever see him? I think he's more or less settled at Big Sur now, and the state of Europe would be enough to keep anyone at home these days. I suppose the next war will break long before you have time to answer these jottings. Can you tell me anything about Giordano Bruno's influence on the Elizabethans?

I wonder if you have read Evelyn Waugh's *THE LOVED ONE*, a devastating satire on the burial customs of Hollywood. It would amuse you I think. It's the most macabre thing I've ever read—I can't believe it is a true picture of what actually goes on, and yet it seems to be: life of the mortician in Hollywood—It's certainly the best thing of its kind since *Brave New World*, and unlike most of his work it doesn't play down to anyone, the English gentry or the Catholics or anyone. In its curious way I think it's a masterpiece—the first since *Vile Bodies*. I'm afraid I must bring this letter to an abrupt end. Work.

Yours

Lawrence Durrell

To Mary Hadkinson

The British Council
190 Lavalle, Buenos Ayres
[June ? 1948]

Well, we have found a flat in Cordoba and a mutton-headed slavey and now await furniture from the British Council. But really Mary, Kenya! What an extraordinary thing to happen to you. Ah! but in a week you'll feel you could scream with boredom as I do here and want to get back to the banditry—What a terrible picture you paint of it all—Incidentally you harangue me as if I were a communist which you know I'm not. I was a republican-Sophouliot, and I believed in REAL INTERVENTION, not this mealy mouthed disgraceful shambles we've created. O of course I know that Russia is to blame and that now we MUST fight to keep her out of Greece: but my Greek politics date from when we first went into the country. Now I'm out of date, I expect, the situation has been allowed to deteriorate. Ifs and Buts won't cure it: nor will kings—though if it has got as bad as you say I now believe in keeping the King there, and sending 10,000 BRITISH AND AMERICAN Troops to clear up, build roads, etc. Incidentally 200,000 Greeks did quite well against the Italians and Germans. If you want to know why the Gk Army won't fight ask the British Military Mission— But now it has all gone far beyond the situation I was fulminating over when we were last there(You choose the cures for it: but I still believe either policy RIGHT OR LEFT if wholeheartedly applied would have quieted Greece down: it's the neither norness that has done it: and this pathetic belief that Greeks are not natural bandits at heart— which I never believed. Read Napier's despatches from Cephalonia. There was a man who knew what he was at. 'If I went to Greece I would take a gallows, plenty of tarred rope and a sufficiency of foreign troops.' Otherwise it's a WASTE OF TIME, GET OUT, LEAVE THE BLOODY PLACE. It is not strategically important enough anyway for all this nerve-strain.)Which is of course the last thing you or I really want—I mean personally. I still think I shall live there some time—perhaps after the next war—looks pretty imminent doesn't it? I wonder why we don't get it over now? Russia can't be allowed to take over where Hitler left off—that's obvious. Meanwhile—the Argentine—O dear, this boring tedious town. Food very good. Easy life, but the climate is desperately exacerbating—electrical storms four times a week—temperatures going up and down—One new delicacy as fine as anything the Chinese thought of—called Palmita. It's the white heart of a small Brazilian palm tree, tastes like a mixture of oyster and asparagus—a lovely taste—yes, horses and cows, there is nothing else—We ride one and eat the other interminably. Sorry about Patmos—Yes, I will consider it as soon as I finish my ½ done Rhodes book—Mary, it's so hard to write about Greece from here: one's feelings don't rise in this climate, the death-dew settles on one, one don't nostalge enough. Even England is far better—But if I can raise a spark of marble-dust and blue nostalgia I will do Patmos. Another thing—reference-books! I need the British Museum. Meanwhile do you send all your pictures to VIVIAN RIDLER CARE OF CONTACT 24 MANCHESTER SQUARE LONDON, and offer him reportage will you? Don't be shy now, nothing was ever done by shyness, forward into the breach. I've suggested to Tambi that RUNCIMAN might do a small Patmos book to go with your pics? *POPE JOAN* is due in October; that's a marvellous book—What else? *Cefalû* is being done here in Spanish. Nothing else. Heat. Vapour-trails of cows on the pampas, desolation, Cunninghame Graham, green tea, big belly, much sleep, no exercise, force majeur, British Institute. Me one time lecture-man. Me givvy lecture Shakespear. Shakespear him velly fine big-speak sing song man, velly wise, velly pure, velly clean.

Larry.

To Mary Hadkinson   Argentina [1948]

Mary,

This brief scrawl may reach you before you leave—it's just to acknowledge your last note with the cracker mottos from St. Winifred's. I don't know if Kenya's like this place—if it is, I give you six months! By the way, look out for an astonishing woman writer living there in great secrecy. Her real name is The Baroness Blixen and she writes extraordinary short stories under the name Isak Dinesen. Several of her books have been done in U.S.A.—the latest *Winter Tales*—no, *Seven Gothic Tales* are excellent in their genre. Nobody knows anything about her. She must be queer to live in Kenya—and she a Dane!

. . . We have just travelled 300 miles thru a wall of yellow dust to TUCUMAN to lecture, past a dead salt lake which is worse than Sodom and Gomorrah to look at, thru a landscape so flat and barren and dusty that it was really a nightmare. Tomorrow I fly to Mendoza—at the foot of the fucking Andes to perform the same office—gabble, gabble, gabble. Next to Rosario—in the heart of the dust-bowl ugh! We pant for air. Here it is *cold* bitterly cold, but dusty and windy. Imagine an Egyptian Khamseen for 4 winter months, not a drop of rain, and freezing point! The air is so dry that you wake with a sore throat and a skin like a rhino—England will be all golden balm after this. Let it rain! Let it snow! Let it freeze! I have half a book about Rhodes written—very bad. Must be redone. No other plans or projects except a book, a play, a film, a poem, climate permitting.

All the best to you. Learn to ride in Kenya. It's wonderful for the Oedipus Complex—and shoot big game. Have just seen Gregory Peck doing it with great charm.

Love—Larry D.

Yugoslavia

To Theodore Stephanides   British Legation, Belgrade   [1949]
Theo,

Just a brief line to tell you we've arrived safely. Conditions are rather gloomy here—almost mid-war conditions, overcrowding, poverty: As for Communism—my dear Theodore a short visit here is enough to make one decide that Capitalism is worth fighting for. Black as it may be, with all its bloodstains, it is less gloomy and arid and hopeless than this inert and ghastly police state. Our own situation however will not, thank goodness, be as gloomy as that of the Yugoslavs—as soon as we find a house to live in, and as soon as our little car arrives from England. Diplomats live well everywhere as a rule—and here they suffer only from claustrophobia. There will be a chance of some shooting this winter and perhaps a trip to Salonika by car. But for the rest we are marooned in a large hotel—together with the rest of the press and fragments of diplomatic missions. *I wonder if you could send us a heap of Vitamin tablets* (*ABCD*) to keep our flagging spirits up. The Summer is hot—hot as Cairo; and Belgrade lies at the confluence of two damnably dirty and moist rivers. I hope to crack down on the Rhodes book some time this year. Any news of your book?

Love

Larry

To Theodore Stephanides   British Embassy, Belgrade   [1949]
Dear Theodore,

Just a brief line to thank you for the Vitamin tablets which arrived yesterday and which I am dishing out to our avitaminosed staff. I've also started to take them myself experimentally as I was beginning to suffer from insomnia and I think they are doing me a certain amount of good.

. . . . .

There is little news except that what I have seen here has turned me firmly reactionary and Tory: the blank dead end which labour leads towards seems to be this machine state, with its censored press, its long marching columns of political prisoners guarded by tommy guns. Philistinism, puritanism and cruelty. Luckily the whole edifice has begun to crumble, and one has the pleasurable job of aiding and abetting this blockheaded people to demolish their own ideological Palace of Pleasures.

Tomorrow we move into a house and perhaps there'll be a chance to do a little work later on this year. But the climate is foul.

Love
Larry

To Anne Ridler   British Legation, Belgrade
                                  21 September [1949]

Dear Anne,

We have just come jolting back from the Zagreb fair and found your letter. Letters are very welcome behind the curtain. One almost forgets in the sabbatarian gloom of a Communist country what life in the west is like. Never mind. Our car is supposed to be on the way and we shall soon start travelling madly. We have a trip laid on to Salonika in October though I don't know really whether to take Eve down with me coz we have to traverse Yugoslav Macedonia to get there and things down there are obscure and full of portent. However we'll see. Zagreb was a bit of a rest—a lovely little Austrian university town with good walking hills round it, and forty miles to the north some really lovely lush landscape with wide-eyed brightly-dressed peasants; gay jolly and sensual after the central European pattern. The whole of the corpse diplomatic was taken up to Zagreb in a special train. It was a scene from a Waugh novel. The Nederlands chargé d'affaires slightly tipsy on the platform; the ministers shaking hands and cooing like doves; the Argentine Ambassador in a frock-coat got locked out of his pullman and ran shrieking beside the train for a hundred yards, paced by a couple of taciturn guards with skeleton keys, each leaping up in turn and trying to open the door. The wife of the Brazilian Ambassador got locked in the lavatory and had to be set free with axes and dosed with peppermint. The coaches which conveyed the corpse diplomatic had been specially made for the occasion by the Yugoslav Light Industry. It was a compliment to us that we should be the first to try them: or was it something else? At all events the lavatory didn't work and the whole superstructure rocked so much that the Egyptian Minister's wife was thrown out of her bunk and spent the night on her knees invoking Allah. I must say there were several occasions on which I was sure we were going over. As the lights fused almost from the beginning we passed the night hours in anxious darkness roaring across the Croatian plain in a trail of sparks from an Emett-like engine. At Zagreb a red carpet had been laid down and we dawdled out to our cars under the clickety click of news cameras. Luggage was lost. Porters and flunkeys fought and cursed. We shot our cuffs and drove off to our hotels. The fair was most interesting and very well done; there was a prototype of almost everything from refrigerators to motor-bikes on show—none have so far been seen outside the fair: certainly none are for sale anywhere. But the impression created was that Yugoslav light industry was running America a close second. Enormous crocodile like speeches were made; we overate and over-drank; and then escaped to spend two days making friends and touring the surrounding landscape with my number two in Zagreb. Little Dorian Cooke was with us, on his first visit for years and we had some pleasant boozing in various taverns and met a number of his friends. All prices had been halved for the duration of the fair so that one had the very faintest illusion of being back somewhere—in the Tyrol say before the war. There is no other news of any weight that you won't get in your morning press; the country is comparatively calm—the journalists think ominously. We don't think. Not paid to. We answer telephones and wait for leave. Glad to appear in your appendix. I think some of the short poems in the last book were as good as anything I could ever do—Christ in Brazil and Pomona de Maillol etc. but you are the chooser. No news of *Sappho* or the apologie for poetry yet. Love to V and the children.

Larry

To Anne Ridler

Dear Anne,

A brief note from a troubled spot to wonder how you are and what you are writing—despite the patient motherhood 5 year plan. We have been travelling rather hard all this past week. The hardest trip was to Sarajevo—crossing the dusty plain and bumbling over the Zvornik bridge to climb the stone ladder into Bosnia. You would love the upland country—lovely smooth grassy slopes and pine-trembling mountain peaks all round. Cold air. And the Bosnian peasants in their dramatic costume—can you imagine the quaintness of Tyrolean costume stabbed here and there with an oriental touch, giving a rude masculinity to it. A whole day you crash across this great alpine plateau and towards evening the road begins to fall, to hesitate, to follow water like a hound through two beetling ravines. Torrents rushing, eagles flying. You come around a shoulder of rock and—guess what? A Turkish town—pure 1795. Soft pearl bulbs of minarets and trellised houses built up the steep sides of the mountains above a tinkling river that jingles through the town to chime with the clink of stirrup-irons and the soft blackish chatter of the veiled Turkish women. All the houses in the Turkish quarter have musharabaya trellis windows for purdah-ed girls. The cafés are fenced in with coloured wooden trellis. The older houses look like charming birdcages hung about the hills. The whole town gives the air of being some late 19th century drawing by Lear, say. Mosques, minarets, fezes—holding the gorgeous East in fee while the river cools the air, splashing through the town and the bridge on which whatsisname was assassinated (now called the People's Bridge) stands gracefully but ominously where it has stood for some 80 years. After this filthy dank capital with its cloddish inhabitants Sarajevo was a treat. One was back in Jannina or some town in Epirus again. At least I was. It is by far the best trip we've done to date (in a borrowed jeep) and I was sorry to return here. Northward the great flat Hungarian plain stretches away interminably through its ugly villages—to some final oblivion. But the hills are west and south—and how one longs for them in Belgrade.

As you probably know we are enjoying a lovely little crisis whose end is as yet unforeseen. I have been trying to give London the impression that the whole thing is my doing. I somehow don't think they believe me. Meanwhile however, not a line of poetry or prose—O Lord. I can't work here.

Love to Vivian
Larry

To Theodore Stephanides   Belgrade   10 May 1950

Dear Theodore,

A line by this bag to thank you most warmly for the medicaments which arrived safely and for which I enclose a cheque. Would you be an angel and send me the prescription mentioned on this form. It is for another sufferer—I think the TB rate must be round 80% here. A few gifts of this kind are such a godsend to the wretched people who are starved and terrorized almost to death. . . . And Yugoslav security is so tight, and friendship with foreigners so discouraged, that we cannot make friends normally without great difficulty. We are so looking forward to leaving for Ischia. It would double the pleasure to see you again with Zarian. Surely you can conquer your travel phobia? Xan Fielding is going to meet us in Naples. It should be enormous fun really and give me the rest I need. No chance of doing any work here— though I must say it is the most interesting assignment I've had so far from the purely political point of view—I shouldn't be surprised if it all piles up in a new Spanish war this summer. However, better than peaceful Argentina much.

Much love to you from us both.

Larry

To Anne Ridler   Forio d'Ischia, Ischia

[June 1950]

Dear Anne, I have been owing you a letter
From furrin parts—from Ischia, where better
To spin the odd iambic in your name
And tell you something of this island's fame?
We came originally here to see
A character from Prospero called C.

[104]

(It stands for Constant) Zarian,
The wild and roguish literary man
Who with his painter wife lives on this island,
A life romantic as one could in . . . Thailand.
Together we have tasted every wine,
Most of the girls (I mean the Muses Nine)
And some small favours accident affords
To such poor chaps as we—as deal in words.
Sure provender of every sort's to hand
For us old roués of the writing brand—
The island is decidedly volcanic,
Quite different to Greece though quite as 'panic',
The soft blue vapour hanging over the bay
Gives tones of blue you don't see every day
While the volcanic rock is all contorted
As if an island goddess had aborted:
But limestones soften into sparkling bays
And geysers everywhere contribute haze,
So soft and sweet and indolent it lies
Under its Naples' picture-postcard skies.
They've lodged us in a wine-press high
On a lighthouse point—a window in the sky
Hidden in vineyards where the sunburnt girls
Shout blithe as parrots in their darkling curls,
Sing bits of opera at me all day
With mad Italian generosity.
So far, however, no real offers of marriage.
If Eve weren't here I would have had a barrage (Sorry!)
Despite advancing years and stoop and paunch—
You get here by a super motor-launch
Crowded with chattering girls from Naples O
Such animation such colossal brio
It makes one feel much younger just to see,
At least so Zarian says. (He's sixty-three)
He scales a mountain like a wild chamois
Despite a certain—bulk—avoirdupois
And swears Per Baccho loud as any peasant:
Together we've enjoyed a very pleasant

[105]

Month of mad cookery and writing talk,
Such food, such wine—a wonder we can walk.
The Master with his silver flying hair
Cooks like a saint and eats like a Corsair,
In octopus and scampi and red mullet,
In hen and hare and cuttlefish and pullet
We've eaten round through past and present tense
Right through the heart of time's circumference,
And now, a week from leaving, in cross-section,
I look like—what? Old Mercator's Projection
That used to hang upon the schoolroom wall
And puzzle us when we were very small.
Puzzle no more—as Groddeck says: 'The wish'—
But what imports his counsel when a dish
Floating in some extraordinary dressing
Comes to the table? None of us needs pressing.

This then the sum of all our news is,
Apart from gastronomic self-abuses,
We've bathed and boated and collected pumice,
Lain on the beach sunbandaged as black mummies,
Tasted the salt good Mediterranean blue
Which is as much as we had hoped to do.
Good company, good eating and the sun—
The indulgent patron of this island home
Have all contributed to make the spell
Unbreakable—so leaving will be hell.

Of literary news there is a lot.
Ischia it seems has fast become The Spot.
Capri is finished, everyone is here,
Poets and painters too from all the nations,
And some of curious sexual persuasions.
Among the giants Auden, the great peer
Of all us little moderns, he's acquired
A villa for himself and lives retired;
We've met the great man more than once or twice,
Eve is indifferent; I thought him nice.

A place for exiled writers hating fuss
This seems; why in a little country bus
Jogging to Panza yesterday who should I see
A man I'm sure you reverence as much as me,
Old Norman Douglas, worn as if by sea
Like some old whorled and rubbed-out ocean shell
Still holding shape and life and living well;
Eyes a Homeric blue and hands quite firm,
An air of indefinable ancient charm
Like some old Roman talisman's patina
His Italian pure and deft—I've heard none finer.
But look—the bottom of my second page.
To read this all will take you quite an age;
Time to sign off and tell you we are well
Beneath the ocean-swelling spell
Of *mare nostrum;* how's life treating you?
How is the poetry, housework, knitting, stew?
It is high time for me to take my leave,
And wish you everything from Larry and Eve.

To Theodore Stephanides   Belgrade   Friday [Winter 1950/51]
Dear Theo,

Yes, it must seem churlish on my part to send you nothing but prescriptions—I'm sorry to be so Keatsian: but you must think of me as someone who is serving a 3 year sentence in Pentonville, from whom you get little news but many demands upon your attention. Nor would you blame me if you could see the amount of oakum I have to pick—journalists' brains are lined with oakum—and I have to wine and dine them until my own brains are beginning to resemble theirs. Such news as there is Eve will already have given you. For the rest, we are sinking slowly into the frozen mush of a Central European winter—It is very gloomy I find. And the inhabitants of this benighted country are facing starvation—which sets our appetites on edge, living as we are in the lap of a positively pre-war luxury. Our own little domain (the internal politics of this place) competes in dreariness with the landscape, the dirty streets, the shaggy, forlorn crowds. To change into a dinner jacket and motor to a reception where the combed and scented ladies of the Diplomatic corpse (sic) await, is to experience the pleasures of Babylon (the surfeit of which is hellish). Eve is struggling with the first signs of a child which she proposes to produce sometime in late spring. She is spending a few days in Zagreb where the air is better than it is here, and I've just done the long drive up and back to carry her there. No Russians in sight as yet on the *autoput*—and no flying saucers neither. Don't know why it is that we dislike most of the countries we get sent to—never happy unless we are in Greece.

Yes, the price of that medicine is certainly prohibitive. Unfortunately I couldn't read the prescription or judge the contents. I send you another tenner to keep the account square. I've started a new play—but there's nothing enlivening in the atmosphere to set it floating so I imagine it will just bog down like the Rhodes book.

Best love
Larry

To Anne Ridler   British Legation, Belgrade
                  15 February [1951]

Dear Anne,

A brief line to let you know that Eve is coming to London for a fortnight in order to scout around and see what she thinks about having the baby there; I've told her to drop you a line and perhaps when she comes to Oxford you'd be good enough to give her tea and tell her roughly what the form is. She is still a bit undecided about everything, so I thought the best thing was for her to have a looksee for herself—.

There is no news to give you much that you don't see in the papers; ah yes! I have struck a great blow for poetry. While in Trieste I found, hiding in a garage, too big to be used, a perfectly gigantic car—a Horch: the German Rolls Royce. Eight cylinder, forty horse power. It used to belong to Goering and then to the general commanding the area. I bought it for a song and brought it back. It is lovely, silver-grey, sleek and with a funny old-fashioned look. It makes you feel like a film-star of the twenties. We call it Herman and are planning one mad summer of plutocracy in it—before the war breaks out. As a matter of fact you have often seen Herman in the newsreels—do you remember the entry into Prague etc. with one of the big shots standing up in the front and giving the boys the salute. That's how I go to the office now. Everyone is speechless with rage, and few will speak to me these days. But the Belgrade police force is deeply respectful. There are two horns on the car, bass and tenor. I say that I've struck a blow for poetry because it is an ideal poet's car: too large for any purpose except triumphal entries, and so expensive to run that only a lunatic would buy such a thing. I shall sell it to Tito when I leave. He already has one but not as nice as mine. Wish you could come out and admire it.

Eve will give you the rest of the news such as it is!

Love

Larry

To Alan G. Thomas   Belgrade [1952]

Dear Alan,

. . . Meanwhile as usual I'm off on a tangent. Can you lay hands on *Sappho* and *Nero* by Arthur Weigall (Hutchinson): I owned both once and sold them back to you. Now Margaret Rawlings has made such a success of her public reading of *Sappho* (did you see *The Times* notice on the 22nd?) that she is raving mad for me to tailor the text to her character: she wants to try and get it produced properly. I want to work myself back into the proper frame of mind and these books, though trivial, give a very good account of everyday life. God! this place feels so far from the Mediterranean. Flat, land locked, inhabited by pigs undistinguishable from Serbs and Serbs vice versa: no olives: blank stupid geese: dust in summer and fog in winter. This week terrific snow. Leave your car outside the office for an hour and it disappears into a giant snow-drift. Icy wind from Tartary. And I've missed Greece thanks to a number of unlucky things—chiefly not being successful enough as a bum-sucker. It always came hard. But by dint of sweat I've somehow finished the Rhodes book and now I want to fix *Sappho* for M.R. and give her a chance to act the great lady on the stage.

I am also interested in a translation of Aeschylus (but *not* verse on any account: prose. Bohn if possible: Blackwell is full of Bohns.) Also, if you still have it, that copy of *The Sexual Life of the Ancient Greeks* (which I always see lying glumly in a corner when I visit the shop, price rising steadily). Have you any cheap histories of early Greece—between Hesiod and Sappho? And in my book-box isn't there a *Daily Life in Ancient Greece*?

Best love to you both
Larry

To Anne Ridler   Belgrade [May 1952]
Dear Anne,

 . . . This country has withered me with its Utopian present (40% of the children have t.b.) and the even more Utopian future it promises for all of us. I don't see how we are going to get through the next few years without a war. The only hope is that Russia fears the USA enough. Anyway, next week we are taking the car, tents etc. and hobbling down across infernal roads through Macedonia to *Greece*! Six weeks of blue. We are going to amble down past Olympus in search of a fishing village with a good cold spring, rent a peasant house and hire a village girl. Our tent we'll pitch on a shady headland and olive glade near the sea. To spend the days sleeping and swimming—I hope I'll get enough energy to do a spot of writing—I'm bursting with ideas for a new play, a new novel, a new book of poetry. Ah well: we shall see! We have done several camping trips along the Danube—fine landscape, noble, copious—but not my style of thing—too much of it for one thing. And the sky is thick as an eggshell. Sleepy, flat lush land stocked with geese, pigs and sleepy peasants. Hans Andersen goose-girl landscape. How suddenly it all changes when you come to the Vardar Valley and quicken into Greece. Base rock. Olives, wild flowers, sweet limestone with hidden rivers rolling underground. Me for Greece! But I don't seem to be able to get a job there. You see, I know the language! 'A *serious* defect in a diplomat!' Pfui

 Sappho-Jane is great fun and awfully pretty now in her first puppydom. She adores camping and has her own little tent of light-blue campeen—vivid as a sky. She loves every moment and is tremendously well-behaved. Last week-end we camped at a ruined and deserted monastery in the Fruskazena called Ohopovo—sunk in a secret dell full of bees and cherry trees and a terrific thunderstorm came up over the Danube at dusk. Spurts of rain and livid sparks of lightning. I

[110]

thought Sapphy would be scared but she slept through it all quite soundly. Is learning to walk now and can say three words.

To Anne Ridler   Bled   17 August [1952]

Dear Anne,

I was able to fly to Belgrade yesterday in the Embassy courier plane and collect my mail, with your letter amongst it. Many thanks for the Herculean labour, I hope the wretched book reads the better for it.* I went completely stale on it—too many changes of scene and five years of unlucky postings. Not sure you're right about cutting the second siege: there were some six or eight and I chose the two greatest as historical milestones, one for ancient, one for modern Rhodes: it was pretty perfunctory as it was. The trouble is that there is too much history, and I selected only what a visitor would like to know as rapidly as possible. The 2nd siege is really a great turning point, apart from being the greatest ever in modern times. *Must* it go? If you say so okay. I would rather have out other parts: the ghost stories which were bad though true. You see, modern Rhodes *town* is a living replica of what it was at the last siege, and the visitor simply will feel a frightful let-down: what about thinning it out into its barest essentials? Somehow I can't help feeling that when you spend a week in Rhodes, using the book as a companion you'll say 'Hell! Not a word about the medieval town: and here it all is before my eyes!' And the map I want to repro-duce, so carefully showing every site—such a lovely map! Think it over, will you? Imagine a book on Oxford which ignored the present-day buildings and only touched Anglo-Saxon remains, mostly not visible to the naked eye?

. . . We are meditating a small house in Cyprus with 50 olive trees as a corner for S-Jane, who is turning out very prettily—like a small dark partridge. I must say Bled is the only place in Yugoslavia I would think seriously of revisiting—a wooded lake set in thickly-thatched Alpine meadow-scenery, and girdled by Alps; every ten days of sun-shine is punctuated by one day's soft polishing rain which brings up the whole landscape like a chamois leather does a car. Cool and peaceful. Little villages in orchards, their balconies built deep against snow like

* *Reflections on a Marine Venus.*

[111]

house-martin's nests: narrow openings with deep wooden balconies behind. From inside you look at the landscape framed as if it was a mirror. The mountains thickly studded with stars and pierced every-where by hoarse icy torrents—*Lovely*—and the Slovenes are blond as buttercups and bloom warmly in the sunshine to gold and cinnamon. Lovely girls! And such flowers.

All the best to Vivian and thanks.

Larry

To Alan G. Thomas   Belgrade [1952]

Dear Alan,

Just got back after a very tiring but wonderful visit to Greece; the wilder part; Chalcidice, the promontory which ends in Mount Athos. In a grove of giant plane-trees next the sea. A wonderful month really. Found an old woman to cook for us. Just swam and sat about eating fruit, thinking about nothing. Consequence is masses of work waiting for me here. We were offered an island for sixty pounds, called Olym-piada (Alexander's mum was exiled there after poisoning someone—her husband?) It is 8 sea miles from Stavros: water, harbour, several hundred olive trees. If interested apply care of the Harbour-master, Stavros. Nearest village 1 sea mile from the island is Olympia; rugged country.

 . . .

Love to you both

Larry

[Enclosed in above letter:]

Letter to Anaïs Nin

Anaïs, on this smashed and rocking skyline,

Through vermin, cinders, teeth of houses,

We wake and walk like nerves unseparated,

Within the body of our parent, man.

Now unprotected by the skill of lies

Watch in the turbid glass of these canals

Reflected like conceits each others' faces,

By the foul waters of an Egypt's hope.

[112]

People who have reached the end of themselves
In new beginnings verify their ends.

We move upon the measure of this hope
Where women and mattresses from windows—
The discoloured tongues of pleasure, hang.

And the romance of open sores—the noble savage
Squats by his waterwheel to worship
And only wakes to piss his barbs and fishooks
Against the politicians' promises.

Here all who find their sweet distraction in each other
By these canals go down in hope
On the green diagrams of land,
Choked with dead leaves and setting sails, find only
Passion that by its own excess divides,
And foreign on the ash-heaps of a city,
Garments for children roaming like the germs,
Fragments of umbrellas, cooking-pots,
The weather did not give them time to try.

A few of us here, a very few,
Are critics of these causes,
Besides the dead, within their snoods of stone;

We move in the refreshment of an exile,
A temperature of plenty served by want
Subtracting nothing in the formal science
Of verse: the art of pain by words in measure.

We ask only
A statement of the nature of misfortune,
That by the act of seeing and recording,
We may infect the root and touch the sin
That the new corn of Egypt springing
From the lean year in a time of triumph
Deliver the usurper from his coffin
And let all that might be begin.

To Theodore Stephanides   Belgrade   4 November [1952]
Dear Theo,

Excuse my total neglect for some time past but I have been working awfully hard as well as travelling up and down this bloody country with various nobs. The last was my boss Eden whose much advertised tour was publicity-managed by little me, which resulted in my getting nearly as much publicity as he did; and included an invitation to the White Palace to meet Mr. and Mrs. Tito, and also two dinner parties at Bled where I was able to examine the leaders of this country at close quarters. Seeing is believing they say.

. . . I've turned in my resignation and we are clearing off in December to Cyprus. I've asked George to look around for a plot or a tiny villa for us to buy. We prospected in Greece but really the economy is so chaotic and prices so fluctuating. What do you think of Cyprus yourself? Is it as pretty as other islands? Water? Grass? Where would you live if you had to live there.

I have no idea what I am going to do but I suppose I can write a book a month for two years as a start—you'd better send me your plot-book.

Meanwhile of course we are in awfully good heart, and feel about twenty years younger at the thought of quitting this place which we have now examined from north to south and found full of savage beauty but quite impossible to live in. There are two special places which no one has been to which I think are worth while but apart from that— travel is too hard on the tyres and the mind.

                              Love
                               Larry

To Alan G. Thomas   Belgrade   [1952]
Dear Alan,

Amusing myself doing a scenario of *Cefalû* for a U.S. Film company which appears to be interested in buying it! We leave for Cyprus on Xmas Day all being well. Two things I would like you to do for me 1) Could you assemble the fragments of my Alexandria novel for me and post it to G. Wilkinson, (care of) Villa Christina Kyrenia, Cyprus. Mark it 'To Await arrival'. It consists of 1) little loose leaf notebook with a black buckram cover—some bright doodles in it 2) E. M. Forster's book on Alexandria, yellow cover, limited ed—signed by EMF 3) I think one or two white lined notebooks, official Foreign Office Stationery labelled OHMS. S.O. Book and marked Supplied for the public service. Written up a bit in pencil I think.

Then I would like you to cast a mental eye over my hoard of books, mentally box or bale them compute the weight, and ask your clerk the cost of shipping them to Limasol in Cyprus—Would you be an Angel? Apparently I can take anything into the place if I am settling, provided that it comes in within six months of my own arrival.

Write you from Trieste when I'm shot of this job—Ouf! Relief!

Love to you both

Larry

Cyprus

At the last moment, just as they were about to leave Belgrade, Eve, the strain having been too great for her, suffered a breakdown and was sent to hospital in England. Durrell, accompanied by his infant daughter, Sappho, travelled on to Cyprus alone. Here the release from official duties and the escape from the claustrophobic pressures of a communist country to the knock-about freedom of a largely Greek community caused his spirits to rise. He bought, rehabilitated and furnished a charming old Turkish house near the abbey of Bellapaix, and his mother came out from England to keep house.

Many friends came to visit Bellapaix. Cyprus had become a cross-roads where philhellenes and travellers in the Middle East paused before or after their journeys or while writing their books. Many of these were old friends, either from pre-war days in Athens or Egypt in war-time: George Seferis, Lord Kinross, Patrick Leigh Fermor, Sir Harry Luke, Freya Stark, Rose Macaulay and many others. And there were new friends both among the English colony and the Greek and Turkish inhabitants of the island.

But the dual expenses of supporting Eve in England and making a home in Cyprus ate into the savings on which Durrell had planned to live for 'a golden year of freedom for writing', and he was forced to take up teaching in a Greek school. 'How did you manage to do your writing in the days when you worked in a bank?' he once asked T. S. Eliot. 'In that precious hour, when you first get up in the morning, before the day comes crowding in.' Every morning Durrell rose at 4.30, and, fortified by black coffee, sat down to write by candle-light, then, as dawn broke, he drove to the school in Nicosia. 'I'm pushing my book about Alexandria along literally sentence by sentence,' he wrote to Henry Miller. 'Every waking moment is possessed by it so that by the week-end when I type out my scribbles I usually have about 1500 words.' Normally Durrell works on the typewriter from the very first, but in order not to disturb the sleeping child he wrote much of Justine *by hand, pausing from time to time to make cryptic drawings in coloured inks on the opposite page or on the covers of his notebooks.*

For almost thirty years, while Durrell moved around the world, his papers and considerable collection of books have been stored in the loft of my house. From time to time, during his infrequent visits to England, he climbs up through the trap-door and spends a morning sorting his effects into order; and while he is abroad I send out the books which he needs for work in hand. On three occasions, when he has bought a house and put down roots, the whole collection has been posted out to him. This has always been the signal for violence, war and revolution on an international scale. In 1941, soon after the parcels had arrived, Greece was invaded by the Germans, and a considerable collection of unpublished typescripts was used by the occupying forces to kindle fires. Charles Eldecott, my packer, had hardly despatched the last parcel to Cyprus when the crisis of ENOSIS flared up, and within a year or two the books were all back in Bournemouth once again. Naturally I felt some trepidation when, in 1957, we sent these, by now well-travelled, books out to Provence; sure enough trouble flared up in Algeria, and there were riots in France itself; fortunately the Algerians did not have sufficient power to invade the South of France, and Durrell has now remained in possession of his books for the longest consecutive period since the nineteen-thirties.

But to return to the situation in Cyprus; when the ENOSIS crisis had developed in violence and intensity Durrell was pressed, once again, into the service of the Crown. His fluent Greek, previous experience as a press officer and sympathetic understanding of the Greek character ensured his fitness for this difficult and often dangerous post. Among other activities he devoted a good deal of energy to reviving the Cyprus Review, *pressing his friends Freya Stark, Sir Harry Luke, Patrick Leigh Fermor, Lord Kinross, and other writers on the Middle East, to contribute. As the bomb explosions and assassinations were stepped up, only to be matched by the execution of captured terrorists, Durrell's position, torn between conflicting loyalties, became more and more excruciating. On the one hand he was an Englishman working in Government House, yet his sympathies as a philhellene and his devotion to the Greeks extended back for almost twenty years. Friendships were strained to breaking-point and beyond, fellow villagers were afraid to speak to him and it became dangerous to live in his house at Bellapaix. But amid all these difficulties and hazards he snatched time to work, generally at night, on his writing, and by 1956, when he left the island for good,* Justine *had been completed.*

To Alan G. Thomas   Ionian Bank, Kyrenia, Cyprus
                                    10 February 1953
(Postcard)
Just got here and am in a frightful mix with the child a house a job—It
seems a hopeless thing to satisfy all these demands—place is lovely—
would like to stay if I can. Will let you know about the books—I've
forgotten how many I have—approx. what would the whole shoot
cost—just the books of course?
Love

Larry

To Alan and Ella Thomas   Cyprus [1953]
Dear Alan and Ella,
    . . . Meanwhile I'm getting on with the bloody house, some days
gloomy and despondent, and on the point of selling it, some days full
of optimism. I calculate it could be really lovely for about £1500—a
Turkish house skilfully and unobtrusively modernized inside. Rather
an inaccessible position but a really glorious view. I wonder if you could
get me the catalogue of a stained-glass manufacturer. Can one just buy
panes of coloured glass—or perhaps single panes with not too hideous
a something painted on them? I wonder. Also have you any idea what
woodwork costs in England. It is expensive and bad here. I'm toying
with giving Sapphy a Turkish bed—a dais in one corner of the room
with a carved wood balustrade running round it—I often saw clumps
of carved rails for sale in junk shops. But perhaps transport would make
the sending of it too expensive.
    As soon as I'm organized I'll ask you to start sending the books.
Love, Larry

To Alan G. Thomas   c/o Ionian Bank, Kyrenia, Cyprus
                                    15 October 1953
Dear Alan,
    Forgive me being such a lousy correspondent. We are on the last lap
of the house and I've started work—terribly tiring—another fortnight

should see the house done. I wonder if you could be an angel and order me a dozen panes of coloured or stained glass—small—the size of half this page, in as many different colours as possible. I have two small windows—fanlights—and though the whole island is plastered with Turkish glass none is imported now. If you could airmail them to me I'd be grateful as the first rains are expected in 14 days. I think any little jobbing builder could tell you a glass-maker who would get them for you. *Please* would you? We are all as yet unearthquaked and well. Mother is bearing up. . . . I have no place to work and am going mad with frustration. Simply dying to get on with my novel—The girl's VI form of the place where I teach send me about six red roses a day anonymously, which is a good boost for a battered ego. I'll ask you to start posting the books soon and send you a cheque.

Love to you both

Larry

To Dr. Theodore Stephanides   Bellapaix, Cyprus
30 October 1953

Dear Theo,

It was good to hear from you again. Thank you for all your snake-dope. It came very appositely as we killed a viper just by the Abbey yesterday. Sapphy was within a few inches of it, playing with a cat which was hunting it. Yes we had a mild quake here but so far touch wood the house is standing up. Glad the Rhodes book amused you—cut in half as it was—I can't bear it.

Marie Millington-Drake should be in London this week and is going to ring you up about the shadow-plays. You will like her I think. She returns in November—so please give her the material you can for me —I will look it over and we might get out a ground-plan. At the moment I'm dead beat with teaching and building but I've written 25,000 of a corking novel about Alexandria which no doubt everyone will deplore but which engrosses me. Yes, my mama is here, and sends her love to you. She was very alarmed by the snake episode. Cyprus is charming but the climate is nearer Salonika than Mykonos—but it has a very real beauty of its own—it lies in the great soft hush of the Levant—The house is beginning to look quite pretty—I hope you will come out and stay soon—Zarian is going to settle and we are expecting Seferis from Beirut any day now. Paddy Leigh Fermor is here at present and we are having riotous evenings together. The trouble is that I have to get up at five and be at work at seven—you will sympathize I am sure. The Cypriots are awfully nice but dead in a peculiar sort of way— Security? Lack of real freedom and responsibility? Riches? I have not decided as yet which. Perhaps all three. But they are more honest than the metropolitan Greeks—though somehow so mentally sluggish it is unbelievable. . . . I'm dying to finish this book—such a strange mixture of sex and the secret service! Love to you. Embrace Marie warmly from me. She's a good girl.

Larry

To Alan G. Thomas   Bellapaix, Cyprus [1953]
Dear Alan,

   The coloured glass was a great success and every bit arrived safely. I have had the troublesome ground floor window of the dining room glassed in—it looks a bit like a Belsize Park Synagogue but really awfully nice. I've discovered that you can be as Betjeman as you like with Turkish houses without ruining them. Will you let me know what I owe you? I am standing by for the books now—how wonderful now the winter is setting in to immerse in the Elizabethans. I wish I could have afforded the huge £125 collection of reprints in your last catalogue. If you have any old books too shameful for the 2ᵈ box even make me a present of them and I'll pay the postage on them. Anything at all. Also please for Xmas dig me up a few bright books for Sapphy—full of animals, please. I have started a back-breaking teaching job but otherwise am happy—no chance to write as yet—however a good novel cooking. . . . I keep farmer's hours now—4.30 I'm up and away. Such beautiful dawns as in Cyprus I have never seen—better even than Rhodes. Paddy Leigh Fermor whom you'd love has just been through and John Lehmann: Adrian Seligmann is wintering here to write his Turkish book; Freya Stark is coming for a few months to stay with Harrison—who is awfully like you—and has (he's an architect) built up an old Turkish house into a sort of *biblio oikion* [book house]—we

[120]

are becoming terribly arty—like Cairo during the war—Send my beloved Eliza's will you when you can?*

Bless you—Love to you both   Larry

Did I tell you what fun Sapphy and I had with old Rose Macaulay? She adopted us and whizzed us off to bathe in her old car. She is a sweet thing—and went off vaguely towards Syria. Zarian is coming to settle here ('My boy we will immortalize Cyprus'). Armenians have given him a whole monastery to live on in a bluff beyond Buffavento. He threatens to give parties to which we shall have to ride 3 hours on muleback. Last night there was a knock on the door and in walked Seferiades—from Beirut holidaying here—you see we are not alone. Every one is arriving or planning to arrive and I am busily furbishing up a spare room for chance guests. Diana Newall is coming from Beirut to spend Xmas and 2 Yugoslav ballet dancers—one the ravishing and ever beloved FOSCA—have booked for August next. Miller is coming for a month next September. Why don't you?

Larry

To Alan G. Thomas   Cyprus 22 December [1953]
(Postcard)
Dear Alan,

Thank you so much. I'll tell Grindlay to transfer you £10 to cover postage. I'm on the last lap of the house and it is really awfully pretty. The books will perfect it, I hope. All sorts of artists coming through— why don't you come next summer. We have camp-beds etc. Henry Miller and wife are coming in Sept. Paddy Leigh Fermor and Joan in June; Ines Burrows in June—hosts of people. It will make the island quite perfect. If only I didn't have to work so hard.

My book has gone by the board now unfortunately. Never mind. Sapphy is well and my mother who sends her love—Love to you both for Xmas.

Larry

* For more than thirty years Durrell has contemplated writing a book on the Elizabethan writer. To this end he has collected reprints of scarce works by minor authors of the period—reprints which are now very hard to find, hence, 'my beloved Eliza's'.

To Alan G. Thomas   Bellapaix, Cyprus [1954]

Dear Alan,

The local bookseller in Kyrenia has been pestering me to help him re-arrange his shop. He has suddenly woken up to the fact that Kyrenia (which was the size of Corfe) is now being heavily Charminsterized,* prices are rising, people coming in. He really runs a small stationery shop with a counter-trade in mags. He smells the boom and realizes that in a year or two there will be several more enterprising people trying to open up here—Meanwhile he has by far the best position but is at his wits' end to know what to do. He stocks a few Penguins, post-cards, papers, stationery and text-books for the Greek schools. In fact a stroll round Charminster will tell you exactly the sort of shop he has, and a glance at your own windows will show the sort of thing he dreams about. He wants advice as to stocking. There is only one big bookshop on the island which is a huge emporium, an inextricable jumble run by a Turk, but which has a large stock and is consequently famous. People motor 18 miles into Nicosia for a book rather than visit my friend.

Meanwhile his potential public is as follows:
1) 3,500 English residents
2) Visiting tourists and troops—say 5,000 a year
3) Schools anxious for books on simplified English, Texts, Eckersley etc. (Longman's)

The stationery side is well established and the shop pays its way on it; but I think books, both new and second-hand, particularly travel and guide-books would sell steadily and quietly. How shall I advise my friend? How much capital should he put into a larger stock? Second-hand books? Is there any sale or return system? I imagine his problems are those one would face in expanding a business in Winton or Boscombe. Would you be interested in selling him chosen stock? Let me have a note if you are interested. Perhaps it might later appeal to you to be a managing director of a shop in Kyrenia (Business Trips). I am confident that if his little shop is carefully nursed it could rapidly expand —so many people spend the summer and winter here—and as I say the town is expanding horribly. The US Radio Station has produced a number of Yank families too. Let me have your views will you?

Yours

Larry

* Charminster Road, suburb of Bournemouth.

[122]

To Alan G. Thomas   Bellapaix, Cyprus
                                     13 February [1954]

Dear Alan,

Thank you for your good essay on bookselling the contents of which I have passed on to my eccentric friend in Kyrenia. He is most grateful. At the moment I am working so hard that I can't contemplate opening up another venture or I shall break a blood-vessel. But I shall keep your offer in mind for future ref. It has been a most tiring year and I am not out of the wood yet. To build a house, mind a baby, find a job—and write 25,000 of a good book (alas stopped), has taken all my energy. But the house is really most attractive. I do hope some time you'll come and stay with us. At the moment Freya Stark is preparing for a journey to the Black Sea here and we see quite a lot of her. She says that one bookseller sent in a query about her last book and thought the title was '*The Cost of Incest*'!* She's nice. All sorts of other people seem to be coming out so we should not lack for friends. By the way would it be impossible for you to order me a printer's dummy the size of a large novel—is it crown octavo, with some decent though not super paper—I shall make distinguished visitors write me something. I have an old dummy with quite a lot of interesting autographs in it. If this one is nicely bound in buckram could you have lettered on the spine

                    Bellapaix Abbey
                      in Cyprus

. . . . .

The books are coming in nicely. Thank you. They will make such a difference to life as Cyprus is terribly provincial and utterly cut off— No music, no theatre, no nothing. But there are some v. nice people settled here—an old architect called Harrison whom you'd love, a descendant of Jane Austen, and an artist or two.

If I have any money over I'm going to ask you to send me a few books later—but as I can't quite remember what I already own I'd better wait. I do hope I haven't sold all the psychology I once owned— particularly a psychoanalysis of Baudelaire.

                    Love to you both
                        Larry

* *The Coast of Incense.*

[123]

To Alan G. Thomas   Bellapaix Abbey, Cyprus
                                                     14 March [1954]

Dear Alan,

I must write you immediately to thank you for the munificence.
The book is simply beautiful and could not be better adapted to its
purpose. I will kick off with Freya Stark and Sir Harry Luke today and
get Rosemary Seligmann to do a drawing. What a beautiful parchment
bag for it. Since my new address people have been reacting in a most
favourable way; it has been given out that I have bought a huge
ruined monastery and am living therein with 275 concubines. It's
shocking how people exaggerate. I've only got 235. But I'm having a
press photo taken of myself in Carmelite rig, 'tonsured like a "man-
dril" ', dictating Pope Joan to a couple of pretty nuns. . . .

I'm working so hard these days I have no time to think. The clock
is just striking six—I'm off to work.

Many thanks for the lovely book. I hope you and Ella will come and
write in it before the Greeks push us into the sea.

Love   Larry

To Freya Stark   Bellapaix, Cyprus
                                                     1 June [1954]

Dear Freya Stark,

Thank you so much for your letter from Turkey which was full of
characteristic touches which made one feel the weird bare splendour of
it. I do hope the book is shaping itself steadily in your mind's eye. I
have, as usual, been working terribly hard and only snatching moments
for my book which I have begun to loathe because it is nagging at me
all the time and I feel I haven't the strength and concentration to deal
with it as it deserves. We have also been simply inundated with visitors, mostly old friends I haven't seen since my pre-war Athenian days.
Pleasant meetings enough but I feel the wretched book reproaching me
when I get up in the morning and stagger down the hill to the car!
Sapphy is enormously well and happy and Lucia is still her favourite
doll, though she has developed a faintly spastic left knee which we do
not dare to examine for fear of making it worse. On the second we are
expecting Ines Burrows to stay for a week en route for England, I am

sure you remember her from Cairo. Bernard B. [urrows] was Head of Chancery when you were a Friend of Freedom, and indeed it was he who introduced us one afternoon long ago. They are at Balukesir now—Bernard has his first Embassy. Xiutas—the Right Rev—was delighted by your card, and continues to swear and recite his way round the island. He has unearthed a charming little Turkish verse which, recited in a dark incinatory tone, seems to me good even in translation. It goes like this:

> And if you go to Kyrenia
> DON'T GO INTO THE WALLS
> And if you go into the walls
> DON'T STAY LONG.
> And if you stay long
> DON'T GET MARRIED
> And if you get married
> DON'T HAVE CHILDREN!

Try reciting it aloud. It is quite haunting. My mother sends you her best wishes as does Marie [Millington-Drake] who is building an extraordinary encampment of grass huts down by the sea while she decides about the ever more problematical house.

Every good wish and do come back soon.

Yours Sincerely,
Larry Durrell

To T. S. Eliot   Bellapaix Abbey, Cyprus [1954]
Dear TSE,

How delightful to find your inscribed play waiting for me in the pouring rain at the village pub. Couldn't have been a greater thrill. I sit down at once to thank you. I'm still working infernally hard as a schoolteacher but I have managed to put what little money I have (had) into a tiny but lovely Turkish house in a tumbledown village built round a huge ruined Abbey. A lovely village. Cyprus is rather a lovely, spare, big bland sexy island—totally unlike Greece with a weird charm of it's own—I haven't yet seen it properly. . . .

I have no time to write alas! And I'm teeming with books at the moment. I've got the guts of a good book on Alexandria out on paper:

but I have no time at the moment to induce the necessary nervous breakdown without which one can't get the little extra power into it which embalms. . . .

I'm getting old. Can't write poetry anymore—too tired. Only things which really please me are making love and lying in the sun—To realize the importance of pleasure and get contemplative enough to really enjoy it is something achieved. . . .

Every good wish

Larry Durrell

To Freya Stark   PIO. Nicosia, Cyprus
                                                       [1954]

Dear Freya,

I learned with dismay from Austen [Harrison] that you had not had a word from me. I answered your letters and addressed by hand the envelopes—to Asolo—as you seemed to be moving about a great deal. Rumour said Baghdad. Then came a cryptic post-card from Paddy with a less drunken looking note by you in the corner. And news? Surely you must be back and have my letters. I have been working like a black—they have made me a pasha and I am grappling with the moribund Information Services of the island, trying to make our case against the united howls of Enotists, British pressmen and fact-finding M.P.s. It has been no joke and all writing has had to be put on one side. How I envy the sense of space and leisure and meditation you are getting into your new book. . . . Later on you must send me some pictures and a short article on some Cypriot Turkish subject for the *Cyprus Review* which I am trying to revive. . . . As for us, we are cleaving fast to this politically 'jumbly' island. How I long for a short holiday somewhere. But, materially things are looking up and the work, though hot, is more congenial than teaching. Only my own real writing beckons and leers at me from the subconscious—but there's nothing to be done about *that* for the time being. We are doing £25 worth of alterations to the house while we live in the Government House in Nicosia which they have given us. The usual troubles with Cypriot labour. But at last Marie's problems are settled for Austen has agreed to build her the sort of house which will put an end to wander lust.

Endless conferences and telephone-calls. Endless discussions on concealed patios and fountains. Soon there will be half a dozen nice people settled here and we can begin to work on the doughy shapeless mass of Cyprus social life and give the island an identity. You must really help in the pages of the Review. Important people coming here and bothering to write about it will make life seem all the more worth living for us Cypriots. As soon as I have got the Review on its feet I shall write you a formal editorial letter making you an offer for an article. I also hope to entrain that tireless and delightful globe-trotter Sir Harry Luke—and others like Osbert Lancaster who know the island well and who deserve to be better known in the island. In about six months I hope to be able to relax—Sapphy is well and happy.

Much love from us all
Larry Durrell

To Freya Stark,   PIO. [Cyprus December 1954]
Dear Freya,
    Thank you very much for your letter. I am glad you liked the book —glad indeed that it arrived safely. Your offer of a little excerpt from your new book is simply thrilling and will be so useful from every point of view. I am planning to give the government a really good Middle Eastern review. It really does need something to project Cyprus and to give some standing to British culture generally. Quite a lot of people have now been roped in, Paddy [Leigh Fermor] and Patrick [Lord Kinross], Sir Harry [Luke], Lehmann and so on that you need not fear to appear in bad company, or tower high above a series of nonsense-reportages. By all means send us photos too if you have them. We primarily aim to be a picture magazine. . . .

Sincerely   Lawrence Durrell

To Freya Stark   PIO. Nicosia, Cyprus
31 March 1955

Dear Freya,
    Delightful to hear from you and to learn that a contribution is on the way. You have all been a tremendous help and the little Review

is struggling towards a satisfying final form. It will be something to stand the government in good stead—something worth owning. The Governor is very pleased with it but the Administration tends to grumble and regard it as frivolous. But the troops are buying it out and incoming tourists like it. Austen is I believe in London designing clock-towers for Nuffield College and Marie is in India consorting with rajahs and elephants. Her father flew in for a week and gave some lectures. My young and very successful brother Gerald arrived this morning for a two month stay to finish a book and make a couple of television films in colour. He is bursting with energy and enthusiasm. Sapphy is as charming as ever and has grown up into a most graceful little creature with lots of allure and intelligence. I am still working terribly hard and hope by midsummer to have completely made over the Information Services including a new radio station better by far than Athens. Then a little rest of some sort I hope. The Bellapaix house is spring-cleaned and [we] are all spending our first week-end out there this week. Sir Harry L. is here, in fine heart and sends his love, as do we all. I shall worry Xiutas.

Sincerely
Larry

To Freya Stark   PIO. Nicosia, Cyprus [1955]
My dear Freya,

I have been working and flitting about so fast that there has not been a moment to tell you how much I've enjoyed the selection of the new book,* parts of which we are so gratefully carrying in the *Cyprus Review*. At every turn one confronts the self-questionings of a mature spirit which has quarried its own experience in solitude and patience and charity. Nowadays writers' reflections only reflect bright surfaces of the mind; your prose has the overtones you sometimes see in the sea at noon when the sun is at zenith—a second floor below the surface. There is little news I can give you from here. We lurch from one crisis to the next. What a hedgehog of a problem Cyprus is! Eve has taken Sapphy to England and I must say it is a bit desolate. My humble

* *A Book in the Making* by Freya Stark appeared in the *Cyprus Review* June-July-August 1955.

official residence feels as if there had been a recent death in it! I'm awfully tired too and feel a very dilapidated old dung-beetle poet treading away at the meagre resources of time at my disposal. Perhaps something magical will happen to me next year. The Bellapaix house is shut up, empty and dusty, and all the toys in the cellar including *Lucia* with the spastic knee. However one learns about the deeps and shallows of one's own feelings this way so I feel that at the worst I'm gathering useful information.

My best love to you
Larry Durrell

To Alan G. Thomas   PIO. Nicosia, Cyprus [1956]
Dear Alan,

I'm tidying up here against my departure in August and I thought I'd send you a clutch of letters from writers and others worth keeping. Also the Mss. of *Justine*—the new novel that Faber's seem quite excited about. It may amuse you to read the first draft. My plan is to get to France for a couple of years—don't ask me how it's to be done. But after this long spell of Balkan service—nearly seven years flat I feel I need Debarbarizing and re-gilding. Could you, if I come down, put me up for a few days in September. It would be fun to see you again. Did you get the disc?

Love
Larry

The Midi

*During the latter part of his stay in Cyprus Durrell had met and fallen in love
with Claude, a Frenchwoman from Alexandria, who was destined to become his
third wife. Soon after his return to England in 1956 they set up house together,
for some months, in a Dorset village a few miles from Shaftesbury. Here, living
in a tiny cottage, Durrell wrote an account of his experiences in Cyprus:* Bitter
Lemons. *This was written, of course, with the remarkable capacity for rendering
Greek life and landscape which had characterized his two earlier island books,
but the drama and topicality of the ENOSIS struggle brought it to the attention
of a far wider public, while the tension between his own dual loyalties, and his
capacity to see the struggle from both sides, gave an additional vitality to its
structure.*

*Durrell very rarely discusses his work while it is being written; when a book
comes to fruition in his mind, he writes with exceptional speed, often for long
hours at a stretch, and while this happens he is virtually incommunicado. I well
remember the week-end after* Bitter Lemons *was finished. He came down to stay
with us, and we forgathered with his mother and sister Margaret who were also
living in Bournemouth at the time. He was relaxed and exhilarated by the relief
of having finished the book, while at the same time he was full of both the tragedy
and humour of life in Cyprus; after a few bottles of wine had been consumed, his
conversation leapt and sparkled like the fountains of Versailles.*

*Never really content when living away from 'the wine-drinking countries
which surround the Mediterranean basin', Durrell and Claude set out to look for
a home in the Midi. Financially he was at a low ebb, his savings all but exhausted,
and with no immediate prospect of a job; but, although he did not know this at
the time, the great turning-point of success in his life as a writer was at hand.*
Justine *and* Bitter Lemons (*and the first volume of Antrobus stories,* Esprit
de Corps, *and the adventure story for the young,* White Eagles Over Serbia)
were all published within the same year; Bitter Lemons *was chosen by the
Book Society and won the Duff Cooper Memorial Award, and, in the words of
Faber's advertisement, this was 'Durrell's annus mirabilis'. By the end of 1957*

he was world famous; within the next few years his books were translated into Arabic, Danish, Finnish, French, German, Greek, Italian, Japanese, Norwegian, Portuguese, Spanish and Swedish. He would never need to look for uncongenial employment again.

The ambience of southern France provides a very sympathetic setting in which Durrell has made his home and put down what may well be lasting roots. Its shores are washed by the Mediterranean, it is a wine growing-country, and the local people have many of the qualities Durrell found so congenial in the Greeks; while, on the other hand, Paris can be reached by overnight train. And although, to a large extent, the coastal regions have been exploited, vulgarized and in many ways made intolerable to the sensitive eye, only a few miles inland French provincial life continues undisturbed as it has for centuries.

Durrell and Claude settled at Sommières, a small town some miles west of Nîmes. Here they rented a modest house; it was somewhat primitive, there was no lavatory, cooking and heating facilities were rudimentary; but these details did not disturb their happiness, and they soon made many friends among the Sommièrois. The butcher's wife, waiting until their backs were turned, would add pieces of meat to that which had been already weighed, and, as one would expect, there were soon a number of cronies among the regulars who frequented the riverside café; among them Louis Legrand and Marcel Ranage. During the Occupation Louis and Marcel had been members of the Resistance. In the last weeks of the war they had been captured, red-handed, by the Germans; and had expected to be put up against the nearest wall and shot. But the German officer contented himself with taking away their automatic weapons and telling them to beat it, remarking: 'The war is virtually over now, and we can't win. I don't want any unnecessary blood on my hands.'

In due course the annual reunion of ex-service men, class of 1936, was approaching. The organizers discovered that if they could swell their numbers by only a few more they would be entitled to a better dinner at the same price. They were of the same age as Durrell; indeed, had he been a Frenchman, he, too, would have been of 'the class of 1936'; so they enrolled him as an honorary member. The dinner was a great success; in the ensuing conviviality Durrell put on a straw hat and sang Maurice Chevalieresque songs. By the end of the evening Louis was considerably the worse for wear and Durrell volunteered to see him home. This was made the more difficult because Louis had reached the stage at which he was unable to recognize his own house. He kept peering at one house after another. 'That looks like it . . . no it isn't.'

The dinner had taken place during Durrell's early days in Sommières, before the spread of his reputation as a writer. In later years when he appeared, from time to time, on television, facing some top interviewer, his confrères would turn to one another and say: 'And to think, he's an honorary member of the Sommières class of '36!'

The landlord, wanting the house in Sommières for his own family, refused to renew the lease, so Durrell and Claude moved to another home, a mazet *just outside Nîmes, which they rented with an option to buy. A* mazet *is a peasant cottage on a small piece of ground akin to a smallholding, generally owned by someone who has another home elsewhere, as a week-end cottage or summer house. The Mazet Michel is situated in an area which was rich in olive trees until, some years ago, they were all killed by a ferocious frost. The district immediately around looks rather stark, littered with millions of slabs of stone, gleaming in the sun, and dotted with thousands of apparently dead tree trunks. The house itself, a cottage of four or five rooms, stands on a little eminence. Durrell developed, as an afternoon occupation, the habit of building dry stone walls from the ample materials which lay around on all sides, until it almost seemed that the* mazet *lay within a fortified* enceinte. *Tiny green shoots began to sprout from the blackened and twisted carcases of the olive trees, whose will to live is, it seems, invincible. With increasing affluence the house was made more comfortable and attractive, a lavatory and a bathroom were installed indoors, while a deep cistern on the edge of the courtyard provided a pleasant plunge in hot weather.*

In the Midi Durrell wrote the three other parts of The Alexandria Quartet —Balthazar, Mountolive *and* Clea—*the* Antrobus *stories and two more verse plays,* An Irish Faustus *and* Acte. *In 1961* Sappho *was produced at the Edinburgh Festival with Margaret Rawlings in the title-rôle; she had long admired the play and took the leading part in a rehearsed reading as early as 1952. Meanwhile, Gustaf Grundgens produced all three verse plays at Hamburg, to much greater acclaim; Elizabeth Flickenschildt taking the title-rôle in* Sappho, *1959, and Anna Maria Gorvin appearing in* Acte, *1961.*

Nothing, it seems, succeeds like success, and while the unrecognized author is left to starve, offers of highly-paid commissions are thrust from all sides upon the author who has already achieved fame and fortune. Among other articles, broadcasts, television appearances, and so forth, Durrell wrote the travel pieces for Holiday Magazine *which are reprinted in this book.*

Old friends called as they passed that way, among them Sir Walter Smart, who, forced to leave Egypt, to which he had retired at the end of his distinguished career in the Foreign Service, now considered settling nearby, and wrote enquiring about possibilities. Henry Miller spent a summer, together with his wife and family, at Sommières. And there was a new friend, Richard Aldington.

Durrell had admired Aldington's writings from early days, and I well remember the enthusiasm with which we both read All Men Are Enemies, The Colonel's Daughter *and* A Dream in the Luxembourg. *Once, as a young man, before the war, Durrell had written to the* maître *about some point which I have now forgotten and received a courteous reply. Now neglected, Aldington was living at Montpellier, while his daughter Catha was studying at the University of Aix. Aldington's power as a creative writer had deserted him in later life and he was writing no more books which could rank with* The Colonel's Daughter; *but he remained an able man of letters capable of turning out well-written pieces of craftsmanship, a* Life of Wellington, *translations, anthologies and so forth. However, he had become very embittered and this estranged many readers who should have been his natural sympathizers. The climax came with two savage books attacking Norman Douglas and T. E. Lawrence, both of whom have a considerable body of admirers. I was in the new book trade at the time, and remember subscribing these books among the enthusiasts before publication, only to have them hurled back at me by enraged devotees. There was T. E. Lawrence, the intellectual and archaeologist, who had shown up the 1914 professional soldiers as the pack of bungling amateurs, which, by and large, they were. Aldington himself had written one of the best accounts of the disillusion which came upon the young men who had volunteered in 1914; and here he was, blasting away as if he were a senior member of the Cavalry Club. After that no publisher risked giving him a commission, and the backwash affected the sale of his earlier books, however good.*

Durrell gave to Aldington a warmth of friendship which only those who know him well can appreciate. His admiration for Aldington's creative work remained undimmed. Now that publishers on all sides were badgering him, almost daily, to write for them, he spent endless time and energy in the effort to place Aldington's work instead. It is only just to add that Aldington's bitterness was, to a large extent, an outward shell. The warm, deeply cultured man remained at the core. One of the happiest experiences of his last years was the Christmas that he spent with Durrell and Claude at the mazet. *He wrote his last letter to Durrell in 1962 and walked out to post it. By a coincidence Durrell was reading this letter when the news came over the telephone that Aldington had died.*

Another good friend that Durrell made at this time is F.-J. Temple, Director of the R.D.F. radio and television station at Montpellier. He supervised the production of two of Durrell's privately printed pieces: Beccafico, *a vignette of life in Cyprus, and the surrealist* Down the Styx, *adding translations into*

*French by himself. These were printed in limited editions at Montpellier and are
both reprinted here.*

*During the summer holidays there were gatherings of children; Sappho, and
sometimes Pinkie, joining Claude's children by her first husband, Diana and
Barry. And the party was even larger the year that Henry Miller's children,
Tony and Valentin, were there as well. They bathed in the river at Sommières,
or all drove in convoy to the sea at Stes. Maries. On some days they explored the
Camargue and on others they watched bullfights in the Roman arena at Nîmes.
In 1964 the annual reunion took place in Corfu, Durrell and Claude going out
first to establish headquarters in a villa at Paleocastrizza. This was the first
time that Durrell had been in the island since 1939 and there were many
reunions with old friends, as described in his essay* Oil for the Saint.

The little mazet *was becoming overcrowded as the children grew well into
their teens and possessions accumulated; so in 1966 Durrell and Claude moved
into a new home in Sommières. This is a quite large nineteenth-century house,
somewhat mysterious and romantic, hidden behind high walls, with a conservatory
and an overgrown garden. Diana Menuhin described it as exactly the kind of
house one would imagine as belonging to Madame Bovary. After considerable
re-decoration and the installation of central heating they moved in.*

*Ella and I were invited for the first Christmas in the new home. Claude wrote
a lively and enthusiastic letter, urging us, as we were coming so far, to stay
longer; there was the excitement of the new house, many places which we had
not seen to explore, and so forth. Then on December 9 came an express letter from
Durrell. Arrangements would have to be cancelled; Claude had not been too well
for some time, nothing very serious, but the local doctors could not pin it down
and they were going to consult a specialist in Geneva. A little later Durrell
wrote again from Geneva: the trouble had been identified, the treatment would
be a bit tedious and last for three weeks, however there was no need to worry. He
returned to Sommières in order to collect various things which Claude needed for
the longer stay. When he got back to Geneva there were long faces; Claude was
not reacting to the antibiotics. On New Year's Day, 1967, she died.*

To Freya Stark

51 St. Albans Avenue
Bournemouth, Hants.
20 September 1956

My dear Freya,

How good to hear from you again. As usual I am bedevilled by women and babies and lack of money. I'm trying to get to France for a few months but I am saddled with Sapphy whole time at present and must take her too. Much as I enjoy her the strain of trying to write with a small child on one's hands is v. great. I'm still waiting for news of a lodging near Paris where I can finish my Cyprus book: poor quality it will be I'm afraid and done at speed. How I would love to visit you— but alas! And of course I didn't resent your letter. The Greeks are quite mad today. Politically they are parrots you know. Of course a lot of blame attaches to our original refusal to take the Cypriots seriously. But now it's too late for parleys.

I'm living in dreadful confusion writing this on my knee and reading Sapphy Lewis Carroll as I go. Hence the dispersed and scrappy letter. I'll write you at length from France.

Bless you and thank you.
Larry.

To Freya Stark

Stone Cottage, Brookwater
Donhead St. Andrew, Shaftesbury
Dorset 21 October 1956

My dear Freya,

I was just writing your name when your letter came—with its delightful invitation. How I wish I could accept it, but at the moment I am heavily encompassed by problems which can't be easily solved unless I stay here for a few months. I should by now have been in France but my luck is at low ebb this year. Never mind, I have contracted to finish a book on Cyprus by Xmas and have been simply obliged to find a corner in which to do it. Hence this old thatched cottage near Salisbury, rented to me for a few months by a friend. Sapphy is with me, adorable as ever. A six year old is even more work than a baby in arms! And the questions. Daddy, what does God look like? Daddy, what is the moon? What is 'a sake'? (For Jesus' sake, Amen.) I am nearly driven wild by this cross-talk!

With any luck I shall be over the channel this Spring—and if S. is settled in London may venture down to Asolo for a week or so.

Good luck with the new book. Sapphy sends her love. She remembers the doll Lucia very clearly.

Love,

Larry Durrell.

To Alan and Ella Thomas

Villa Louis, Sommières
Gard, France   [1957]

Dear Alan & Ella,

I'm writing a short note in round robin form to give you our news. We are still camping in this villa trying to clean it up. It is still cold and windy up on this hill behind the medieval castle. We went first to Nice and Cannes but found them awfully like English seaside resorts and heavily geared to Tourism, not very nice; so we worked back to Marseilles, Toulon, and round the horn to Arles, Montpellier, Perpignan. All this bit is flat alluvial marshy with some pretty villages on the coast but again full of tourist shacks and villas. The odd thing is that three miles inland everything is deserted and ancient and quite quiet. We thought the best thing would be to find a place on a big river for summer quiet and bathing. This is a medieval town with a river flowing right through it; very pretty. The valley is vine-planted away to every horizon and is going to be delightful in a month. It has a single line railway to the biggest of the nearby towns, Nîmes, which is full of Roman ruins and where the Spaniards come to give bullfights every year. The villa we have taken provisionally for six months with a view to looking round the country; it is solid and modern but without internal water and lavatory so we are more or less camping for the moment. But in every direction there are small villages with houses for sale at between two to six hundred—huge rambling peasant houses built over curved doorways and immense stables. The rooms are twice the size of Margaret's drawing room and very high. Palaces in fact, though without any sanitation and water except wells. But with electric light. . . . It would be wonderful to settle here if possible and try to nab a rambling old house full of odd shaped rooms. We shall see.

Love.

Larry

[136]

To Sir Walter Smart   Villa Louis, Sommières
                                           Gard, France [1957]

My dear Sir Walter,

. . . We have been here since February only; we had one week of
teasing north wind and some rainy spots, but really marvellous weather
since. And here on this river it smells good and healthy, better than
Cyprus; not quite as douce as Rhodes. We don't fear heat ourselves if
it's dry. The damp in Egypt and Cyprus got me down terribly, not the
temperatures. I should think from a winter look along the littoral that
summer was dank and marshy there, but inland not so. The part I haven't
examined is the Hyères side of Marseilles. You see we have been careless and rather poor, travelling by village bus, and tied by one serious
consideration. If we went broke Claude who is French, and unbelievably
resourceful for an Alexandrian, was prepared to work until I straightened
out the boat. We had to be near a possible work-point, so we chose
midway between Nîmes and Montpellier; tho I must admit I have seen
nothing prettier than Sommières, and the river will offer us all the
bathing we need. The most likely seaport we found (bearing our preoccupations in mind) was Sette, but as a free port it is already being
exploited though I imagine that you could get a reasonable villa for
twelve hundred there still. If you go to look at it call on a delightful
estate agent we know and he will give you the form. M. De Brunel.

But while we were thinking of this year we were also keeping eyes
open for the chance perhaps of buying, and now have the technique.
All around here in the smaller villages there are enormous barn-like
wonderfully solid peasant houses going. We have looked at two in the
next village—Auchargues. They were shapeless and rambling and
HUGE; water and light. But I think would cost between six and eight
hundred to turn into the lovely houses they could be. No plan, no
design, no doors in the right place etc. Marvellous high-ceilinged
rooms with beams—*grenier, écurie* and God knows what else. They were
four hundred each. Position not good I thought; but the man who
showed them to us, a local lawyer called Nègre, said he could find us
dozens like that in almost every village. Of course had we had a car we
could have ventured further afield—or money for that matter. In
Nîmes there is a charming estate agent too who turned us up slightly
more expensive ones with water laid on and light—his cheapest was
one which, owing to other problems, we did not get round to seeing—

at St. Bonnet. It was five hundred. I gather that the technique is to call at the *Mairie* in a promising village. They not only rent but sell houses of owners who die without heirs—seems quite a lot of people do. And this also goes for apartments, lodgings etc. We tried this out of curiosity in Sette and turned up two possible flats at 15 pounds a month in one afternoon. As to weather: I don't know. It seems absolutely lovely country and I can't believe the mistral is worse than the khamseen—but I have no direct experiences of it yet. I'll ask Richard Aldington about it next week; he lives in Montpellier and has been years down here. I suppose all river mouth deltas are windy and unpredictable—

Of course no lavatories and *salle d'eau* a rarity. Even in this lovely villa we wash from a bucket and crouch among the vines *à la Grecque*. If my money affairs straighten out (hollow laughter) I aim to put one in. Is there any chance of you coming this way? Remember that we could put you up for a couple of nights but I'm afraid it would be Albanian fashion, washing in a bucket and trotting about in the undergrowth with a shovel! But a pleasant room and two little beds. It might fit in if you were doing a fighter sweep over this area. Do you know Aldington? He might be of use?

Love to you both
Larry

Later in May we'll have children here alas so I'm trying to get this book finished as soon as possible.

To Ella and Alan G. Thomas

Villa Louis, Sommières
Gard, France
[Postmarked 4 April 1957]

My dear Alan and Ella,

. . . yesterday we went down to Montpellier to visit Richard Aldington. He is in a very bad state, sixty-five, and I think in bad shape owing to the terrible state of affairs arising out of his Lawrence book. He has pulled the whole house down about his ears and is virtually under a boycott. His sales have stopped abruptly; publishers and editors won't print him—even letters to the press. Worst of all he seems to have undermined the readership which has been supporting him all these years at a single blow. It is no joke for a man of sixty-five, and he's now under medical supervision for the usual writer's *surmenage intellectuel* etc., sodium amytal and so on. But it is clearly the moral effect of having ruined his whole career—even in the USA where his biggest public was. The demon of TEL has risen from the grave. I'm terribly sorry for him, although you know what I feel about the Lawrence book; but it has killed ALL his books stone dead, and publishers won't put them back into print—a really frightful position for a man living by his pen and with a charming sixteen year old daughter to support; and in poor physical shape. I am doing what I can to help and have reviewed his Mistral book for the *New Statesman*, but with sinking heart—because what he has done can't I think be repaired by a dozen good puffs. He has to win back his readership, write his way out of this mess, and I don't feel that at the moment he has it in him. Would you ask Bill Woods when next you see him whether a film scenario—say a French or ancient Greek love-story under his name would appeal to anyone? Claude thinks the only hope—he obviously can't write six more novels—is a film in the standard romantic Aldington style. But I know nothing about the market. Ask Bill, will you. The poor chap is sadly down and eager to grasp at any way of restoring his position; pity, he was a good scholar and in his robust slashing style a readable novelist. I am tackling several other people about him, but you see it's not easy—as apart from the fury of Lawrentians everywhere the bloody *public* he had has been ruined. However I must do whatever I can.

Claude has finished her second novel and started her third; I must say it's rather good, the second; and writing prevents her from talking too much. Which is healthy. I have no word from Gerry about the gorilla nuptials as yet; I fear that one of the party may get raped if they get too close with their camera. I hope it isn't Jacquie or the secretary. . . .

Much love
Larry.

To Richard Aldington

Villa Louis, Sommières
Gard, France. [1957]

Dear Aldington

I'm so glad the little thing passed muster. I hope they'll carry it to tell a few people what a delightful book it is, and specially visitors to

Provence. I have enjoyed it. We are getting on quite well—villa is nice but no bath and no lavatory—we have showers from a watering-can (weather somewhat cold for this): as for lavatory, I am of course a firm supporter of the Old English Humus group (Massingham) and believe in giving mother nature back as good as I get but—It remains to see how long the vines stand up to this Rupert Brooke treatment ('Corner of a foreign field which is forever England'). We are now having a marvellous correspondence with an earth closet specialist in Arles. Sommières is terribly funny—strongly touched by the spirit of Raimu and Fernandel; I can see a pancake novel forming in Claude's mind on the pattern of *Clochemerle* with the Vidolade as the high spot. The flood stories are really a scream; we have collected hundreds of first person singular accounts. I do wish I had a tape recorder.

I am now trying to get the Treasury to baptize me 'resident abroad' and the French to accept the idea; I know nothing about Income Tax etc. here. We have seen a number of lovely peasant houses for three and four hundred pounds and perhaps next year we might buy one and make it over; but conflicting ideas beset us. We might go seriously broke in which case Claude, who is a tremendous speed-everything-executive girl, would get a job in the nearest big town; so we should have to be within commuter's distance of one. The seashore I begin to fear is out—and Perpignan way would be too far if C had to find a job in Toulouse. The best combination would be a house about five miles from Nîmes or Avignon on a swimmable river. (My daughter and Claude's two will want to come out this summer—perhaps both my daughters: the elder by the way is nearly as old as yours and is on the way to becoming a ballet dancer.) Well, all these little beasts will have to be lodged and fed for the summer holidays—

I mustn't bore you with these problems. I never met Lewis alas; but of course he is great. Only with the Ape I felt the personal pleasure of the pejorative made the book good satire but somehow not on a 'universal' plane—don't know how to say it. It sinks under the weight of its own spleen. Will it outlive its subjects? And I felt this immoral because I always felt Lewis to have a greater equipment than Joyce, and he should have spent his time making some art instead of complaining about the lack of it! What a tremendous proser! I suppose the cultivated meanness that you write about is a sort of childish hangover —what children do if they feel unloved; be naughty and get slapped—

that at least is some sort of attention. I knew someone awfully like that. I was told the humiliation of going bald worried him terribly. Just as the 'small man worry' was the central Lawrence problem (T. E.) His brother told me: 'He could never forgive himself for being tiny.'

Yours
Lawrence Durrell.

To Alan G. Thomas   Villa Louis, Sommières
Gard, France [May 1 1957]

My dear Alan,

Thanks for a delightful letter full of good sense and good anecdote. Today is Labour Day dear fellow Marxist, and consequently an appropriate day for me to address an epistle to you. In France the Catholic Church, which in some curious way entirely missed Marxism as a potent form of absolutism which it could have used, is setting out to remedy the defect. For days the press has been full of exhortation to bring your tools, all ye who are heavy laden, and we will get them blessed. Consequently today there is going to be a regular turn out of tools, better I imagine than a flower show. The French peasant has a deep and reverent respect for his tool—as who hasn't? Consequently he will not be slow to respond to the Church's appeal. Incidentally the only reason for the French affection for Churchill is the pregnant phrase 'Give us the tools and we will finish the job', almost the only thing the great man said which translates directly into French without a circumflex, and which stirs the French heart to the echo. As for tools, in principle I have advised Claude to stay indoors after the blessing service as there is no tool like an old tool . . . And so fellow Marxist I take my leave of you. . . .

Roy Campbell dead! It sounds so silly. What a loss to us the old carbonaro and mischief banger. They won't have no more joy of Roy in heaven—first thing he'll do is to write an unpardonable epigram on the Holy Ghost and break up a prayer meeting; and what's more he'll eat garlic all the time to the intense annoyance of the angels who are all Maltese British subjects.

I am now on the last three or four pages of Justine II, which may not be as bad as one always fears; at any rate the form is really original—

[141]

the same book written from a different point of view. By Xmas either I have the centre panel done (a straight novel) or I'll be in a home or both. Have you come across *Zen and the Art of Archery*? You ought to have a look at it.

Love to you both
Larry

To Alan G. Thomas   Sommières, Gard, France
[Received 3 July 1957]

Dear Alan,

. . . Claude left for England last night and doubtless you will have seen her before you get this; you can tell her I miss her. She warned me I would but I didn't believe. Anyway I have been much consoled by seeing Lady Chatterley in French at the open air cinema—Avis Important: ce film ne recherche pas le scandale mais il traite d'un sujet délicat. But it is curious how they have rationalized the whole thing. Stripped of its highly pressurized prose it goes something like this: Autrefois il y avait un certain bonhomme Chatterley qui se trouvait dans une situation affreuse. Il manquait des cuillons, le pauvre. Et sa pauvre femme a passé des jours entiers en se plaignant parce ce que—Eheu! Mais à la fin c'était beaucoup mieux parce ce qu'elle a trouvé un autre bonhomme qui en servait des couillons immenses, blafards, exfoliâtres etc. etc. The fat man's cousin in front of me asked him: 'Mais qu'est-ce qu'il a pour l'amour du ciel?' He told her once, but she didn't get it; he told her twice, she was still puzzled. He told her thrice and she sat back with pleased amazement sucking a sweet—Ah! She understood! He had no balls! Down here in Sommières one wouldn't make such a song and dance about it—So long as French film-lovers look like greyhounds sickening for distemper everyone is happy.

I agree with you about the French; it is the disparity between their character and the character of France itself which is so strange. It is a masterpiece by a grumpy man. But they have a far higher regard for freedom than we have, complete disregard for 'face', and a profound sense of values. I think Claude is right in saying it is because there is still genuine unfeatherbedded peasantry and the values of ordinary life flow from them—in food and similar things. Here one does not feel so

[142]

bitterly about the mob getting all the gravy—because they spend it unerringly on whatever makes the heart glad. You should see the old workmen spend their wages—the care with which they select a good bottle of champagne—champagne at 12 shillings—or even an ordinary rouge at a shilling. You should see them going over a counterful of cheeses with their horny fingers touching them like Menuhin does his Strad. The intellectuals here are really outside ordinary life— nobody looks to them for physical values, only spiritual. It is taken for granted that nobody will do anything to seriously impair the quality of Camembert. *That* will go on. The rest is ideas—and they don't care where the ideas go if they don't get into the wine. Of course the motor-bike and telly barber-shop moronic world is catching up here— but very slowly; and somehow when any lout on a motor-bike can discuss wine and cheese in broken tones with tears streaming down his cheeks you feel less sad about the motor-bike. In England you feel everything is a *cult*, life itself is a sort of ritualistic cult, sex a fertility rite etc. One is conscious of the tabu. And much as I deplore the lack of lavatory sense here I'm convinced that their healthy attitude to ordure is the basis of their psychic balance; the balance in sex relations too. It's good to get men and women using the same lavatory, getting used to the smelliest part of each other; it keeps the crops in perspective. Then there are two other things unique of their kind—the reverence for love and the devotion to artists. There isn't anyone who doesn't gaze admiringly at you if you say you are a painter or poet; even those who can't read. I think these outweigh the bad qualities in a final judgement. I can't think of another nation quite like them at their best. Anyway, this suits me fine; and ask Claude to tell you about income tax etc. It is damn civilized the way they go about things.

Love Larry

Don't keep *Justine II* too long as there is a hope of selling serial rights on it.

To Patricia Rodda   Sommières [1957]
Dear PR,

. . . We got back in good fettle from Aix where we had a good three or four days with David Gascoyne, whom I hadn't seen for about ten

years. He is Paris 1938 vintage so we had plenty to recall, and punished
the bottle a bit. He was staying with a painter Meraud Guevara in a
lovely big Provençal house: large car too. Splendid luxury, so we drove
around Cézanneland: almost every corner is a ready made Cézanne. I
began to understand the technical problems he had set himself much
better by surprising his pictures *before*, so to speak, he'd got them down.
But Aix is—well not spoiled but full of *artists*—which means tourists.
And I was rather glad in a way to get back to dusty bony Languedoc
with its sleepy *un rusé* people, and crawl back to this splendid vineyard.
Here it is still eighty years behind the times; and the nearness of the
Little Argentina (Camargue) with its swamps, mosquitoes and wind
should effectively drive off tourists for a while yet; we are just out of
mosquito range and fairly high off the floor. And all in all damned
lucky. As for devaluation—it's marvellous! Twenty per cent more for
every pound I transfer. You see I have technically 'emigrated' and am
allowed a transferable account out of which I can whistle pounds over—
if I can earn them. People on a *travel allowance* will get hit backwards,
buying their francs in London. That is why your friend is justifiably
worried. But if you need francs in France next summer I can provide—
if I'm not dead broke by then. It's going to be a struggle but for the
first time now the books are beginning to slide—not very steeply as
yet; I must nail *Mountolive* to the barn door before the form of this
nonsense becomes clear. The American *Justine* has started to pull away
from the shore too into a third edition. Seems I'll have enough dough
this year to stay on and beat it out on the machine. *Esprit de Corps*
should be along soon. I've told them to send you one. It is a joke—
rather coarse material; but these short stabs sell frightfully well.
Think of it—500 dollars from the *Atlantic* and ditto from *Playboy* in
the States—nearly a year's food and lodging! Not with British income
tax though; but as from January I'm opting to pay French (one third)
so the British will have to hand me back what they've stolen to keep
their funny little misery hatch afloat—all goes in painting the front
door as far as I can see. The French are so much more sensible I find.
Not a penny on clothes or keeping up face; they dress in rags—but eat
like fighting cocks and drink like Pomeranians. And they are sensible
about love making too. Things like *The Wolfenden Report* make one
snort with laughter in Europe; I'm surprised that *Canard Enchaîné*

hasn't run it as a comic. And we talk about liberty of the individual! Well, I guess I've always been a consenting adult! . . .

                    All the best L.D.

To Buffie and Gerald Sykes   Sommières, Gard, France   1957

Dear Buffie and Gerald! . . . If you come back to France *don't* go to Paris, it is terribly expensive and crowded. Cheaper to choose a backward province and visit Paris as and when needed. Prices are exactly a third; but of course the one proviso in France is EAT IN. We get by about the same as England—but the food is regal and the wine good; even the cheap *gros rouge*. But of course we have chosen an unpopular department, Languedoc is bleak and stony, and the wind and mosquitoes from the Camargue keep tourists away except in summer, then only a month. But of course we are fairly robust, used to camping about the Balkans etc. so these hardships seem trifling compared to the spiritual joy of living in France—so winy and sexy and mad about ideas! *Justine* comes out in November in French and German! It is very exciting; and the whole series has been contracted in advance by Germany and England with Duttons now following up most generously. I had a splendid personal letter from E. Macrae of Dutton—President— saying how delighted he was with *Justine* and with the MSS of *Balthazar*, the second volume. I'm embedded in the third now—a big straight naturalistic novel; the last one will revert to the *fleuve* style again and tie up all the ends (I hope). Anyway, with enough in the larder until next summer, the baby paid for for clear through next year, I can draw breath and work without looking over my shoulder at the Foreign Office or the Council of Europe. Anyway I think after my book of diplomatic sketches I'd find it hard to lobby a job now! I'll be sending it to you shortly. It's rubbish, with a giggle here and there.

    . . . Signing off, to rush to the post, love to you both—no, all three.
                    from
                    Larry Durrell

To Theodore Stephanides   [Sommières]   [1958]
Dear Theo,

. . . I have seen an old abandoned *mas* in the wildest part of the
garrigues between Nîmes and Avignon and may succeed in taking it on
a v. low rent for a period of five years. The property is enormous and
quite ruined—several hundred, no about a hundred, olive trees dead
from frost, but sprouting round the roots; pine, cistus, wild flowers
etc. In climate not unlike a desolate corner of Crete or Cyprus. I think
that with a few chickens and goats we could live frugally enough, but
I'm wondering whether the regrafted olive trees, the sprouts, mightn't
be capable of reviving, and also whether I couldn't plant a carob or
two—unheard of here. If they did well I would rent a large strip (£2 a
year) and grow pig food. It's wild and desolate heath, calcareous,
stony, bony. It once bore vines but they are gone. Springs, though, and
holm oak, hares and foxes. Do you get the idea? With the exception of
the mistral (very severe) it is exactly like a desolate bit of Attika. The
French, who work till they drop on anything that will yield two francs
a day, simply disregard this sort of terrain as unproductive. Now what
crops would need no looking after? Origanum? I thought you might
have some ideas—or at least be able to suggest a line of sensible reading
which might enable me to dig an interesting project out of this waste
and wuthering land?

Love Larry

To Richard Aldington   [Sommières]   [1958]
Dear RA,

. . . We have found a tiny *mazet* on the Uzès road, on the edge of
the *garrigue*, windy folorn and rather Brontë where I hope we'll be
moving in September; but it is completely unfurnished and it's tricky
work planning for basic furniture etc. But I'm going to take a plunge,
rent for a ten year lease with an option to buy if I can, and . . . well:
once more into the breach. . . . But things are, if not rosy, better than
they were. The quartet is sold in four languages which is something,
and the Yanks are going to put all my books into print at the rate of
two a year. I calculate that with ten chickens and the excellent *potager*
out there I shall just squeeze by!

[146]

. . . Now that I have formally put poesy aside until I can earn a living with prose people are pestering me for it, the BBC intoning it and other smile-making things—what is one to make of the British? In *Mountolive* the only cut they insisted on was the word '*fellatio*' which I shouldn't have thought anyone knew, save the late Havelock E. and Norman Haire—It baffles me to be unable to get a sense of rapport with the way they think; they shy like a nervous horse at a piece of paper in the road—Anyway, what the hell; if I have to do six more thrillers to stay here I shall do them with a good grace. I have now cased up this joint, as Henry would say—To live within bike-shot of Nîmes, and with the Stes. Maries as my summer resort (I have two excellent tents) seems heaven to me, mistral and all. Ouf! I suppose I'm getting old, but I'm sick of travel. As always, everyone is trying to make me start travelling again; *Balthazar* has had quite an extraordinary *advance*-press, for it isn't out in USA till next month, and next year in France, while the Germans have lagged behind with translation-troubles over the blood-clots in *Justine*. But the book has been reviewed in three languages on the English ed and the result is two invitations to tour America, one Holland and one Sweden! But I'm going to stay with my chickens; they need me (and I need them until I see how the money shapes)! . . .

Every good wish
Larry

To Richard Aldington

le mazet Michel Engances
Chemin d'Uzès
près NÎMES GARD [1958]

Dear Richard,

A swift line to thank you for the unexpected and welcome gift; I thought at first it must be an EOKA bomb and so made Claude open it! I am sorry that we won't see you yet awhile, but the stocks of dead olive will hold out until you come. Meanwhile, too, we are working wonders with this little *mas* and I shouldn't be surprised if you found it an ideal hideout for a couple of boozy writers. But of course the prospect of actually being able to buy it next year has made us look at it with entirely new eyes; I've got quite a little building project in my head.

There is a mountain of dry freestone to play with and I can do the work myself; I have an awfully good mason friend who comes and brickles whenever I need something really professional done for the pleasure of borrowing Chauvet's books which he wraps up and carries away reverently. They are extraordinary people—*all* of them anxious to paint and write, the artisans. The plumber's wife is a lauréat of the *Beaux Arts* and the painter who is rather languid does appalling but very professional water-colours. But one senses quite clearly here that one is in the Panurge country—they talk endlessly of belly wearying meals with emphasis on quantity always—a thousand oysters, a million pigs of garlic, a fifteenth helping; and they are always down with ferocious liver crises! But delightful honest chaps (deeply suspicious of each others' honesty!) Yes, this was a good ploy indeed. I gather Antrobus is going well in London. I am hovering about like a wet hen before beginning *Clea*. Ouf! I'm tired by the thought. I'd so much rather be a plumber or paint in oils! Another ten days and we'll be quite straight and then the merry rattle of typewriters! No, I haven't had any bites from the movies; I nearly sold *Labyrinth* once but after two attempts at 'treatment' they gave up.

Every good thing
Larry

To Alan G. Thomas

MAZET MICHEL
ENGANCES   PRÈS *NÎMES* GARD
FRANCE
[Postmarked October 1958]

Dear Alan,

Claude has found some excellent old bookshelves cheap and we have plastered them up along one wall; a queer sense of whatsisname they gives me after three years of homelessness (symbol of homelessness for me is books on the floor, under the bed and in the granary). What I wonder would it cost me to have you send me out a few slowly, bit by bit? It was about a tenner to get them all out to Cyprus wasn't it, and about fifteen to get them back home. I think I could invest a tenner in the project now—about which there is no hurry whatsoever. Do you

[148]

feel able to do a tenner's worth of sending or are you absolutely work-bound and staffless? I don't want to trade on your good nature.

If you can and do; please make small parcels, preferably a single book as the postman is a hundred and twenty and has to cycle four kilometres uphill. I have to give him wine and fan him with my hat after every book.

ALSO PLEASE DON'T FORGET TO MARK EACH PACKAGE THUS

Gratuit. Service d'Auteur.

Otherwise I shall have to pay customs!

I'd be most interested first in books of reference, or anything on the Gyppos about whom, damn it, I shall have to start writing; the Elizabethans can stay put for the nonce.

This place is awfully wild, mosquito and gypsy ridden, and suffering from the recent floods which were v. bad; Sommières was sunk up to its waist in riverwater. We luckily are on a hill like a draining board. In an awful mess still, trying to set everything to rights.

Latest joke was a telegram from Hollywood saying I was the only man to do a script on life of Cleopatra and would I go at once please! Will I hell! But it is curious to think of those cigar stuffing moguls reading *Justine*.

Love to you both

LARRY

To Alan G. Thomas

le mazet michel engances
chemin d'Uzès NÎMES GARD
FRANCE [Spring 1959]

Dear Alan,

Very many thanks for the happy letter and the prompt despatch of the books. The old postman puffed up the hill with them this morning. I am beginning to wonder whether I won't be able to take everything readable off your hands this summer; I've now masses of bright new empty shelves with nothing but hideous copies of *Justine* in six languages. The English only send you six complimentaries; everyone else 15. I've been trying to cut this generosity off at source but an occasional parcel comes through full of Durrell. You should hear the

[149]

groans. Nothing in them to *read*. I am steadily moving out into the fairway—*Clea* is half done; eight languages in all. But the Americans and Germans saved me by handsome advances which enabled me to continue with them; though I've had to do a lot of dirty chores as well of a journalistic kind. My windfall in the autumn will enable me to pay Saph's school on the Composition Fee Schedule for four years in advance, thank God! And also to put down perhaps the whole sum on this house which is tiny and in rather a mistral-swept corner of Provence, but suits me fine. But until I have something saved I won't consider myself really free; it's tricky living abroad and trying to earn at home! . . .

I can't move from here until I've finished this blasted book. Everyone wants to send me everywhere; the Americans up the Nile for *Holiday* Mag, and the *Observer* back to Cyprus; meanwhile *The Times* wants short articles—but about what I ask myself! Ah for a moment in that loft of yours!

There are now three Egyptian society ladies in Cannes claiming to be the original of *Justine*! I'm tempted to go down and try them out for size. How could they refuse?

Every good thing
Larry

To Alfred Perlès

Masmichel Engances
Nîmes Gard France
Thursday 26 March   [1959]

Dear Joe,

. . . I was glad to get your sunlit letter from Crete. . . . I hear from Charles [Holdemann] that your Greek is absolutely terrific; this delights me. I knew the country and people would thrill you. It's a climate that strips the bark however old you feel and pushes out green shoots; I peel ten years off me every time I touch down at Athens. I have never discovered why. But apart from a general meeting up of all the old 'sea-green incorruptibles' I had also something else in mind. If I could find some old house on an island I could give the children a Greek holiday for a change this year. I had in mind to motor down and show Claude the Ionian islands before making a definite move for this summer. (She is mad about Rhodes, but hasn't yet seen Corfu, Zante, etc.) In the middle of all these pleasant dreams Cyprus flared up again, and I have been watching the developments carefully, very fearful that the result might well be a wave of resentment and annoyance against the British and Americans; as usual the UK is going to play its stupidest hand and suggest partition; now if in UNO you have Russia voting for Enosis, and the Anglo-American team voting for partition, our good name will be mud once more; hence I hesitated. I was not thinking of anything more specific than unsmiling faces and the lack of courtesy without which Greece is never quite Greece. And having been through all this once in Cyprus I didn't want to have a repeat performance for a summer holiday. Hence my hesitation. I want the children to see Greece with her smiling face and not her wounded pouting one. . . .

I have a hundred other things to tell you; but they'll keep—*geia hara*!

Larry

To Alan G. Thomas   Masmichel Engances
Nîmes Gard France
[Postmarked October 1959]

Dear Alan,

. . . I have enough work for two full time secretaries. Stuff is piling up all the time; and the French and German press has broken all records on the first two of the quartet—*Mountolive* isn't even out yet! Pray to goodness the bubble doesn't get pricked too soon. Yesternight a 40 minute live programme in the French national hook-up with Henry and I. My French sounded quite respectable to my surprise. NRF are doing a study of *The Black Book; Encounter* and *Paris Review* are doing two long tape recordings of me. There have been some long articles in Holland, Italy and Sweden which I can't read. My dear chap all this is very well but I am so busy explaining my genius to chaps that there doesn't seem a moment to think about any more work for the time being; and I really want a corner to do some Elizabethan reading.

. . . I am trying to avert further crowd scenes in Paris when *Mountolive* comes out; they offer me parties and television appearances and a formal signing of me own work at the biggest bookshop in Paris. Jean tells me that Gagliana had a blow up picture of me life size in their window between Proust and Stendhal! Up like a rocket, down like a stick. Anyway Sapphy is paid up to the age of twelve and we can eat for two full years ahead; I certainly didn't hope for anything like that when I crossed the *Manche*! Devoutly thankful to the dear Europeans for taking the wandering boy to their bosoms in so unequivocal a fashion. A fluke! But life is made up of such flukes and windfalls. I'm sorting Henry's letters to send you; they are muddled and many handwritten; don't know how you will microfilm them at all. But in my rummage I've discovered a number of letters I thought I'd sold or lost from Dylan Thomas, Shaw, etc. Only alas not the nice insulting one from Sitwell; what can have happened to it. I'd like to have quoted it in my memoirs.

I'm not giving you this dope to bore you, but for bibliographical curiosity. *My Family and Other Animals* has had a good press in France chez Stock; but the man who published it nearly lost his job because he turned down *Justine* in the same batch on the grounds that they didn't want two brothers on the same list! HE is much abashed; and Stock apparently have put (*frère de Lawrence Durrell*) on some of their advertising (I'm quoting Jean) which is an amusing topsy turveydom. But then—The new CORREA list had a front cover with four pictures, Pasternak, Jung, Miller and yours truly with a banner THE GREATEST EUROPEAN WRITERS ON OUR LIST. *Tiens*, I thought, swelling like a frog with pride, I'll pinch one to send the family; but then I realized that probably the only familiar name would be that of the wicked Durrell himself!

All this goes to show that fortune is a fickle jade and not to be trusted; every penny I make will go into bricks and mortar and ground, and not in nightclubs.

Dear Alan and Ella, it is hard to thank you adequately for such royal hospitality; to leave you with such a savagely punished cellar—I don't know what to say except to thank you a thousandfold for it; it held the ring and gave Claude the necessary time to *réagir* and climb to her feet. I'll be sending along a lot of bumph soon. . . .

More soon

Love

Larry.

[152]

To Alan G. Thomas

Masmichel Engances
Nîmes Gard France
[Early Summer 1960]

Alan dear,

Did I ever write and thank you for the bibliographical data? I hope so. If not herewith warm thanks to you. Incidentally in Paris yesterday I ran into Larry Powell quite by chance and was able to thank him. *Clea* has gone with quite a big bang in Paris—scads of publicity, television and all sort of papers thrown open to me—and *fan* mail! Such a lot from all over—lots from U.K. *Two* mathematicians have written to vindicate my notion of the form; altogether the old quartet has really I think got by. By the way the boys of King's School* were so angry about the *Observer* sending me to school there that they asked for an article for the school mag. It is completely unpublished—May interest you? It is quite funny. Miller and Katsimbalis are both weaving about down here and we are expecting a visitation any day. I'm writing a scenario for Elizabeth Taylor on Cleopatra!! It means money for my Piero della Francesca book next year.

Just got back after 10 hectic Paris days—I am becoming quite a celebrity in Paris. It is surprising and pleasing to have young kids mobbing me at cafés in St. Germain.

Love from us both
Larry

To Diana Menuhin

[Written on menu: 'Dîner D'Adieu du Commandant'. Menu dated 24 September 1962.]

Dear Diana,

I believe our paths crossed by a few hours recently—a near graze! What bad luck. I have been sent on a journalistic assignment for a brief tour of Israel and Greece. As you can imagine the Greek visit was most exciting though Israel was interesting and rather moving and I hope to write something about it. But Athens gave me back at a blow all my old friends whose touching warmth was really like a home-coming; made it like one I mean. We did a swift autumn tour of the Pelopon-

* King's School, Canterbury, confused with Durrell's own school, St. Edmund's.

nesus—deserted bare and blue! Dug out old taverns, discovered new. Above all had Katsimbalis and Seferis to ourselves for *days* on end. Such stunts, such gales of laughter, such memories exchanged! It was like a gasp of rare air and I felt twenty years younger. 'Fifty years seemed but a day'! And now we are back to the problems of country-folk, leaking roofs and cisterns, damp wood etc., etc. I won't bore you with them. I'm glad you've found Mykonos. I first went there in 1936 and stayed with an old lady called Poppeia—there were no hotels and no tourists. I shared a lavatory seat with a hen and a bed with 1000 fleas. . . .

Larry D

To Freya Stark

Masmichel
Engances par Nîmes
Gard   France
14 November 1962

My dear Freya,

The pleasure of getting your delightful Trojan letter was mixed with a sense of chagrin at having missed you in Athens by a few—a very few days. If you managed to see Austen he will have told you of our brief visit: we made a 'crochet' to spend a few days with old friends. It arose quite by hazard out of an invitation I received from a film man to spend 3 weeks in Israel and write him a short story about kibbutz life there. It was a handsome offer and it gave us the first travelling holiday (*congé payé*) that we [have] had for ages without the question of the children. It turned out to be more tiring than I'd guessed but much more interesting than I'd dared to hope. We saw a great deal in a short time and went round all the crazy deckle-edged frontiers. Disconcerting often to be looking down the barrel of an Arab Sten gun: in Jerusalem for example. What a sad mess—a neither-nor of a place—typical fruit of British intellectual cowardice! But all in all I was glad that we were now out of the Muddle East and living in France. Greece was an unmixed delight—my fears of being disappointed faded like snowflakes. Nothing of value has changed and much that I remember as shabby and nasty had been ameliorated. The restoration of monuments and the accommodation of an expanding tourist trade have been admirably and tactfully handled. And the Greeks themselves have lost none of their gay kindness—even though they have now learned to respect traffic lights!

And so back to this windy cottage on the moors with the mistral howling and the trees bending double. It has turned cold. Time to cut wood and keep the fires going all day. We are expecting to spend Christmas with my family and other animals in Jersey.

Every good wish for the birthday and for many more of them; keep up the good books which nourish the age!

Much love from us both.

Larry Durrell

To Alan G. Thomas   Zefiros Beach Hotel
                                     Paleokastritsa: Corfu
Dear Alan,   [Received 22 June 1967]

I hope you got my card and forgave the delay. I was doing a very tiring drive across Europe. Well, here I am for a day or two. I leave for Athens Sunday. There's hardly a soul about except for Durrells and there are rather too many of those about—Margaret is also here spreading sweetness and light. Theo as well. I've been round about a good deal looking up old friends—it's been melancholy in a way. Claude was so very much loved here that it's been watering-cans all the way. This last three years so many friends, etc., have died that I feel ringed about with graves. Another sad epilogue—that peaceful house at Kouloura with its gay and industrious family—I noticed that it was all shuttered and barred, through my heavy glasses. Today I learnt that Athenaios, that sweet man, in despair at the paralysis gaining on him committed suicide. He drank the olive spray insecticide—terribly painful death. Little Kerkyra has abandoned the house and gone to Jannina to live with her daughter. Spiro, the boy, my godson, has gone to sea again on the China run. I went up yesterday and sat about on the rock below the house. Niko, the sailor, was away. *Pas un chat.* How strangely things turn out. I expect you feel rather as I do, vague and scattered—as if one were convalescing from a major operation. Damn everything.

Love
Larry D.

Landscape and Character

Published in the New York Times *Magazine section. June 12, 1960.*

'You write', says a friendly critic in Ohio, 'as if the landscape were more important than the characters.' If not exactly true, this is near enough the mark, for I have evolved a private notion about the importance of landscape, and I willingly admit to seeing 'characters' almost as functions of a landscape. This has only come about in recent years after a good deal of travel—though here again I doubt if this is quite the word, for I am not really a 'travel-writer' so much as a 'residence-writer'. My books are always about living in places, not just rushing through them. But as you get to know Europe slowly, tasting the wines, cheeses and characters of the different countries you begin to realize that the important determinant of any culture is after all—the spirit of place. Just as one particular vineyard will always give you a special wine with discernible characteristics so a Spain, an Italy, a Greece will always give you the same type of culture—will express itself through the human being just as it does through its wild flowers. We tend to see 'culture' as a sort of historic pattern dictated by the human will, but for me this is no longer absolutely true. I don't believe the British character, for example, or the German has changed a jot since Tacitus first described it; and so long as people keep getting born Greek or French or Italian their culture-productions will bear the unmistakable signature of the place.

And this, of course, is the target of the travel-writer; his task is to isolate the germ in the people which is expressed by their landscape. Strangely enough one does not necessarily need special knowledge for the job, though of course a knowledge of language is a help. But how few they are those writers! How many can write a *Sea and Sardinia* or a *Twilight in Italy* to match these two gems of D. H. Lawrence? When he wrote them his Italian was rudimentary. The same applies to Nor-

[156]

man Douglas' *Fountains in the Sand*—one of the best portraits of North Africa.

We travel really to try and get to grips with this mysterious quality of 'Greekness' or 'Spanishness'; and it is extraordinary how unvaryingly it remains true to the recorded picture of it in the native literature: true to the point of platitude. Greece, for example, cannot have a single real Greek left (in the racial sense) after so many hundreds of years of war and resettlement; the present racial stocks are the fruit of countless invasions. Yet if you want a bit of real live Aristophanes you only have to listen to the chaffering of the barrow-men and peddlers in the Athens Plaka. It takes less than two years for even a reserved British resident to begin using his fingers in conversation without being aware of the fact. But if there are no original Greeks left what is the curious constant factor that we discern behind the word 'Greekness'? It is surely the enduring faculty of self-expression inhering in landscape. At least I would think so as I recall two books by very different writers which provide an incomparable nature-study of the place. One is *Mani* by Patrick Leigh Fermor, and the other Miller's *Colossus of Maroussi*.

I believe you could exterminate the French at a blow and resettle the country with Tartars, and within two generations discover, to your astonishment, that the national characteristics were back at norm—the restless metaphysical curiosity, the tenderness for good living and the passionate individualism: even though their noses were now flat. This is the invisible constant in a place with which the ordinary tourist can get in touch just by sitting quite quietly over a glass of wine in a Paris *bistrot*. He may not be able to formulate it very clearly to himself in literary terms, but he will taste the unmistakable keen knife-edge of happiness in the air of Paris: the pristine brilliance of a national psyche which knows that art is as important as love or food. He will not be blind either to the hard metallic rational sense, the irritating *coeur raisonnable* of the men and women. When the French want to be *malins*, as they call it, they can be just as we can be when we stick our toes in over some national absurdity.

Yes, human beings are expressions of their landscape, but in order to touch the secret springs of a national essence you need a few moments of quiet with yourself. Truly the intimate knowledge of landscape, if developed scientifically, could give us a political science—for half the political decisions taken in the world are based on what we call national character. We unconsciously acknowledge this fact when we exclaim, 'How typically Irish' or 'It would take a Welshman to think up something like that'. And indeed we all of us jealously guard the sense of minority individuality in our own nations—the family differences. The great big nations like say the Chinese or the Americans present a superficially homogeneous appearance; but I've noticed that while we Europeans can hardly tell one American from another, my own American friends will tease each other to death at the lunch-table about the intolerable misfortune of being born in Ohio or Tennessee—a recognition of the validity of place which we ourselves accord to the Welshman, Irishman and Scotsman at home. It is a pity indeed to travel and not get this essential sense of landscape values. You do not need a sixth sense for it. It is there if you just close your eyes and breathe softly through your nose; you will hear the whispered message, for all landscapes ask the same question in the same whisper. 'I am watching you—are you watching yourself in me?' Most travellers hurry too much. But try just for a moment sitting on the great stone omphalos, the navel of the ancient Greek world, at Delphi. Don't ask mental questions, but just relax and empty your mind. It lies, this strange amphora-shaped object, in an overgrown field above the temple. Everything is blue and smells of sage. The marbles dazzle down below you. There are two eagles moving softly softly on the sky, like distant boats rowing across an immense violet lake.

Ten minutes of this sort of quiet inner identification will give you the notion of the Greek landscape which you could not get in twenty years of studying ancient Greek texts. But having got it, you will at once get all the rest; the key is there, so to speak, for you to turn. After that you will not be able to go on a shopping expedition in Athens without running into Agamemnon or Clytemnestra—and often under the same names. And if you happen to go to Eleusis in springtime you will come upon more than one blind Homer walking the dusty roads. The secret is identification. If you sit on the top of the Mena House pyramid at sunset and try the same thing (forgetting the noise of the donkey-boys, and all the filthy litter of other travellers—old cartons and Coca-Cola bottles): if you sit quite still in the landscape-diviner's pose—why, the whole rhythm of ancient Egypt rises up from the damp cold sand. You can hear its very pulse tick. Nothing is strange to you at such moments—the old temples with their death-cults, the hieroglyphs, the long slow whirl of the brown Nile among the palm-fringed islets, the crocodiles and snakes. It is palpably just as it was (its essence) when the High Priest of Ammon initiated Alexander into the Mysteries. Indeed the Mysteries themselves are still there for those who might seek initiation—the shreds and shards of the Trismegistic lore still being studied and handed on by small secret sects. Of course you cannot arrange to be initiated through a travel agency! You would have to reside and work your way in through the ancient crust—a tough one—of daily life. And how different is the rhythm of Egypt to that of Greece! One isn't surprised by the story that the High Priest at Thebes said contemptuously: 'You Greeks are mere children.' He could not bear the tireless curiosity and sensuality of the Greek character—the passionate desire to conceptualize things metaphysic-ally. They didn't seem to be able to relax, the blasted Greeks! Inci-dentally it is a remark which the French often repeat today about the Americans, and it is always uttered in the same commiserating tone of voice as once the High Priest used. Yet the culture of Greece (so different from that of Egypt) springs directly from the Nile Valley—I could name a dozen top Greek thinkers or philosophers who were trained by Egyptians, like Plato, Pythagoras, Anaxagoras, Democritos. And the 'tiresome children' certainly didn't waste their time, for when they got back home to their own bare islands the pure flower of Greek culture spread its magnificent wings in flights of pure magic to astonish and impregnate the Mediterranean. But just to hand the eternal compliment along they invented the word 'barbarians' for all those unfortunate savages who lived outside the magic circle of Greece, deprived of its culture. The barbarians of course were one day to pro-duce Dante, Goethe, Bach, Shakespeare.

As I say the clue, then, is identification; for underneath the purely superficial aspects of apparent change the old tide-lines remain. The dullest travel poster hints at it. The fascinating thing is that Dickens characters still walk the London streets; that any game of village cricket will provide us with clues to the strange ritualistic mystery of the habits of the British. While if you really want to intuit the inner mystery of the island try watching the sun come up over Stonehenge. It may seem a dull and 'touristic' thing to do, but if you do it in the right spirit you find yourself walking those woollen secretive hills arm in arm with the Druids.

Taken in this way travel becomes a sort of science of intuitions which is of the greatest importance to everyone—but most of all to the artist who is always looking for nourishing soils in which to put down roots and create. Everyone finds his own 'correspondences' in this way—landscapes where you suddenly feel bounding with ideas, and others where half your soul falls asleep and the thought of pen and paper brings on nausea. It is here that the travel-writer stakes his claim, for writers each seem to have a personal landscape of the heart which beckons them. The whole Arabian world, for example, has never been better painted and framed than in the works of Freya Stark, whose delicate eye and insinuating slow-moving orchestrations of place and evocations of history have placed her in the front rank of travellers. Could one do better than *Valley of the Assassins*?

These ideas, which may seem a bit far-fetched to the modern reader, would not have troubled the men and women of the ancient world, for their notion of culture was one of psychic education, the education of the sensibility; ours is built upon a notion of mentation, the cramming of the skull with facts and pragmatic data which positively stifle the growth of the soul. Travel wouldn't have been necessary in the time (I am sure such a time really existed some time after the Stone Age) when there really was a world religion which made full allowance for the different dialects of the different races practising it: and which realized that the factor of variation is always inevitably the landscape and not the people. Nowadays such a psychic uniformity sounds like a dream; but already comparative anthropology and archaeology are establishing the truth of it. When we think about such formulations as 'World-Government' we always think of the matter politically, as groups of different people working upon an agreed agenda of sorts; a ten-point programme, or some such set of working propositions. The landscape always fools us, and I imagine always will. Simply because the same propositions don't mean the same in Greek, Chinese and French.

Another pointer worth thinking about is institutions; have you ever wondered why Catholicism, for example, can be such a different religion in different places? Ireland, Italy, Spain, Argentina—it is theologically the same, working on the same premises, but in each case it is subtly modified to suit the spirit of place. People have little to do with the matter except inasmuch as they themselves are reflections of their landscape. Of course there are places where you feel that the inhabitants are not really attending to and interpreting their landscape; whole peoples or nations sometimes get mixed up and start living at right angles to the land, so to speak, which gives the traveller a weird sense of alienation. I think some of the troubles which American artists talk about are not due to 'industrialization' or 'technocracy' but something rather simpler—people not attending to what the land is saying, not conforming to the hidden magnetic fields which the landscape is trying to communicate to the personality. It was not all nonsense what D. H. Lawrence had to say in his communion with the 'ghosts' in the New World. He was within an ace, I think, of making real contact with the old Indian cultures. Genius that he was, he carried too much intellectual baggage about him on his travels, too many preconceptions; and while the mirror he holds up to Mexico, Italy, England is a marvellous triumph of art, the image is often a bit out of focus. He couldn't hold or perhaps wouldn't hold the camera steady enough—he refused to use the tripod (first invented by the oracles in Greece!).

The traveller, too, has his own limitations, and it is doubtful if he is to be blamed. The flesh is frail. I have known sensitive and inquisitive men so disheartened by the sight of a Greek lavatory as to lose all sense of orientation and fly right back to High Street Clapham without waiting for the subtler intimations of the place to dawn on them. I have known people educated up to Ph.D. standard who were so completely unhinged by French plumbing that they could speak of nothing else. We are all of us unfair in this way. I know myself to be a rash, hasty and inconsiderate man, and while I am sitting here laying down the law about travel I feel I must confess that I also have some blind spots. I have never been fair to the Scots. In fact I have always been extremely unfair to them—and all because I arrived on my first visit to Scotland late on a Saturday evening. I do not know whether it is generally known that you can simply die of exposure and starvation in relatively civilized places like Inverness simply because the inhabitants are too religious to cut a sandwich or pour coffee? It sounds fantastic I know. Nevertheless it is true. The form of Sabbatarianism which the Scots have developed passes all understanding. Nay, it cries out for the strait-jacket. And sitting on a bench at Inverness Station in a borrowed

deerstalker and plaid you rack your brains to remember the least pro-
nouncement in the Old or New Testaments which might account for
it. There is none—or else I have never spotted the reference. They
appear to have made a sort of Moloch of Our Lord, and are too scared
even to brush their teeth on the Sabbath. How can I be anything but
unfair to them? And yet Scotland herself—the poetry, and the poverty
and naked joyous insouciance of mountain life, you will find on every
page of Burns's autobiographical papers. Clearly she is a queenly
country and a wild mountainous mate for poets. Why have the Scots
not caught on? What ails them in their craggy fastnesses? (But I
expect I shall receive a hundred indignant letters from Americans who
have adopted Scotland, have pierced her hard heart and discovered the
landscape-mystery of her true soul. Nevertheless, I stand by what I
say; and one day when I am rich I shall have a memorial plaque placed
over that bench on Inverness Station platform—a plaque reading
'Kilroy was here—but oh so briefly'!) But I must not fail to add that I
have always admired the magnificent evocations of Scots landscape in
the books of Stevenson; they are only adventure tales, but the landscape comes shining through.

So that I imagine the traveller in each of us has a few blind spots due
to some traumatic experience with an empty tea-urn or the room-on-
the-landing. This cannot be helped. The great thing is to try and travel
with the eyes of the spirit wide open, and not too much factual information. To tune in, without reverence, idly—but with real inward
attention. It is to be had for the feeling, that mysterious sense of
rapport, of identity with the ground. You can extract the essence of a
place once you know how. If you just get as still as a needle you'll be
there.

I remember seeing a photo-reportage in *Life* magazine once which
dealt with the extraordinary changes in physique which emigrants to
the U.S.A. underwent over such relatively short periods as two or
three generations. Some of the smaller races like Chinese and Filipinos
appeared to have gained almost eight inches in height, over the
statutory period investigated, while their physical weight had also
increased in the most extraordinary way. The report was based on the
idea that diet and environment were the real answers, and while
obviously such factors are worth considering I found myself wondering
if the reporters were right; surely the control experiment would fail if

one fed a group of Chinese *in China* exclusively on an American diet? I don't see them growing a speck larger myself. They might get fat and rosy on the diet, but I believe the landscape, in pursuit of its own mysterious purposes, would simply cut them down to the required size suitable to homegrown Chinamen.

One last word about the sense of place; I think that not enough attention is paid to it as a purely literary criterion. What makes 'big' books is surely as much to do with their site as their characters and incidents. I don't mean the books which are devoted entirely to an elucidation of a given landscape like Thoreau's *Walden* is. I mean ordinary novels. When they are well and truly anchored in nature they usually become classics. One can detect this quality of 'bigness' in most books which are so sited from *Huckleberry Finn* to *The Grapes of Wrath*. They are tuned in to the sense of place. You could not transplant them without totally damaging their ambience and mood; any more than you could transplant *Typee*. This has nothing I think to do with the manners and habits of the human beings who populate them; for they exist in nature, as a function of place.

Pied Piper of Lovers

Published by Cassell & Co. 1935

As so often happens, much of Lawrence Durrell's early life is reflected in his first novel, Pied Piper of Lovers; *a somewhat 'prentice' effort with no great intimation of what was to come. The hero, Walsh Clifton, is also the son of an engineer working in India, and in the first extract, printed here, father and son are travelling to Kurseong where the father is to build a railway. After an Indian childhood Walsh is sent 'home' to school and there are descriptions of the impact of England, suburban London and life at a minor public school. Walsh is bored rather than embittered by his schooling. A chapter in our imperial history might well be written, now that it is virtually over, analysing and recording the emotional price paid by the children of empire builders torn from their real home and sent 'home' to the care of unwilling relatives, generally, it would seem, spinster aunts. Durrell's fictional account of this experience is far less bitter than the appalling picture, etched in acid, which Kipling drew of the evangelical household in Southsea where he spent a miserable and tortured childhood; or the grim description given, in the memoir of her brother, by Saki's sister.*

During a holiday in Devon Walsh makes friends with Gordon and Ruth, young people of somewhat uncertain private means who are staying nearby; he falls in love with Ruth, but at the end of the holiday they part. Clifton senior dies from the effects of a snake-bite, whereupon Walsh leaves school and goes to live in Bloomsbury on the small income which he has inherited. Disgusted, after a time, by the squalid and purposeless life of his fellow bohemians, and especially by a sordid party which he attends, Walsh, unable to subsist on his inheritance, looks around for further means of support, and discovers that he can turn his talent as a song writer to effective purpose. He meets Ruth again, by chance, in the Library of the British Museum, and they join forces. But he soon learns that she is afflicted with a valvular disease of the heart and that her hold on life is precarious. In an epilogue Walsh and Ruth are seen living together in a cottage in Devon.

PROLOGUE
set in India

He remembered, for instance, standing on the deck of the *Endeavour*, craning over the side to watch the paddle-wheels. A ship was a more frightening thing, he reflected, than a motor-boat. It was nicer to sit nearer to the water, and feel it spin away under you unevenly, and trail your hand in it. When no one was looking you could lick your fingers. Salt water had a lovely taste: but the paddle-wheels of the seaship were very alarming things. The bleached white wood made its laboured rotations in the water, each paddle emerging with an increasing speed, as if released by a spring, and hurling itself up at you, threatening you with a crack over the head: deceptively it turned aside and rolled over into the water again, uttering a sinful chuckle at having made you timid enough to duck back. It flung a small, playful spray over you. A great hiss it made, flinging pert wavelets across the acres of still sea, with enormous disdainful gestures.

The *Endeavour* was very old. Her timbers creaked like the stays of a very old lady forced into some unwonted activity. The captain had called him 'Sonny', and had said that she (the ship) would soon have to be broken up; there were lots of new white clean steamers now, stealing all the passengers. Walsh had nodded very sagely, and had asked if the new steamers had wheels. It appeared that they had not. Then how, in the name of heaven, did people go on them? Did they have interesting things on board? Apparently the only things the *Endeavour* had in common with her newer competitors were engines, and even these, explained the bewildering old man, were different. Walsh wondered, rather bitterly, if grown-ups had any real sense.

Later on in the voyage he had been sick. That too was an experience which he would not have missed for anything. It was so easy: and the fuss the women made before embarking!

It had happened like this:

He had stood for hours looking down at the paddles: bracing his feet under the tilt and heave of the deck: clinging to the rail like a limpet. His head hung down over the water. Greens and blues and browns mixed, blended and dissolved in the confusion under him; a magic so swift and facile that it deceived the eye. He wondered if he would see a whale. How queerly the water frothed away from the pad-

[165]

dles, showing its teeth in a white snarl! He spat not once, but several
times, with gratifying precision right into the heart of the white
turbulence. From time to time, when the blending of colour burst
upon his sight and vanished in the green sameness of the major water,
he smiled, a smile of pure happiness. It was then, in his memories, that
the great moment came. How swiftly the water rushed! He spat again
with more abandon. If you stared at it you became giddy, as if you were
falling . . . falling . . . falling . . . He shut his eyes against the
first insidious nausea, but that only seemed to make it worse. He was
whirled round in a chaotic darkness, punctured by sharp lights. Then
the feeling left him. He opened his eyes and was frighteningly, but rather
happily sick over the side, lolling his tongue out like a puppy to feel
the wind cool upon it. The water seemed very near to his face. . . .

It was a magnificent feat, his being sick with such ease and pleasure.
It placed him far, far above all those blowsy women who lurked in
cabins with basins, retching and groaning, and hiding their shame
from the menfolk: but then, of course, he was a man, not a girl, and
that altered things considerably.

Some of the women had continued to be sick long after they had
landed; they had been compelled to stick their heads out of the rattling
carriage windows. That, of course, made it dangerous for him to look
out: but he had stuck his nose hard against the glass and stared out
across the leagues of flat dry land across which they clattered. Miles
and miles of forests, paddy-fields, swamps, through which the unfaltering engine lugged them: bridges and signal-boxes and towns, all silent
under the aching noonday heat, with the sun flaring on the tin roofs.
Once they disturbed a flock of wild duck from where they had settled,
in a paddy-field by the track. What a wild trumpeting, squealing,
flurrying, as they sprang into the air, wagging their heavy wings!
There were cranes, too, standing pensively in the shallows of the river,
mincing delicately around on their slim legs in search of food.

It was at this point that his memories became jumbled and confused. He remembered the great houses in Calcutta; very tall and made
of stone, and the dusty streets with the cavalcades of carriages, rick-
shaws, trolleys; Europeans dressed in white clothes; a cool hotel with
a lift and a newspaper-stall; white napery spread upon a table and
beautiful foods served by a host of impassive servants; a zoo with a
baby elephant that shook hands with its trunk; a place where sickly

ice-cream was given him in great quantities; a rickshaw in which he had been (naturally enough) sick; a leper whose skin had peeled off in little white flakes and to whom he gave a rupee, and a host of other things, fugitive and unreal, probably founded as much on imagination as fact.

But when he came to the second part of the journey, it grew more distinct, more exciting still. His father had told him one night that he had got a job. That, of course, meant less than nothing to him, but it had transfigured his father. They ate an enormous dinner together, tipping all the waiters with a reckless prodigality that mystified him even when he remembered it. His father had given him round shiny coins and told him to give them to everyone he met. It was curious, but inexplicable. Grown-ups behaved in an extraordinary way when the mood took them. He had been rather afraid that they would both starve if they gave away all their money, but his father had assured him solemnly that he was going to get a lot more, so that it did not matter very much. His father was a '*decenchap*', whatever that meant. A travelling companion had told him so, and he had always remembered it.

Two days later they left by train for the northern frontier, and it was during this time that they were forced to ride in a crowded carriage. Among their fellow-travellers was an old man with a happy face and a monkey which he carried perched on his shoulder, secured on a strip of rusty chain. The monkey was called Amos, and it looked very like the governess they had left behind. It indulged in an eternal search among the pockets of its master's coat for food to eat—monkey-nuts—and chattered and showed its tiny white teeth in a grin of rage when it was stroked. Walsh joined it in a meal of nuts, to which he too was very partial, and made friends with this fascinating if treacherous companion.

Once during the journey a man entered with a terrier which he placed upon the floor, not observing the monkey which had wrinkled up his ferocious little nose and begun to bounce up and down on the floor. There was bound to be trouble, but when it came, it was so unexpected that it took the boy's breath away. That admirable monkey! When the dog lunged across the carriage at it, it bounced up to the lap of its master, and from there sprang upon the luggage rack. Then, from its secure perch, it uttered creaks of malignant triumph, and began to urinate, directing the flow with deadly accuracy upon the dog. Of course, they were all splashed a bit, but Walsh didn't mind. He was so astounded at the trick. He wished for a minute that he had as sure a way of dealing with his enemies: but his father was silly enough to be annoyed and grumble. The master of Amos dragged him down and punished him, making him apologize to everyone in the carriage, which he did with an air of humiliation and sorrowfulness which softened the hearts of even the most moist among them. He took a finger from their hands, very much as one takes a banana from a cluster, and very gently put it to his teeth. Then he removed the small green woollen cap which was perched on the back of his brown head, and swept them a bow. Amos was enchanting. He had been really sorry when the happy little man left with the animal clinging to his shoulder. What would he not give now for a pet like that? He had asked his father, but he was told that monkeys were wild things which grew sullen and spiteful in captivity. There were plenty of them in the woods above the cart-road, and he made up his mind to trap one. He wondered whether his father was really a '*decenchap*', and if so, was the title *important?*

At any rate he was Master Walsh Clifton, and that was marvellous enough.

That was, I suppose, as far as he ever got with these tantalizing and beautiful memories. Certainly when there was so much to do in the garden of the old house, so many new moths and butterflies to discover, that he found little time for day-dreaming; the mood took possession of him without any conscious effort of will, and left him before he had either need or desire to drive it out. One minute he would be teasing a nest of red ants with a twig and the next he would see the whole panorama of his adventures roll out before him on the brown earth, like a picture-show; he would stop and sit dead still on his haunches, staring at the rows of angry defending soldier ants crowding to the shattered ramparts of the nest. His dark eyes would widen as he impressed upon himself the astonishing importance of these visions, and correspondingly, the huge importance of himself.

At such times when he considered the relative importance of others in relation to himself he smiled gently and sorrowfully, as one who looks upon a piteous and silly sight: only a God or a Pharisee could have managed a smile like that.

At Kurseong, their ultimate destination, they were installed in a house as old as the Lucknow Residency, and very nearly as dilapidated; a crumbling fortress, it was spread over a level jut of the hillside above the town, squinting down at right angles upon the pink and white straggle of the newer houses. From its upper windows it commanded a view of some thirty odd miles of mountain country, across the valley in which the heavy Balasun dragged its way, curdled and jade-green in winter, tooth-white and broad in summer, across the tangle of paths on the green fertile crest, dotted with pines, to where Kinchinjunga and her sisters climbed out of a grey and blue wilderness. You will find the town on the map (if you care to look) almost exactly in the middle of the bottle-neck territory of Northern British India which is jammed into the wide cavity lying between Nepal, Sikkim, and Bhutan.

The greater part of the permanent population of the town, at the time when Clifton got his job on the narrow-gauge mountain-railway, consisted of tea planters whose narrow brick houses were built, for the most part, on the outer flanks of the hill-spurs, from where they overlooked mile upon mile of symmetrically planted tea-bushes, bright green even under the coating of summer dust; but beyond these flat territories of bushes the hill range was successful in its defiance of cultivation; isolated patches of sugar-beet and an odd garden of sickly vegetables here and there were all Nature allowed in a country which was almost utterly subject to her caprices, and in which she suffered warm, luxurious vegetable life on one square foot of ground, and gave to another a sprinkling of shale and chalk fit only to nourish dry and brittle stalks of grass. The soil.had been flung as a cloak is flung, carelessly across the mountain, falling deep here and there where a crevice allowed it depth enough to cherish the roots of the gigantic forest-trees, the oak, the ash, the simul tree, and the tufted tree-fern, and in other places only thinly covering the frame of rock; here and there shoulders of rock had pierced the covering and emerged into the daylight, standing up in their smooth bulk as if in defiance of the soil-coverlet that had hidden them for so long. Occasionally, too, they would shake themselves loose and start trundling down the hill: more than once boulders the size of a whale had crashed into the sleeping village and demolished half a dozen or so of the rude dung huts of the inhabitants. But whenever such a thing happened, the village elders would gather

[169]

together and, after a long session of sage discussion, announce that such a thing could only be the work of evil spirits, ghosts . . . their own expressive word, *bhuts*. After this first declaration another would be made which forbade anyone to lay a finger on the boulder for fear of drawing the malice of the *bhut* upon himself; prayer and the necessary acts of propitiation alone, if they would not actually repair the damage done, would at least prevent a repetition of the offence. That was how it was. The huts which hung together on the edge of the penultimate crag above the river, which had been blessed by the collective designation 'Kurseong', were for the most part leaning among a nest of boulders against which other small huts of wood or dung leaned. It possessed a main street, through which ran the railway-line, and which served as a bazaar for the inhabitants, and a tethering ground for children and cattle alike, from which yet another row of ramshackle huts had been built back up the hillside.

Above this rabble of houses stood the old house, detached and cynical, as incongruous and striking as a museum would be in a mining colony. The jut of its massive cornices, the peeling scabs of stucco on the walls, gave it the appearance of an over-ornamental, garish relic; bore witness to the passing of a style of architecture the characteristics of which were a sprawling stability and a superb insolence. It stood out sheer among the firs, dominating the ridge, like some incubus left over from a lost age.

A long veranda shot out to the very edge of the cliff-side, bounded with stubby mock-Corinthian pillars of great girth, and weighed down by a broad-windowed corridor which it carried. Above the façade a row of almost obliterated scrolls set the visitor wondering what arms had once been graven there, what knights had lodged under the heavy roof, what carousing and revelry had brightened the lowering silence of the enormous dusty halls.

The blind lower windows looked out across the overgrown pathways, and the moss-clothed stones that edged in the rows of flower-beds. The walks were redolent with the sharp smell of rottenness, as though centuries of decay had not managed to stifle the scent of the dwarf rose bushes.

The gate, a writhing ornamental tangle of iron, was covered in a coat of barley-coloured rust: it opened squealing upon a hedge of rhododendrons, while on either side of the path which led to the porch stood a row of sentinel nightshade, the white flowers drooping in the languor of the silence.

No birds seemed ever to fly about the garden. On the hillside below it grew a tangled profusion of ferns and wild flowers, heavy with scent, and here all day in the summer you could hear the twittering of a hundred junketing sparrows: but from the garden the sound seemed deadened, dim: even the ear-splitting *scraw* of the mina was a small beat of sound in the pulses of this silence. It was a queer illusion, this muting of all sound, this anonymous garden softly absorbing and deadening all voice, all utterance. It was as if one had unwittingly intruded upon a submarine life miraculously existing above the sea: the rotten drooping plants, with the water settling upon their leaves, the still earth gathered into a fine hair-net of weeds, and above all, this idiot half-sound tantalizing the ear which had been led by memory to expect a greater volume.

The front door was studded with all manner of brass ornaments, knockers and letter-boxes, all unrecognizable under their tarnish, and possessed an inlet window of blue and red glass: it cast an octagonal shadow across the bare boards of the hallway. All that had been left in the house was a wide smudged lithograph, framed and hanging upon the drawing-room wall, which depicted the 'Stand of the Royal Scots', at some famous action or other, long since forgotten.

The house was called 'Emerald Hall', though who had given it the name no one could tell them. On the front gate was a lopsided plaque of rotten wood bearing the mystic letters EM . . . LD . . . LL: symbols which seemed to bear the same quality of mysterious decay as bore the unkept garden and the rambling house.

Clifton had said: 'It'll be quite all right when we get some furniture in and cosy it up a bit. You see.' But his tone lacked conviction.

The small boy had made no comment at all, but remained standing quite still, awed but not frightened by the silence. He had wondered why his feet made so great a noise on the gravel. A fat, beautifully marked caterpillar hung like a bright emerald ring in a crumpled rose: in his nostrils ran the dank smell of the earth: these were strangely exciting things.

'It'll be all right,' repeated the man, pressing the small hand of his son, 'what do you say?'

The boy offered no comment. He stretched his puny arms and

yawned: his eyes filled with tears: he replaced his hand in his father's and smiled slowly, shuffling his heels in the gravel.

'It'll be fine,' persisted the man, but he did not believe in his own assertions. He wished that there had been some other accommodation in this cursed hill-station than this hulk of masonry. Would any amount of furnishing ever reduce this atmosphere of deadness? Impossible: and he was right, for no amount of furniture made the rooms appear less cavernous, and the regular ministrations of a gardener only served to produce small isolated patches of tidiness which were soon swallowed up in the conflict of decay.

But for the first few weeks the boy was too absorbed in the exploration of his new surroundings to be oppressed by them. The melancholy that brooded about the old house did not affect him; indeed, if he was aware of it at all, it was as something which heightened the colour of his daily discoveries in the garden, giving a sense of permanent mystery to these new experiences. The garden was full of all manner of strange flowers that he had not seen before, among which he was most conscious of the nightshade. He had been told it was poisonous, and the terrible poetry of the name haunted him with a fear that one day, unthinking, he would eat some of those bluish berries and die an agonizing death. But there were compensations for this fear: there were so many other things he could touch and pursue without fear. Half a dozen different varieties of beetle, ranging from the walnut-sized coprophagous one, to the sheeny grey-green rose-beetles. Caterpillars were enormous, banded with every colour of the rainbow; moths and butterflies, blue, brown, slate-coloured, and bright yellow, busied themselves all day about the corners of the bushes. He explored these mysteries as thoroughly as he was able, wandering all day long through the deserted pathways, upon the carpets of moss, whispering to himself or talking to his companion, the *ayah*. She who had been engaged by Clifton to look after him during the day was a slender middle-aged woman with the characteristic secrecy and silence of the hill-people; her flat Mongolian features were broad, good-humoured, and lacking in any great animation. She was loaded with ear-rings, nose-rings, bangles, and heavy brass anklets that clipped monotonously as she walked. She tended the boy well, suffering his rages and irritations with the patience of a woman who has borne many children of her own.

[172]

She was tactful, did not intrude, and was never officious; indeed, she did no more than her job, following him about to see that he came to no harm, giving him his meals, and explaining as best she could the nature of those things which baffled him; why the hill-people collected donkey-water in bottles; why the roof of every house in the village was covered with circular pats of offal, drying in the sunlight; why her husband beat her.

She would sit on her haunches and smile kindly as she related these things without shame or reticence, as though these phenomena were as curious to her as they were to him, and her understanding of them something superficial which did not really touch the heart of things.

Together they walked miles, exploring the country round the town, from the heights of Victoria Hill, to the bleak wind-haunted muzzle of Eagle's Crag overlooking the plains. She taught him how to rid himself of the leeches: to avoid pulling them off his flesh, as they left round sore holes: to place instead, a pinch of salt upon them. He was amazed to see them quickly dissolve into blood and drip from him. She taught him to sing the crooning songs of her people, told him queer folk-stories, and first made him acquainted with the unusual intonation of the hill-tongue.

Some evenings, when his father was late back from work, he would wander to the edge of the garden to watch the sun set behind Eagle's Crag, and the veined rivers twinkle in the shadowy carpet of the plains that lay outstretched before him. The scattered legions of fir trees would stand very slim and erect, as if poised on the brink of some precipitous movement, while the colour-tones of the rock-balconies would change from blue to grey, from grey to silver, until the first webs of darkness blurred all defined outline and gave the uncertain body of objects the significance of a panic. In the dissolving half-light whole companies of trees would seem to change shape and position, the hulks of rock to recede slowly into themselves, and the thunder of the Balasun River in the valley to become subdued and merged in a monotone of plaint; a dirge only lightened by the sound of voices in the village, laughter across the dim roofs, and the final hard clatter of his father's footsteps on the road below the house. He would run to meet him, happily confident of the inevitable greeting:

'Hullo. You still up? It's high time you were in bed.'

They would walk up to the house arm-in-arm laughing and talking, and his father would shout to the servants to light the lamps, his voice a riot of cheering and comfortable sound in the silence.

Sometimes Clifton would bring with him the illustrated journals of the month which he had bought from some station bookstall; he would hand them to his son with a sense of obligation, as though he were trying to lighten the loneliness of his surroundings, and in some way satisfy his own acute sense of guilt. Yet he was conscientious enough to feel the need of excuse. He had said:

'It won't be for very long . . . a month, or so and then your Aunt Brenda'll be here to look after you.'

Walsh had politely and without interest agreed. In actual fact he was as happy as anyone could be whose activities were superintended by a bland and self-effacing shadow, and whose territory of activity was not restricted to the limits of a garden, but to as much rocky country as he chose to explore. This fact, and the fact that each successive day he became more and more amazed at the inexhaustible hoard of marvels revealed to him during his explorations, made propitiation a farce.

He had wandered, without realizing it, to the curving ridge of trees above the burial-ground. He recalled with a start that it must be long after tea; he would probably be late for dinner, but it did not matter very much. He screwed up his eyes and estimated that the sun had another half-hour to live. It was just hidden behind the snout of Eagle's Crag, and the shadows were beginning to lengthen across the glades. The moss was soft and springy under his feet.

He decided to stay there awhile, judging the time by the height of the sun, and then to take the short cut home. There was the thrilling prospect of danger in the act of racing to get home before darkness fell; after dark it was unwise to take the scrubby and tortuous path down the hillside for fear of snakes. Even with a lantern and a stick the prospect was not too pleasing.

The leeches fell from the trees about him with the heavy noise of rain-drops. Lucky it was not damp, otherwise there would be millions of them swarming all over the place. He carried in his pocket a soiled twist of paper in which were a few pinches of salt. Now as he sank down on the moss the action of habitude was the removal of this twist of paper from his pocket; he laid it beside him. However hot it might be, he reflected, there would be one or two at least of the pests upon you; that could not be helped.

Sure enough you would find the small rubbery creature coiled on your skin, sucking the blood from a vein. When you put the smallest pinch of salt on it it trembled and released you; turned on its back, wriggling protestingly, and began to slip from you, dissolving slowly to blood. It left sticky red smears all down you, so that you had to go and wash them. It was more pleasing, he thought, to let the blood congeal, and then to pick it off with your fingers. . . . Sometimes when the leech had been feeding for a long time it became swollen and shiny and the salt acted almost immediately. Amazing change! One minute there would be the drowsy, sated creature moving gently upon the wound as it grew fatter, the next a gout of blood falling and catching on the points of hair. . . .

He sat up in sudden alarm as a flying fox-swerved past in the trees. In the woods about him a small wind broke into mournful ragtime, drumming the leaves together and creaking the trees. A squirrel came down to ground level and set herself diligently about collecting food. He had always wanted a squirrel for a pet but had been warned that they did not survive captivity.

He lolled back on the moss, clasping his hands behind his head. A slow melancholy took possession of him. He seemed to see himself lying there, looking up at the green leaves, as if from a great distance and from a totally new personality. He was plunged in a consuming self-pity.

He drummed his heels on the ground and murmured defiantly:

'Sala . . . swine . . . sala,' as if to drive away the mournful fancies that grew in his mind.

The brown earth of the burial-ground was silent, with its circles of ankle-deep ash; brown and pitted. Why did people die? Illness? He too had a body, strong and healthy. He pinched his thigh as if to verify the fact. If you got ill and died, you were either buried or burnt. The little European graveyard below Eagle's Crag was chill with decay and silence, the lettering on the tombstones pricked out in hectic reds and phosphorescent greens. He would hate to lie under the ground in a closed box; more particularly in that silent plot of ground. His father could not save him. He could buy him presents but not save him; nor could Father Calhoun. That was a terrible thought. He shuddered suddenly, imagining his dead body in a box, and Father Calhoun standing over it, praying. His eyes would be shining and his cassock would be dark in the light of the candles about the room; he breathed more quickly, imagining his pale face under the flickering candleshine. He wanted to cry at the thought of it, but the tears would not come. He knew that his father would be sorry and much too shy to come and see him as he lay there in the loneliness of death. His father would smile, showing his white teeth, and talk very quietly about something. He felt, for probably the first time, utterly lonely; desperately in need of an ally, someone who would help him. He gave a little moan and turned over on his side. He could not cry; he felt hot and strained.

Then, out of the murmurous evening, echoing in the hollowness of distance, came the sound. He heard and started upright; took a few hurried steps through the trees and stopped, listening. A mina screamed somewhere near at hand, and he started, oathing softly and volubly under his breath, telling himself that he had been mistaken; there were so many sounds that meant nothing, so many sounds that picked up echoes and . . .

Heavily the sound rolled up again through the trees, large and clear, as if to echo and refute the futility of doubt. The trees about him broke into a trembling at the sound of the conch. In that second's certainty the boy too was seized with a fit of shivering. He muttered to himself and looked about him.

On the shelving edge of the table-land a great boulder had plucked itself away from the earth and fallen twenty feet to the circle of trees, laying bare the shoulder of the hillside: out of the rubble of shale that had dropped away from his wound, hung the leaning trunk of a sickening birch tree. The boy ran towards it, muttering. . . . 'Should be high enough.' With the nervous agility of dread he swarmed up it, climbing higher and higher until he could lean, swaying perilously upon the highest branches, and look out over the road.

He picked up the landmarks that he knew well by sight: eastward from Eagle's Crag the tin hut of the station was recognizable: to the right of that road. Empty. It came into view again by the disused shrine, a long strip of cobbles flanked with boulders. That too was empty. He swore fiercely and gripped the swinging branches.

On each corner of the road lay a slab of grey rock. The boy stared until his eyes ached at as many of these slabs as were in view, but could

[176]

not see clearly enough to determine whether or no they were sprinkled with rice and *pan* leaves. He had almost decided to get down from the tree and make a bolt for home when the procession came into view from behind a clump of trees. They had passed Emerald Hall. In front of those who bore the corpse walked a gigantic Bhutia, carrying the conch-shell. At each corner of the road he threw back his head, and placing it to his mouth blew a long terrible blast on it. The sound scattered a million echoes in the hillsides, prolonging itself into a wild cry that dwindled rumbling into the farthermost fastnesses of the mountains; each small gully and coign of rock caught the echo and flung it back, magnified to the farther summits of crag.

Behind him trailed the bearers, staggering under the burden of the corpse that had been placed in a sheet, the extremities of which were fastened to a length of bamboo pole. As they made their uneven and erratic way up the hill, the dead man jumped and bounced in his scanty covering, and seemed to be protesting at the horror of being buried alive. His outlines were clear against the sheet.

The boy drew his breath sharply in relief at the sight. Horror had been only in the knowledge that the funeral cortège was approaching nearer and nearer, and that he could not tell exactly where they were. He dreaded passing them on the road. Now, with the problem solved, he slid nimbly down the tree, and struck through the woods towards the boundaries of the Keen plantation, where he would be able to pick up the track home without fear. He whistled as he trotted along, trying to forget the wailing of the conch, and obliterate his knowledge of that staggering procession who were about to consign a corpse to earth; or ashes.

Later, as he neared home, a huge Columbian moth, furred blue, and measuring about six inches from wing-tip to wing-tip, fluttered across his path and away into the evening.

He cursed himself bitterly for a fool. He should have brought his butterfly-net.

≈§ §≈

ARRIVAL IN ENGLAND

It would perhaps be impossible to define accurately the feeling of disappointment he experienced as he stood on the deck of the liner and watched the pearly cliffs insinuate themselves out of the light sea-haze; at any rate, he was not impressed by what he saw, and as he leaned his chin upon the rail, he told himself bitterly that it was *smaller* than he had imagined! Since he could not see the whole island at once it must be concluded that this observation implied some sort of intuitive deduction based on as much of the coast as was visible.

To the right, where a sickly sunlight had penetrated the haze, the cliffs curved away, trim and lacquered. The towns, threaded like beads on the string of white road diminished in size as the cliffs curved and diminished under them into an ultimate hinterland of blue fog. The nearest houses, insolently dressed in their vulgar reds and greens, perched in rows: as haughtily self-assured as a line of prize brooding-hens; behind them, to the west, a factory-chimney accused the sky; and behind that again, so far distant that it was a mere speck, an air-plane nested in a single cloud, the sunlight running liquid amber down its wings.

He sucked his orange noisily and wondered why he did not feel gloriously happy at the thought that he was actually looking upon England. The others were happy. Oh, beyond all doubt. They had crowded to the side and leaned over, peering out upon the promised land, laughing and pointing; but those who shouted, pointed, and exclaimed were in the minority. A great number stood silent, gripping the rail, and experiencing that emotion of country-love which is occasioned in exiles by the sight of the Dover cliffs.

But though on this particular occasion the sight of Dover affected more than half of those men who were on deck, it did not affect in the slightest the solemn-eyed, orange-sucking manikin who stood with them. A concourse of soldiers, representing every rank of the Indian Army, engineers, planters, all stood dumbly at the rails and stared upon Albion, with few signs of outward emotion, but with pleasurable and very muddled memories of Matthew Arnold's poetry, and the more throaty stanzas from *Marmion*. They were mostly tall, sunburnt men, with cropped hair and fuzzy moustaches: men to whom sentiment was a source of discomfort: men who should have known better.

'There she is,' said a stout major, puffing out his cheeks, and hooking his thumbs in the loops of his trousers.

'Yes. Yes,' chorused the voices softly.

'White as white.'

'Dover. . . . See the airplane?'

'And the breakers.'

'There she is.'

'How long before we dock? How long?'

'Yes, yes,' chorused the voices softly. A hedge of arms waved over the side pointing. Hundreds of feet, clad in canvas shoes, shuffled the clean wood deck.

'Five years since I last saw them.'

'I remember them distinctly since nineteen.'

'Impressive——'

'There she is.'

'White as white.'

'Yes, yes,' chorused the voices.

It would have taken a small effort of imagination to metamorphose them into a company of weary crusaders, blinded by the desert suns, rough of skin and infirm of body, to whom the ubiquitous mud of the London kennels was more than welcome after a long sojourn in Moorish deserts, and the green forests of Hampstead a divine blessing after the parched deserts of another continent. Perhaps there was something a little touching about it all; the crowding to the rails, the silence, the intent expressionless faces gazing out upon the cliff-lines. Perhaps there was!

As for the boy, he felt galled by his own lack of excitement: by his own apathy. Was it right that he should remain in a solemn detachment, unable to respond to a moment which was supremely important in his life? But he could find no tribute to answer the lavish tributes of those who were neither sufficiently carried away by sentiment to remain silent, nor too disabled by sea-sickness to be forced to remain below. Beside him stood a waggish young engineer, unfeignedly glad to be home again. He repeated from time to time in a hollow voice: 'Jolly old England. Soon, soon for wine, women and song.' He smiled round idiotically at intervals and punctuated this incantation by blowing his nose loudly. He was in great spirits.

⇛ɻ ɾ∽

A toy forest waved its tiny trees in mocking ovation, as though rejoicing in its own sparseness; not like the Terai, which swept in a dense green cloud of interlacing forest, dizzily away to the first uplands, the first walls of black rock, dwindling gradually in thickness until it lay, a mere scrub of pastel-shaded vegetation about the lip of the ultimate icy horn—Mirik. No, he was accustomed to a different dimension, a different space. How cramped England was.

A puny train, dragging a dozen grimy carriages, stumbled away inland, with little shrapnel-puffs of smoke swinging up from it to an empty sky. The water beneath them was glazed and still, and the air so still that you could hear the faint hurdy-gurdy of the propellers shaking the decks.

He rubbed his sticky hands on his coat and coughed. Then he looked down at his feet which were clad in a pair of new brown shoes. Brenda had bought them for him during the voyage. 'There!' she said, 'they're real English shoes.'

Certainly they were excellent shoes: new and very expensive. They had an ornamental tracery of holes punched in the leather which stretched from toe to heel; and a disastrous habit of squeaking when he walked.

The only trouble was that they were a little too small for him, and made his feet sore and hot. Now as he looked down at them, reflecting on their excellence, he wriggled his toes about, and rubbed his ankle with his hand. It was a great pity they did not fit him.

He shivered slightly in the breeze. It would be no use, he thought, to keep on looking at the coast and trying to pinch himself into enthusiasm. It would be much more fun to go into the lounge now that it was empty and make a noise on the piano. But as he walked his shoes hurt him, forcing him to limp slightly.

They detrained (in the full military sense of the word) at Victoria, and were both secretly alarmed at the thunderous noise of traffic that sounded under the great sheds. Unused to the English porters, it was some time before Brenda mustered up courage to ask one if he would mind their baggage. When she did so, however, it was with such an air of deference that the man (as becomes Englishmen who detect inferiority in anyone) was exceedingly rude to her. He performed the job with an air of sullen stupidity, and looked at the half-crown she gave him with insolent hauteur, trying it between his teeth to see if it was good.

They were bundled into a taxi which jerked its unsteady way out of the station in the direction of Russell Square, while the two of them

[180]

sat back on the seat like frightened children and gazed out disappointedly upon the slushy streets. The air was heavy and poisoned, a kind of dust-fog that was irritating to the throat and the nose. Hyde Park, of which they had read so much, turned out to be, on first sight, a foggy sector of threadbare grass, fringed by a line of damp green chairs.

❧

LONDON AT NIGHT
(Walsh in Bloomsbury)

Some nights, when sleep was impossible, and he had lain awake for hours watching the yellow pools of light on the ceiling as they flickered, and listening to the growing quiet of the streets, he would get up out of his bed and stand at the window. The café opposite stayed open until three o'clock and through the steamy glass of the swing-doors he could see the groups of men and women sitting round the marble-topped tables drinking coffee; mostly tall, sallow Jews, he noticed, with long dark overcoats and rakish hats; their clothes were padded out about the shoulders to give them the appearance of physique which they did not possess. And the women, mostly Euston Road bawds, with their loud market-place voices and disease fast hollowing out their eyes and melting down their features. Across the clear sound of voices in the silent street he caught clear scraps of words, unfinished sentences which hung for a moment in the air of the darkened room, and disappeared, leaving only the ghost of meaning in his watching mind. And from this polyglot crew of ruffians and bawds, lustrous Jews who waited in the shadows of every street-corner, and loud-mouthed taxi-drivers who drank tasteless coffee as they awaited late fares, some few he selected as worthy of remembrance. He knew from habit the times of their appearance, and waited to see them come down the street and shoulder their ways into the steamy den. At eleven, for instance, a tall negress walked through the street, limping with fatigue but with a face cocked up to the sky. She hummed a song as she passed in a low, nasal voice, very melancholy but not displeasing, and, surprisingly, held a beautiful silvery-coated whippet on a lead, which followed her softly, its arched body taut and docile. Every night, as she passed, she stopped at the entrance of the café and pushed the swing-doors aside, peering around at the seated people as though seeking someone; but she never went inside, only turned back each night with a little shrug of annoyance and continued her walk. Later, shortly after two, there appeared the figures of two men, one tall and powerful, the other smaller, but sturdily made. The larger was always without a hat, and his face was small and twisted with knobs of curly hair trained back across his poll. His shoulders were large enough for him to do without a padded overcoat. His companion was dark but in a more pallid Israelite, way and carried a huge, ebony-handled stick which seemed thick enough to house the blade of a sword. They walked slowly, with a kind of nervous nonchalance, and always stayed in the café until a quarter-past three when they both swaggered out and called a taxi to them from the cab-rank at the corner of the road. They seemed never to speak to each other.

Some nights when he found it impossible to sleep he would dress and go out for a walk in the streets, slowly treading out the deliberate sound of his feet upon the pavements, smelling the stale night smells and hearing the noises, and imagining himself in a new world—a world of which half-silence and fear were the keynotes. The stale earth in the window-boxes, sterile and exhausted, unwilling to put forth more small flowers for the dust to choke, had a sharp, rancid smell that mingled with the stale odours of basement kitchens. When he walked thus, in a land where noise was so sharp and disturbing, he found himself able to notice things and comment on them, compare and associate groups of ideas. Even if the nearer silence was unbroken there was the great purring sound of distance, the mighty pouring of blood through the arteries of the city that was never silent. He wondered how many diverse sounds, how many different causes, went to make up this giant uniform growl of silence; the gurgle of water in the underground sewers, the wailing of sirens on the river, the swishing of the late trains as they moved out on their journeys, the groan of an early cart as it crawled down through the city, the chatter of the prostitutes at the street corners, the drone of taxis, the scratching of paper as it drifted upon the pavements—all these were absorbed and became components of that blare of silence; even the small flat sound of his feet upon the pavement was absorbed into it, and made a millionth part of the activity. Sometimes he would stand quite still and strain to distinguish the separate sounds of the vast orchestra—strain until his head ached for those indistinct siren-calls, the roar of trains, but he could never distinguish anything; always a nearer sound would break down his effort, laughter from the next street, or a cry from some shuttered window.

Yet from out of all the bewildering diversities of the night-life some sounds and smells remained constant and unchanging, and for these he treasured recognition as he did for those two or three inhabitants of the café opposite his house. The wheels of a taxi on the smooth black road never made anything but the sound of a choir of gnats, even in wet or frosty weather; and those gaunt men who wheeled their barrows of fruit through the dark squares never looked anything but furtive and hunted; their filthy cloth caps were pulled down low over their faces, and they lowered their voices when they spoke as though there were something shameful in the act of peddling their rich merchandise through the midnight city.

In a little street off Fitzroy Square there was always a light in the basement, and if you stood on the gleaming glass slab fretted with metal, your body was shaken by the pulsing of the machines that baked bread all night; and at each fresh throb of sound the wholesome smell of bread came out upon you from the grating in great heartening whiffs. He would stand upon the pitted glass and let the hot draught pour out around him, permeating his clothes, while he sniffed the sweet odours of the bakery. Once, as he stood there, taking great breaths of the pure warm air, a man, clad in a white smock, came to the grating and handed him two huge hunks of newly-baked bread on a long fork, inviting him to eat it, smiling very kindly upon him:

'I get lots of you poor artists round 'ere. Always 'ungry, aren't yer?'

And as Walsh let his teeth sink into the warm crumbly richness of the bread he said, after thanking the man:

'That's settled it. I'm going to be a baker.'

But there were other things that he hated. Down by Leicester Square, in the little burrows behind the theatres, he found many a bundle of rags that had once been a human being curled up asleep in the doorway where tomorrow it would be turned away to make room for a pit queue; and once, a ragged little old man with a tabby beard who was burrowing in a dustbin. Beside him on the pavement lay a very old and very worn violin with only three sound strings, and a minute parcel of his belongings, girded up in a stained handkerchief. Walsh gave him a florin, but the poor creature seemed hardly to comprehend the meaning of the act, and he stared at the coin as it lay in his creased brown palm. Then, with a sudden quick gesture, he nodded his head and turned back to the dustbin, rummaging among the scattered paper and filth. His little frog-head was ducked flat as he tried to reach some object deep in the bin, while unconsciously with his boots he trampled the little round parcel which held his belongings, trampled and tore the red handkerchief.

On these late walks Walsh would often be filled with the feeling that he alone among the living trod the gloomy streets; his moving body and the feel of his clothes hanging on him, they were the only knowledge of substance in an illusory world. Even the sleek and silent men who stood night-long at the street-corners, and the women with their chalk-pale vermilion-rouged masks hiding what little self was left them, were but puzzling symbols of actualities that existed only in the squalid turbulence of the daytime. With the knowledge that so many activities, so many interests, so many personalities lay submerged in the second-sleep of dawn, his own perceptions quickened and briskly demanded food, as if given a freedom which the day denied them.

Corfu, Greece, Cyprus

A Landmark Gone

Published in Orientations, *Vol. 1. No. 1. (A Forces Quarterly, edited by G. S. Fraser.) Cairo. n.d. (War years.)*
Privately printed, in an edition of 125 copies, for Lawrence Clark Powell, Los Angeles. 1949.

Somewhere between Calabria and Corfu the blue really begins. You feel the horizon beginning to stain at the rim, the sky seems to come a little nearer and into deeper focus; the sea darkens as it uncurls in troughs around the boat. You are aware not so much of a landscape coming to meet you invisibly over those blue miles of water, as of a climate. Entering Greece is like entering a dark crystal; the form of things becomes irregular, refracted. Mirages suddenly swallow islands and if you watch you can see the trembling curtain of the atmosphere. Once in the shadow of the Albanian hills you are aware of this profound change. It haunts you while you live there, this creeping refraction of light altering with the time of day, so that you can fall asleep in a valley and awake in Tibet, with all the landmarks gone.

This is perhaps why we chose Corfu to live in: the island is a sort of ante-room to Aegean Greece with its smoke-grey bare volcanic islands like turtlebacks on the water. Corfu is all Venetian green and spoiled by the sun. Its richness enervates. Its valleys are painted out boldly in heavy brush-strokes of yellow and red, the Judas trees line the dusty roads in terrific purple explosions. Everywhere you go you can lie down on grass. Even the rocky northern end is rich in mineral springs: even the bare rock here is fruitful of water.

About the town one should use the past tense. Angular Venetian architecture, arcades, colonnades, shutters—peeling shutters holding back the sunlight which bounds off the bay and strikes upwards in a terrific dazzle. You lie in bed and see the sea spangling the cracked Venetian ceilings with their scrolls and cherubs. There are other curiosities. The remains of a Venetian aristocracy living in overgrown baronial mansions deep in the country, surrounded by cypresses; a patron saint who lay (a cured mummy) in a silver casket in the church of his name, and who performed terrific miracles; festivals, dances, olive-pickings, holidays, storms, births, deaths and magnificent murders. And outside everything beyond the charm of accidents and persons, the hallow-blue rim of the world pressing in on the outside edge of the crystal.

We took a fisherman's house built on the bare craggy northern point of the island, almost in Albania. The people were sailors and the village small. The whole landscape was metamorphic rock—great layers of laminated stone on which clung precarious symbols like the olive and cypress, myrtle and arbutus, persisting like anachronisms in this world of bareness. We built a top-storey to the house costing £43 10s, a balcony overlooking the deep curve of the bay, where we could gaze, like Jesus, on the cities, over the sloping verdant lowlands in their haze. To sit by the bare rocky border of the sea and gaze into the land of milk and honey was ideal. I had work to do; and my wife had a lot to think about.

Here we lived—though 'live' as a word takes an unfair advantage of the steady dropping away of time. Days dropped away from us like pebbles from the walls of a deep well. I wrote a good deal, burned a good deal, corrected a good deal, and went on writing.

Our skin became slowly black, and our hair coarse with salt and very bleached. We began to learn Greek—to discover the rotation of the fruits—white and red hill-cherries, prickly pears, grapes, tangerines. We marked off a section of the bare white rock, walled it in, had some soil transported, and declared it a garden. The peace of those evenings on the balcony before the lighting of the lamps was something we shall never discover again—the stillness of objects reflected in the mirror of the bay; a mirror ever so slightly swinging, its surface ungrazed by the fishes moving about its lower floors. It was the kind of hush you get in a Chinese water-colour. The darkness leaked in over it all without disturbing anything; the proportions all remaining the same but the light changing. At last the sea would rise up to meet the sky and they would merge into a single warm veil. Everywhere you smelt the sage bruised by the feet of the sheep on the mountain-side.

The invisible shepherd would lie under an arbutus and start playing his pipe. Across the bay would slide the smooth, icy notes of the flute; little liquid flourishes, and sleepy quibbles. Sitting on the balcony wrapped by the airs, we would listen without speaking. Presently the moon appeared—not the white, pulpy spectre of a moon that you see in Egypt—but a Greek moon friendly, not incalculable or chilling; like the flash of swimmer's arms out in the sea. Immediately the water was transformed into a tract of silver coins; a grampus puffed and was still; the flute stopped its meditations. We walked in our bare feet through the dark rooms, feeling the cool tiles under us, and down on to the rock. In that enormous silence we walked into the water, so as not to splash, and swam out into the silver bar. The black cutter lay motion-less on the glaze. We touched the deck and found the wood still warm from the sun—like a human body almost. We didn't speak, because a voice on that water sounded unearthly. We swam till we were tired and then came back to the white rock and wrapped ourselves in towels and ate grapes. Perhaps we walked for a while on the hillside in the moonlight under the cypresses.

It is astonishing how little of the past can be recaptured in words. I have been trying for a year to rebuild that white house by the water's edge in a book; the taste of the little yellow grapes—a particularity of the island—the private and forgotten cove under the red shrine of St. Arsenius where Dorothy and Veronica, two ballet-dancers, invented a water ballet by moonlight; the cool white rooms with my wife's lazy pleasant paintings of our peasant friends looking at us from every wall; the little black boat riding at anchor outside the window, its masts grazing the balcony.

The day war was declared we stood on that balcony in a green rain falling straight down out of heaven on to the glassy floor of the lagoon; we were destroying papers, drawings, packing books. We were still inside the dark crystal, as yet unconscious of our separation. We refused to read the omens.

Last April as I lay in pitch darkness on the packed deck of a caique as we nosed past Matapan towards Crete, I thought back to that balcony in Corcyra, that green rain in the shadow of the Albanian hills. I remembered it all with a regret so deep that it did not stir the emo-tions; seen through the transforming lens of memory the past seemed so enchanted that any regret would have been unworthy of it. We never ever speak of it any more, having escaped. Time has done its stuff, the house is in ruins, the little black cutter smashed. I think only the shrine with the three cypresses and the tiny rock pool where we bathed is still left. How can these few hastily written words ever recreate more than a fraction of it?

Panic Spring

Published by Faber and Faber, 1937.

The setting for Durrell's second novel is an imaginary Ionian island, Mavro-daphne, owned by Kostas Rumanades, an immensely wealthy Greek who, from the modest beginnings of his father's currant business, has built himself up into a merchant and financier of international power and importance. Deprived of friend-ship by the ruthless nature of his career, for even his wife has deserted him, he finds it lonely at the top. So, in order to secure company and conversation, he has fitted up a number of villas, scattered about the island, which he places at the disposal of any guests who show some sign of originality and character.

A modest boat brings supplies of all kinds from the mainland, and its captain, Christ by name, is commissioned to watch out for congenial travellers likely to provide Rumanades with good company and bring them to Mavrodaphne. As the novel opens, Marlowe, an English schoolmaster, is stranded at Brindisi by the Greek revolution; bored, after a few days of close contact with his compatriots in the hotel, he seeks refuge in a dockside wine shop. Here he is found by Christ who offers to take him to Greece.

On arrival at Mavrodaphne Marlowe meets members of the colony, guests of Rumanades; Fonvisin, a Russian doctor, refugee from Bolshevism, Francis, an English girl, a painter, who is supposed by her employers to be combing the Middle East for textile designs, and two young Englishmen, Walsh, who supports him-self by writing jazz songs, and Gordon who has independent means. In due course Marlowe meets the great man himself, and is offered a villa.

Nothing of great moment occurs; Rumanades entertains them all at his luxurious villa, gives concerts by means of his E.M.G. gramophone and a fire-work display in honour of the local saint. He starts to repair the church and commissions Francis to decorate it with frescoes. There is a great deal of conversa-tion and longish flashbacks depict the earlier history of Marlowe, Francis and Walsh. Towards the end of the book a great storm rages, during which Rumana-des dies, and as it closes the characters are about to leave the island and go their several ways.

Walsh, the reader will remember, was the leading character in Pied Piper of Lovers, *and both Gordon and Ruth also appear therein; indeed, the chapter entitled 'Walsh' might well have served as a coda or small sequel to that novel. It is interesting to observe that, as a young man, twenty years before the publication of* Justine, *Durrell was already experimenting with the exercise of writing at two levels of time.*

CHAPTER III

RUMANADES

The Ritual of the Fireworks, as it was called, had been Rumanades' own idea.

In the old days, the annual church procession in honour of the patron saint, led by the village priest and two senile deputy-acolytes recruited from the monastery on the top of Leucothea (of which they were the sole inhabitants), had been enough to satisfy his national and personal sense of honour. But with the arrival of foreigners he had begun to feel that something more was demanded of him; something more in the way of entertainment which would reflect favourably not only upon himself as the owner of the island, but also upon the patron saint. Hence the fireworks.

More than this (since any fool could buy a box of fireworks and let them off on the beach for the entertainment of foreigners), it was necessary and fitting that the whole business should receive, as it were, ecclesiastical sanction. It was the Punctilio, the Large Gesture, that the old man was after.

The village priest was asked if, before the ceremony, he would be good enough to give a short address, offer up a brief prayer—in short, indicate in some way that a definite connection existed between the bona-fide ecclesiastical ceremonies and this informal one. And here was the rub.

The priest, who was conscientious, crawled up the precipices leading to Leucothea on his hands and knees, and was hauled up the sixty-foot cliff-face fronting the monastery, in a basket to which a rope was attached; which itself was attached to an antiquated windlass propelled by the two senile, perspiring, verminous old gentlemen who were his acolytes in times of ceremony. A grave conference was held; the priest wondering all the time whether he would live to announce its results to Rumanades.

The two monks, who were jealous at being excluded from the invitation (this was a grave tactical blunder on the part of the old man), spent the whole day arguing the matter backwards and forwards, stopping for a glass of wine and a rest at five-minute intervals, during which the question was pondered with a grave silence.

'Let us not be in a hurry,' one of the old men kept repeating. 'We must consider the question from every angle.' With the air of hardened medieval Sorbonnières they settled down to resolve the tangle of opinion with a wealth of dialectic that did them considerable credit, when it is remembered that neither could read nor write. At sunset, when the priest was finally deposited with a crash at the foot of the cliff, they were still at it, primed with wine, and really grateful to have something which they could discuss for an indefinite period of time. Looking up indignantly, he caught sight of one of them leaning over the terrifying drop, waving genially at him with one hand and unsteadily clawing his vast beard with the other. As he stumbled down through the dusty woods he caught the sound of an aged voice blithering: 'We must not be in a hurry. We must consider it from every angle.'

That night he presented himself at the Villa Pothetos, and informed Rumanades that the procedure demanded of him would not be seemly in the eyes of either God or man. By 'man' he implied the two garrulous anatomies he had left behind on the cliff-top; God, even after twenty years of diligent search, still withheld a single clue to His identity.

Rumanades sighed, raised his eyes, and drummed his long fingers on the glossy wood of his desk. He would have liked to accomplish the business with tact and diplomacy, but in the face of refusal so blank he felt called upon to exert what pressure he could still apply.

The church, he said, after a long and stealthy silence, was in a very bad state of repair. The priest agreed. There were holes in the walls, the damp had rotted the painting off the walls, and the woodwork of the altar was rotten. The priest agreed. Did he (the priest) think it was fitting for services to be held for the glorification of God in a temple which was only distinguishable from a stable by the bleached cross on its door? At this point the priest opened his mouth to speak, but the old man with a gesture silenced him and continued quietly. Did he (the priest) not realize that they could be of great use to each other, and between them assist in the general advancement of worship, to the glory of the patron saint and all concerned? The priest knew he was beaten.

In the silence that followed, Rumanades scrutinized him closely, from the top of his grubby stove-pipe hat, to the uneasy black shoes that peeped nervously out from time to time under the soutane. Then meaningly he said: 'Would it not be to the glory of us all if I were to restore the church?'

He knew only too well that the priest slept on a straw mattress behind the damp altar: and that he suffered from rheumatism; that another winter in the dank, unprotected barn was more than even the most practised ascetic would stand. Accordingly he drummed away at the table-top and smiled: and called for a bottle of wine to seal the pact.

And it was so.

CHAPTER IV

PHAON

There are moments in the intercourse between men, when qualities of ease, silence, content become, not the jealous property of one person, but the common pool of all; and it was in such a silence that the three of them, Marlowe, Gordon and Walsh, set out to walk down the road to the bay. Food (and Gordon's cooking was really excellent) had put new life into them. They lounged down towards the beach, lazy and comfortable in knowledge of their companionship, talking triviality with the zest of veterans in friendship.

In the electric hush of twilight which preceded positive darkness and followed the quenching of the sun, the highroad had become peopled with peasants from the mountain villages who had come down to watch the fireworks. The throb of donkeys' hooves in the thick dust, the voices, the bright passing of coloured clothes, the curtain of drifting dust—all contrived a soft, orderly pageant of colour and sound, through which the hush of twilight contrived to break. Then, lingering, trembling, like a new lover for the world, the night slipped down upon them, and the pageant was swallowed up, annihilated. In a moment they were marooned on the stony cliff-path, groping for sure footholds where a minute before they could walk upright and at ease. Gordon stumbled and swore with fervour. Somewhere to the left on the darkened beach a maroon stormed up to the sky and, after the preliminary crash, loosed its five or six pattering yellow flares.

'Good God,' said Marlowe.

'I know,' panted Gordon between blasphemies. 'Seems to go off between one's teeth up here.'

'We're late,' said Walsh. 'The priest's beginning.'

A beautiful bass voice like a gong now took up the tale. Slowly and with infinite relish it began what seemed to be some sort of liturgical incantation, dwelling on and tasting the lovely syllables of language, rising and falling in the perfect expression of the sense. From the terraces of olive-trees came an occasional muttered response. Soft shapes moved like pieces broken from the darkness, and the humid silence was penetrated by whispers, and girls' quiet laughter.

'Look,' said Walsh suddenly, 'do look.'

To the left and above them, in broad silhouette against the sky, a ledge of rock curved out sheer from the level of the cliff-face, and on it, sculptured in black, fixed in a rigid sitting pose, the figures of the two old monks were visible. Leaning forward in a vain attempt to see the palpably invisible, their bodies were clenched in scornful anger. They seemed the very substance of rock carved into a caricature of scorn. Gordon chuckled.

'The poor old dears,' he said. 'They're as jealous as hell.'

Walsh, giggling as he stumbled down in the chasmic glooms ahead, turned up his face to Marlowe and explained that they lived on the top of Leucothea, in the ruined monastery. 'How they both manage to get back into the nest is a mystery to me,' said Gordon. 'It's bad enough when one stays behind to work the windlass.'

'Oh, I saw them doing it once,' said Walsh, 'through the old man's telescope. Quite by mistake. They both got into the basket and started to pull the rope. Like a couple of demented prophets, with their old beards flapping over the side. Crashing against the cliff at every pull. And ducking down, too, as if they were afraid of bashing their craniums on the sky.'

'Do they do anything?' asked Marlowe. 'I mean, besides just winding themselves up and down the cliff?'

'Hold hard, the path turns here,' said Gordon. 'No. I don't think they do much. Pray a good deal, I suppose. And they love considering things. Simple things for preference. It's their own brand of work; that and drinking white wine. They're perfect medieval relics. If only they could write I'm sure they'd spend their time composing long tracts determining the exact number of camels that could pass through a needle's eye, or ditto angels stand on the point of a pin.'

'Rubbish,' said Walsh. 'They're too simple-souled to be casuists. Christ! The old man's started blasting.'

For a second the darkness was broken by one tiny flare: a match: and in its flapping light the domed face of Fonvisin was visible, puckered about a cigarette. Then a flight of saffron rockets fizzed wildly up into the night, and the bay of Nanos rocked in a wild sheet of colour; a pungent cloud of smoke fell to the level of the water, and lolled drunkenly inshore. A rapturous murmur of applause greeted this effort, and from the higher terraces a sharp burst of clapping. In the few seconds of light Marlowe caught sight of the little band of privileged sightseers grouped round Rumanades: Vassili hopping with uncontrollable delight on one gaitered leg; the priest, lounging in an attitude of resigned boredom, chin on breast, Fonvisin supine on a rock, motionless and somehow contemptuous; and Rumanades himself, with Francis and Christ at his heels, fussing about among the mounds of seaweed.

Any introductions at that time and place were bound to be cursory. Rumanades was for a moment nothing but a handshake with darkness, until a shower of gold rockets gave him a lean, bearded face, shyly arrogant in expression, and a lank body clad in fusty black; a shower of white light for the grave face of Francis, with its deep eyes, and sleek, unplucked black eyebrows; red for the bony dome of Fonvisin's head.

'This is Dr. Appolyon Fonvisin. Mr. Marlowe.'

In the red glare their eyes met, and Fonvisin's smile belied the sober stare of the eyes, considering, criticizing, assessing. . . .

'You must really forgive,' said Rumanades nervously, 'my preoccupation with the ceremony. The day of our Patron Saint, you know. If you don't mind . . .' and he fussed off.

Fonvisin lay back on his rock, and his nostrils gushed cigarette smoke. Pillowing his head on his arms, he stared fixedly up at the sky. Marlowe sat down near him and presently Walsh came and joined him with a casual: 'Hullo, Fonvisin. You still alive?'

For a minute the Russian smiled grimly up at him. 'I am alive,' he said. 'Yes. I am alive. If you want to know.'

'So am I,' said Walsh with a sigh, perching himself on the rock and swinging his legs.

Yellow, green and red, flight after flight of rockets fumed up to the dark ceiling of heaven, and loosed their showers of coloured rain. The hollow bay flung back tremendous echoes in the face of the still water. The roar of applause swelled with the crash of clapping from the olive-covered slopes above them. A great throbbing pall of red smoke wavered among them, and with each successive flash the bright silhouette of the priest, standing with his chin on his breast, was lit with a bright phosphorescent outline.

Flight after flight of rockets. The darkness which, undisturbed, gave the illusion of being limited to the small radius of sight, bulged elastically in all directions. Each new comet plunged its colour, like an avenging knife, into the black. Great lovely, faltering trajectories were carved out above the cynic impassivity of the sea; and from the natural amphitheatre terraced upon the cliff-top round after round of applause seeped into the vacant seconds of silence, demanding more and yet more.

Francis danced up from the confusion, her face an unholy cipher of delight in light, a shadow against shadow in darkness.

'Isn't it lovely? Oh, isn't it miraculous?'

For a long moment their eyes met and she stared down upon Marlowe's small, rather fine ascetic head, lean and pointing away to the chin: his eyes were small but very bright, a clear salt blue, and seemed to be built deep in under the heavy ledges of bone. They were full of that evasive anguish of his generation; and the evasion in them made her smile and counterfeit ease.

Through the reek of gases the voice of Rumanades called vaguely: 'Nearly over now. Nearly finished. Finale.'

There was a moment's lull. Then the last fuse began to giggle and splutter, and, gathering impetus from the fiery commotion in its vitals, lurched up into the night with a wheeze, splendidly bound for heaven in defiance of all gravity. Up it went to the top of its curve, unfaltering,

[197]

and then, after a preliminary stutter, shot a loop of gold stars outwards towards Epirus and the hills. Neatly and cleanly the stars lapsed, waned and were extinguished and only the reek remained, and the faint slap of a discarded stick on the dark water. Then a grudging applause broke out, disturbing the night.

There was a sudden gap at the heart of things. Speech, which had been keyed to its highest pitch to carry in the inferno, sight, which had been tormented by alternating noon and midnight, hearing, which had been well-nigh blasted—these faculties were suddenly restored. Quite what to do or say they did not know. The applause from the olives, gradually growing in volume, gave them their cue.

'Finished. All over.' Rumanades lowered his head and peered in their direction. 'All over,' he said, 'my dear Mr. Marlowe. Please forgive my bad manners, but I am a sort of high priest to-night.' Marlowe made the appropriate reply, in the appropriate voice.

'Bed for me, I think,' said Walsh, yawning and knuckling his eyes.

The peasant audience were on the move. Laughter and animated talk, mingled with the fresh scent of flowers, came clearly down to them; the priest bade them good night in his rich voice and swept off into the darkness; the ledge on which the two monks had sat was empty. Fonvisin yawned and stretched with insolent ease, and picked his teeth with a matchstick. 'And I,' he said in his careful exact English, 'have a little adventure waiting for me before I go to sleep. Eh?' He smiled vaguely around him and unknotted the handkerchief from his bald head. 'A little adventure.'

'You and your conquests,' said Francis, with a certain contemptuous emphasis.

'Conquests!' he mocked, twinkling with glee. 'What a Puritanical woman. "Your conquests", she says.' His imitation of contempt was delightful. Puffing out his lips, he gave a snort of laughter.

'Er . . . Mr. Marlowe,' said old Rumanades nervously, 'if you will take a little walk please, there is something I want to speak to you about. . . .'

When they were out of earshot he sighed and shoved his thumbs into his waistcoat pockets so that his fingers dangled down across his abdomen. His jaws moved slowly as if he were chewing his tongue.

'I would consider it a great honour', he said at last, 'if during your visit you would live in a little villa which I have empty. It is called

Phaon, up there on the cliff, among the trees. It is a nice little place. . . .'

Marlowe, who had been coached in his part by Gordon, stopped and protested that such generosity was more than he could allow. 'I am already in your debt,' he explained. 'I have landed on a private island, and you have given me permission to stay a while. . . .'

Rumanades became exquisitely nervous, stabbing his pocketed thumbs downwards, and hanging his head.

'Nevertheless', he said doggedly, 'I would consider it a great honour if you would accept my offer. It is really not very much to ask . . .' and Marlowe, taking pity on his embarrassment, accepted the offer with a gratitude which he expressed as delicately as he could. The gesture had been achieved. They shook hands with grave formality. 'I can only hope that some day I will be in a position to return your hospitality,' said Marlowe, and Rumanades thanked him solemnly as an owl. 'I am sure you would,' he said. 'My dear Marlowe, I am quite sure you would.'

CHAPTER V

MOVING IN

The move from the inn to the Villa Phaon fulfilled all the necessary conditions of a musical comedy finale. It was infectious with gaiety, and Marlowe, to whom ceremony—even such well-wishing and spontaneous ceremony—was anathema, was a trifle dazed by its extravagance.

He awoke about dawn to the brief sight of sunlight topping the olives and moving across the sea, and was puzzled by the unfamiliar scent of flowers in the little room. Before he could bring his mind to bear on the subject, however, he had dozed off, and it was only the familiar roar of Gordon's laughter that shocked him into a sitting posture, hands to his head. Embarrassed by the intrusion of faces in the low doorway, he stared about for signs of their laughter, still half asleep; and was aware that he lay, couched in an absolute nest of flowers, fruit, vegetables, and eggs; orchids and anemones, cherries and wild strawberries, beans and giant tomatoes—the room was swarming with them. On his trousers lay a pyramid of red festival eggs. A bunch of vermilion pomegranate blooms sprouted from the pocket of his coat.

'Gordon,' he said, 'what is all this?'

The wrinkles crowded about Gordon's laughing eyes, and crawled upwards across his forehead. Leaning sideways against the door-post, he answered: 'Bribery.'

Marlowe soberly crossed his arms over his chest and stared.

'It was magnificent,' said Gordon: 'you lying there sleeping, surrounded by a harvest festival.'

A dado of grinning faces bobbed around his head in the semi-gloom of the passage-way, corroborating the laughter. Marlowe was suddenly filled with a shy annoyance. He huddled down in the clothes and frigidly requested privacy. The faces vanished like snuffed candle-flames, and Gordon, serious of a sudden, apologized fervently and closed the door, leaning his broad back to the wood as a safeguard against intrusion.

In silence Marlowe began to dress, carefully examining his clothes for signs of the ubiquitous vermin which had tormented him all night. Pausing as he lifted his shirt to his shoulders, he half turned, and caught the eye of the young man. Gordon smiled mildly and apologized again. 'It was thoughtless of me.'

'My dear man,' said Marlowe, '*that's* not what worries me—it's all this.' Standing there, between perplexity and annoyance, he swung his arm wide, indicating the tumbled bed, with its load of market-produce, the chair, the floor. . . .

'It's all this,' he added, and smiled gradually.

Gordon crossed to the bed, and cleared himself a place to sit on. Elbows on knees, he said: 'It's bribery. You'll find this stuff useful, though, if you're moving into Phaon to-day. Save you a trip down to Christ's place.'

'But, good Lord, do I accept it?'

A brief examination proved that the donors had left no clue whatsoever to their several identities; fruit and vegetables, as Gordon remarked, could hardly be traced back to their owners.

'It's pure formality. I imagine they want to bribe you to buy fruit and vegetables and stuff from them. Anyway, we'll see.'

[200]

Breakfast for Marlowe was purely an affair of coffee and a cigarette; and the duration today was determined by the perplexity caused by these agricultural phenomena; yawning lethargically from time to time, he sat beside Gordon on the bed, and puffed smoke up at the dingy ceiling.

'Tomatoes and broad beans.'

'Even, my God, a cauliflower. I must have had my head on it.'

Prodigiously yawning, he followed Gordon out, to where the crowd of suitors talked together in the hollow echoing bar-room, and shuffled their bare feet on the flags. The room was swimming in colour against the vivid sunshine of the doorway. Christ's cousin, more blowzy and drab than ever in contrast to the gay head-dresses and the swirling skirts, dispensed equal quantities of black wine and garrulity, making the best of the time and the trade.

At the moment of their appearance they became the focus of all interest, the pivot upon which the whole gathering circle of humanity turned and whirled, in its swarming and squeezing towards the door.

Voices fluent with necessity beseeched, cajoled, insisted. Scarves danced and swayed, profuse with colour. The heavy dresses twirled and snapped at their ankles, instinct with a disturbing life. Heavy and sickening, the smell of garlic rose on the air. Gordon, head and brown shoulders above them all, laughed in the fresh laughing faces of the women, and shouted for them to make way. Maria, Chrysanthe and a horde of others shouted him down, beseeching him, with a familiarity that horrified Marlowe at the time, but which he recognized later on as a natural trait of the peasants, to intercede on their behalf.

Down the road they went, hedged in by the women and followed, at a respectful distance, by the men who carried the suitcases; a cavalcade of noise and colour centred on Marlowe, pale, blue-eyed, and nursing his northern reserve. Only Gordon was laughing unfeignedly, and bargaining noisily. The fine dust of the road rose in a cloud about their ankles, and the sun, as yet not uncomfortably hot, warmed their backs.

'Chrysanthe will bring you eggs and milk.'

Marlowe nodded perfunctorily.

'Maria wants to be your servant.'

'Which is Maria?'

A broad figure, electrified by the mention of the name, pushed nearer to them, leaping across their path on a pair of stodgy brown legs. Leaning towards them and repeating her name, the woman smiled in a sort of humorous anguish of speechlessness, and drew her green head-dress back from her black hair. Her white teeth were set evenly in a broad, kindly mouth, devoid of almost everything but laughter and a certain casual sensuality.

'Maria?' he said, and she, nodding her head in recognition, twinkled her brown eyes at him.

'Malista.'

Talking, and chattering, the women still followed them, across the path to the road, and down beyond the ruined stone bridge and the iron spring, from where Phaon was visible, glittering on the hillside.

'It looks as if it were carved in salt,' was Marlowe's comment, when Gordon pointed it out to him.

'That', said Gordon, grimacing, 'is a poor compliment in this part of the world. They use sea-sand sometimes in the building, and in the winter the walls of your house have such a large quantity of salt in them, they suck up the rain like a sponge.'

From the parapet flanking the road a path had been cut, and a white concrete stairway mounted to the villa's porch. A trellis of vine, Marlowe noticed, shaded the cool green porch; and at the back of the little place a deep volume of colour, dashed with bright gold spots, receding to a pure sky, established the identity of the orange-groves—green freaked with gold, already dusty and tremulous in the heat.

The procession followed them doggedly to the very terrace in front of the house, the men groaning under the weight of suitcases. In the shade of the vine-lattice, Marlowe turned to watch the womenfolk, brilliant in their colours, mounting the long flight of steps, casually conscious of their own kinetic beauty, direct and assured. An hour of negotiation followed, during which Gordon, with his mixture of lame Greek and fluent Italian, did the talking.

Chrysanthe was to bring him eggs and milk when he wanted it; Agathie and Sophia romped off in delight at the thought of having a regular customer for their vegetables; Maria made a point of beginning her job at once, swaying off to the spring with a pitcher on her head, to get them a drink.

Marlowe and Gordon sat down on the uncouth wooden bench under the dapple of sunlight.

'By the way,' said Gordon, 'what books have you got?' and Marlowe, kneeling on the ground, unhasped his battered suitcase and groped among his treasures. Molinos, Guyon, Bossuet and a crowd of others he lifted and placed in Gordon's brown hands, smiling up a trifle diffidently.

'Mostly quietist people,' he said, without further explanation.

Gordon was silent, turning the books over, opening and shutting them. Long slants of sun picked up the sheen in his head of unkempt yellow hair and his heavily marked eyebrows.

'Oh! dear,' he said slowly, 'I want something to read, and I can't stomach metaphysical pinpricking.' He smiled up suddenly and leaned back so that the sun shone on his great gold thumbs.

At that moment Maria reappeared with her pitcher and they followed her into the house to find glasses. It was small, but very clean and cool: a mere two rooms and kitchen, with a lopsided house or office added, it seemed, as an afterthought. It was scantly furnished for one, with good shaggy unpainted wood—a table and a single bookshelf—and sturdy peasant chairs. On the low bed lay a pile of utensils and odds and ends which Rumanades had sent down from the Villa Pothetos: a pair of sheets, some dusters, a saucepan, several earthenware pots, a tin oven for the charcoal fire, a kettle, and a bundle containing a knife, a fork, a spoon and a tin-opener. These Maria took immediate command of, refusing positively to leave them where they were until Marlowe had made an inventory.

'They don't understand a conscientious soul like you,' remarked Gordon, and laughed at his glumness. 'Never mind.'

Pacing the bright tiling of the floors with a fine sense of ownership, Marlowe busied himself with the opening of windows, the throwing wide of shutters.

'Good heavens, Gordon,' he said dramatically, 'the Sea!'

'It's always there,' said the young man negligently, asprawl on the bed, 'and it's never the same.'

Marlowe's eyes followed the long line of the coast, laid out, it seemed, for his inspection, like a relief map: squared in colours that were bright and positive in sunlight. To the north there was a giant growing ruffle of tides, being pushed round the point of Lefkimo. Otherwise the long slab of water was immobile, impervious it seemed, to the single lateen-rigged fishing boat which rested upon it, showing

[203]

no sign of trough or flaw. Eastwards the misty mountains brooded. Very faintly, as if doubtful of its powers, a wind, whose path had somehow missed the water, tested the suppleness of the two dwarf cypresses in the garden, rocking them.

'I suppose it's always like this,' he said at last, with the uncomfortable feeling that he had broken the silence stupidly.

'It's taken for granted. For my part I'm sick to death of it. . . .'

Turning, Marlowe saw the smooth abstraction of the brown face, and for a moment was himself filled with a gust of nostalgic yearning for greenness. The North, at that moment, as he gazed out from the vine-porch to the pure flamy landscape, ripe and positive in tone, seemed an inconceivable distance away, tucked down under obscure landscapes, misty and wet and remote in its forests and marshes: a land of gnomes and shadows, which could produce no vivid memory here, where the fruit burned ripe on the trees, and the glossed green of the olives achieved a hundred subtle gradations from green to green. No, the North was unthinkable, and as yet the South was barely comprehensible in its vividness.

'It's funny,' he said, 'habit.'

Sombrely Gordon agreed, his gaze fixed unwinkingly on the slender tips of the cypresses, which moved in a grave rhythm against the sea-line. In his imagination (the heroic deception of memory!) he was confronting a wide English prospect, lush and delightful undulations chequered with crop and arable and fallow. Wheat like gold foam; the ashy rectangles of oats, the mustard crop, spittlebright: these were tantalizing images of coolness and ease focused against the blue water and the distance that hid Epirus.

CHAPTER VII

WALSH

Grey days in the south of England. Autumn with the long mounded fieldways in a crush of rotten, sweet-smelling leaves. Prodigious quilts set for the feet of winter. Down by the lake, on the damp margin of hummocks, pitted and perforated with old mole-burrowings, the de-composing stubs of horse-chestnuts indiscriminately littered, like the relics of feasts, significant of feasts to come. The lupins in the cottage garden were burnt out. Their colour heavy and patched with decay, sodden brown patches with the stumps rotten. Why is it that lupins burn up heavenward from the feet, like martyrs? How fine it must be, she said once, to feel the flame of life eating one away upwards, out into space: burning up the body from the toes to the face, and short life flowing electrically upwards. Baucis and Philemon should have been changed to asphodels, so that their mouths could meet finally above the flame that swept up their bodies. Trees are clumsy in death.

Autumn, I give you late Autumn, like a once bright playing-card, now softened and blurred with the damp: its painted significance now indistinct. The bright inks running wet, with all the hard outlines gone. Late Autumn like a bedraggled parrot, moist in the declining season. The popjaye royalle. Smoke from the cottage chimneys, from the farms, lifting and merging across the hill-slopes where the sodden grass lay crisp all summer. Now we have a sopping scalp of green to the earth, easily peeled, easily torn by heavy boots or the brute feet of the cattle that crowd the gateways. Southward, if you look from one of those hills among the farms where all night long the dogs tug at their chains and bark at nothing, you will see the long grey form of the sea stirring through the mist. Uneasy grey patrol of waters round the coast, eternally vigilant.

And then Ruth. Dozens of pictures of her: dozens of shapes and lights which were her. Ruth, particularly, under sentence, like the lupins and those lissom early flowers that flagged the April hedges. Ruth smiling, elbows propped on the wood window-sill of the cottage, staring down across the slopes, seaward. Ruth angry. Ruth in quiet nakedness beside him in the heavy bed upstairs. Ruth shaking the hair out of her eyes, smiling again—the red oval in her face, fringed with teeth, and the bright soft rim of lips about it. The eyelash, particularly, fluttering in soft terror against his skin. The terrific interchange of gestures, the great flux of lightning that swept them, drinking them up, while the eyelash beat and beat. The tides, the recession, the final music of nakedness. Yes, but he had seen her face turn back, folded in painful crying, half laughter, half tears, and her mouth actually moan-ing. Surely the lupins had voices for the final fire that consumed them, surely the last spasm of life shivering in them made them moan like this, upwards?

There were so many images that it was no use to apply method to them, to go back step by step, stratum by stratum and reconstruct them: memory was a sudden gift out of nowhere, as if a child should turn and hand one a bright playing-card of himself and Ruth, static and fixed in the eternity that was two years by the calendar reckoning. Two years in which he could watch the progression of a million springs, summers, winters, for time itself, all continuity, had utterly vanished. The one big division in the pattern was Ruth dying: her lapsing like that into quietness, like a gift of faithlessness. There was only time before that and after it. An infinity in which her going was the one clean partition.

Before the events it was nothing but bright colours to remember, crowding in on him, without method or progression. Ruth, for instance, in summer, her hair wet and salt from swimming, shaking down the apple blossom from the tree, standing in the shower of petals shouting with laughter. Apple blossom. And then himself—how unreal that dead self—breaking through the wet fringe of hair at the nape of her neck with his mouth. Or himself again, as they lay on the clean hard sand of the cove, naked, filling her sleeping nostrils with fine sand. How unreal themselves, laughing and tangled in each other's arms on the warm sand! But we are talking of Autumn, and the last fruit.

They walked in the rain together, among a torrent of wet dead leaves, wind tugging their hair back on their scalps, rain in their mouths and the smell of dead earth. Little splashes of mud coming up on to the rim of his corduroy trousers, and congealing hard. Rain falling from the elms. The vicarage with its damp red stone sweating water and the limp trees smoking round it. Her icy hand stuck inside his coat for warmth, burrowing like a mole through his red pullover, his shirt, his vest. Icy contact with skin!

They walked together in the rain, across the long meadow, in heavy grass, their footsteps cutting a long trail of fallen rain-drops, until they reached the long last lichgate on Trimmer's Hill. Crouched on the wet gate, hooking their heels in the bars to keep them balanced in the wind. He spread his mackintosh over them both, and under its shelter they smoked cheap fags and sat silent. Below them, half a county curved away to the sea, laced with lines of road and hedge, toned here and there with long tracts of woodland. Cars spinning along the shining black lines in a flutter of water, like wild geese dragging their toes along the surface of a lake. Small cars like uncouth baby bears, and coloured monsters as well, but all in a flutter of rain-water.

Then the long race back to the cottage. The gate with the latch that stuck. Ruth dancing about impatiently while he wrestled with it. Indoors, Dolly, the rosy farm-girl, had built up the big log fire and laid tea. Fresh bread from town, butter from Dail's farm, icy milk with three fingers of cream on the top. Honey, muffins, toast. Stampede in the great flagged kitchen, slipping out of their sodden clothes and shoes into dressing-gowns and slippers while Dolly poured the tea.

Rain again, lashing the windows, scuttling in the gutters. The fire smoking blue and crackly. Sparks, gold-starred, flashing along the tough forest wood. Drops of resin, burning blood bright, falling from the wood in a pother of smoke, hissing among the embers. Butter and resin, warm slippers, toast, the rain falling outside, and Ruth. Oh quick, draw up the long couch to the fireplace, and put the tea-table beside it. Pull the curtains across the big bay-window to blot out the rain and the closing darkness. Ruth gobbling the muffins with the melted butter running at the corners of her mouth. Kiss the warm buttery mouth and slip your fingers inside the warm blue dressing-gown at her breasts. The slow even bumping of her heart at your fingers. Capricious metronome. The delicate mechanism faulty; quiet heart ticking itself away into the silence, consuming itself, consuming him, consuming this rapt world of toast, wood-resin, warmth in slippers, butter mouths, breasts, loveliness, stars at night, and the wake of liquid nightingales which sang in the elm all summer. Everything being poured out and consumed by just this inexorable movement. Systole, diastole. The dance of life in the imperfect body. And her rich mouth and breath, fit to blow in the nostrils of an aeon of lovers. O God, O God, I know that my Redeemer liveth. Kiss the yielding mouth again in silent panic. Squeeze the small breasts again until they hurt.

> *O to forget this gnawing memory*
> *That where I have invested love is only*
> *Perilous and woundable frail flesh. . . .*

And Ruth, for the moment not thinking, not noticing his fear, not allowing her own perpetual fear, saying: 'Tell the girl to light the candles, will you? The bitch always forgets.' And the wrinkles that ran along her nose, drawing up the fine mockery of her smile.

Soft lamplight on them both now. Candles in a long iron stick, and one softly radiant oil-lamp. Feet spread in luxury before the fire. The infinite quiet, the infinite rest. Mouth to mouth it was no good in the silence; they would be masks moving each to each. The torsion of subcutaneous muscles, the shape of the eyes set back against the brown forehead. The mouth as senseless to his want as the rubber lip-mask of a dentist's gas-apparatus. Only that chill, half-second's pause before orgasm, when the skins trembled and tangled like a pouch of snakes together, when the voice broke haunting in among the summer nightingales and the dogs, rattling their chains and barking at nothing, only that moment, above all others, held the mystery. Then she was lost in himself. Not the daily and imperfect osmosis of ordinary life. Feeling percolating through a membrane. In that moment the walls were broken down, and the fluid rushed together, like the meeting of seas.

But what did she know of these fascinating abstractions as she sat, trying to pretend that she did not know that he was staring at her: with her stockinged toes curled under her, reading herself into a doze? For himself, in an amputated world, there was only the slow crumble of toast in his mouth. The warmth crawling over his feet on the coloured carpet and up his legs. Little draughts and eddies of air in the room behind him. Dust on the shelf of books. A cheque for thirty pounds on the mantelpiece and a letter from Garland saying: 'Do you mind selling your soul? You do it well. This last tune of yours is good. As I see it you'll be rich before long. *Ecstasy to be in Love* is still selling mildly. But I anticipate bigger things from this one, *Never come Back.*' Does one mind selling one's soul? Does one mind anything when she is trying to pretend that she does not see me looking at her with grave eyes? Why can't I weep? And his diary.

So many abstractions in that one brown face, and the eyes moving like synchronized insects along the lines of black type. So many faces in one face. If I sit down and try to write of her the thoughts fly into splinters, and my brain numbs, while the images of her fall across my body like burning rockets. These very white, senseless, bloodless typewriter keys refuse to chatter of her. They become so many dissimilar white faces of her. Let me count them. Thirty-two keys to her, and all lost, all sterile and lost by words. Yet one goes on, for no discoverable reason except this insane desire to make oneself real, to understand the splintered mirrors in oneself, and through oneself to reach out for that twin world, whose discovery is lost in a single second of two bodies in friction, heeling over like toy balloons whose strings have snapped, heading for the spaces among the planets.

'Forget these dreary milestones, the commas, the hyphens, the exclamation marks, the colons, the full stop which lies at every sentence, whether it has the flux and ecstasy in it, or whether it is some drab and meaningless cliché, down-at-heel, sucked dry like old orange skin, and tossed into the mind's limbo as soon as comprehended. Open and close the inverted commas, though the words of her mouth can never reach another mind except through perhaps some turn, some artifice, which another's words place over them. Reality of her, I suppose, must run like a thread in a worn carpet, here and there bright, visible and new. The carpet slippers of old men, the dust of ancient ankles have blotted out most of it, will blot out the rest. Even these banal lines can only blow across the mind like a casual scent of March flowers, soon lost, soon disseminated, and the breath of a lover's mouth in darkness on your tongue, becomes for an instant her breath, significant. Otherwise we meet across acres of ink, of paper, of corrections, ink blue, red, green, violet, vermilion, ink running in the veins of the head, the mouth gushing ink in poetry, the hearts of our lovers filling, pausing, gushing ink again into the body to complete the endless circuit. I think if I took a bright knife to you, my darling, and split the artery which bulges above your elbow, your arm would spout ink like a tiny fountain, running across my wretched papers, across the wretched type-heads of this machine which tries and tries to hammer out an image of you; one hard medallion of you on to the senseless paper. Perhaps when I kiss you, your mouth is only wet with ink, where I have pressed shapes in you, printed my own longing indelibly across your body, hammered these dancing type-heads into your very pith. . . .'

But the playing-card of their last Autumn had more than one face on it; or rather, the faces changed, merged, swapped. Dolly, with the red cheeks and the hefty loins, Dolly the dour potential baby-maker who could not marry until old Vole skipped into his coffin. What a four-foot tyrant the old man was, hovering on the edge of the grave!

And the big stout harness-maker's son, with his blue eyes fixed long-ingly on the old man's second daughter. They courted now. One could see them on Sunday, holding raw red hands, dressed in their best (he in a black suit, she in a red dress), standing like rooted stumps by the cornfield gate, immobile, gazing with a queer gentle puzzlement on the earth bursting into life. The atmosphere would go thin some time, and cut them like knives, and goad them to action. So gentle they were, so puzzled, with the mud sticking to the soles of their heavy shoes. Their desire, one felt, if it ever got hold of them, would submerge the whole household, would sweep away all the furniture of old Vole's life; all the gimcrack paraphernalia which helped him to maintain his autoc-racy over the female.

The kitchen range, with its stirring pots and pans over the bright fire, the mantelshelf with its two sere photos of an ice-age Mr. Vole and his big-fingered, now-dead wife. The little tea-caddy, with green and gold patterns on it, in which he kept his shag. The guns hanging up on the wall. The cherrywood stick behind the door. The sink where the thick cheap plates were washed up. His innumerable soiled waistcoats in the bedroom. *Whitaker's Almanac.* A shovel. Boots like iron, whose toes had curled upward with damp, and to whose soles hung the dry mud of a hundred winters. His little insect hands, finger and thumb dredging his waistcoat pocket for loose matches. His feet on the fender. Dolly herself, standing for an aeon over the sink, staring numbly out of the window across the farmlands, with a plate in one hand. The warm cattle, whose breath stirred one with its sweetness and volume: the loose black mouth of a foal she could take in her rough hand and kiss with great winsome smacks. All of this, one felt, would be swept away giddily, loosely on the torrent that waited to break forth from their stony bodies. Yet the flood never came. Old Vole, oblivious, could think of nothing but his crops and his bitter beer. Ruth would have liked to see him playing Noah, sailing away on the wrathful flood of his daughter's life. But the flood never came. To-morrow, I think, if it is spring or summer when you read this, you could go down and see them still there, Dolly and the red-faced youth, rooted by the edge of the cornfield, quite dumb, quite still, puzzled by the silence and calling of cattle. They will stay there until the first midges begin to bite her red arms. Then they will say good-night like wood-carvings by the edge of the corn.

So much for Dolly. But a half turn of the card in the light will give you the Rev. Richard Pixie, the parson. Here was a six-foot pixy, bowed down by the cares of religion, who called and was drearily friendly, in the name of our sweet Saviour, etc. He insisted on calling Ruth 'your wife'; though he knew they were living in sin, he still had some vague idea of helping them to avoid sinning in life. He would come so dreary, so weary, so lax, debile, anile, frustrate, gnawed, and unwind himself into a chair by the fire, stretching out his wretched black boots, and accepting cigarettes with both bony hands. He stank faintly of all the mouldering relics of his caste and occupation, much as the brick church smelt—of damp vegetables and flowers—after the harvest festival. He was a confirmed reader of the sporting page, supporter of the party policy, subscriber to conventions, coloured bathmats made of cork, mother's meetings, lads of the village brigade, football on the green. He did not even preach his own sermons and give one the chance to have some fun at his expense. He read them out of a book. He had never heard of Donne, piles, the Reformation, Duke Ellington, the cosmic ray, Remy de Gourmont, Henry Miller. The top of his head was flat, matted with light red hair, the shape of a snake, or some reptile. Sometimes he brought his wife, sometimes he came alone. He seemed happier when he was with her, perhaps because the endless rushing of her conversation completely obliterated him, allowed him to take refuge in a corner by the fireplace. She was a thin woman, with a body like a pencil. Her mouth was a purse of solecisms which was continually tearing and allowing the clattering, bouncing stream of old pennies to run out among the company. Such a stream of coins, and every one old, with the face rubbed off it by long handling. Not one bright bronze newly-minted coin in the collection. Nevertheless out they all flowed, in the drab stream, rolling across the floor, hitting the legs of chairs, the wall. Stunned, one bent down and groped about for them, collected them. Handed them back to her and hoped for the best. Alas! within a moment, bang went the mouth of the purse, and out rolled the stream again, intolerably tedious.

She had big rough hands and slack breasts, long since laid up against her, useless: stacked like late autumn windfalls. Their only child, which had been named Maud Alexandria Helen Pixie, died when it was four. Since then they had had five dogs, Rufus, Whisky, Bill, Rufus and Whisky; two cats, Betty and Annie; and an Austin seven, which she had called Victor III, after her now deceased father, and on whose faulty tin bowels she spent her most cherished maternal treasures. She decarbonized it herself, cleaned it herself, mended punctures, recharged the batteries, fitted new rings when necessary, boasted about it, added up its insignificant mileages, painted the wings, corrected a slipping clutch, knitted it a radiator cover, and only used it when she had to. In spite of this, however, the bloody thing only went about once in every five times.

Besides this occupation of hers, there was nothing else worth noticing. She showed a clear inch of petticoat under her dress when she walked, and left cigarettes in her mouth until they fizzled right away up under her nose, without touching them. But she once said to Ruth, looking significantly at her, as she got into the car: 'You'll regret all this one day, dear. Believe me, I KNOW.'

Now what in the name of heaven (as Ruth said) could that mannish tubular parson's wife know about 'all this?' Walsh was sure that the answer was one of the largest zeros ever drawn. Nix. Nothing. He had a good eye for the symbols of private tragedy, and once, when the vicar was showing him the excellence of the interior architecture of his home, he had penetrated the fastness of the bedroom, and let his eye wander across all those signposts to domestic decay.

Pixie obviously gargled in permanganate before going to bed. On the shelf above the wash-basin were two identical tooth-mugs, each holding a spare set of witty false teeth. An atomizer for Pixie's tonsils. A corn-cure. Embrocation for the lady's rheumatism (probably the result of lying out all winter on the damp garage floor under the Austin). A prayer-book; a cheque-book; a bank-book; a *Daily Mail Year Book*; a Bible, and a collection of unpleasant male neck-refuse—collar studs. A photograph of a Herculean maiden aunt suggestively flanked by a print of the Colosseum. Two pairs of worn slippers. In the corner, with the dust thick on them, a pair of fantastic skates. Obviously the domestic ice had never been firm enough for him to skate on. Perhaps the way was effectively barred by the shelf full of preliminaries—permanganate, Milton, Sloane's, and the atmosphere of Swift's lady's dressing-room. Over the bed-head, on the wall, was a text, such as one sees in hikers' hostels: *The Lord is my Shepherd.*

At any rate, then, the Pixies were honest enough to admit each night, as they went to bed, that they were sheep. The good shepherd protect them, and keep his fingers out of the mincer, and his wife out of the mangle, for I have done with them.

Trigger, I suppose, was much the same—but in a different way. He was the village doctor; very large, heavy, with a face full of pores the size of pin-heads, and a fan-shaped ginger moustache which seemed an absurd Edwardian relic fixed on a face that was medieval in its obesity. The face was the face of a Renaissance prelate, the voice was the voice of Gargantua. One could imagine him eating pilgrims with the salad and not noticing them. His laugh was infectious, rousing, under the fan of whisker. His great paws were always full of chilblains, and smelt, (*a*) of absolute alcohol, or (*b*) of embrocation. The folds of his tweed shooting-coat swung wide as he walked, spreading a faint damp whiff of tobacco, lint, spring onions, and damp dead pigeons.

His life was built on two passions: killing and curing. When he was not indulging either of these he was bored with a terrible annihilating boredom. When there was a long spell of saving life ahead of him, he would go out with his gun, and shoot the stuffing out of every man, woman or child in sight, by way of compensation.

Trigger was majestic. In the simplicity of his tastes; in the crudeness of his ideas; in the sparseness of his opinions; in the profound singleness of his purpose. While the philosopher was meditating; while the fakir was sitting on a trolley-full of pins; while the poet was fulminating, the painter daubing, the pedant, like an elderly hen, scratching around the barren mud of his natural backyard, the letter page of *The Times Literary Supplement*——Trigger had quietly and with system arrived at simplification of life which defeated them all.

They used to go out a lot together, he and Walsh (the latter with an old twelve-bore he hired from Vole), and rough-shoot across the parklands. The squire had given Trigger permission to shoot where and when he liked. Explaining this, Trigger said significantly: 'I once treated him successfully for constipation, y'know.' Quite seriously, with his discoloured blue eyes fixed fiercely on a hedge from which something might be put up by the sound of their boots in the mud, or his own loud voice.

Walking across country, stopping for a rest and an occasional cigarette, one could find out a lot about Trigger's passion for medicine; in the consulting-room, at the sick-bed, in the surgery, one could not get him to talk of anything but shooting. His mind hinged into two watertight compartments, which functioned, as it were, inversely.

'And look'ee, my lad,' he said one day, as they skirted the long meadow by Dail's Farm to get some rabbits, 'don't go expectin' any bills from me, 'cause I won't be sendin' you any, see?' He cleared his throat loudly and hawked. 'Young Ruth is worth mints to me in a dead practice like this. Mints. Nothing but greenstick fractures and scarlet fever to keep me busy. And old Verey's piles. I ought to be paying you.'

For all his adoration of Ruth he could never quite see her as a person or, for that matter, imagine anyone else doing so. She was a 'dooced interestin' case'. One felt that he could see her only through the transparent walls of a test-tube. But it would have been intolerable had he been one of those grave, sententious, mourning cockroaches, which batten on death.

No, Trigger was some sort of gent, in a peculiar way of his own. A mixture of rube and gent which it would not be difficult to find anywhere in England. Tact, as far as he was concerned, was non-existent.

'Know anything about surgery of the heart?'

'No. Nothing at all.'

This, while they were sitting under an elm on the further slopes of Trimmer's Hill, in the grass of a long meadow, with a dead pigeon beside them. Walsh squinted along the black barrel of his gun, turning it now on this target, now on that. He held a cartridge to his nose and inhaled the fine smell of a past explosion. The pigeon had a strange green membrane over its eyes. Its beak dripped eloquent bright blood.

'Dooced fascinating game. I read of a case the other day of a fifteen-year-old. Mitral stenosis and regurgitation. Bloke laid open the heart by a flap job. Clamped the bottom of the appendix. Couple of sutures shoved in, appendix incised and pulled over his finger like a glove. He found he could poke around inside the auricle as much as he liked. Amazing, what? He found that stenosis wasn't too bad, valve wasn't as thick as he thought, so he just stretched the damn thing with his finger. Ligature, and there you are. Chest-flap closed. There you are. What do you make of that, eh? Amazing, what?'

'Amazing.'

'But, I mean, really amazing what they can do to one these days, what? I mean, it's amazing when you think of it?'

'Amazing.'

Trigger contemplated infinity with his cigarette burning away under the tabby fan of moustache. His paunch rested comfortably against the inner wall of his plus-fours, his hands were plumply spread-eagled to support the weight of his body thrown back. The grass was very damp. Sideways, Walsh could see the slight prognathous starting of his underjaw, fixed in an attitude of concentration. The whites of his eyes were discoloured by fine veins such as one sees in those rich Blood Royal children's marbles.

Several times he called with his car to take Ruth into town to the laboratory of a friend of his. His gallantry was profound and a little embarrassing. His laughter set up pin-point answering vibrations in the elms, in the dead leaves along the ditches, in the trembling nerves of the girl herself, in his own hanging suit of clothes, heavy with damp tobacco and pigeon smells. His big teeth shone their yellow film of cigarette-stain, and the veins twinkled around the circular blue vent of meaning, the iris in each eye. Trigger was being tactful. In the cold his laughter clouded into jets of uproarious steam as it left his lips, ringing like a spade on the frosty earth. His hands were blue meat, heavily chilblained.

The girl in her rough tweeds and black beret, perched beside him on the front seat like a substantial bird, could feel the cold thrill of leather run along her thighs; could smell the warm engine smell; and could smile among red cold lips as the car gathered way down the lane, among the plundered trees—cold algebraic patterns on the dark sky—across the shivering countryside into winter; into the winter which closed on her like the cold black wooden lid of a coffin. Sometimes, as he turned his head and looked at her, hunched and queerly male in the seat beside him, he was flushed with a queer bright emotion that was half fear and half pity. There she was, after all, beside him, with her brown socked legs stretched out under the dashboard, smoking his cigarettes. How strange the eyes of the girl when she turned to him! The light fell slowly, deeply into them; they showed strange moods, half-flickers, dyings of colour. The moist lips shaping themselves about a cigarette. The broad thinning curve of eyebrow, hooding the secret nose, evasively wrinkling its laughter upward.

Ah well! It was a different Trigger who could stand, in white X-ray guards, watching the ray turn her bloodless; a spindle of bones in a white jelly. He was admiration itself for her afterwards. I think, if he had been able, he would have put her into a little test-tube, labelled it, and contemplated her with reverence and adoration for the rest of his days. Men have strange goddesses. Ruth as Ruth only existed in pieces: minute spaces of feeling in acres of objective vision. She was only real to him thus, as a marrowless framework of transparent bones, swimming in jelly, a machine which symbolized the only mystery which was real to Trigger. To his own way of thinking this was Love.

Walsh would never go on these expeditions, though the girl pleaded with him once or twice to go with them. He knew that his own lack of composure would startle them both, would annihilate that reticence between himself and Trigger on which their relationship was based. Trigger might come awake with emotions too barely uncomfortable, sentiments too threadbare to stand his vocabulary. He would go instead for a walk, dropping in on his way home at Tarquin's cottage. Tarquin was the schoolmaster.

Sitting in the threadbare armchair, puffing his pipe, with his feet crossed at the wide fireplace, he would be again amazed at the huge, bald, gentle cranium of his host; the twists of silver at his ears. The mild eyes, almost olive-purple, with their fine lashes. The ease with which one could escape, as it were, through Tarquin, to ages long past, to traditions, pomps, splendours, colours, pageants, against which his own age appeared shabby, bigoted and mean. Tarquin was interesting because he was a splendid medium: through him one could reach history. No, it was more than that, for Tarquin *was* history. The perfect refugee to whom any age was more immediately accessible than his own, he lived between the fireside and the long shelves of dusty books, which fed his insatiable taste for the living death. The ghosts of Greek boys, more real to him than ever Walsh could have been, haunted the low windows of the cottage; sandalled strangers from the dusty Ionian waited in the porch, respectfully alive in the precious music of his voice. Tarquin had drifted for centuries down the vivid Nile, among a pageant of barges, with his attendant Nubians, black shining midnights, while the long spokes of moonlight cartwheeled the still waters and sunk in the smoky flare of torches. Women more delicate than Cleopatra had been his abstractions, with the shift of light along unguents, resins, salves; the fume of balsams hung in his nostrils. His feet had been laved in lotions more purely astringent than grape-juice or the rank liquid pith of olives. He had been disembowelled by Ptolemaic embalmers, cured and mummified, and had risen again on the third day. The colonnades of white Mediterranean villas had heard his slow footsteps, pausing in peripatetic meditation; Lucretius had bathed with him; Epicurus kissed him as a brother. The long blue Ionian nightfall, splintered by lights among stone columns, had given him the vision of Greek women, ripe as marble, natural as fruit to be plucked, lingering among the shadow of the waters, laughing upon the mouths of the young men. The high-riding disc of full moon showed the leaning, falling torsos of young men, swerving down into the spray, with the laughter drifting up on the spice-ladened air: mimosa sweetening the still air across the bays and islands, and the girls with pomegranate flowers in their mouths. Tarquin kept these images of his life stored in that deep, shining cranium of his. As he talked his long hands released the stem of his briar, and built up the cool breathing statues for you—bodies of the young men now dead, and Greek girls.

Quiet and precise he was, while his language was as sure and cold as the technique of a lapidary, as he snipped away at the cold pebbles of thought. But the light shone in and through him, in a shaft of clear thought illuminating lost ages. His talk had the quality of some ancient and unhappy epigram, written by an anonymous lover to a lover as anonymous, holding all the bright and eloquent pain—eloquent as the bright blood dripping from the nose of the dead pigeon—of an age dead, but still strong enough to wound us. His Love was different from Trigger's, but as poignant.

December came in that last year like a long breath of cold from one of the poles, settling frost along the farmways, the pumps, icing the bare trees, leaving a white finger under the dripping taps. The fruit was all laid up in the lofts at Dail's, snug with straw, and a log fire blazed all day in the little hall. Dolly's arms had become red and raw with cold as she walked among the steamy breath of cattle. At night, lying with Ruth beside him in the bed upstairs, watching the cold distant flicker of headlights on the arterial road tinting the raftered walls, he could feel the season closing down on them like a suit of ice; could hear the ringing stamp of hooves on the rimy track which ran behind the cottage. The strawberries were laid under straw. At night the candles beside their bed winked and smoked in the cold draughts of air from the tiny window. The season was gathering its forces to sweep them both away in a whirl of snowflakes, into an eternity. The blood was slow in their veins, black arterial rivers congealed along the body's canals, now viscid and almost still: like the desire. Laid up under straw like the scented apples in the loft, whose fragrance drifted down from time to time to them as they lay in the stupor of half sleep. Why had they need to make provision for next years' cider? All this was a remote world, in which the real poignancy was numbed; a world of ice, spiked crowns of thorns, dead rotten leaves, shadows of bare trees now innocent of birds, fires guttering below the chimney-pieces, candles in raftered rooms, cold breaths on their cheeks. In the darkness, in the pale shadows of winter along the walls, in the light of lanterns, among the scented steam of animals' breaths in byres, sheep moaning beside fiery thorns, what room, what feeling was there left for the sharp spikes of death or desire or loss? In darkness their breathing mouth to mouth (so far between bodies, so distant the space between planets of flesh!) was the breathing of white cadavers already, laid in the velvet-lined caskets of a remote charnel-house. No longer they had electric lips, eyes, knees, loins: but only the cold mesh of veins, running cold and heavy with the dark blood. At night she would read to him in that clear voice, ringing like a shadow of truth among the truths and falsehoods of other ages; while he, with his hands folded across his still body, his eyes closed, saw too deeply into the mysteries of her personality ever to weep, or grudge her the natural deceptions she held before him. The candles burned away on the pages of their books. The voice of winter was vague with warning. For his own part, beyond deception, evasion, beyond the talk and trembling, the lies and happiness, with a hard serene conviction he knew the end: with a conviction as cold, stern, as the rim of ice which had formed across the lake, he knew it all. He could hear her reading without emotion now, while the candles beat down their tracks of gold across her throat and her moving lips, and the small breasts in her dressing-gown.

'Every revolution which the sun makes about the world divides between life and death; and death possesses both those portions by the next morrow; and we are dead to all those months we have already lived, and we shall never live them over again: and still God makes little periods of our age. First we change our world, when we come

[218]

from the womb to feel the warmth of the sun. Then we sleep and enter into the image of death, in which state we are unconcerned in all the changes of the world: and if our Mothers or our Nurses die, or a wild boar destroy our vineyards, or our King be sick, we regard it not, but during that state, are as disinterested as if our eyes were closed with the clay that weeps in the bowels of the earth.'

The heavy blankets which covered them so warmly might have been the layers of sod, cut finely and shaped by the patient spade of the old sexton. In the dark the walls of the great upper room shrank down to the dimensions of a six-foot coffin. Yes, raising the pads of his fist he could beat and beat on the polished walls of the blackness that was obliterating them both, until there was no reason or sense left in his breathless, stifled mind: only the doom hung over him like a curtain and he was inarticulate.

For a time the frost scouted for the season. A St. John the Baptist time, with bright berries on the hedges, robin vermilions fluffed on every paling, like financiers puffed with wrath at an economic winter. A St. John the Baptist time, minus scrip, locust and wild honey, but vivid with berries and hungry sparrows crowding for food. They walked together down among the crisp spikes of grass, by the lakes, and watched the ice crust over. A blue membraneous scum first over the eye of the water: then green, muddy black, like a gangrened wound. And then the steel surface upon which the feet of the wild duck found no purchase. All night long the wind ruffled the woods. The noise of stones flung on the ice by passing farm-boys squeaked away, diminishing, into the further woods, across the iron-bound fences, northward. The winter had been announced.

One night when Dolly went into the yard for wood it was snowing in large velvety tufts. Ruth and Walsh watched from the upper window when they went to bed. All distance had vanished, had been broken down by this manna. Columns of turning, tossing, leaning whiteness drifted out of heaven like feathers out of a sack, settling easily upon the cowed world. There were no stars, no planets, no signs, no wonders, no orange comets, not even shapes material evolving laboriously through this soft pile. They were quite alone now, in a sunk world of snow, penned in a little house among woods and hills which existed only in their memories. Four hands over a dead fire, and all the candles low.

Episodes of decay. Numb feet in boots on the snowy road. Sunlight so watery that when Ruth breathed across the window a rainbow sprang from her mouth across the light, a slanting prismatic portent in a deep curve. Perhaps a pot of treasure at the end of it. Largesse as gold as urine. Hands, bright hands and flushed cheeks nestling in wool. Hands kneading snowballs. A parcel of dribble-nosed schoolboys on the way up to Tarquin. One orange-haired imp with bloody knees, pressing bruised hands in his armpits, blowing on his nails to warm them, after a fall on the frosty road. The snow put deep shadows on the world, in the corner of the bedroom, across the walls like webs. Looking out across the garden, like seeing a negative of a known photograph. Christmas card December. Signals of ice hanging in delicate fingers from a tree. The voice of birds quipping, a little shrill with cold, a little anxious with fear. The racket of milk-churns being loaded on to a six o'clock lorry. Episodes of decay. The old thumbed notebook of Ruth's which held all her poems.

> *'I am so plunged in you, God knows,*
> *There's no redemption but the falling,*
> *Spirals of terrible water, my princeling,*
> *Snatching the life of me, cold,*
> *Colours of water about me, calling. . . .'*

Wretched stuff, with here a line, there a line, skip a page, skim a page. Then suddenly,

> *'You are my only logic in the cold world.*
> *I, a graft to your tree, following, merging,*
> *Fruiting as you, flowering as you.*
> *The thorns of winter spike us both.'*

Poor bright pages with their tributes fluttering past under his thumbs like successive kisses. Out of one's mouth came the words. The frost made a witty steam of them.

A letter from Gordon, Ruth's brother, with a beautiful Greek stamp, and a pen-drawing of men drawing a boat up a sand-beach.

'It's silly to wish you a merry Xmas, isn't it? When the oranges are ripening slowly on the stalk, I mean, and the tangerines sport a green and yellow glaze like the finest porcelain. Occasionally the old man of the sea gets up, wraps the north wind round him and prowls down these coasts, havocking. Old man *maestro*. And then I think it's winter. But the olives aren't fully gathered yet, and the fishermen still skip barefoot into the water. Sun, life a long coma. No, I can't think clearly or continuously about you two. Are you happy? Please be happy as long as you can. Why don't you make a dash and come down to this Island? Coral and sea-gulls, sponges and octopus, and a patron saint who's represented by a decayed tibia. Please darling Ruth bring Walsh down south. I haven't seen you for such ages I don't know what you look like. Yes, it was a Greek girl in Athens, but it didn't last. We strained the litany of sensualities until our voices cracked. I don't care. I recuperate in a long sun-convalescence from a disease more lovely than T.B. Chastity like a pure dream, for ever and forever, as long as one sun lasts. And then? The rest is silence.'

Episodes of decay. Dolly proud of a ring on her red finger. Her mouth broad with slow, amazing laughter. Old Vole had consented. A robin found dead on the path. Pompous even in death, fluffed out its red stomach. Lying in Dolly's laughing hands. They put it on the fire and stoked the wood. The fiery bird. Robin into Phoenix. Would it be born again and vanish in a red ruft of flame up the wide chimney?

Then one night a snow-storm came down out of forests, with a big insane wind to guide it. Past midnight. The slow clock from a steeple sounding foggily through the blanket. Wind at the shutters, at the oak front door.

Something had happened in the field outside. Cattle trouble. Something dead in the long swirl of snowflakes. Lanterns shining out in a dim parade, and men's voices.

Inside it was so still he could hear himself thinking. Dust sleeping along the books. The oil lamps sleeping yellow. The yawn rising up in his throat. Feet sleeping along carpet slippers. The fire sunk to embers. The dead body of a book in his fingers.

Then the silence became so profound that thunder, or artillery leaping into action from the hills, could not have been more utterly paralysing. For a minute he was afraid to look at her face, as she lay on the long sofa, a book folded between her breasts. His breathing, the dim noise of voices, water-music from a tap in the kitchen, insects moving in the musty wood of the rafters, all insisted on the silence.

Looking, then, he saw Ruth staring away heavenwards, quite pleasantly remote, but terrifically motionless. Snap went a crazy spring inside the mechanical brain, quite cleanly and perfectly, without pain, but something like relief. His own fingers on a book, his cold thighs against the chair, his own breath flushing the lungs, infinite processes along the nerves coming into play. Light scorching his eyeballs. The mouth hung open from his face in concentration, dribbling. Casually, without urgency, formed the desire to urinate in his mind.

Episode in numbness. Standing in the stern of the big liner as it loped southward across a heavy sea, smelling the wide smells of salt water, scourged by the March winds.

People passing at his back. Talkers. The drive of the engines under his shoes. The clean sand-scrubbed deck. The long beautiful arches of spumy water, slipping away under them.

Off the shores of Portugal a flight of brown, queer-billed sea-gulls pulled out to meet them, ravenous, curving with a splendid velocity to the wash of peel, sticks, cardboard, bread, peelings, offal, soup, fish, meat, ham-fat and big-eyed potatoes.

When they were off Cadiz a wind swept the white horses out from the land at them, deploying beautifully. At night on the gusty dark upper deck you could swear you smelt the warm South coming nearer, ever nearer.

One night the wind, like an offering, brought them the smells of apples, guitars, neck-cloths, donkeys, dust, mimosa, jonquils, voices, garlic, desire.

Nevertheless the great ship, undistracted, nosed down Gibraltar way, through the neck, into the blue Mediterranean.

CHAPTER XII

ATQUE VALE

During the same week the weather, which had hitherto been so perfect, produced a few quirks and freaks from its repertoire. Waking one morning, Marlowe found that his bed was soaked in the rain which was beating down across the open window. An ugly wind dragged at the panes of glass and drove them chattering against their frames. Securing the window, he stood, his body glistening with water, and noticed that a great width of cloud hung above Leucothea, menacing the channel. Lightning slanted down out of the sky from time to time creating apocalyptic gulfs of blue light on the hillside, and the thunder followed it.

Below the villas the sea was piled up in furls of water, dashing now this way, now that, unable to decide upon which side of the channel to explode: while the seaweed in the bay was carried out in layers, like floating mats, and dumped on the end of the rocky headland. Such manifestations were inexplicable at this time of year.

The rain had ploughed gutters in the earth banks of the hillside. In the road itself were hundreds of puddles, spinning round and round in the wind, winking and bubbling. The air was crisply cold.

Breakfast that morning was a dull affair. Maria crept about her tasks like a whipped dog, muttering and crossing herself from time to time, when the lightning flashed. Her clothes were sodden on her and splashed with mud.

She served him that morning with an averted face, and a far-away look in her eyes that seemed half fear and half concentration on some distant event—perhaps the next flash of light, or beat of thunder. He did not speak but ate moodily, staring out across the tossing waters whose end was chipped off soft by the curtain of damp mist which hung down, obliterating the mainland. When he had finished he remembered that Francis had promised to show him some of her canvases before she roped them up, ready to send back to England. Wrapping several thicknesses of newspaper round his head and shoulders outside a thin mackintosh, he tugged open the door and ran down the steps to the road, leaving the muttering woman to close it after him. The first drag of the wind nearly pushed him off his feet, and the rain rapped holes all over his swathed head until the newspaper was pocked like a sieve. He could hear the olives moaning and dragging at their roots as he scuttled down the hill.

Huddled in the doorway of her villa, he rapped long and loud before Francis heard and came to open the door. He flung off his pulp of newspapers and pushed into the hall, shutting the wind-swung door with his shoulder.

'Heavens, what a day!'

'Appropriate for the business,' she said evenly, and led the way into a room where Gordon lay on the floor smoking.

'Hail to thee, blithe spirit,' he said sombrely, pleased with the pun. 'Is it still hailing outside?'

In the corner of the room stood half a dozen or so large canvases, loosely roped together, leaning against the wall. On request the girl undid the ropes and presented her productions one by one for his approval. They were pleasantly designed scenes from the life of the Island, for the most part carefully and cleanly painted. It was distracting, however, to attempt an appreciation of them when the light was so dull.

'Francis tells me she's going,' said Gordon slowly.

'Yes,' said Marlowe, still staring at the canvases, 'so she says.'

The girl stood by the window, expressionless, with a curious tension in her pose, turning now this canvas to him for approval, now that.

'Yes,' he repeated softly, concentrating.

The flashes of lightning silhouetted her long body across the running window-pane, livid.

'When are you leaving?' she asked at last, deliberately forcing herself to the question.

'I?' he said, surprised; and for the moment he had forgotten the haunting decision which demanded fixed dates and times for his movements. 'Not yet, I hope. Not for a bit at any rate.'

'What about the critical intelligence?' said Gordon. He got to his feet and stamped out his cigarette in the fender. As Marlowe opened his mouth to say something he turned and cut him short. 'Wait. Tell me something first. Don't you think there's a lovely sense of colour and design?'

'Yes,' said Marlowe carefully.

'Thank you. I must be going.'

From the corner, where he had flung them, Gordon produced a gigantic mackintosh cape and sou'-wester in which he proceeded to imprison himself. Then he said, with camaraderie: 'Well, you sods. So long. See you at the party.'

'Party?'

'She'll tell you all about it,' and he commenced his wrestling with the door. Putting a booted foot in the aperture, he inserted his face into the hall again and said, 'Marlowe.'

'Yes?'

'Try and convince her that she's got no feeling at all for the *form* of those bloody things. Not a trace. So long.'

Marlowe turned slowly as the door crashed to, and the noise of Gordon's running feet diminished from outside it. He went into the room where Francis sat uncomfortably on the couch, staring out at the lines of rain on the window-sill. Very expressionless and stiff was her pose. He sat down beside her silently, disinclined to talk.

She said slowly, with a half smile on her mouth, turning her head to him: 'Do you believe in omens?'

'No. Why?'

'Look at the rain.'

Looking out of the window, on the panes of which the water squeezed and trembled, he had the sensation of looking into the glass plating of an aquarium. Dim and liquescent, the fringe of trees and the background of churning sea slipped across their vision. Their ability to stand there, on one side of the glass, dry and untouched by the weathers, seemed almost as much of a fiction as the dark landscape outside.

'Omens?' he said nervously. 'What do you mean?'

'Gordon was at the wine-shop to-day and a peasant told him that bad weather at this time of year meant the death of somebody. Everyone is awfully upset in the village.'

'Oh,' said Marlowe, compressing his lips in a prim line.

'Yes. And Fonvisin had to go up to Leucothea again today because the old monk had a relapse. I expect he's properly caught in it.'

Somehow the darkness of that morning, the force of the storm, suggested something plausible and frightening about these beliefs. In the gulf of a thunder-clap his answer was swallowed up. He repeated his words as the noise rolled away:

'Do these things worry you?'

She turned to him with a smile. 'Lord no. But this weather depresses me. Doesn't it you?' He admitted that it did; and, realizing for the first time how weak and pointless it made his motives, his fears, his decisions seem, he was again cast down. On his desk he had left Fred's letter. The lightning would be flashing on it from time to time. He wanted to sit nearer to the girl for comfort; no longer to kiss her, for action so definite would commit himself; simply to sit near her so that their shoulders might touch, or their knees.

'What are you thinking about?' he said at last.

She was thinking of the vicarage at home, with daddy writing his sermons; the smell of damp; the cold rooms in which the fires had not been lighted. Mother sucking her teeth over her knitting. Andrew had died long since.

'Nothing,' she said.

'Nothing!' he echoed and got up, walking over to the window to stare out of it.

By leaning his head forward he could see at an angle down the hillside to the right. It was very melancholy. The rain jumped a foot from the road, furiously, and little water spouts were snatched up off the sea and whirled hundreds of yards before they dropped. The village looked deserted. The trees heaved and shook above the cluster of coloured huts.

'What about this party?' he said, wondering how appropriate revels would seem in such weather.

'Oh, that,' she said, almost contemptuously. 'That's one of the old man's ideas. Seems a good day for the *Ave atque Vale* business, doesn't it?'

⋙ ⋘

He [Rumanades] stood at the front door and shook hands with each of them as they passed, with his head down upon his chest, as if fearing to look at them. One by one they ran through the doorway into the rain, muffled in coats and papers, like curious grotesques: and each turned in the rain swept light of the doorway, cried out and raised a hand, and then was spirited away by his shadow. The old man stood, backed by the line of jumping candle-flames, gripping the shaking door and watching them as they were lost in the blankness, one by one. Their voices sounded from very far off, crying 'Good-bye,' and thanking him. The wind wrenched their garments out on their stooping bodies like wings. 'Good-bye,' they cried: the voices of Walsh, Marlowe and Francis.

He shut the door securely upon the weather, and, assuring himself that the servants were long since gone, walked from pillar to shadowy

[226]

pillar, blowing out the candles, until the hall was dark except for the lightning, and silent but for his own slow footsteps on the stone.

He mounted the stairs slowly, one by one, breathing hard, as if the effort needed were a great one. Somewhere in his mind he was searching for the idea which would govern his actions. He did not know what it was. Something was needed. Something was there at the back of his mind, which he must wait for: an agency which would direct him. This body of his walked in a dark trance of weariness and confusion, without direction, up the flight of stairs to the music-room. The candles dripped and dripped until he puffed them out, with a gesture like a kiss: and left the acrid smoke from burnt wicks hanging in the darkness. They were burnt right down to the black wood sockets of the sconces. He felt, of a sudden, very ancient and whimsical, and a little weary. With a quaint little smile he stopped and put his hand to the left breast of his coat, reassuring himself that his heart was still beating. A minute bumping communicated itself to his fingers. He gave a sniff of approval and pushed open the door of the music-room. The room was just as they had left it, with the lights still burning. His footsteps made very little noise upon the smooth wood floor.

He seated himself in the armchair, facing the dying fire, and with his face in his hands, concentrating. What was it he was waiting for? From where would it come? The occasional thunder seemed a hint of the nature of the things with which he was trying to establish contact in his mind. He waited in painful respect. Would it be a voice? As he waited he heard the sharp strokes of a bell wafted up to the house through the noise of the wind and rain. Uncertain, he went to a window, and drew the curtain across in the face of the lightning. The olives had gone mad, jumping and twisting, and flinging their bodies up, raving at the sky. Against the light from the window the rain fell in lemon showers. The dim straits were humped and twisted in dark torsion, and the waves in the blow-hole below Phaon beat like tomtoms. It was funny that all this energy should be let loose around him, and he, of all humanity it seemed, safe and dry from it, in his little ark of masonry and plaster. Noah must have felt like this, looking out from the ark as from a watch-tower across the immense waters of the world, snug and dry, but ineffably alone, with the soul weary in his old body, crying out for the symbol of a dove. The cypress trees, with an air of dignified lunacy, bent now this way, now, like pendulums, that, touching their toes. He gave a chuckle, and his eyes turned from side to side in his head, as he watched the landscape, start up at him and disappear again, swallowed by the night.

Again the sound of the bell. Running his dry tongue round his teeth, he stared out, trying to establish its identity in that world of chaotic sound. Illusion? Perhaps there was a fishing boat caught in the storm, and the priest was invoking the aid of the saint. Perhaps it was the bell in the church-tower.

There was a sharp sound of footsteps on the path of the house, retreating, soon lost; and then the bell sounded again, beating across the valley and up the slopes. He knew then that in the monastery on the top of Leucothea the old monk was dying, or already dead. He could imagine the dead man's familiar, distracted by the weather-symbols of judgement, dragging the long bell-rope which hung in the yard, his eyes closed against the stinging rain, his beard turned to the sky, crying out the warning of God to the valley, and to mankind. So the monk, after all, was dead. For some reason he felt cheered by the thought.

He drew the curtains together again, shutting out the view, and returned to the armchair, rubbing his hands together as he might have done after a successful business deal. The fire shone boldly on the glass bottles, though itself dying, and on the black piano. The fire was dying, the priest dead. Seating himself, he poured out a glass of the red wine, his especial favourite, which was brewed for him in one of the southern villages from grapes specially grown. Raising it he drank, letting the tepid sweetness of the liquid cling on his tongue, curdle along his palate, and send its fumes to his brain.

Sitting there, in all simplicity of mind, he contemplated his own death as something new and delightful; a divorce from the present which was perplexing, always perplexing, with its trivialities. Death, once beyond that partition of physical pain and fear, seemed to him made in the shape of his own desire. It would be a place of infinite understanding, in which there would be no bars for the roving intuition; everything would be open, and explored. Death must be a very spacious place, he heard himself think, in which so many heroes can be accommodated, so many mysteries solved. And thinking like this, in the warm first flush of exultation, he recalled to his mind all those things which before had done him hurt, trying to prove that the new strength was proof against them. As a man will press a bad tooth to see that it still hurts, he filled his mind with the unhappy things, but was at peace. Somehow the death of the monk had assoiled him and annulled his fear.

Still smiling, he got to his feet and blew out the candles. In the silent corridor he paused for a second, looking at the floor, and then went to Manuela's room.

The shutters were drawn, and the musty air lay warm in it, and dark. He groped his way across to the French window, with a sense of impish excitement, and unlatched the window, letting the rain beat in upon the expensive tiles, and the lightning flash down, lighting up the furniture—the great bed and its counterpane decorated with the phœnix, the polished wardrobe, the line of bottles on the dressing-table.

For a time he stood at the mirror, watching his own smiling face light up with every flash from the wide windows.

Presently he went to his own room, leaving the window wide and the lightning playing upon the silk phœnix.

That night Fonvisin could not sleep. Sick, wet and weary, he had got back to his room in the tavern to find that the roof was leaking on his bed; and that one wall had absorbed the water like sugar, until its surface was coated in large dark stains.

The frightened peasants refused to get up and do anything to help, so that he was obliged to move the bed to one side and sleep in it as it was.

Outside, he could hear the rain and the wind playing their duet, and lying there, in the damp sheets of the great bed, he ground his teeth in rage and annoyance. He too heard the bell and wondered what it was; he did not think of the monastery at Leucothea, or the monk. Putting one arm over his eyes, he tried to sleep, but the dinning of the rain on the tin roof pierced his consciousness like riddling machine-gun fire. The lightning shone even through his closed eyes. From time to time he was partially successful, sinking into a troubled state of semi-coma, but no sooner would he find himself slipping into clear sleep than he would start up again at some sound, magnified by imagination or the imperfect functioning of sense. A bough of a tree beat and beat against the loose panes of glass in the window.

It seemed to him as he lay there that, sleeping, his mind was full of a nervous expectation, which these sudden wakings dispelled. There was something, just beyond the reach of his mind, which was tantalizing him with a message. What it was he could not tell.

Presently it seemed to him that he was being called, though from where and by whom or what he could not tell. Across his closed eyes flowed a stream of disconnected images which gave him no clue. Sleep. He must sleep. He was still feeling sick.

It seemed to him then that the face of the old monk rose up out of the darkness at his bedside, with an expression of demoniac concentration on it. The old lips were drawn back angrily talking, while no sound came from them.

He reached forward to take the old man by the arm (for he should have been lying down, resting, not walking about in the rain) and found his own fist clutching vacancy. Immediately a cock crowed and he heard Walsh playing the piano. He reached out for the matches which lay on the chair beside his bed and lit a candle, thinking that these impressions must be produced by overdrinking and weariness. For a little while he sat, propped up in bed, reading, and then dozed off again, to the accompaniment of rain and the rapping at the window. The bell rang again, once, twice, in his dream, and, when he had begun to think that he was too far gone in sleep to be worried any more by the quirks and inconsistencies of his mind, he saw a sudden picture of the lightning flashing along the white sides of the Villa Pothetos. A voice said: 'What was that?'

'Nothing,' he croaked with a dry throat.

'There's something wrong.'

'Nothing,' he said again.

'In the light there.'

'Nothing, I tell you. Nothing.'

A black panel seemed to slide away before his eyes to show Francis and Gordon dancing round and round, madly, while above him, truncated, the figure of Marlowe laughed loudly. He laughed himself and dipped his fingers in the wine-glass, tilting his head and letting the drops run on to his tongue. They burnt like an acid. As he did so there was a sudden confusion outside, a door was pushed open, and a voice said: 'For Christ's sake, Fonvisin, for Christ's sake.'

He had hardly realized he was awake before he found himself out of bed, in the centre of the floor, putting on his clothes in great haste. Taking the matches, he ran down the passage and out into the night.

Out in the rain, for a moment the impulse which had been directing him seemed suddenly lost. He ran twenty yards down the road, and then halted, panting, in the shade of a tree. Drawing his coat round him, he felt the water spinning round his boots in the roadside puddles; the rain drilling his coat with spots of wetness. It was a terrible night and he cursed it, looking up to the sky and shouting in the face of the wind. As he waited he knew that the impulse would return and govern his actions.

All of a sudden he was off again, running heavily in his big boots, this time in the direction of the Villa Pothetos, without hesitation, and certain in his own mind of the direction. He crashed up the path, stumbling among the loose stones, and swearing as his footsteps threw up splashes of moisture on to his calves.

At the edge of the plateau he stopped and listened, holding back his own gusty breath to enable him to hear more clearly. Nothing. Only the wind in the cypresses. He stumbled on, his hands stuck in his pockets, his hat pulled down over his eyes.

As he came out of the crowding shrubbery he happened to glance upward, and knew what his forebodings had tried to tell him in their imperfect way.

It was like this:

The French window was wide open, and the room behind it bright with electric light which cut a broad yellow swath on the darkness. On the terrace stood the old man, naked, holding the parapet with both hands. He was staring out to sea with a fixed and gentle concentration which nothing could shake. Even the ugly lightning could not make him flinch. He looked very nice and naïf standing there, his naked body pouring with rain, and the drops hanging in his sodden beard.

Fonvisin called, Fonvisin whooped, Fonvisin danced about on the path raging at him, but it made not the slightest difference. He stood, looking out at the tormented sea, moving his lips very silently as if repeating a prayer.

Seeing it was no good, the Russian ran round the side of the house to the front door, swearing. The door refused to open, so he drove his fist through the coloured glass panel, and, shoving his arm in, unbolted it. The hall was dark territory which he crossed in a couple of bounds. Up the staircase he went in the dark, not thinking to switch on the lights which must then have been working. He burst into Rumanades' room and ran to the old man's side, putting an arm on his shoulder, his mouth drawn up in anger. The skin was wet and cold, and unresisting.

'Come,' he said imperiously, and the old man, turning, wavered, as a tree wavers before it falls, and put his arms across the Russian's shoulders. He was very happy in a gentlemanly way.

Once inside the room (the few steps took him an age to accomplish, even with the Russian's help), he leaned sideways with one hand on the dressing-table, looking mildly at his own reflection in the glass. He began to tremble slightly and his teeth to chatter in his mouth. He seemed vaguely reproachful, and his lips still moved very slowly.

Fonvisin forced him down on the bed and, seizing a rough towel, enveloped him in it and began to curry his pleasant old body, hissing between his teeth like a groom at work.

'What . . . did . . . you do that . . . for?' he grunted at last, towelling the bony back. And the old man sitting there quietly, jogging his body about under the roughness of the Russian's fingers, only smiled sweetly, as one who does not properly understand, and scratched his neck.

'The rain,' he said at last, like a child between ecstasy and wonder. 'It was only the rain.' And he drew a deep shuddering breath from the very bottom of his lungs and lay back softly with his mouth twitching among his beard.

Fonvisin left him there, on the bed, and ran down the corridor, switching on the lights as he went. In the music-room the bottles of wine and spirits lay in different places, where the party had left them, and running here and there, he found a bottle of brandy, lying on its side half empty, in Gordon's chair. He grabbed it and, taking a wine-glass in the other hand, went back to give the old man a stimulant.

He opened the door, only to find the bed empty, the covers laid back. The window he saw at a glance was still as he had left it, fastened shut, but the other door into the corridor was wide open. He dropped the glass and the bottle on the bed and ran back into the passage. Empty. Looking down from the head of the stairs he saw the old man below him, walking down with great slowness and caution, chuckling as he did so. It was a splendid joke.

Fonvisin skipped down the flight and caught him up, talking to him as one would to a child. He carried him back to his room and put him in the bed, soothing the hair of his brow with his own hard hand.

'Ha. Ha,' said old Rumanades playfully, and began to cough inside himself.

'Now you stay where I tell you,' said Fonvisin roughly, wondering whether his forehead was hot enough for him to have a temperature. 'That's right.'

He went into Manuela's room and with great difficulty managed to bring her precious bed in and place it beside that in which the old man lay. Then, slipping off his sodden clothes, and taking a sip of brandy, he crawled in between the delicious sheets, and prepared himself to doze beside his patient.

The night passed very slowly, and by the time the first faint inches of dawn had reached the sky behind the hills of the mainland, the rain had slackened off a bit, and the thunder had slowly begun to roll southward.

Once or twice the old man woke and, sitting up in bed, gave a short, discursive and intelligible lecture on the flora and fauna of the island. And once Fonvisin woke to hear him weeping away to himself, snuffling under the bedclothes, and talking in snatches to a woman. By four o'clock, however, he had sunk into deep insensibility. At six, to his own and (subsequently) everyone else's surprise, he was dead.

Very weary, and with a foul taste in his mouth, Fonvisin lurched over to the window and unfastened it, intruding his bleary and drink-smelling carcase on the morning. The air was sweet as spring water, and the scents which the storm had crushed out of the flowers and foliage came up to the balcony in great whiffs like incense. To the east was the omnipassionate morning, opening its rifts of blood upon the water. The air was bitterly cold. From the east the light opened in long chinks and filters of wounded red, as if the morning were a pomegranate, casually prized open by the childish world.

In the hills the water still flooded the banks of the springs, sucking at the stones, skipping the rock-torrents. The shepherds, still fearful of snow, drowsed in their sheepskin cloaks. The sun which must be shining on the domes and minarets of Constantinople would soon shine for them too.

Nearer, there was the rough sound of footsteps on the road below

[233]

the house. A man in a coloured smock, yawning, passed on his way to the village, praising the light. Fonvisin called to him, telling him to take the news of Rumanades' death to Christ. As he talked he found himself smiling and stretching his arms, gulping in the icy air, purging his weary and dirty body. The man crossed himself and, dropping his spade, ran down the hill with tears on his cheeks to call the priest and deliver the message. Fonvisin turned back into the room, laughing with tenderness at the morning, and patted the dead cheeks of the old man, saying: 'Now if you don't mind, I'll have a bath.'

He bathed at leisure, and, when the priest came, made him wait in the room while he dressed. The poor man was snivelling with cold, and aching in every bone with rheumatism and the fear of death. They sat on the bed beside the dead man and drank what remained of the brandy, while Fonvisin neatly disposed the slack limbs and performed all the necessary duties.

The priest stood for a long time at the window, saying: 'Death is a terrible thing. It comes so suddenly. Death is a terrible thing.' But he drank his brandy to the last drop and enjoyed it as a creature should.

While the priest prayed loquaciously at the white bedside, Fonvisin stood on the balcony consumed with the freshness and tenderness of everything, humming to himself an old song which he had not sung since he was a child. In the village the dogs had begun to bark, and a man's voice shouted something, indistinct. From the bay came the tattering of an engine and in a few minutes Christ's boat came nosing out into the still choppy water, heading for Corfu. He had instructions to wire the news to Rumanades' lawyers in Athens, who would notify the dead man's relations, if, indeed, he had any.

The Russian folded his arms tight, gripping his fingers under the arm-pits with a kind of ecstasy to feel his own life so secure in his body; from somewhere deep inside him the laughter poured gently up through his lungs and his mouth, as if from some fountainous source of warmth and mellowness. The stone was wet with dew and the rain which still hissed along the wide gutters of the house. He put his arms inside the sleeves of his faded corduroy jacket, running his fingers along the newly washed flesh of his arms, so smooth and warm and hairy. Presently he went to Manuela's dressing-table and dashed sweet-smelling talcum on his freshly shaven jowls: and pinched a drop of eau de Cologne in his fingers before applying it to his nose as if it were snuff. Then back to the terrace again, to draw the icy morning into his very bowels and sing for well-being.

The priest came and stood beside him with a long face, telling him that the old monk had died in the night. It had been too wet to go up, but a shepherd had brought the news in at early dawn. At this Fonvisin laughed outright.

'It is a terrible thing,' said the man reprovingly, 'a terrible thing.'

'Yes?' said the Russian and turned to stare curiously at the grubby man, with his belly-to-earth mien, his tangled black hair, and his festering shoes. 'Yes?'

The priest returned to the dim room. The morning was too much for him. He knelt again, as one who was himself unworthy to perform the office. His beautiful voice, in tones of meek entreaty, began to pray for the spirit of the defunct Rumanades; the old man who lay there with many smiles on his mouth, enjoying some ancient and whimsical joke of his own.

It is a pity, thought Fonvisin, as he stood and watched the sun come up, that a corpse cannot laugh.

Presently Agathie came down the road, treading as proud as a peacock, with the pride which only that woman knows who has wearied and buried many husbands. Her skirt was prussian blue, spinning at her bare and lovely ankles, her loose blouse coffee-brown, with particoloured frills, and round her black and arrogant features she wore a vermilion head-cloth. In her left hand she carried a vast bunch of black grapes, with the dew still fresh on them; she sucked them one by one, spitting the pips grandly among the dust.

'God praise you, woman,' said Fonvisin in a deep voice, and intensely. 'Be happy. Your clothes are as beautiful as your body.'

She turned up her bold face and stood there for a while, speaking to him, with the whole richness of life and fertility moving in her strong body. Then she raised her hand in agreement, with a powerful gesture, and went down the road again, sumptuous in the sunlight.

The contract that they made, he standing on the balcony, and she below, with her face lifted to him, shall not be revealed. But he was satisfied, and later, walking down the road, he too flourished his body, turning its massiveness from side to side, feeling the power to move in his loins and the heavy muscles of his arm. He too stopped and broke himself a hanging bunch of black grapes, wet on the skins and cold, and eating them, tramped onwards, ripe as nut for life, and content.

CHAPTER XIII

THE CURTAIN

By tea-time that day, life for the five of them had resumed its normal rhythm; but it was soon to be altered. Vague and evanescent their plans had been, and this simple one-act death on the part of the old man would force them to reconsider the chances. They were all at once a dispossessed court, left without a succession to save them. To Francis it mattered least: she had been going away in any case. Death she could not try to understand. Being told of death so near, she had gone frozen and mute inside herself, avoiding everyone except Walsh. To Gordon death had not very much force. He spent the day at the Villa Pothetos with Fonvisin, interviewing the hordes of peasants who came from the distant villages to make a gift to the dead man and weep at his feet.

But Marlowe, curiously enough, spent the day working as he had never worked in his life. He had slept late into the morning, been woken with the news of Rumanades' death, and after breakfast, without giving it much more than a passing thought, had sat himself down to his work of self-expression. Occasionally, from outside the armour of his scurrying thoughts, the words came to him, 'Rumanades is dead. Have you heard?' but they created hardly any impact.

In the village there was weeping among the young and the middle-aged. The old men, glad of the sun, sat themselves outside under the trees with great placidity in their rush-bottomed chairs, lit their smokes, and fell into pleasurable drowses, occasionally waking to take their nip of *ouzo* or wine. These, the real darlings of death, had seen enough of life not to fear it.

In the sunset, a scarlet seaplane of all things blew up from the south like a dove with an olive branch, and skidded into the Bay of Nanos. The entire peasantry of the island lined the cliffs and terraces to watch it disgorge two passengers: one, a specialist from Athens, complete with gold teeth, a fountain pen, a black suit, and a small bag; the other, Rumanades' lawyer, sober and dour as a deathwatch beetle.

Late into that night there were consultations with Fonvisin, and discussions with Gordon, and exhortations to the peasants. The two business men moved about the great house with the assured decorum of vultures or mourners, trailing their grave coat-tails behind them.

A coffin was made, and while the doctor busied himself over the corpse, attended by the jaunty Fonvisin, the lawyer went about with a hammer and chisel breaking open cupboards and cabinet-desks with an air of slightly insane geology on his face. In the end, after he had cut his thumb and taken the creases out of his trousers, he found what he had been searching for—Rumanades' will.

Sitting down at the desk, he read it through several times, absently dusting the lapels of his coat with one hand as he did so. Nearly everything was left to Manuela [Rumanades' wife]. He sniffed and raised his hands in the air, as one who would say: 'What can you do with such a man?'

For years he had been trying to trace the girl, by advertisement, police, and private detectives; and it had all been in vain. She could have come to no good. Ah well, these Spaniards! What could one expect of them? They would have to keep up the hunt for a while longer, and if no trace were found of the girl, he supposed the whole estate of Rumanades would be claimed by the Government. He deplored the waste of so much good money. He toyed for a moment with the idea of falsifying the will; of inserting, say, a clause which would benefit him to the extent of several hundred thousand drachmae. But then, he remembered, as the family lawyer he could hardly do that; he must content himself by presenting a really fat bill for his professional services. Looking up, he caught Fonvisin's eye. Enigma.

There was one other clause of significance in the will, recently added. It stated that Francis was to receive annually the sum of two hundred and fifty thousand drachmae, with the good wishes of the deceased; and that the body was to be taken to Ithaca for burial.

'It will be obvious to you', he said to Gordon that evening, 'that it would be difficult for you people to continue living here while the estate is being cleared up. You understand?' His English was as faultless as was his taste in clothes. 'After the island reverts to the Government, of course, it will be different. Visitors will be welcome. But just at present. . . .'

[237]

'Yes. I understand,' said Gordon impatiently. He was thinking of the legacy to Francis which the lawyer had just read out. He turned to Fonvisin, who was standing by the window picking his teeth with a match-stick.

'Where will you be going from here?' he asked curiously, and the Russian scratched his lip, replying: 'Not sure yet. Perhaps to Italy.'

That afternoon, as they walked down the hill together, Gordon was elated by the knowledge that once more all the roads of the world were open to him. He would go south this time, Constantinople way, where the sun came from. He felt very strong and happy about it. Onwards again, into the blue!

'When is the funeral?' he asked.

'Tomorrow morning at dawn. He's going to lie in state in the church next to the saint all night. In the morning the boats are going to row him across. The seaplane with the madman in it is going on to Ithaca to make arrangements.'

'Shall we be going across too? Etiquette and that kind of thing?'

'On the contrary. The lawyer was angry when I said I would go. You'd have to get permission.'

'I see,' said Gordon. 'Well, I only wondered.'

They walked down the hill to the corner of the road, and paused for a moment as their ways diverged.

'By God,' said Fonvisin with something that was remotely panic, 'I might not see you all again. I'll be away a few days in Ithaca. Fancy that.'

Gordon's elation vanished of a sudden, and he began to feel the fear and wonder of new adventures and places crowd his heart. It was the penalty of wandering, he thought, that there should be many good-byes at every stage of the journey.

'True enough,' he said shyly. 'We might not meet again. Christ goes north tomorrow evening. I imagine we go with him. In case we don't,' he held out his hand stiffly, with a frozen propriety, 'good-bye and good luck.'

Fonvisin gripped his hand in his fist, wrung it hard for a moment, and gave a crooked transfiguring grin.

'Good luck,' he said, all in a breath, and turning, swung down the hill.

The following night there was an unintentional festival in the village—for so many people had arrived that there was no accommodating them, and they either slept in blankets under the olives, or spent the night sitting about in the arbours round the wine-shop, drinking. They had come from everywhere, from the villages to the north and south of Nanos, in boats and by road, in all the colours of funeral and festival. With them too had come the beggars, who wandered in and out of the groups of seated men, doing a brisk trade in witticism. The old wooden-faced piper, who plagued Francis twice a day whenever he came down to Nanos (because she had a godly face), walked about, a little drunk, but in fine form. Every now and then, for the sheer fun of the thing, he would unbutton his vest, produce his pipe, and give a few toots and twirls.

Under the olives, here and there, lay dark groups of sleepers, while from the wine-shop door, blazing in lamplight, came roars of male laughter and the greasy slicking of cards. A stream of men entered this door. Festival was in the air.

Donkeys wheeled wearily down the road from the hills, stumbling among the boulders, and setting up wings of dust at the heels of each cavalcade. More people, and still more. In the bay a whole fleet of fishing boats and oil-driven coasters had dropped anchor. The stone-shifters were in again with a fresh load, and the still air was bright with their commerce. In their flower-yellow straws they staggered up the slope with the materials for the church, helped by the women, laughing and chattering among themselves—a polyglot crew.

Outside the inn door, along the dusty wall, was piled a long row of melons, waiting for the ripening sun. The lamplight fell smoothly over them as they lay there, like hundreds of bland faces, green and yellow, fat and round, long and tapering, with the uniform expression of a coroner's jury sitting in judgement. The women moved across and across the yellow doorway, motley as birds of paradise, stepping proudly and with the assurance of their own colours and their duty to the dead. Someone had a guitar out there among the olives, and the plangence of its strings, slowly twacked, was joined by the fine tones of a voice, singing as if the limping, rising, falling melody would go on for ever world without end. There was a deep suppressed excitement in the voices of the girls and the men under the olives, as they took up the burden, raising their faces to the roof of leaves from which shone yellow-green reflections of the light. There was devilry in the laughter

[239]

of the lovers who prowled along the top of the cliffs, above the blank sea, linked of body and spirit.

The little barn-like church was full of the reek of candles and incense. It had been newly swept and garnished, and the tin-nimbused frescos of saints had been polished so that they shone with dark malevolence. The women, red, blue, saffron, yellow, mustard, cinnamon, magenta, walked about under a forest of candles as thick as a man's arm, each going up to the right-hand nook by the altar to kiss the case in which the rib of the patron saint was locked, before moving across the line of frescos to gaze upon the dead face of Rumanades, and leave their offering of fruit, flowers or vegetables with the remaining Leucothean monk. He stood, poor man, with his red-rimmed eyes half closed and his beard on his chest, half asleep with fatigue, but doing his duty, on the left of the altar, with a candle in his hand, and appropriate prayer forming in his mind. He had buried his comrade that morning, with the help of a peasant.

The little anteroom at the back of the church let out strong earthy whiffs of fruit and flowers, whenever the door was opened. The offerings were stored there; and in the gloom it resembled the dressing-room of an actress, full of the gauds of a great success.

The priest, hollow-eyed from sleeplessness and rheumatism, moved about among all this with the dignity and unction of his office, now stopping to speak to someone, now turning aside to arrange the flowers, or snuff a curving candle.

At about midnight Francis and Walsh walked down to the church together to look at Rumanades, arm in arm, for they were both a little nervous.

They paused at the door, staring wide-eyed at the congregation of men and women who had made the pilgrimage to the dead. The priest, seeing them, came across and complimented her on the unfinished fresco which covered the short back wall of the building. In that yellow light it looked very bold and strong, in ripe colours, and she herself was proud of it.

They walked up the aisle together, hand in hand, for she had never seen death, and he still feared that motionless passivity which visits the human body when it dies. Their noise on the wide stone flags of the floor, newly swept and sprinkled with sweet water, was nothing in the soft hush and fall of voices around the altar.

[240]

In the side wall (which was being demolished) there were gaps in the brickwork, and outside these they could catch glimpses of children playing in the light from the tavern door. In a clear space among the olives someone had lighted a small fire of sticks, and round it squatted a circle of old women, laughing and talking, happy of an event which excused the wearing of their best clothes. The town was a hive of chatter: and above it, from time to time, threads of melody from the pipes pierced their ears. The old piper was in excellent form by now.

In the doorway at the other end of the church Vassili stood in his uniform, blear-eyed from weeping; while Christ, in his ceremonial shoes, creaked up and down, talking with gravity to anyone who would listen to him.

'Dear sir,' he said brokenly to Walsh, gripping the boy's arm with his little brown fingers, 'dear sir,' squeezing his eyelids down hard in an effort to bring the tears to his eyes, 'what a tragic, my dear sir. What a *tragic*.' The light flapped down on his brown face from the swinging candles. They breathed in the hot sweet stink of molten wax. The old monk leaned heavily against the doorpost, weary of death itself, with his eyes drowsy red zeros in his matted hair. He nodded to them, bowing his head in a gentlemanly way, and folding his mud-grimed fingers over his chest.

They went slowly up the two steps, past the altar-rail, holding each other's arm, to join the little cluster of peasants who waited their turn outside the holy of holies.

The rib of the patron saint lay in a large ornamented casket of the size of a child's coffin. At each side of the church-altar was a tiny nook, about five square yards in size, whose wall-surface was covered by a fresco of saints. In the right-hand chapel lay the patron saint; in the left, Rumanades.

They waited while the peasants kissed the pictures outside, and then, muttering a prayer, ducked into the dim doorway to pay the same tribute to the casket in which the saint's bones were reputed to lie. In the restricted space the fumes from the candles made it almost impossible to breathe. The line of dim saintly faces, circled in bright tin, glowed with a kind of ascetic malice. They waited in there for a few moments, in a kind of stupor, watching the swirl of women in the doorway, entering and kissing the silvery plates which circled the casket, running their lips round the ornamental flutings and knobs with a passion of religious fear.

Christ came in while they stood there, and began to kiss the silver-work with ostentatious loudness, smacking his lips against the metal which had been worn smooth by generations of hands and mouths.

He came across to them again when he had finished, smiling and saying, with a certain pleasure: 'The saint is kind to us, dear sir.'

'Christ,' said Francis quietly.

'Yes, missy?' He was all attention, his violet eyes wide with expectation, his hands ready to gesture.

'What time do you leave tomorrow?'

'Very early morning. At sunlight.'

'Come,' said Walsh, and hooked his arm again through hers. 'Let's go out now.'

They walked past the front of the altar and the row of framed pictures, almost completely rotted away by the damp and neglect. In the semi-chapel on the opposite side of it, they paused staring in on the coffin which held the body of the old man. In detail this second nook was like the first; an ordinary bed had been placed in it, under the crowding brown faces of paint, and covered with cloth of some dark velvety material. On this lay the smooth coffin.

They entered together and stood for a long time, without nervousness, looking down on his white face, composed and yet not severe. There was a slight compression at the corners of his mouth, as though a smile were about to break out on his face at any moment. The only unhappy thing was the stare which made his eyes so expressionless. He lay there glaring up at the fresco of saints above his head, like an absolute stranger in a strange place.

Francis withdrew her arm, and stood loosely beside the boy, staring at the enigmatic old man's face, without fear or prejudice: quite alien and strong in herself again.

The interminable muttering continued in the body of the church at their backs. The monk snoozed against the door-post, waking occasionally to give a little shiver of fatigue. He was beyond sorrow by this time; and beyond showing even the polite forms of it. Very far away, in the infinity that was night outside, a voice took up a song of lovesickness, with a slow lift and drag about it that suggested physical pain. The guitar, almost inaudible, squeezed the melody out drop by drop, as one would clean a wound. Through the hole in the wall they were able to see the circle of old women round the fire stir with the warmth of approval, warming to the lure of the sweet words. The singer was dying for them: and the old flesh on their bones ached for lovers. Not for the dead and forgotten men, the shades which lurked in grimy corners of the memory, but for new ones, young men with the brightness in them, haggard for women and the bodies of women. The singer was giving himself to them as Juan is said to have given himself, from pity, to an old woman who importuned him; and they, like that old and lovesick woman, were become new again and fresh for lust. Their faces were turned to the singing so that the firelight shone on the folds and pouches of their flesh: and they caught their hands together and squeezed them between their knees in a delight that was painful.

Inside the church the candles still sparkled, while the smoke of incense went up to the ceiling like steam. The boy and girl stood for a long time, staring at the face of Rumanades, rapt.

They were none of them awake at dawn to see the final ceremony, except Fonvisin, who was taking an active part in it, and Gordon; Marlowe had worked so long and so hard that he slept on well into the afternoon. Francis, through the numb content of her body, and the dreams which passed in her mind, heard the noise and bustle of the preparations.

At three o'clock that morning Gordon had packed some food in a knapsack, taken his binoculars and climbed the long cliff-paths to the Jump, alone, and very happy.

Now, at early dawn, he sat on the edge of the dancing-floor, dangling his feet in space, smoking.

Eastward the light crawled up the flanks of the mountains, and brimmed over slowly until it flooded the death-still sea. Inland it had penetrated the valley, shining on the chequers of olive and vine, corn and barley.

In the village noise was growing up dimly out of silence. A man sang a few bars of a song. A door banged. Three ants in scarlet set out on the road to the bay.

Nanos looked like a glass bowl of water in which fruits floated—

grapes, cherries, figs. The coloured boats bobbed gently, while from under the awnings sleepy men appeared, stretching themselves and yawning, stiff with the chill of damp. From the tethering-grounds among the olives came the sniggering of donkeys. A woman shouted something.

Gordon watched keenly, and saw the confusion growing, until the town looked like an armed camp preparing for an attack. From the white gates of the Villa Pothetos three dark figures emerged and began to walk down to the village. He guessed that they must be the lawyer, the doctor, and Fonvisin. Half an hour later the procession started.

From the door of the church pressed a coloured multitude of people, clustering round the black figures which bore the coffin on their shoulders. The priest and the monk were in full ceremonial costume; over their black soutanes they wore beautifully fringed and embroidered stoles, reaching almost to their ankles. In the right hand of each was clutched a tall candle, while the priest held one of the sacred books. Behind them came the crowding peasants, holding aloft the sacred ikons of the village, laughing and talking among themselves.

The procession went on down the hill, centred on the coffin and its bearers; down through the olives and past the lemon groves, until at last it left the cliff-paths, and emerged safe and sound on the jetty. Alongside the line of bobbing coloured ships there was a halt and conference while Christ manœuvred his boat into position to receive the privileged mourners with the coffin. The others began crowding into the boats, laughing, with a great swinging of skirts and twirl of scarves.

Then the long line of boats set out southward in the keen air of morning, to Ithaca.

THE END

Zero

AND

Asylum in the Snow

TWO EXCURSIONS INTO REALITY
(written in Corfu)

'*Asylum in the Snow*'. *Published in* Seven. *No. 3. Winter 1938.*
'*Zero*'. *Published in* Seven. *No. 6. Fall 1939.*
Zero and Asylum in the Snow *privately printed by the author, Rhodes 1946.*

'*Astu*

'*What is unpleasant and a strain on my modesty is that fundamentally every name in history is myself. And with the children I have put into the world matters stand thus: I ponder, with a certain amount of suspicion, whether all who enter in the kingdom of God also come from God. This autumn I was obscured so as to become as insignificant as possible and was twice a spectator at my own funeral, the first time as Count Robilant (no, he is my son, in so far as I am Carlo Alberto, and untrue to my nature) but I myself was Antonelli. Dear Herr Professor you should see this edifice as I am wholly inexperienced in the things I create, so that you are free to make every criticism, I am grateful without being able to promise that I shall profit thereby. We artists are unteachable.*'

From the letters written by Nietzsche after he became insane.

ZERO
(for Henry Miller)

$$\sin \frac{2\pi (x + 3a)}{a} = \sin \frac{2\pi x}{a}$$

EVERYTHING ILLOGICAL IS GOD: AND I AM GOD!
The night opens with a Tibetan delicacy; the shadows fall across the

[245]

long-nosed sun-dial and tell me that I exist, I exist. I have decided to speak, not for those who in their fervour are aimless and lunatique, those who run magically, whose ankle-bones are chaotic with reality; nor for those who paddle in their own urine, or knead their dung into delicate torsos. I will tell you who I am and what I am doing here. I will speak with a nicety of language that would give ears to the blind, and eyes to the deaf who hear me, but do not understand what my glossary is. If I am bitter it is because the asp has stung me; it is because the vial was emptied into my ear while I slept. (Actually it is great pathos—do not smile at the wringing of hands, at the torpor I exhibit when I meet you. By request of the management, do not smile. . . .) You weep, my darling, you take my hand and press it to your mouth, completely fatal; I feel the segment of white teeth touch my knuckles through the great grin of tears you wear. The snow chimes about us and I can do nothing, nothing. I cannot find words, only a sort of music which is cold comfort because I do not hear your answers. You see me sitting here like a Prussian with tears standing in my eyes. They never fall. They are always there. Two tears of rock carved on the canthus. Rather than agonize you lean over and tuck the motoring rug under my knees. The black trees open, the wind climbs, and the vortex of language comes up in my throat like a soft ball of blood. The memoryless hysteria of the snow closes on us like a man-trap, your arm is in my arm. Do you think I do not understand? I see myself sitting here stiffly, like a robot, behind the taciturn driver. I am a figure of fun perhaps because I cannot find the right word, and you do not dare to speak to me: because I can only manipulate an algebraic thunder in answer. Laugh if you want, it does not touch me: only you weep to see me groping among the syllables for a platitude of comfort, the naked bodies of lost words which would heal. If I try I can almost cross the gulf. What have you been doing? Are you happy? Why do you smile, weep, wonder, etc.? Are the apple-trees still knotted in their own hamstrings? You see, I can almost manage it. I am almost speaking after the manner of men. Almost. That does not alter my sitting here, like an incubus beside you, knowing that you are trembling under the striped rug. I have confused you with the loose-black-mouth-of-the-foal: the entity of the farm. I take in imagination always the wet, loose lips in my hand and kiss them, breathing in the cordial scent of the cud. It would be fatal to my peace of mind if I had a mind. In the madhouse even the wireless shuts down at twelve. Good-night everyone, and the moment is yours. I speak to you with simplicity then, because you are neither the foal nor the seal, and I am not myself. The apple-trees are growing in my mind: the earth opening all her pomp and liquors under the snow. In the Spring we will go down to the pool, and I shall meditate the miracle all over again. Are these pieces of the explored world banal? It is a sort of gathering up of threads, a finale, a vale—before the adventure begins. It is necessary to put my affairs in order before I go to meet my father. It is necessary to empty the old wine in meditation and reverence before stiffening the skins with new. I think you understand. . . .

On Tuesday you will come with the fourteen horses and four coloured wheels, and enter the monastery bravely. Your fear is childish and obvious. In your jaunty clothes you are afraid. I draw you aside to the corner and put my hands on your body, to assure myself that you are a woman, and to recollect what you mean.

As I write this I realize that Tuesday has become solid, a girl's body in coloured silk with stiffened nipples, fear, and the attitudes of pathos. The rules forbid us to enter the white bed and carry this exploration to its conclusion—the unimaginable outposts of feeling when you are a cool-bodied fish in the sheets, palpitating in the oblique current, gathered like fucus, slippery, thawed, thewed as the leopard. My little ape! You and your tribe are like coloured children, so transparent in feeling. I turn towards the solid Tuesday of hips and flesh, smooth buttocks and pectorals, with a momentum that is the eternal theme for us all here. The week glows towards Tuesday, the storms plunder the outposts, flocks of wild birds empty themselves over the lamps: secure in the lighthouse I wait for the Tibetan fiat to sound. Vasec waits with me, he does not know for what, and the intangible Dancer. The rest have gone. All the time, at night, lying in our beds, we can hear the dim roar of the looms, the factory where the empty calendar is woven and painted with heraldic beasts. The beating heart underneath us, weaving its Sundays and Mondays, the bobbins dithering in a frenzy of activity. The night.

On Tuesday there will be a jewelled hush, an audit. The walks will be dressed in snow, the bushes incandescent with birds. Everything fallen in a divine abyss of lull, poem, zodiac, frost, butter. Perhaps today is the day, I do not know. I find it difficult to tell until I hear the motor, the fourteen horses crushing the jewels, and the doors of God opening.

Vasec says you must bring the canary: he will not believe until he sees it with his own eyes. He is an experienced countryman, he says. So how can he believe that the cage was created round it by God? It is slightly redundant: if God gave it wings, then why the cage which is too small for it to use them? You will have to answer this when you come. We are very much at rest on the point, however, because I am teaching everyone how to experience phenomena. In this sector of experience there is only the creative activity. We are nothing ourselves: we do not let our imaginations even imagine that *we* have a part in the cosmic dance. It happens like cinema. Kiss the children for me, and see that they say their prayers—it is ridiculous, *ridiculous!* Today I said to the old man: 'I am a free man, thinking free thoughts, why must I suffer?' Inevitably he did not understand. But he went away and searched his whole library to find a name for my suffering. He is a good soul, but frugal—terribly frugal and meagre. My opulence makes him fear me. He looks in my eyes and trembles—so deep they are, so sad and assured, set deep in my glum sockets. At times the symphony that runs through my arteries like a river reaches him, touches him, scalds like a live wire. He sits there like a domestic rabbit in his white apron, surrounded by pencils and paper, shaken with an anonymous agony for me, for my passion and crucifixion which he begins dimly to understand. When he sees you the tears come into his eyes, and he locks himself in the library, trying to find a way out of it all. Why, when you are so young, so debonair, so much one with your slim silk clothes, the caryatid, the green girl? For my part I am happy, I touch your clothes and hair: I break little morsels of desire from you and share them with Vasec and the Dancer. It is a charity which costs so little when I am so rich in you, so Arabian with bullion.

Did you know? Hamlet is dead, the little one, the black cardinal. I must break the news gently. Vasec came to me in the night crying like a bull because the little one was his pet. Vasec was disfigured by a divine love, and when I lit the candles his nostrils were carved in ink. His hands dredged up the sheets with weeping. It was a personal pain under the heart: the loose dewlap quivering like a jelly under his tears. He was like Lesbia with the dead sparrow. The old man thought it was appendicitis for a long time, until he entered, and experienced the ghost. In the starched bed the little man was supine, his little fingers yellow and little, clenched like the claws of a dead bird. The lines on his face meant nothing. He had died in the future—how far ahead of us all we could not tell. Even the physicist could not tell. It was a moment of great nicety—because we could not bury him until he joined us in the present. Ophelia was not present by request of the management, and there were few flowers. Everyone was puzzled. However, we decided to keep to the form, even if he was without substance for another fifty years or so. It was a wonderful night.

We buried him in his own country, following down the long lines of cypresses, the lions regardant, the double-axe, and the eagles. The priests were plangent with victory, and their black soutanes glowed like insects in the candles. A wild cold night, with a full moon hanging aloft, as clear as a bugle-call. The earth was mystical all over Europe at our ceremony, opening the mother to receive her Hamlet, the western dead. Forgive us our sins. The little men with bony skulls and knuckles made of bark descanted our mimic with real fervour. The beards rose and fell. Decorum was emptied in our spirits like a salve, while the sea spoke on our left, the headlands were torrential with the moaning of the wild olive, the juniper, the walnut, the cedar of Lebanon. I knew in those moments the worth of everything, fell like a carving to the clandestine cobbles, bowed, broke, emptied in all utterance to the sea by wild music, the cataleptic jargon of tongues, the pneumatic gifts. My soul was full of broken weals and stars of the third magnitude. I kissed Vasec's lips, slippery under their hairs, because I am Yorick for ever and we are brothers in Hamlet, and the sea drives on whatever we do, to Crete. Understand me, wherever you are, lying in whatever null bed, hearing the wind climb in the trees and the cranes negotiate Sicily. I am no longer fish nor fruit, vegetable, mineral, oracle. Weep for Lycidas, dead ere his prime.

The problem is serious. For in spite of the ceremony, Hamlet is in the room, dead, but waiting for us to catch up with him. What everyone wonders is: will he stay fresh? We touch his lips, draw them away from the jawbone like a dog. They are stiff relics—a bunch of dusty grapes left over from a forgotten summer.

Vasec and I sit beside him and play draughts. This is just right for Vasec because he can spend his intelligence completely on the game, he can exhaust himself, his passion, his nerves, his intelligence; as for

me—well, I have a reserve over to go on with. We sit here precisely and
have orgy after orgy of game until Vasec leans back exhausted, dribbling with concentration. All the while Hamlet is perpetuated in the
little white cot in the corner, his claws holding the sheets, his face
settled like a quicksand: if you stare down on him you are drawn down,
in ever-widening vortices, to a level of concentration which is magma.
The lotus-depths in which my mind is the only one really at home.
The others are shy of it, even the old man. He allows me to say
insolently to him 'You have mistaken your role. I AM THE HEALER:
and you are destroying all that is curative in me.' He scents truth, but
is too clandestine to concur. How quiet the others have been since I
entered. The dancer does no harm, poor gazelle. In the moonlight he
waits for the flock of terrified deer to catch up with him: and they go
down together among the lilies. Their hooves have beautiful gnomic
patterns. Even Vasec is spending his virtue to a small degree these
days, his dome enters heaven like a turret and bewilders Ararat. I teach
him about Tibet, about the monasteries hanging there and the terrible
cogitations of the necromancers opening over the icebound lakes, the
shawls, the dragons, the aura of mind brooding in the atmosphere of
snow: the butter-lamps smouldering by the shrine, the prayer-wheels,
the yak and the hermit. It seems that sometimes he too has met God.
A little yellow man in a wash-drawing, brooding over a motionless
swanpan. Enough.

I record this, not out of agony but simply that when you come on
Tuesday you will have no fear: you will be more or less acquainted with
our grammar. I saw you sitting in the chair last night. Dear, he meant
nothing: Vasec is a sacrificial lamb. To touch your knees under the
coloured silk—was that culpable? The Dancer is agitated by the delicate thwarted silk in which you are sheathed. They have given him
some of his own: he has made his lips up and now dances for us with
grave delicacy, like a performing child. Last night he came running to
me gravely with his hands on his chest: 'Look,' he said, 'she has given
me breasts to perpetuate. They are growing. Feel.' He is luckier than
Fifi or I. He is more adult than Pieter or the Starfish. That is why
when you sit on the chair and do not know how to speak to us, I want
you to realize our blood-brothership. Do not stammer and blush—you
are beautiful enough as you are. It is impossible to believe that you are
tribal: that you are a member of the sects which carry cancer with them

and sordes, anoia and mucilage, syrtes, tabes, Glaxo, compound interest and compound fracture. Are you one of them? If you were not you would not puzzle over this . . . actually it is great pathos, do not smile. By request of the management, do not smile. Weep for Lycidas, neither fish nor fruit, vegetable, mineral nor oracle. This is my crucifix. I am taken down roughly. I think of you, and my mind is whirling with a million chisels, I am apostate, heretic, traitor . . . would you say 'hallucinated by the absolute?'

The nights now are full of the snow's jargon and the beatitudes of the frost; a million inimical jewels bathed in suds and set in the gleaming ouch of the lawns. The Dancer is the artificer of moonlight as I told you; his felicities are incarnated in a world where there is no obstructing flesh—ankle, thenar, palm, wrist—but only a flight of Mind in a hollow alphabet of symbols. Only the indestructible atom of spirit in its lawless method. Only the moon. He has covered the last crater alone, his foes cherishing the last raving crater of Copernicus, of Vega, the Milky Way ringing under his fingers like the stops of an empty flute. Is it I who am too precise for you—or is it *your* mind in which the real is partitioned off from the symbol? The Dancer knows that it is not only the polarized light which causes his method. Observe the mild, hairless face—the lips carbonized by laughter. I tell you he knows.

For the rest of us they have reserved a label. There is amusia, aphasia, aboulia, alexia, agraphia, and anoia. When the men in white coats want, they go to market like so many ducks for them. We shrug our shoulders and turn away. What? On the evidence of some printer's devil, a charred syllable of Roman-Greek origin, are we incarcerated here among the snow? It is too true, I assure you. I have thought of writing to *The Times* once or twice: but what use? *The Times* itself is one of the causes of the trouble. I content myself in drafting out the invitations to the garden-party, to be held at the fool moon, among parasols and inanities. I shall appear among them disguised as a bishop. It will be ironic—among these starched churchmen who faint away if they catch a glimpse of a real man of God. I shall offer a first prize for the mind which is most orderly in its arrangement: the mind that most resembles a vegetable garden. The tea-cups will be brimming with polarized light, the parasols hectic with dinosaurs. There will be speeches to memorize. Unaccustomed as I am to public speaking,

[251]

etc. . . . I shall carry not a batch of notes, but simply a fountain-pen in my hand. I shall say, without fraud: 'Come. Enter into the creative activity in which you do not need your understandings. Do not mistake truth for the possessive process any longer—ratiocination, knowledge. The real desire is *to be possessed.*' After that chaos will reign, followed by silence in which nothing is heard but the creaking of dowagers' corsets. Local boy makes good!

But all this writing is embezzlement. I am avoiding news because everything topical has become dangerous with the images of you. At night I climb the lighthouse stairs to where the great lamps burn, and peer out on the novelty of the horizons which for others *do not exist.* Tibet laid out like a rotten jawbone among the foot-hills, the vertiginous polarized greenery, the scabs of emerald moss, the deodar, the leopard, the snows exploding in space, exhaling rainbows. . . . A breath of numen, where the Chinamen sit in the lotus pose and the nights are fuliginous with fables. Underneath me I can dimly hear the shuttles weaving the calendar: the looms creating Tuesday, which is solid flesh, hip and ankle, and half-mine at that.

Beside me I have Judas, who whispers incessantly all night, as the continents roll by in a vertigo of heraldry, and the clouds numb visibility. He too is owned by a label, more seriously than the rest. It is so certain, his symptoms, that they cannot see him any more—only the label. It is a medical horoscope they devise for him, situated comfortably in the middle-brain, the hind-brain, and the semi-circular canals. Sarcoma is his middle name, while he is allowed to sign his cheques KATATONIA. Actually he is an old seraph with a congealed back, who every morning washes his face in the chamber-pot and flings the bed-clothes out of the window. This is to air the room thoroughly. His moustaches are so long that he is forced to draw the ends up round his ears. He sits by me in the lighthouse with immense care, as if he were piloting an airplane—which proves that for him also the scenery changes. But he will not tell me what he sees. Speech has become too imperfect a foil: has snapped off at the hilt. Only this susurrus, which is gnomic, tribal, ritual. The birds wheel up against the lighted glass in heavy flocks, but he does not utter. There is a moving sea of wings beating outside, a cataract of sea-mew and petrel and albatross, but I am alone in my visual I. Towards dawn he will creep up and kiss me softly on the cheek. Then run away immediately crying, 'Betrayed.

Betrayed.' If my face could move in the right way I could manage a laugh.

Where there is conscience there is schism. Judas is not consoled by the vistas, but walks all day chinking the blood-money in his trouser-pocket and looking for the place of skulls. He has no notion of you when you come to see us, which makes me angry because I cherish you in the light of their envy. I delight in your impact—the silk throwing its colours among our insane white. When Vasec touches your cheek, verifying the delicate aligned plates of bone in your skull under the malleable flesh, I blush with you—but for joy and exclusion. Cheeks as soft as yeast, and powerful. You are amazed at our candour? I tell you, now that the defined limit of language has fallen open on its hinges, there is no room for chicanery. We are more valid than human beings—in a gentlemanly way. We beat ploughshares into words, with all purity of diction. It is a state of being more lucid than Euclid. We are an insoluble proposition, to which the hypotenuse has been lost. Perhaps you will enter Golgotha one day yourself in a tragic attempt to find me. All this is data which I gather up for you: a chart written in a fine deft hand: but the treasure is buried. X marks no spot at all.

Last night I was writing again: the intangible glyphs from the new book of the dead. You see even here there are lucid moments for us—though perhaps not in precisely the sense you and yours would sanction. But lucid, lucent, hallucid—yes, I am sure. The whole of my life was fallen suddenly on paper, the apple-trees, the farm, the hot garrisons of pied daisies, the children incessant, the piercing innocence, the cattle-like camphor-scented mummies in the opaque evenings. Lucent. My God, we had recovered the world in which the old millwheel thumped its million candlepower concussions under the bridge. You climb the rusty girder, naked. Flex back the arch of spine, gather the clouds, staunch back the fine ankles, poise for the dive. The pool glows back its membrane of ink: the dermis studded in the scorched kissing of kingcups. Then fall, the flesh of body like an axe into the underworld, and I am woken from my paper in this opaque room, this white sanity of winter, to grovel on the floor, whimpering, trying to gather the broken components of water up into a reasonable image: a still-life from the land of the no longer living. This is too curt. The last service of the body, I suppose, is in the Death: the music-room where is the absolute counterpoint of God, unrolling its empty dialogues of silence

[253]

into time. Death is that white status which it is no longer necessary to contemplate. For me, there remains only the journey, the outbound express into the wilderness of lightwaves, clocked by no milestones, fooled by no flags, the red and the green, stopped by no signal. Arctic Ultimate. You see? At last I have learned the bitter lesson—to speak for myself. I have recovered from the wounds already—other men, they were my wounds. I speak from the sharpened pencil of the self now, vicious as graphite, as keen—tragically, only as durable. Giant, you are mortal! I accept the kisses of Judas now with reserve, swing a glove, and ask patiently what wood they have chosen, what time it begins. The journey has begun. In whatever direction I move it is travel, the anatomy of voyage.

With the others it is not so. With Vasec it is only a cog missing in action. He will drink ink because he knows it is time for his milk, and sit there smiling with a black mouth and African teeth. With Pieter you know what it is: little ailments in the hip, sciatica, rheum—until the Lord of Hosts tells him to take up his harmonium and walk, when he is reborn in rather a hideous way. The Starfish wonders why his mother does not call. It was April, the first clean jewels. The girls were at table, rich with pigtails and humour. He saw her over the food, and knew she had eaten his life. 'My darling,' he said, 'My darling,' and took down the whip from the antlers of the black-buck. In the bedroom she was pregnant. He was choking with divine love, his woman, his hearth, and the fine children like saplings. The peat was stopping his throat, the winter highlands, the hard earth, dour, dour as porridge. In his passion he saw the red, worn hands, the murky circle of gold, the nails peeled away with dishes and greasy plates and tedium. In the room downstairs the children were silenced like a brood of owlets, when he began to whip the unborn generations, the hanging fruit of her womb. Terror climbed the stairs, but his love was too much, until she went all silly like a doll and the sawdust ran out of her neck, and the price went up from sixpence to half-a-crown. Do not judge as easily as twelve good men and true. There is a supreme justification in action which you cannot understand. Honour the monster in him, if you expect the miracle. Do not judge, by request of the management, do not judge.

It is the same with Hamlet when he came to us last night, unannounced. It was difficult not to judge, to see the threads that had snapped, and still distinguish them from the threads that were whole. He came walking with that delicate Elizabethan tread, like a guilty child who has stayed away too long. 'There is a moment or two of time left me,' he said, 'before I go into my little black box. I come to you (that was I) because you, more than anyone, understand. With Vasec there is love, but no understanding. I come to you because I do not want to go away into minus quantities and be forgotten. I need the fragile consummation of memory. Give it to me as a last gift.'

After that he went away into a quiet contortion of weeping which you would find disgusting: but his silence and utter mask when they screwed the lid down, was anaesthetic with pride. Death, you see. The last status. We did what we could with manners, according to the old custom. From between the bars I watched the procession gather and flow out into its immemorial manoeuvre: the stiff black robes: the language: the cataracts falling between the beds of tall cypress and cedar: Bennu, the phoenix, with the green Nile water heavy in its beak: the sun touching the wing-tips of olive, until the night fell, and nothing moved on the vast plain, but the faint medieval luminous cross with its furniture. The furniture of Christ. Death had become his host. The long lines of insects were swallowed slowly in the west. Last came Ophelia, her face stiff, her yellow hair electric with fate. Her eyes were two silly cornflowers, numb at the roots, after a dry summer. I did not go, but watched from my cage, in order to make my loneliness certain. The procession concerned them: what was cosmic in the drama of bodies was mine. I was jealous of it.

Slowly we are all dropping away into the patient maw of events. Soon Vasec, too, with the great burden of love he owns, and the Starfish with his glamour. All of them, and us, and at the last, perhaps, I. But the target is not certain yet.

When I think like this, at night here, I make a kind of dialogue with you about the hypothetical future. I speak to the empty wall, to the nook where Fifi lies, where the Dancer travels on the moon like a jet of silver soda-water. At my language even the seals, startled among the ice, under the northern lights, sit up in bed and make question marks with their ears.

My life has settled on me like a great lens, focused to a diamond-point of sanity. Would you say I was more lucid, more at home among the ordinary elements? This light burns on the paper, a picture too like a sun-spot for me to look at it for long. You are there in the inevitable room, car, snow, summer, bathing. The supplication thongs me, I cannot move. These eyes, swollen up into mere commas of supplication, the heart with the full-stop written in it. What shall I say to make it plausible? The pen draws fine geometric abstractions round this lonely house among the apple-trees, the autumn smoke in a rusty sky, the cattle. . . .

They will not let me ride away with you when the Tuesday automobile calls. I would be happy in the sodden woods, with the falling leaves and the mild shotgun. Amen. The children crossing the stream. The oats. Here it is so familiar that I am stifled in its tedium. I do not belong here. I sit and suffer the carnage, the havoc of these unhappy people, and speak to them as gently as a doe. Luke, and Malaria, and Tiryns. And Vasec with the enormous head. His skull is a sounding-board of bone. When he eats you hear the resonant crumping of a horse at his oats. The Dancer, on the other hand, is so fastidious that he puts pinches of salt on the back of his tongue before he eats. The salt preserves his balance, he says, and makes all sweet and savoury. It is all so known. They are so cordial they do not notice my boredom. The limbo of egoists. Pieter with his optic disc in a state of atrophy and Luke with the magnets in his pockets. Twenty spines curved over a ravenous dinner-table in a dance of food. Afterwards Vasec's cranium in concentration over a chequered board. . . .

All this havoc of spirit is the product of your weeping: the moment when you grin with tears and put your mouth to my wrist. You are the thong, the mantrap without which I could accede easily, fold up my emotional baggage, and cross the border into a landscape so still that it might be painted. A beathless, coloured territory where the hermit sits forever, bowed over a butter-lamp, and Mind is luminous in every shrine. I reach over, but find I am hobbled. In the night I struggle to untie the bonds, break prison. You are there like a desert of agony, and I think of the car, the escape we will have on Tuesday if I can speak. It is hollow wishes, the old skeleton of escape. The old picture is so silent, so familiar in its austerity. We were glorious men and women in days of yore, etc. Look, there is the husband, there is the happy man. She is warm and filled with scented bread. The children sleep like birds. The little house broods on a moonlit triviality and falls asleep. Deep ash in the woods the deep note of the night-jar, the oak and the ash. The peaceful skein of living gathered up and put aside in the coloured basket among the knitting-needles. Two plain and one purl. Do not stir, by request of the management, do not stir. We are asleep in the deep armchair, the windows are moist, the fire breathes underneath the bed of ash. T-h-e D-o-g A-n-d T-h-e C-a-t S-l-e-e-p O-n T-h-e M-a-t.

I escape from the chain-shot and stumble up the steps of the lighthouse, trembling with fear. The birds are still falling. Judas sits in his original place, the eternal pilot of continents. We do not have correspondence. If there were a fraction of my spirit to be carried in words, in paint, in music. . . .

It has all fallen away from me: it is all falling away, lapsing, loosening. You and the picture like a painful inevitable amputation. My clothes stick to the wounds. I tear them away. I would be free, but for the machinery of familiarity which you start with your gauds, the cavalier with breasts and soft hair, terrible with silk. The new country waits, sunk in its own terrible finery of mountains and glaciers: the dove and the panther: the spirit forcing the roof of the skull in its flight. The prayer-wheels twiddling their charms. The ambience of will, the monopoly of God.

Shut in the tower I am shot with sanity: time does not pay her dividends. A man can only stand so much. The farm, my God, the hot ash of dead fires, the kettle urbane, the lantern on the hook, the breathing of cattle, the marl and mulch of January, the rime and ribbons of March, the dividends of corn. . . . I am ruined by the delicate bodies of men and women who haunt the house, their delicate days and ways, somnolent with mud and patience. The serfs. The roaring girls whose lusts are almond-seed and seams of quaint shale. The terrible patient hunger of the landed men, whose bodies were trees and the gestures of history. I would enter my lineage if it were not for this. The pith of my thought is the silk girl, trampled in the late corn among the poppies, stuck in a framed oil-painting, out of date as mud, but instinct with pain. It is suddenly as if a loose driving-rod were clanking between my eyes. I run to where the old man is. I am in great agitation: 'Look,' I say to him with the old gesture, 'I throw in my hand. I am not understood here. Let me go, I will be as other men are, talking of ordinary things in the ordinary way, I cannot stand this equilibrium between two worlds. The continents fall between my fingers like sand,

and I cannot grasp them. Send me back into the painting. I am really a ladybird after all. I must fly away home, my house is on fire, my children will burn. Also I have an appointment with the vicar Seriously.

I hiccough terribly, but he does not speak. For the first time there is an understanding in him, but it is hidden in fear. He will not utter.

'It has been a mistake,' I repeat to him with more pathos. 'I am a husband and a husbandman. You mistook me for a disciple. For that matter I thought so myself. I am wrong. I can never cross the border. My papers are not in order. See, the passport was faked. The ticket-collector was a royalist. For God's sake. I shall never enter. Never. I shall never get through to the other side.'

Then he says, more sternly, with great vacuous orbs: 'Give me the writing.' I give it to him, whimpering, but saying, as if novel, 'I shall never get through. Never.'

The breath of the Word enters the rooms and fills the flowers with scent. Life is so godly, waiting behind the apparatus of a few papers, some ink, a white wall. Life is solid flesh, warm hip and loin, and more than half mine. He reads while I smile the lethal smile. Then he says fondly: 'Be at peace. You are there already, but have no compass, nothing magnetic. March on Orion and be happy. You have nothing to lose, because all is lost. Look. Here in the paper is written. You have already said it on the first page. The first sentence. Turn back. There is no way forwards. Turn back.'

ASYLUM IN THE SNOW

(for Anaïs Nïn)

(Strictly in confidence), there are five of us. I am not counting Vasec or the Dancer or the magic man; I am not counting the other flesh and blood who are like arrows, running here and there in the gardens, digging holes in the earth to bury the hatchet: or crying like birds. Not them. Not the red man who is lying exhausted on the lawn in the morning, elegant starfish: they are all so silly that they are allowed to run all day in the garden. It is we who exist. From the window I watch the children pushing bags of sweets through the railings. Fifi is feeling her breasts and calling for her milk. They will bring it to her in a glass

soon and tell her to stop saying those things. This makes us all laugh.
The walls are very thin and made of dust, so we can laugh elegantly
towards each other, and the other understands. You see it is a sort of
blood-brothership. Our bloods are full of little animals and songs which
call out, or tickle us and make us laugh. The people in uniforms never
understand. At first I was a bit afraid. Now I am so hugged by the
secret that I close up like a knife with laughing. Well, there is the snow.
All night I could feel it falling on my nerves. For we five who exist in
these rooms it is a kind of signal for faith, hope and hilarity. In the
morning they take away the little tin pots. Mine is nearly full of
laughter, I am such a happy fellow. It comes out of a brass spigot which
I keep in my trousers with my loose change. It is never the change that
comes out, but the laughter. Green laughter. Vin ordinaire. Kümmel.
Soda. Milk. Orangeade.

Towards evening the hunchback goes and rolls in the snow. We
look the other way because we are embarrassed. No one dares to speak
of him because he has become mute. His eyeballs are all scraped with
cold. They turn him the right way up, so that even the sky can see the
change. He has become God. He is the fifth of us when he rolls in the
snow, but otherwise like a mouse, not speaking, not laughing, not
saying anything. His face is crucified, and a certain thing comes out of
him. I try to write it but I cannot. Then, after that, all night it is
psalms falling from heaven so white, and huge shafts of harps and
angels and psalms, on my nerves in concussions of harps and angel-cake.
(Look.) Here is the pen they gave me and some sheets of paper. I used
to go quicker, quicker, until it was no more pen and paper, but a sort
of cinema inside my breast, a sort of mass: black candles, Irish whisky,
stoles, soutanes, bell, book, and choirs of violet bats. This is quite true.
I was an inevitable conjurer. In the spring I used to impregnate everything with my paper and pen, until the whole earth was stifled: it
couldn't come up. I couldn't live. Then I was so happy because I was
sowing the death everywhere, and the virtue was growing inside me.
I was master of plants, bees, hills, fishes—everything walking, creeping, rooted: in the air or the sea. Everything acknowledged me. I used
to make a list of the earth and read it over. Very little escaped. A few
weeds perhaps, or deep-sea fishes. But the rest was a chaos of broken
paper, tissue, gum, ink, clips. And I? I was the magic man. I would

breathe quickly and murder my wife with language and heavy instruments. Vasec laughs when he hears this, and scrapes the window. In the snow it is so queer to hear Vasec scraping, scraping, all night long like a mole in the darkness. I can't get over it. He is so copious, Vasec the butcher. They said he was a fat man, but really he is so little, so minute, so utterly one of them. A needle in a haystack of flesh. If you give him paper and pen he will sit in front of it all day, while the sealing wax falls from his nose and puts little burning flags on the table. He is useless. We have given him up for lost long ago. Amen.

The snow is growing upward from the earth. There is a quiet light in the passage. Life is passing into us like the light, through a filter. I make my feet like compasses and draw Ptolemaic universes on the floor, skating to make him envious or angry. Our conversation through the walls is gaudy. I am speaking to Fifi. The eastern star. The magic apples on the fire. The magi burning in eleven thousand trees, in eleven thousand Chinese wash-drawings on the tents of the philosophers. The polished piano. Brass criticizing the music, forests of bugles, critical brass complaining: and the violins ripening. Fifi is opening her legs and saying to the doctor: 'Lift him up. Lift him up.' There was so much water that it was an easy birth. The star is brooding over the manger. Soon the egg will be laid. The cattle thrust their great faces into the crowd of wise men and are indistinguishable from them. The morsel can feel the damp noses on him like sponges. The dewlap laps the dew from the Virgin. A bovine arson of faces in the light of the eastern star, the wise men with their pipes, falling asleep like skittles. It is enough. Then the snow coming down in many psalms on Vasec's fingers, filling his enormous eyes with fate, soap and barbarity. And we five so lonely, so simple and lonely, lying on a back bed, saying her name and feeling her in the pillow: and drinking the cry as it comes out of our eyes. Her backbone was eaten by mice, and the auricle and ventricle broke off relations. I say it in the paper (but in strict confidence). Very well. She opens her legs, but before you can lie down across her she becomes the snow, the snow like the uniforms, and Christmas comes out of her, with toy trumpets, and pork, and holly, and the mistletoe, and the face of the hunchback, and the children saying prayers over an empty stocking. It is frantic that she should appear cold snow running down the legs to the belly, the pork, the valentine, the little brass spigot where the wine comes from. I am excited by this writing. They say it is not good. They sweep it up like old snow and burn it, I remember, tomorrow. It is silly, but the old man is weary. Too much paper. Too much ink. He likes the bead work better, it is restful. Soft colours with many saints and something artful in it he has a name for. A name? What is that? When you are afraid of something, or you want to hate it, you give it a name out of the alphabet. Then you can let it into the house and it will not hurt you. It is covered in a name, and you do not see it properly, you only see the little black letters. In this way you can lie quiet beside your wife in bed and have no fear: when you put out your arm or leg you will not find a Christmas tree, or a Chinaman, or amputated holly in many bloody berries, but the thing you are looking for. I mean the snow; the time when you cannot see, but it is beautiful, and the snow touches you with many rubber bladders: and behind your head the pulse begins to beat. And you know it is mammal, warm with pith, juice, and another kind of charity which isn't just a word, but an alphabet of essence. This again I cannot write. I could show it to you in my face, but I cannot write it. It is too ancient, drawn on the walls of many caves by the bears who never knew what a Christmas Tree was. Leave it alone, or the pen will burst into fire and burn me severely. It is an arsenal in the ink-bottle, so be careful.

All night Fifi is snowing, and today her breasts are more troublesome than ever. They bring her the milk as usual in a glass, but it is frozen: so there is more laughter than ever in my little tin pot. You see when her breasts got slack she said to the doctor: 'Give an actress a change.' So they filled them with paraffin.

Then, of course, the first frosty day she woke up and found they were full of stones. No one seemed to care. They are so heavy and full of pebbles. They just bring her the milk and go away again into the snow.

New paragraph. This is for the little one, whom I call Hamlet, because he knows quite well what he is doing. He is natural. It is other things which seem to ruin him. He is a litany in black. When the snow comes, as you can imagine, this is a very pretty sight. He has some goldfish in a bowl which we share. They are beautiful but unripe. He has a face like a fiddle and speaks utterly about her. On Wednesdays she arrives to worry him, and give the doctor dramatic gold. This is completely false because she does not exist. I will explain it perfectly, because he cannot write for himself. They were together in a house for a number of nights. It was an old house, and he was old. I do not mean his hair was grey. He was ancient to her, because he lived in many clever dimensions. He could do it at will, like a quick dream, but she could not follow him. For instance, he could go into tomorrow and bring her back presents, cake she had not yet made, shawls, bangles, and good news about her parents in a far country. This was strange because he could come back to the Now, having visited Tomorrow. She was afraid. Then one day he vanished. It was a hot day in August. Everything was silent. Cattle. Grass. Dogs. Everything except the crickets. I forgot the crickets. He was gone. It was quaint. He had done it in the night as usual, and reached tomorrow, but couldn't get back. His hands are very white. Vasec touches them and says: 'Snow. Snow. Snow,' over and over again. I do not know what this means, except that he couldn't get back to her. He lived in the house, he didn't move for fear of losing her, but they could not touch each other. Every day there was his pipe smoked from yesterday, his desk used, paper, ink, bed rumpled. It was acute pain. She would fill bowls of flowers from the fields and pray to the little weather ikons, but it was obsolete. The servants would find new money on the mantelpiece and tell her. They followed round the house, standing near the goldfish, because he loved them and had quiet thoughts standing by them every day. But they could not touch, or row the boat, or lie in the sun together. This was fatal. She gave the peasants many obols to find him, but they could not. He was there all the time, but acting in tomorrow. And they did not think of looking for him there. Vasec says if there is enough snow he will go back one day. Because it is cold living in the house alone, and the empty beds and isolated note-books, etc. Vasec is enormously in pain for him, he weeps. He says his womb is poured out for the little one's sorrow. There is not ointment, of course. The old man said: 'Time the great healer.' But Time is the great separator. I cannot bear Time. There is too much time here among the snows.

He began to write to her. Many letters in black, and leave them about the house. But he had soon used up all the words. And she could not answer, because you cannot address a letter—MY HUSBAND, TOMORROW. Besides he was getting farther away. Soon it was a whole day. Then a week. Then so far that the ink faded, and he would carve it in the cliffs where she could find it when she went bathing to remember him. It was frantic. She would lie in the fields and let the flowers strangle her. Vasec is too copious to understand precisely, but he feels it all, like a bull. When the hunchback lies in the snow the little one has a pale face, but with great dignity. He runs solemnly to the goldfish. He is not embarrassed but contemplative.

I say it is the snow, but I mean it is really a partition. The minutes are snow-flakes. One cannot stop to count them. All night, lying in the blond bed we see the snowflakes marked up by the clock. When I think of little machines like clocks or waterclosets, or theories of the universe, or paper on the lawn, or the late final, I am puzzled by myself. It is so completely useless here, this territory where we speak through walls and fill our bowls with laughter. I am writing this with the most absolute precision, so do not be impatient. The men outside and the men inside, for example. There are five of us left to create the world— would you say the *real* world?—but they will not listen to us. They like the sound of the water rushing into the pan, the treacle lolling from the jar, the poets papering their souls in bad taste. Really. They sit beside their wives, who are names, and if I lift a femur to show them what it really is they are outraged. Moral indignation, they call it, but it is fear. It is the little nameless, shameless, timeless thing which has come into the house without its dress of words. It is naked and danger- ous. We who speak through the wall have given over with words, because they destroy all this: snow falling on Vasec's eyeballs, Fifi playing with herself and hymning, speeches through the wall. This banquet of quietness and communion. I am a writer. Yesterday I said to the old man: 'It is getting towards Christmas. I have a confession to make. I am Lawrence Durrell, the writer, who wrote until one day the world came into terrible focus. I am the writer who never really wrote. Because the moment I became a real writer there was no parti- tion of snow or minutes: and I had to come here for a long holiday from myself.' Whether you go to the slaughter-house or the monastery it makes very little difference. This is so much confidential paper for them to gather and puzzle over: for the coroner to put beside the hatchet and the other exhibits as he sends in the only verdict. The only possible comment of the world in which the watercloset is king.

Vasec is here on holiday because he can still taste the blood, whatever he does. You can fill his mouth with snow or sand or balsam or merde, it makes no difference. In his mind's eye (his enormous eye) he is hanging upside down over the slimy tiles, while they empty the blood out of him. Always. So he is feigning a sort of snow-blindness all day long. Pieter is rowing across the Jordan all day long. They are puzzled by the queer apparatus of the man: the hymn-books, the golden sand, the missionaries in the sago-palms, from pole to pole, etc. I fear nothing when there is snow, because the Lord of Hosts is moving in him, powerfully, like a heavy fish in a heavy-stream of flesh. Pieter's twelve stone buttocks and hips so medieval a stuff for the electric Host. Yet it is there. Therefore I do not fear, but watch the unlucky ones running in the garden, like solitary arrows. For the others I will not answer. I will speak only for Fifi, Hamlet, Pieter, Vasec and the Dancer. The last two we include from courtesy, as disciples. The Dancer is so fragile that his audience quivers with him, and becomes a membrane. He is blown like a trunk of silk in the wind. I must speak for these five because the disease of the little black words is my disease. In the night I wake up and see a great spirit opening above me: truth, or desire, or God. I take it eagerly to the table and open it. It is always full of these little black maggots which have eaten away its centre. That is why I have fallen into a long disuse and silence towards the new year. The doctors are puzzled and fearful at the mystical essence which is pouring from my exhausted body. They fear I may be sickening for an attack of influenza. But in the mirror I assure myself and close like a penknife with laughter. The secret. They will never discover, dull merdes that they are, for they have no faith. I no longer write on the pieces of paper they put for me. I take them instead to the watercloset with me, as a more appropriate symptom of what I feel. It is useless, you see, when a big free spirit like death or love is placed at the mercy of a coroner. Poor little mortal, he is so afraid of it that he micturates all over it, urinates on it with fear. Forgive them, for they know not what they do. All the writing the doctors will get out of me these days is the little daily parcel I leave for them. They are so droll with their machinery of language and spirits clothed in little black words that I fill my bowl with laughter at them. There is no other answer to them but this wobbling bowl which they must come and carry away from my room of snow.

It is essential when it snows to keep a firm hold on your sense of laughter. Specially when the moon is born and the shadows of ink fall across Vasec wherever he moves. The Dancer swerves into a sort of illusion when he goes outside. His tremendous fingers conjure out of air, among the inky trees, and the soft liquid ink which melts on his boots. His body is an inky fluid, spinning in many madrigal worlds. His long face means nothing, but has been given him by the moon. In my disuse and silence I realize this: we have no firm friends, we five, but a catalogue of spirits to breathe through us. The little one, for example. His eyes are so blue, it is simply the pieces of moon filling his empty cranium. With Vasec, when we are given the sun, you can see it shining through him, red his great hands of coral: in the lobes of his ears red. His voice is candent. He will empty his body into the scarlet shirt and stand upright, with his spirit touching the sun at all points. There are spikes of sun in his hair. At the window a private nimbus of darling silver. At night where does the sun go down but into his breast, softening him to peace, pressing him down to sleep in the ugly bed. Myself it is the sleek rain on the orchards, because my wife cries out like the pigeons in their soft purple throats, and the aristocracy of the rain gather about her. The guns are brutal but musical. And the compassionate blood trickles from the broken beaks on farm-land. Enough. Our spirits are all dour, crook-shanked as the apple or the olive. At night the dogs cry on the hills. And in the new year the bugles shadow the fox. The frolic red coats pass the windows and the horses are stifled in their own pollen. It is candid of me to write about the big fireplace where the logs crackle in eternal amusement, or the void bed in a room full of the lights of cars. If I speak to her in the language of the big spirit she will understand, but be too afraid to enter into it with me. Perhaps all this will change.

There is the hunchback's lake in the garden which remembers me, and my farm, and the attitudes of the cattle. We sit by the side of it on the benches and made handsome poems together when he is God. Towards Christmas now they are chopping the trees, which is a pity, because they are great linguists. St. John the Divine and other notable people walk on the ice. Little figures far off on the benches, obscene, because they blacken the action. Pieter is weeping because the Jordan is frozen and he cannot get a single baptismal drop. But we teach him to melt the snow in his mouth and he is soon merry again.

At night it is like a wedding-cake lying there in motionless celebrations. The Dancer makes a silky entertainment on the ice without falling. His agony speaks to the trees who are supine, and he perpetuates them in his thin body and deft legs, and makes them durable for ever. It is necessary to catch him and the woods are full of lanterns and yuletide faces calling. But he is too nervous and explicit in his speed to be caught easily. He speaks a form of terror with his body, so they cannot hold him. They are in boots and sanity, and he is dressed in the spirit of bare feet. Therefore, as you imagine, he creates a whole method of ballet in his elusive fever: little scribbles of his action made with a pencil: how the legs bend at the joints, and the quivering tactual liths of the fingers. His wide feet slobber on the ice as he lifts them. It is Ariel they are subduing with lanterns. Poor cattle, they do not understand in their boots. I shout from the window to explain the logic of motion, but they do not hear. I shout but they turn aside. I shout and the morning star comes up in my throat over the wedding-cake, and I am by the fire, she sleeping in the armchair, warm, mammal; or warm, victorious, in the bed, cherished by pillows, mammal. It is a dark and warm-blooded seal, heavy and plangent, with whom I play these aquatic games in the forever. A seal in bed, when the morning star climbs my throat into the sunlight. It is too much sanity this bare room, with paper, blankets, and the tin bowl. It is so sane that in the morning my eyes grow icicles of pathos and I cannot see any more, only the seal's heavy body broken through a prism of colours. This is an eclogue written with the icicles, which impinges only on my one unit here, safe, captive, among five captive units. Every day with the paper they give me I distil my spirit, and chop away the inessentials by writing them with the gaunt pen, and this little pot of black snow. Then, when I become really a writer, I sit all day with my hands pushed aside, useless. It is not making what goes on outside, I have discovered. It is what occurs in the inside spirits, where the great beings make their territory and the words cannot touch them. In this area everything is explosion, high tension, stand away, a million volts, you are warned not to touch. There are big notices to tell you that trespassers will be prosecuted and there are no paths where it is safe to walk. Consequently I talk to Fifi in the wall and pretend that I am not culpable. Or watch the sun shining on Vasec's great golden thumbs. It is more a bare orchestra of silence, purer than icicles, when I exist this way. I am nearer home, without agony and the passion in the finger-tips. Only I regret the warm blood of the seal, the eloquent bright storage battery, running under the tepid rubber skin of the animal. I have tried to explain this many times in words, from different alti-tudes, but it is useless. I am content now when they bring me flowers, because they see I am peaceful, and speaking after the manner of men. This is a joke! But the flowers make a parody of my childhood for me in this snow sanity, and I adore them as other creatures adore angels. They are so big and rich: the heavy ingots of the roses. Really. Take them to pieces and weigh them in your hand. Nothing at all. But just feel the great lolling heads and you are at loss. You are exceedingly amazed. You press yourself against them, you caress them as if you were a cat. You feed them with snow, etc. But they are destroyed. Ecstasy always leads to destruction. And in this destruction you can feel the bigger things, the spirits which run about the room on fire, like gases. And you are opened all of a sudden like an untenanted house, and the sun makes a progress through you, and the moon brightens your armour, and the nineteen winds chisel out the pure personality for you. You begin to exist. You begin to deserve action.

When you are like that, purified, the logic of the watercloset com-pels you to take a long holiday from yourself, and your seals, apple-trees, farm-lands. You are surrounded by little machines, telephones, watches, gasworks, newspapers, chocolate, tiger's milk, Lent, canned fruit, and buttons. The world makes a wry face at you because you are smiling, *utterly and internally* smiling, without fraud. When you are dancing you are surrounded by lanterns and men with mouths com-pressed like thimbles. Then there is nothing left but to make as much laughter as you can in honour of the occasion, and ask for flowers. Here, my bowl is full of green amusement. Take it away. That is all you are fit for.

[267]

I am thoroughly heraldic when I say this, and it makes them furious. They take away my flowers and the blue man grips his jowls in his fist and wants to knock me down. I have given him many opportunities, because I am a writer, and have many languages on the tip of my tongue, ready for emergency. However, they go away and shut the door, and I communicate with Vasec, who is much worse recently. They can understand nearly everything he says, so they are pleased. The old man looks profoundly cautious, asking questions, and gathering the answers. When they understand everything they will take him to his shop where he is already hanging upside down, bleeding on to the tiles. He has been gutted and executed in the little tabernacle at the back of the shop, with the tiled floor. I suppose there is no hope of them understanding a single thing I say, it is so precise and flawless and immaculate and virginal. There is no hope.

But Vasec was never as chosen as we were. He is included from courtesy, as a disciple more than anything else. There is so little sun in this country that one cannot wonder at it. In the south, among the oranges and the coloured peasants he would learn much more quickly than here: these dull Celtic seasons spinning on the axis of this white glass of milk, little bed, bowl of roses, paper, ink, pen. As for Hamlet, he is in a private act the whole time, so that the scenery is something beyond his book. He is the Black Prince winning his spurs in a stained glass window. At the altar keeping the dark vigil among his empty armour: blind morion, greaves, corselet. And the Grail growing in him, pouring into his arteries, stiffening and budding in his loins. Amen.

Pieter speaks through the wall and tells me that Christmas is coming. In a million coloured windows, the holly season, on a million leaves of greeting, in the park the robin and the hautboy. I am expressionless as a button, because all the pictures he has are of poor quality. In mission houses the harmoniums are snoring. Cheap prints of the Saviour and maps of Damascus. In the hall the coats hang white. And from the front door oozes the mission fog.

I prefer the soft vocal turkeys. The glib wines in the bottles. The archaic cake. The children shouting in the rip of paper, etc. And from the front door oozing the old patriarch himself, the red riding-coated bearded senex, snuff-drunk and roaring, with his nose like a sabre. However. That is a story to be spoken to the seals only, where they spin in the ice floes in an arctic garden, among the commotion of many waters. For others we can only say: It is the dead season. The fires are low. And the black traveller goes across country like the wind, mailed in his suit of ice and terror. And in the old inns they have barred the doors against the spirits, and let the grates glow out. Make many crosses for the saints, for the twelve, for the lichened tombs in the graveyard and their geology of stirring bones. The quick father mounting for comfort, and the virginity like a circle of silver. The hardmouthed lady of the manor in ice, and old ivy-clad parson with Bible at his hip. Make many crosses. They would rise if it were not for the curious lichens that entangle their craniums and fuddle speech. Make many crosses and a brief orison for the dead season when the sun is blood, and the moon ink.

All this Pieter does not understand. It makes him reproving which is a sign that he is afraid of it. He prefers the sable sand, and the nigger-boys diving for pennies, and the sharks hymning, and the poles rotating to the tunes of Bishop Keble. Particularly those winsome harmoniums with yellow teeth and halitosis: from whose guts the maiden's fingers plunder the sacerdotal farts and curvettes of tune. As I say, this is poor quality. Sometimes when I realize it I wonder whether Pieter is really one of us, or whether he too is included as a courtesy. Not as a disciple, because he believes he knows everything already. No one can teach him anything. Once or twice I have hinted that he has yet to exist, but it makes no difference at all to him. None. He sets the harmoniums playing in his waistcoat and that's that. One can only fill one's bowl and hope for the best.

It is not the dead who concern us here, but the living. When I say this I am reminded of Hamlet, acting in his wife's bed in a sort of convulsion that is pure theatre to me. He is beyond her, days ahead, watching the calamities which wait for her. In this dimension it is as if he were suddenly trapped in a vacuum. He writes an occasional note but the words are like stale urine. The unique gift of swords in language is not his. He comes to me and says: 'Write.' And I close my hands on the wood and try for him. But there are only new ways of dressing the spirits for her. The spirits themselves we cannot seal down in a commonplace envelope, under an ordinary stamp.

'Dear Ophelia,

'There are five of us here who would interest you if you could have faith. We cannot see clearly but we are certainly fit to lead the blind. It has rained as usual this Christmas. Old Sam has died. I would send you roses but it costs too much. Fifi broke faith and hung herself in the lavatory. Her breast hurt her a lot and there was a mess on the floor. I hope the kingcups are still signalling to you, because we cannot. We have not art to reckon our groans. Yours, dear wretch, while this machine is to us Hamlet.'

After that the immense ocean in which the goldfish pioneer like elderly clergymen. We keep telling them that everything has been discovered that is worth discovering by their methods, but they will not believe us. They make immense goggling rotations, eternally amazed to find that the world is round, and that two and two goldfish make four goldfish, not counting reflections. And that the poor in spirit have inherited the world. But goldfish, if you could turn your snouts inward on yourselves, what adventuring would be possible! What a superb cartography to see yourself for the first time, filleted, impure, translucent, and ready for the apocalypse. If you could make a scalpel of your love that would cut down to the very juice of the bone, then there would be some hope for you. Alas! You are essentially clerical. It would be useless to make a new set of beatitudes for you and feed them to you like breadcrumbs, or spores, or ants' eggs. Rotate on to oblivion, you shining gorgons. The new numen shall swallow you whether you like it or not, when the hour falls in many melodious strokes from the steeples. Ineluctably.

With Pieter it is so tragic, these harmoniums belching at him all night long. I would get impatient and cross him out, if I were not certain that the Holy Ghost is swimming in his ribs and deltoids at times. Vasec is different. It is no ghost but a kind of luminous thing in him. Towards the end of the journey he would sit quiet, I feel sure, and contemplate his thumbs, plotting against himself. Then a quick act of blood with a rusty chopper, or a secret shotgun. He is like that when faced with verities. Copious.

[270]

Well there is the snow. This damned carpet which makes every-thing sane white. The bed, the walls, the flowers. The robins appear like toys and swell with indignation. It is towards the time of the star that I empty this paper on to the floor, and walk up and down in my little whitewashed slaughter-house maddened by sanity.

The Dancer is hymning over the lake forever, uttering little wild cries. Soon he will fall to earth like a bird and they will have to find him before the rigor sets his jaw in that gnomic smile. He is very madrigal, with luminous eyes and hair like soot. He leaps to the ceiling and returns of his own accord. I am excited by the process of the muscles that make this quilt of flesh for him so easy to land on. He does not fall.

As for me, I am sitting here as usual. Did you think I had gone? Tonight the cattle are full of the nostalgic malaise of the nativity. I am sitting here with my coat on murdering everything as fast as I can write it down. There is a kind of humour in me, but no malice. Only the agony that starts from the hip and cripples one. If you see my wife in Venice, or in Vallombrosa, or in cardinal-crimson Urbino, or in the torrid straits, or in the doldrums, give her my love. I tell you this with my wrists turned outwards to show my sincerity. If you could see my face there would be no need. Every night it is the warm bed, the flesh of the seal, the pure taste of hair in the mouth. This is in confidence. I think you will find her where four oceans meet, in a favourable trade wind, dancing southward under white canvas. I cannot be sure, be-cause from this my slaughter-house, my ark, my monastery, I can see nothing. It is a sort of lighthouse, but it looks over totally unique oceans, Asias in which strange flora and fauna look at me with the faces of a new childhood. It is very lonely, but there is nothing to be done about it. When I speak the words torment the doctors, because there is as yet no vocabulary, no glossary in the tongue I am using. It is a magnificent experiment, but I am lonely.

This morning the old man said to me: 'Come, it is getting on towards Christmas. Have you nothing more to confess?'

I looked into his spectacles and saw once and for all the utter ignorance which he was hiding in his beard. In the strange playground of his mind the apparatus of the watercloset logic laid down like millions of sets of railway lines. All leading nowhere. I was candid.

'I am a writer. This room is the theatre in which my surgery is made complete. I am trying to eat the whole pantheon of spirits, with a dictionary. It is quite fatal to approach me unless you have the faith. Otherwise I can only hand you my little bowl of green laughter and turn aside in sorrow. Why do you fear?'

He said: 'Are you lonely? Would you like a nice bowl of flowers?'

I said: 'There are five of us who alone exist.'

It was not true as I realize now, but he said, being very masterful: 'Come, speak to me. You do not deceive me for a second. I know when you have your lucid moments.'

Then I began to breathe in a certain way and he left quickly, for fear of causing me more pain.

I am sitting here as usual, but in a total loss. This is a lamentation because they have failed me. I said that five of us existed, but it is not true. In the night which is neuralgic with snow I weep and admit to myself it is not true. The Dancer does not. He can dance like a feather, but he does not. Vasec does not. Pieter will not. In the fantastic barracks of the idea I made many coloured regiments, but they have all failed. Fifi was hanging from a rusty nail. She did not either. Then when the curtain begins to descend, in the music, the shuffle of programmes, the applause, I see the terrific protagonist: the last one left on the stage: and it is I. In the final blaze of light, so tiny on the immense stage, and so awake, I kneel down before the annihilating ego who has no id. In this washed white room, among the snows, I kneel down with the pen in my hands. It is nearly Christmas and there is much to be done. There will be great fires, sumptuous with logs and flames: wine: charity. The charity that is a familiar word.

I will be sitting here as usual. The paper is in many sheets, but finished now. The weather is cold, but topical. We shall have snow as the eternal novelty. There will be lighted nobility on the lake again tonight.

This is my carol.

Corfu, December 1938

Delphi

Published in Réalités. *Paris and New York.*
Republished in Venture. *New York. 1965.*

To wander across this country of stone fables, shattered mythologies, blunted statues which have been passed (like wax in a flame) across the sun's burning-glass can be both frightening as well as inspiring. How different from Italy, where the beauty comes out of domestication—the touch of the wise human hand is everywhere. Everything has a history, can be traced, decoded, understood. But Greece . . . everything is confused, piled on top of itself, contorted, burnt dry, exploded; and the tentativeness of the scholar's ascriptions is a heartbreak. It is as if nothing were provable any more, everything has become shadowy, provisional. The scholar begins to stammer; he can hardly tell us anything without using the words 'probably', 'possibly'. Sometimes, greatly daring, he advances towards a phrase like 'it seems likely that . . .'. One feels that one has arrived too late; after all, most of what we know comes from so late a traveller as Pausanias, for whom Greece was as much of a tourist centre as it has become today. But long after the ravages of Sulla, the Emperor Hadrian had tried to revive Greece with gifts and temples, and superficially it must have seemed busy and prosperous enough. But this Neo-Greek revival was a hollow thing.

  Yet if this disappointment persists for the traveller today there is something more certain upon which he can base himself; the landscape remains as unchanging, uncompromising, ravishingly pure and vertical. And each of the ancient sites has its own flavour—expressed from the very ground, it seems. I use the word 'express' since it suggests also the extraction of precious oils from a fruit like the olive. The rareness of Greece lies in this singular purity of landscape-awareness; the historic memories echo on, drone on like the bees that once droned in the tomb of Agamemnon. (Alas, they have been killed off by the injudicious use of a modern chemical spray on the fields of corn and barley around the tomb, where they fed.)

Among these ancient sites Delphi is the most grandiose, as well as the most sphingine; the long winding roads leading away north from Livadia coil like the sacred serpent. The landscape, curled inwards upon itself, reveals itself only in snatches; the mountain ranges come up and recede, recline and rise up. It is almost as if the dose had been one measured by the ancient physicians who built this road towards the centre of the earth—towards that mysterious omphalos which I first found as a boy, lying in an open field above the road. I still have an impertinent picture of myself, leaning negligently against it as if at a bar. . . . But among so many visits to Delphi I have never found the slightest variation in the impression it makes on me; the latest was last year, after an absence from Greece of nearly twenty years. What is this strange impression? As I have said, each site in Greece has its singular emanation: Mycenae, for example, is ominous and grim—like the castle where Macbeth is laid. It is a place of tragedy, and blood. One doesn't get this from its history and myths—they merely confirm one's sensation of physical unease. Watch the people walking around the site. They are afraid that the slightest slip and they may fall into a hole in the ground, and break a leg. It is a place of rich transgressions, tears, and insanity. A few miles away lies dream-saturated Epidaurus, so lax and so quiet; one would not dare to be ill for long if one lived there. Its innocence is provoking. But Delphi. . . . The heart rises as the road rises and as the great scarps of mountain rise on either side; the air becomes chill. Finally, round the last corner, there she is in her eyrie like a golden eagle, her claws clamped around the blood-coloured rock which falls away with vertiginous certainty to the dry bed of the Pleistos. The long thrilling sweep of the olive groves—greener than anywhere in Greece—is like the sudden sweep of strings in some great symphony. And then the ribbon of sea, the small port; for once the sea seems diminished. Behind one the rock climbs, the paths climb, the trees climb with one, until all is bare rock and blueness once again. Up there an eagle flies—one thinks of Zeus! But the atmosphere is so pure that one can hear the stroke of his great wings as he frays the air. A slight wheezy creaking, like a man rowing across water.

Aesthetically there is nothing much to see at Delphi except Delphi itself: would you go to Lourdes to study modern sculpture? Once again the fragments belong to different epochs, different cultures. Moreover they are all votive objects, mere genuflections in stone or terra cotta. Even the famous charioteer is of a poor provenance and hardly gives one an echo of Plato's metaphor.

But the place itself; it is built upon two enigmas and neither of them is easily decipherable—the omphalos and the oracle. In an age looking for both physical and intellectual points of reference these two symbols stand for something important, even momentous. Somehow in Delphi while one is uneasy it is not with a sense of fear so much as a sense of premonition; what is here, one feels, is *intact* in its purity. The force is still there buried in the rocky cliffs. It could speak if it wished and overturn everything with one reverberating statement—but of course one of those statements curled up in a double negative. Is not Truth two-sided? Walking about the hillside in the shadow of the pines, listening to the gentle creaking of the wind and the pleasant susurrus of the cicadas, one has sudden moments of panic. Perhaps this is the moment—perhaps *today* the oracle is due to make its re-entry into the world. If it did, if from the heart of the rock we heard one of those terrific and yet ordinary judgements upon the world of affairs, would we be ready to receive it, act upon it? Delphi is a sort of mute challenge. All the other considerations seem vague, confused. Side by side with the confusion of periods and styles in the Museum one finds in the main street of the little town ample evidence that the Greeks, with their passion for novelty, are still busy accumulating influences. Among the many beautiful carpets hanging up for sale in the little shops along the main street my eye catches something; they hang like dead rabbits in a poulterer's shop. Closer examination reveals them to be the coon skin hats sacred to that great modern god Davy Crockett. His film must have passed this way! The small commerçants of Delphi are not slow to catch on to what the tourist public might need. Indeed the idea is a delicious one. That one should travel from New York to Delphi to buy a coon skin hat for oneself is typical of both modern and ancient Greece. After due reflection I bought one and had it despatched to Henry Miller. . . .

But the oracle, the Pytho? Once again the historians begin to stammer. Apollo killed the Dragon and left the corpse of this gigantic dead beast to rot. Out of this grew the oracular power of the Pytho.

The word means 'to rot'. But what is one to make of this farrago of apparent rubbish? The modern Greek poet George Seferis ventures a thought. 'In such fertilizing compost the power of the god of harmony, light and prophecy took root and sprouted. Perhaps the myth means that the dark powers are the light's yeast; and that the stronger they are, the more intense the light when they are overcome.' One notices above all, the word 'perhaps'; for if anyone should know for certain it would be Seferis. But like the rest of us he is left guessing. This must excuse my own small venture in interpretation. The word 'to rot' for me is symbolical and suggests a spiritual truth into which the Delphic visitor was initiated. One does not know out of what ancient rites grew the notion of re-fertilizing ground with dead flesh. It is older than Athens. But perhaps the 'ripeness' of Shakespeare's 'ripeness is all' is not far from the Delphic notion of 'to rot'. The point at which the body begins to rot is the fertilizing point of death; this manner of trying to make death fertile may have had a symbolic value. . . . From 'ripe' to 'rot' is a short distance in English, as Shakespeare has told us in a famous passage. But there was something special about fruit that had dropped for the Greeks, in distinction to fruit that had been picked. Athenaeius, quoting from a lost writer, says that the Athenians when they placed a ritual meal for the Dioscuri (the twins) made sure that it consisted of cheese, barley cake and *fallen* olives and pears, in remembrance of their ancient mode of life. The gods preferred the perfect maturity of the *fallen* fruit. Even today the oil of the *fallen* olive is reserved for the use of the Church. And as for the twins . . . did they represent perhaps (notice the perhaps) the dichotomy which resides at the heart of man's psychology and which is reflected in his language? The Truth-telling oracle of Delphi never lost sight of the double-axe in man's mind, and the double nature of his consciousness, the double sex of his psyche . . . Even today we have such an idea in the American phrase 'double-take' and the English corruption of French 'double-entendre'. Truth, like the sword, has a double edge. . . . The oracle with all its theological sophistication knew this only too well.

The fact that Apollo created the Delphi we know today does nothing to qualify the confusion, for if you turn to read his biography in the *Dictionary of Classical Mythology* you come upon a God who sprouts attributes as ivy sprouts leaves. . . . Most of them too seem to be mutually contradictory. He is remarkably elusive, uses a number of different passports, while his personal behaviour on many occasions seems quite unsuitable for the god of harmony, light and prophecy. Once again it may be that our authorities are too late; they came here long after an age of darkness had settled over Greece. Now only these fragments remain to echo on in our troubled twentieth-century minds.

Nor will the long excursion to the Corycian cave do anything to clarify matters, though in itself it is worth making if only for the magnificent scenery of the Delphic hill complex, and the taste of the pure Greek air. It is so dry and clear, the atmosphere, that you can hear sounds a great way off—such as a distant shepherd's pipe in the valley and the tonk of sheep-bells; or sounds much smaller in the scale which startle one by their purity. I am thinking of the clicking of a tortoise walking over the burning rocks by the stadium, of the whiplash of a sudden gust of wind in the pines; of the steady susurrus of plain un-stirred air among the dry grasses of the theatre. They utter a faint breath while remaining apparently quite still.

The cave of the oracle was blocked about a hundred years ago by a fall in the cliff, but the famous waters of inspiration still pour out into the glade and rush down the steep precipice to the bed of the Pleistos. Seferis records that the waters of the Castilian spring have a taste of thyme, but for me they have had always the faint flavour of mint. Cold and pure, they nourish the roots of the giant plane-tree which stands guard over this ancient precinct. Last year, peering up into the dense shadow of its leaves we saw a brown paper parcel hanging there, tied with string. A votive object? This was not as unlikely as it sounds for even today the folklore of Greece is full of the habit of leaving ex-voto's in sacred places. Alas! the truth was, though charming, more prosaic. The guide explained that the parcel contained his lunch; he kept it cool by hanging it in the shadow of the huge plane leaves. 'This tree is my ice-box,' he said, not without pride at his own perspicacity.

The traveller who stoops to take up some of the sacred water of inspiration should remember to drink to the poets of modern Greece who have now begun to take their rightful place in the European tradition to which they belong; it is a slender chain of gold links . . . Solomos, Palamas, Sekelianos, Cavafy, Seferis, Elytis. . . .

Perhaps one of them will recover for us the meaning of the oracle we so much need today?

Troubadour

Published in The Sunday Times. *London. 1960.*
Reprinted in Gazebo. *Bath. June 1963.*

Poverty and poetry have been regarded as bedfellows for so long now that I doubt whether I shall be believed in saying that I once knew a poet who made a living from his work. Nevertheless it is so. He was a wandering ballad-maker of Cyprus called Janis, and he travelled about on a moth-eaten motorbike with his saddle-bags stuffed with broadsheets. The Mediterranean has always been full of poets and every village in Cyprus has at least two. It is a communal gift rather than a personal one, and poetry has not yet been completely banished to the parlour as it has with us, though modernity (in terms of movements and periodicals) is fast catching up with feudal life. But village poetry is based upon spontaneity of rhyming, and every year there is a sort of Cypriot Eisteddfod on the Troodos mountains to which each village sends its best poets. They compete in an open contest of sixteen syllable rhymes, the challenger hooting out the first line which must then be capped without hesitation by his rival. Public applause decides the winner. Sometimes these wit contests continue interminably, all through the night, until the winner is declared. The arena is wired for sound and the contestants dress up in the full glory of their traditional attire, proud as peacocks. First one will advance to the microphone and hoot out his line, accompanying it with a vaunting gesture as befits a challenger—twirling his moustache or rubbing his boots on the ground like a bull when it is about to charge. Then his rival must take his place and cap the first phrase with something better. The best poets are full of dirty tricks and frequent linguistic fouls are committed, though there are no referees beyond the audience. Quite a high proportion of the verses are below the belt, which used to raise awful broadcasting problems: for what is regarded as joyful poetic licence in a community gathering was often deemed a trifle indecorous to put out on the radio in the course of a community programme.

But poetry is also still regarded as a solace and a fitting art with which to enshrine marriages, funerals and births. The professional keener still exists. Once I saw an elderly man standing outside Kyrenia post office plaintively singing a song of woe which had something to do with his son being unable to get a pension from the Army authorities. He had had it printed and was selling copies at a millieme each. It was a mournful little thing entitled 'The Sad Case of Aristides Koutsos and his plaint against the British Empire'. It was in the traditional village metre which goes something like this:

> Now listen all ye villagers and I will now rehearse
> The sorrows of a family which went from bad to worse
> Because the British Empire has denied my boy his pension
> And filled our hearts with agony and awful apprehension.

The old man, after finding that he had no redress in law for his grievance, had decided to solace himself in this artistic fashion. He was listened to with deep sympathy and his ballad sold well.

But Janis, compared to these, was a professional writer and the greater part of his ballads were news-ballads as were those of our own early ballad-makers like Nat Elderton (he of the 'ale-crammed nose'). Janis wrote them with the greatest facility and had them set up on credit by a printer in Nicosia. Stuffing the saddle-bags of his motorbike with them he set off on an island circuit made familiar by many years of ballad-selling. He was careful to base his circuit on such country fairs as were taking place at the time, since he knew that a fair tended to draw all the villagers of neighbouring localities into town for the day. In the main square he would set up shop. Putting his bundles of broadsheets around his feet he would start in his pleasant singsong voice to half sing, half declaim, his latest production. He was a small good-looking man in his early forties, always clad in a neat black suit and spotless white shirt open at the neck. Long practice had taught him the strength and staying power of his own voice, so that he was careful always to husband his energies, and never try and compete with raucous hucksters or café loudspeakers. He chose his position just out of the central mêlée where he could be best listened to. He nearly always began with a juicy murder.

[279]

Now listen men and maidens all, at what last week befell
A virgin maid, Calliope, in a lone Paphos dell.
The river ran with blood for weeks, and blood stained all the grass
A virgin's blood for vengeance cries to heaven up above.
In darkness was the dagger sheathed, in silence stole away
The ravisher of Paphian youth, he did not stop to pray
As if the fiends of hell were there to hiss him on his way,
While the poor girl, her life blood spent, just gurgled where she lay.
Now who would cut that soft white throat so neat from ear to ear
But Hadjilouk the barber with a shop right next the pier.
For years he'd lusted for the lass, for years she had refused,
Her brother once spat in his eye and he was not amused. . . .

So the ballad would unroll in that pleasant unhurried voice, while
the villagers gathered round in a tight circle, with many a pleasant
shiver of horror, to listen to him. When he had finished he picked up a
bundle from the ground, crying 'Who will buy?' in a pleasant chirping
voice. His sales were usually good, and his wares not expensive; two
milliemes was a price of a ballad. They could be either recited aloud in
the chimney corner or sung to traditional airs. He had several types of
poem to offer and they were graded according to subject matter; there
were folktales set in verse, or local news-events (usually murders of the
Arden of Feversham type), and there were also a number of what he
called 'Erotika'—rather ferocious songs of naked passion and hopeless
love. These were done up in rather a special way—for on each cover
there was the reproduction of a Rank starlet which the printer had
cunningly overprinted; sometimes she had a dripping heart with a
dagger in it, and gouts of blood dripping down over her vital statistics.
At other times there was a masked man peering over her shoulder with
another dagger, preparing to let her have it from behind. Sometimes,
too, she had a noose around her neck. I often wondered whether Janis
had ever heard of copyright but my native tact prevented me from
asking him. After all, what is such a small matter between poets?
When he had sold all he could, he would usually retire to the
tavern for a glass of wine before resuming his journey. Once I was able
to sit for an hour with him and question him on his work. He answered
my questions with good nature, and with a touch of the resigned
weariness which comes over poet's faces under questioning. He told

me that his poetic skill was a gift which his father had handed down to him. His father, too, had sold ballads but had never been successful at it. He could never make ends meet while he, Janis, the son, was making a small but decent living. It was hard in winter, however. 'What makes it possible,' he said 'for the poet today is the motorbike. You see, in my father's day he had to be content with a camel which is very slow. It took ages to get from fair to fair; whereas now I can often cover three or four fairs in a day and motor from one end of the island to the other in a couple of hours. This morning, for example, I began at Paphos and when I leave you I'll run over to Larnaca this evening for the fair there. It makes a difference.'

I had several meetings with Janis and we became quite good friends; and later that year I got him to agree to let me take some photographs of him to illustrate an article which I had in mind to write. But the wretched crisis intervened before I could do so, and his friendship, like that of so many Cypriots, was temporarily submerged in the hate and despair of the times. We nodded when we met, but I was careful not to force my company upon him lest his acquaintance with a British official might earn him the unwelcome attentions of the nationalists. Once I was in his printer's offices when I saw him come in to pay for his broadsheets. He looked tired and ill. He had a saddle-bag full of millieme pieces which he poured out in a stream over the counter. They took an age to count. He did not see me as I was seated in shadow at the back of the shop.

Later again I had news of him from a villager. He had been forced to give up poetry as all movement was hampered by troop movements and curfews. He had decided to retire to the home of an aunt at Paphos until he could once more resume his trade.

The day before I left the island I bumped into him coming out of a church in Larnaca. 'Janis,' I cried, 'well met,' and for a moment he smiled. But then he checked the involuntary gesture of pleasure and his face clouded over. 'I am leaving tomorrow,' I said. I made as if to shake hands with him but he placed his hands behind his back. He said quietly, 'You did not write the article, did you? I am glad, for it would have made trouble for me.'

'One day I will,' I said. 'In happier times.'

'In happier times,' he said gravely, and inclining his head turned and moved slowly off into the twilight.

[281]

It seemed a hollow enough promise at the time, for the troubles were at their height, and no political progress seemed possible. And so Janis slipped out of sight and mind until last week when I received a postcard from a friend who had seen Janis at work again, reciting in Kyrenia. I wonder what he charges for a broadsheet today and whether the Rank starlets are still doing their stuff?

Beccafico: A Tragic History

Published in an edition limited to 150 copies. Montpellier. 1963.

The sight of a tall glass jar hanging from the ceiling of a Greek grocery store in Marseilles, crammed full of pickled birds, suddenly reminded me. Beccafico! I do not think there is any other place which exports this medieval delicacy today, and there is certainly no other island where this little fig-hunting marauder is trapped in such vast quantities. Those travellers who have penetrated the life of Cyprus at all deeply must, at one time or another, in a remote monastery perhaps or at a village wedding, come upon the delicacy to which beccafico has given its lovely name. In Crusading times it was a favourite comestible and even graced the banqueting halls of kings. The Knights of St. John, who had a very keen nose for business indeed, made it (together with the heavy sweet Cyprus wine called Commanderia) a famous item of export from the island. In Europe this minute bird, duly seasoned and pickled, became something of a gourmet's fad. And even today—or perhaps yesterday—for I do not know if the tragic trade goes on—attempts were made to revive and expand this once flourishing line of business.

The beauty and grace of this small island visitant, however, with its petal-like fragility and brilliantly coloured head makes its fate seem almost unendurably sad. For the beccafico appears in force during the months of September or October to rob the rich fig and vine areas around Paralimni, in the Famagusta area of Cyprus. The birds apparently come in from all parts of the world—Germany, Russia, Switzerland, Sweden: come in swarms like bees, in battalions and squadrons. The air of the villages rings with their chirping. And coming in so greedily they immediately fall victims to the cunningly arranged lime-twigs of the villagers. Paralimni is the great centre of the trade, and it is from here that the trappers set off just before dawn with their great baskets called 'koukourka'. With a systematic care born no doubt of several centuries of practice they organize their limed traps in the trees, and then dispose themselves on long lines as one would do for a 'beat'. The bird-swarms seem so deafened by their own chirping that they show little alarm. They ripple away from the beaters, pouring along the ground like locusts or pouring from tree to tree, until they suddenly find themselves in the traps which await them. At once the air is full of the anguished fluttering of their wings, and their pitiful screaming. And now the lines of villagers advance to gather them by hand, to wring their necks and toss them into the great queer-shaped baskets. 'Once they settle it is like picking fruit,' I remember an old greybeard telling me; and adding 'The bountiful God sends them like manna.' Paralimni virtually lives by this trade, and some idea of the market price of the birds will explain if not excuse the eagerness with which it is hunted. During a good beccafico season the revenue of the village used to be about six or seven thousand pounds. A single beccafico hunter during a fair season can make up to three or four pounds a day. A dozen of the birds used to fetch about seven shillings in the open market. The very lucrativeness of the trade raised a grave problem for the Colonial administration of the island which was most anxious to find a way of preventing this wholesale massacre. Considerations both political and traditional were the major obstacle. It was literally a trade by which at least half the villagers of Paralimni existed, as well as being an important traditional village activity. Many were the efforts made to evolve plans which might ransom the beccafico but none bore fruit.

But to continue: The loaded baskets are then hoisted and the hunters set off for the village where the teams of pluckers await them. Scores of village women stand before the long tables covered in green fronds of palm-leaf. Quickly and deftly, under the attentive eye of the buyers the birds are shredded and cleaned, some to be boiled and some pickled. And so this minute bird, little larger than a wren or robin, finds its way to the table. I must confess that I never found it a great delicacy—for once or twice a Cypriot friend produced a small sealed jar and offered me 'something to enliven the wine' which politeness made me accept. But there was no doubt of its popularity among seasoned village gourmets, and its exportation to various other places in the Levant suggested that the Cypriots were not alone in their taste for pickled birds. The lime-twigs, by the way, are simply treated with a mixture of stout packer's glue and honey, and are freshly set every dawn for the heat of the sun at midday tends to melt the mixture and make it unstable.

One hopes that the new Government of Cyprus will find some tactful way of ransoming this beautiful little creature from mass death every year. I do not know whether the beccafico deserves greater claims on our attention than any other animal, domestic or wild, but its beauty makes a deeper appeal to the heart.

Oil for the Saint; Return to Corfu

Published in Holiday. *Philadelphia. October 1966.*

The return of the native—a good thing or a bad? I am not sure. On principle I have always avoided retracing my steps unless absolutely necessary. It was not, I used to think, a good thing to return to places where one had been exceptionally happy or sad, or where events had taken place that could never be repeated. People vanish, after all; buildings disappear or are transformed, and the time scale begins to nag as one revisits those famous marble staircases that one could once take at speed, three steps at a time . . . the cathedral cat-walks that caused no dizziness. . . .

The extraordinary thing is that Greece has somehow remained exempt from the flavour of such disappointments. Much has changed, yes, but more has remained obstinately and invincibly the same. The radical feel and temper of the land and its people are still what they were for me at twenty. Indeed, many of the changes bemoaned by others have only added amenities that the country sadly lacked before —the inter-island telephones for example, the new roads, the little tourist hotels. As for the people . . . Memory does not grow older by a second per thousand years in Greece. Step off the ship and everywhere you will fall upon remembered faces, be instantly recognized and embraced: and I don't mean only by friends, but by everyone who remembers you, even if his only knowledge of you is that once, nearly twenty years ago, you gave his son a lesson or let him shine your shoes. Because they remember you they possess you, and you belong to them.

But in spite of this discovery about Greece in general, I still tended to regard Corfu as a special case. I avoided it as one avoids touching a sore tooth with one's tongue. After all, this island was where I first met Greece, learned Greek, lived like a fisherman, made my home with a peasant family. Here too I had made my first convulsive attempts on literature, learned to sail, been in love. Corfu would have too much to live up to. Nevertheless I still had many links with the island and with friends who still lived there, so that it was also much less *terra incognita* than any other part of Greece. I plucked up my courage and decided to take the plunge in bright spring weather. There were no special omens or intentions; the idea of the journey had ripened, that was all.

I was up on deck at dawn to watch the first brilliant strokes of sunlight racing along the brindled waves of our wake as we coasted the Forty Saints—once our winter shooting grounds and now barred to Corfiotes by the Albanian communists. The heavy, overpowering range of mountains had only just shed its snow, for the foothills were still green and fresh. The old Venetian seamark was still in place pointing up the deeper channel, and our vessel crossed it before veering south, turning sharply—on her heel, you might say—to point her prow at the hazy Venetian city which was as yet only a smudge of soft smoke. But the north of the island had been my home and here it was, its large-boned rounded scarps of rock and closely trimmed scrub looking like a succession of nude scalps on which the hair has started to grow again. How barren it looked and how strange in the early morning light! But the real strangeness was that it was all so recognizable, down to the smallest detail. It was not so much that it 'came back to me'; I found now that, in a queer sort of way, it had never left me; I had never really forgotten it. The whole dizzy spiral of the road above Kalami and Kouloura veering away towards Kassiopi I had known like my own pocket; sweeping it now with my heavy field glasses it seemed to me that I recognized individual trees, individual sweeps of brake and arbutus. It must have been an illusion, yet it was to persist during the whole of my stay on this (now doubly) magical and precious island. I felt the salt stickiness of the rail under my elbows as I brought the glasses to bear on the sea line, sweeping slowly along the coast from Kouloura with it's bird's nest-harbour toward Agni. I was looking of course for the white house . . . but by now surely the rains had turned it black with iron stains? No, it came swimming into my field of vision as pristine and brilliant as it always had been; moreover, there, posed like hieratic figures, were my peasant friends. Athenaios was on the grey rock outside the house, watching the sun rise as he had always

[287]

done, one hand holding the diminutive cup of Turkish coffee; from the upper balcony Kerkira, his wife, hung out the coloured blanket which would signal the morning caique (the equivalent of the village bus for us northerners) that there was a passenger to be picked up from the landing stage. An octopus hung from a rusty nail. A dog scratched at fleas in the deep dust of the roadway. The daughter of the house performed some unidentifiable task with vigour. (She had been five when last I had seen her in 1948.) A little farther to the left, Niko the sailor-schoolteacher had as always thrown back his green shutters to stand in a long moment of contemplation, glancing sunward and then sideways at his boat where it lay alongside the makeshift jetty. The boat was a new one, though the jetty had not changed. For a minute, caught in the spectrum of the silence, I drank in the whole scene—it was like happening upon a familiar handwriting. Then I shut away the glasses and went down to breakfast in a curious state of utterly calm excitement. The whole thing seemed to be there—quite indestructibly there. I knew that Heleni was dead and Sandos and several others; but their disappearance from the scene of the action had not succeeded in changing the fixed mythology of a glance built up over a lifetime, a taste for a dawn coffee, the cloth on the balcony. I began to wonder whether perhaps it would be I who would exhibit the greatest changes. How would I seem to them?

But now the town was approaching and here once more the early sunlight traversed to pick up the curves of the Venetian harbour, the preposterous curvilinear shapes of its belfries and balconies. We docked to the boom of the patron saint's bell—Saint Spyridon of holy memory who was still working his miracles. I felt quite weak at the knees as I stepped ashore and took one of those little horse-drawn carriages with their fixed parasols bobbing up above. The horse wore a fine new straw hat carefully pierced to allow his ears to stick through; he looked like a prize cuckold on holiday as he jogged and cantered his way up into the town.

I had forgotten how beautiful it was in the early morning sunlight —the preposterous long arcades of the French Esplanade. The deep shade of the trees, the tables, the silence.

It was too early for morning customers, and the waiters were still watering down the pavements and chasing the dust from the gravel of the Esplanade; but there were quite a few youngsters having breakfast, and among them the inevitable painter with his characteristic baggage of easel and colour box. Though the town is a series of unfinished intentions, Venetian, French, British, it remains a masterpiece; I doubt if there is any little town as elegantly beautiful in the whole of Greece. Each nation in turn projected something grandiose to beautify it—and then fell asleep. The Venetians fell asleep over the citadel, though they remembered to leave the winged lion there; the French built half the Rue de Rivoli and then discontinued it. The British elaborated the stylish Government House with stone especially imported from Malta —but did not stay long enough to enjoy its amenities fully. Yet all these motifs blend perfectly and become in some subtle fashion neither Venetian, British, French nor even Greek. They become Corfiote. Day was breaking and shutters were slowly beginning to open like flowers, like eyelids. Nothing appeared to have received even a cursory lick of whitewash in the nearly twenty years of my absence; the rains, like a master colourist, had dappled and fused and smudged and darkened the long façades. The spectrum of their colours slowly changed with the mounting sun—as it always had. I walked about the sleepy town, astonished to find that I was ravished by it all anew. I almost sat down there and then to write another Prospero.

But it was dangerous to linger, for I had many friends waiting eagerly to greet me, and I wanted to cross the island without seeing anyone—to devote my first day to a return visit to the lonely house in the north which had meant so much to me. I felt it almost as a duty. Later I would return and find Marie A. and discuss the little edition of Lear's drawings we were editing together; later I would find the valiant and formidable Countess T. of the sapphire eyes who had once thrown open the hospitable gates of her country house to two gluttonous, penniless and unknown writers called Durrell and Miller. But now, by the logical order of things, it should be Kouloura and the humble peasant family with whom, through whom, I had first got to know what Greece was.

I humped my bundle of gifts and betook myself to the taxi rank, half fearful that I might be greeted by a roar from a fat dusty figure emerging from a battered blue Buick. No, but Spyro Halkiopoulos is dead. Nevertheless his roar remains behind, for a younger Spyro greeted me with it—bounding like a lion from a blue Chevrolet. I did not bother to bargain with him but told him that I wanted to go north and to be dumped at Kouloura. My fluent Greek puzzled him. He looked at me narrowly and said: 'Who are you, sir? I seem to know your face.' I replied evasively. At that moment a colleague called his name and I realized that we did know each other. He had been a boy of ten when I had seen him last; his father had taken me and my brothers fishing with the lamp and trident. But it was pleasant to live for a moment in an anonymity which would soon be stripped from me. A small island is like a small market town. Sooner or later you are recognized. In Greece, at least, the hospitality begins—an unending flow of drinks from the ouzo fountain which plays perpetually in the depths of the Greek soul. Then there is nothing to do but surrender yourself. Strong-willed men break down and cry like babies. No good. The steady flow of hospitality ends only when you are lovingly hospitalized or carried aboard a departing ship on a stretcher. I knew that to declare myself in the town of Corfu at this stage would untruss me entirely. It was not only I who would be fêted, but through me the whole Durrell family which had once inhabited these idyllic shores; I should have to eat and drink for five—my brothers, my sister, my mother; I should have to empty at least a can in each of their names. I might never reach the north at all if I allowed all this to break loose around me. . . . I tried as far as possible to look like an uncommunicative Swiss Baptist who had arrived at the wrong island by mistake.

My driver was still puzzled but disinclined to probe; he drove through the sleepy town, turning me over in his mind, so to speak. Once or twice he glanced at me in the mirror and then shook his head and sighed. No, he couldn't place me. This was all to the good, as it left me free to plunge back into my private reverie, matching the sunlit present with the past. It was as if a film of the Corfu of 1940 had suddenly been stopped in mid-frame and waited for me to come back after twenty years in order to resume playing. Nothing at all seemed to have changed, but nothing. There is, if you wish, the carcass of a new theatre, and the outer shell of a new clinic. But in the long, winding road which leads away through the cypress and lemon groves toward Ypsos there were gentlemen bartering calves against kegs of wine, there were still the sacred idiots being teased by urchins, and the whole symphony of street cries still echoed around us in hallowed cacophony. Plenty of costume, too, and real costume at that; not the detestable, government-subsidized folklore get-up of Provence. Tourists in Corfu still get an honest cameraful for their money, whatever else they may have to complain about. And talking of complaints, I must not forget the holes in the road. I'm not joking when I say that I remembered many of them from my youth—the *identical* holes. This will sound far-fetched, but four years of almost daily motoring over twenty-odd kilometres of road is enough to make you familiar with every bump. Moreover, motoring with Spyro offered an extra method of mastering and retaining a mental hole-map; he had a different swear for each type of hole. The whole family knew the holes by their swears. Once I drove from my mother's villa into town in the dark, and my passengers were able to recite all Spyro's swears like a multiplication table at the appropriate places. Well, they are all still there. In the summer, too, the same crisis still hits the Ministry of Public Works, for the King still visits Corfu to spend the dog days in his summer palace. He must not be allowed to bump his spine, they always think. An army of gnomes with teaspoons comes out one night and very deftly fills the holes with a light mix of cement and clinker—like filling cavities in teeth. This just passes the test of summer weather, but the first thunderstorms of the autumn deftly wash out the fillings and leave us once more with the original road surface—a sort of confluent smallpox effect. But by this time, of course, the King is safely back in Athens and the island can relax again for the winter. I am writing now about the macadamized section of the road only; the rest (and the network of roads left behind by the British is a pretty extensive one) could best be described as one prolonged act of God.

It will sound masochistic to say that I took pleasure in the rediscovery of the ancient hole system of the island. Nevertheless it is true.

Deftly threading our way along, we made excellent time to Ypsos, which lies along the softly curving line of creeks and inlets, chapel-crowned and cypress-stippled islets and lagoons, until with a bump the road comes up against the first scrawny shoulder of mountain rising steeply into the air beyond Nisaki. Here a sleepy policeman flagged us down and advanced to take a suspicious look at us. He recognized my driver easily enough; then he took a look at me and his face flattened out into a huge grin. 'Welcome back', he said, thrusting a large brown paw into the car. 'I have telephoned to the police at Kouloura to tell Athenaios you are coming.' For a moment, so firm was my belief in my own anonymity, I thought that he had mistaken me for somebody else; but no, he uttered my name, and grabbing my hand pressed it to his cheek. It was like black magic. 'I am married to Kerkira's daughter,' he explained.

At this my driver also gave a yelp of mingled consternation and delight and made a grab for me over the front seat. My presents were in danger of being crushed by the force of his embrace. 'And you didn't tell me,' he said reproachfully. 'You didn't say a word. My father, God rest his soul, would never have forgiven me.'

There was nothing for it but to dismount and to be led like a sacrificial lamb to a nearby table, where already the whiskered tavern-keeper, scenting a celebration, had spread his striped cloth and un-stopped his ouzo keg. Here I was, then, unmasked at last by the Greek secret service. We broke into a torrent of reminiscences, punctuating our memories with fiery gulps of the national drink. My driver was able to recount whole sections of my forgotten life on the island—shooting trips, fishing trips, feats of drinking and dancing. Some of these episodes he remembered only from his father's conversation or from hearsay, but some he had witnessed. In small islands, where people do not read very much, the powers of memory never seem to fail, and individual actions take on semi-mythological proportions. We romanced thus with pleasure and emotion for a good hour until at last the ouzo bottle had a sadly punished look. 'Never mind,' they cried, 'there is a whole barrel inside.' I stifled a groan. I was now surrounded by four other policemen, some unidentified fishermen and a neighbour-ing tavernkeeper whose little hotel (according to the scholarly re-searches of my friend Peter Bull) promises the wayfarer 'Hot and Cold Running Waiter'.

I was still curious to find out how (when my anonymity had stood the acid test of the town) I had been recognized in this remote place. The answer was so simple. It amounted to the eternal family bush telegraph of Greece. The policeman explained patiently. 'The uncle of my sister's second cousin was at the pier and saw your name on your passport. He knew you would come back here and he telephoned me. You could imagine how delighted we were after so many years. Have a drink.'

But the sun was well up now and it was time to face the horrors of the road beyond Varvati. We disentangled ourselves from our hosts with some difficulty and after many hirsute embraces we climbed the steep road and catapulted off the macadam into a series of holes large enough to bury an ox. Our average speed was reduced now to about five miles an hour; the shock absorbers whimpered like whipped dogs; dust rose in sheets. My driver swung about, manipulating the car as if we were on a trapeze, and talking with animation of the meals he planned to give me once I returned to town. But how beautiful the drive still is, despite the holes and the dust, for the road runs, now concave, now convex, above the still, hard mirror of the sea, and the silver olives slide breathlessly down in groves below one as if to plunge into it and to swim for dear life out into the blue. Albania frames the whole picture with its huge flesh-coloured scarps. As you climb you realize that the island has two faces, not one. The indolent, luxuriant lowlands with their Venetian scenery give place now to the rocky archaic north with its small bitten-out harbours and scant iron-stained soils. It might be Ithaca or Cephalonia; it might be any of the more rugged island groups that lie to the south.

It is almost forbidding in its stern, unwinking masculinity, this northern end of Corfu. Even the costume changes to chime with its mood—black kirtles and head coifs. This is an island of the seafarer, and wherever you hit the sea and the people who make their living by it, you come upon something hard, something always in mourning, something devout and disciplined.

The faces hereabouts were older and more wrinkled, the smiles quieter, the expressions more sage and more penetrating. Yes, it was in this landscape that I learned many important lessons: the kind you cannot put into words. Even the driver had fallen silent now as we traversed these long, silent groves of ancient olive trees. Here in the north life was a struggle, not a self-indulgence. His face had become grave.

But I had already outstripped our beetlelike progress as we crashed through those silent groves. I raced ahead in my imagination, leaping from cliff head to cliff head, swerving down like a kestrel through the still air to that silent balcony where I knew Athenaios would be standing, gripping the iron balustrade which, twenty years ago, I had myself helped him set in the wet concrete. I knew that from the white house by the water's edge one can hear a car far off on that remote hillside; its noise swells and vanishes, growing gradually louder and louder as it approaches. Finally the sound flows down unimpeded as the car turns the last corner and runs—looking like a toy—along the Kouloura highroad. Yes, he would be there with his hands on the rail, his shoulders lightly hunched; he had always listened with such concentration that it gave him the stance of a blind man. Beside him in the upright chair Kerkira would be busy with her spindle or her darning. There was no time to waste for her: her hands had become almost autonomous in function. One felt that even when she slept they automatically went on working, knitting, plucking feathers, cleaning fish, sewing. At times, almost apologetically, they took a brief moment off to stifle a yawn.

Nor was I mistaken. As the car reached the corner of the mountain I saw the little tableau on the balcony across the blue water. They had heard us, but it was too far off as yet to identify the visitor. We nosed down the steep road toward sea level, winding in and out of the olive groves. The sea lay asleep below us, lime green and enticing. The little hamlet seemed asleep, for nothing stirred in the thickets by the spring; there were no voices of children singing higher up among the olives. Everybody had obviously gone to town to shop. The road ended a good hundred yards short of the old house, and so it was that I approached it at last silently, on foot, with my parcels. By this time Athenaios and his wife had moved from the balcony to the end of the olive grove, from where they could watch the approaches to the house. They stood there in the green shadow of the trees, riveted in poses of concentration, their hands clutched before them. But at my call their concentration broke like a spell and Kerkira gave a sudden wild cry like a seabird. Her husband stood his ground with a tremulous smile on his lips, his arms thrown out as if to embrace not only me but the whole sea-enchanted world about us.

'It is I.'

'It is you.'

'Yes, I.'

'At last you come back.'

One on either side, they put their arms about me and led me, a willing captive, into the house. There was so much to recount that for a moment we were all tongue-tied. But in the cool shadowy interior I saw a glimmer of white teeth as Niko the schoolmaster-fisherman rose like a great fish to embrace me. 'We've been waiting all morning,' he explained, giving me a rib-cracking embrace. 'Welcome.'

Once more the balcony over the water with its plaster stained by the winter rain; once more the little coffee cups and the glasses of kumquat, the Corfu liqueur; once more the familiar voices raised in excited talk, piling memory upon memory, trying to replace the missing fragments of that twenty-year-old tapestry. I had been halfway around the world in this time, while they had stayed here, outfacing wars and floods and family deaths, gathering white hair. Athenaios had had a small stroke two years before which had half-paralysed one shoulder, but Niko, whose white hair betrayed his sixty-odd years, was still the raw-boned Hercules of the past, tanned and sturdy, with every white tooth in his head. The women watched us laugh and talk, rejoicing obscurely in our defiance of time. The past had dealt hard with the family. Heleni, the first wife, had died of starvation during 1940—died keeping her children alive. Some years later Athenaios had married Kerkira, a little village girl who came in to help. She had blossomed now into a plump and handsome matron of a flourishing household with a new daughter of her own to boast of: a policeman's wife no less, which meant that she would one day enjoy a pension. Old albums of pictures now made their appearance, photographs yellow with age, and stained with ancient developing marks. This at least conferred upon the meeting a mild air of improbability. Who was this good-looking and rather cocksure young man who stared out at me, fishing trident in hand? What had he been so damned sure about anyway? It was hard to say. The world he lived in, like our own, had existed under the threat of sudden doom. Everybody had known it.

Deftly the women were laying the table in the shadowy inner room, clucking like chickens with delight and only pausing to replenish our glasses. The talk had turned to village matters, the familiar and immemorial landmarks of lives lived in such heroic seclusion. Niko, it is true, had once been as far as Athens on a teaching course, but the others had never been farther than the town of Corfu, ten sea miles to the south. For them words like Belgrade, Cairo, London sank into the mind like dyes, colouring these far-off places with the richness of ancient myths. They sighed and squeezed their fingers together in their laps as I spoke of them, like children hearing a fairy tale. But for my part I sank into the little world of the village with equal relief and pleasure; this was my form of romance. They could have London and Paris.

The little hamlet of Kalami with its ten families was a whole world

—a total world—whose confines were all there to be enjoyed and measured. It was not limitless like the outside world. It had a formal completeness which allowed the villagers to live their lives in a kind of assured completeness—unfragmented, free from hesitation. Here the chronology too was different. Strangers had come from outside, there had been wars, deprivation and famine, but inside the spectrum they remembered the year when the children of Jani had been struck by lightning, or when Socrates severed his thumb with a knife while cleaning a fish, or when the mason lost an eye from a pinch of quicklime. This was truth; the rest belonged delightfully but uneasily to the world of fable.

When the first glad rush of conversation had spent itself, when the presents had been examined and assessed—and repaid in kisses—we sat down at the long table to eat. The women followed the old-fashioned tradition, standing behind to serve us, but not sitting down with us. From time to time, however, Kerkira would sit for a moment on a chair and sip a glass of sweet liqueur as she listened to our talk. By now I had produced my little phial of green olive oil—the delicious *Vierge* from our Provençal olives. 'How long since you have visited Saint Arsenius?' I asked Niko, and he flashed his white teeth in a smile. 'Last week', he said. 'Why?' I held up the green French oil and said: 'I have brought a little oil for his lamp from our trees in France.' They drew their breath with pleasure and emotion—indeed with a certain pride. Who but a Greek would have thought of such a gesture? Athenaios bowed his head for a moment and when he looked up I saw that there were tears in his dark eyes. 'You have done well,' he said. 'It is not for nothing you are an adopted Greek and the godfather of Spyro.' My godson was a merchant seaman now, doing the San Francisco to Hong Kong run. Niko banged the table with pleasure. 'We will go to the saint together,' he said roundly, 'in my new boat, eh, Athenaios? This afternoon.' Everyone clapped hands and agreed delightedly.

The fare was simple and humble, a fitting reminder that here in the north prosperity was still a debatable concept. But we ate heartily, wasting not a crumb, and the blackish wine from Vigla was good.

'I never cease to marvel', said Athenaios, 'at the way you have brought us trade, just by writing a book about us.'

'A book we cannot read even,' said Niko, mopping up his gravy with a heel of crust.

'What do you mean by trade exactly?' I asked, puzzled.

Athenaios smiled at the question. 'The foreigners that come. So many, you will see. Every Sunday many caiques come from town to see the house. Many British; very nice people. Each one has a small radio which is very loud. It is marvellous.'

Kerkira took up the tale. 'The whole bay is full of them.' she said with pride. 'They swim and make a great noise. Then they come and look at the house and we show them your picture and make them buy Coca-Cola. Yes, we have a Frigidaire now in the boathouse. And for an extra ten drachmas we show them my daughter's trousseau. They go away very satisfied, yes, completely satisfied. And it is all due to you, my dear.' She gazed into my eyes with a kind of lachrymose gratitude and kissed my hand repeatedly. I tried to look pleased by this sinister item of news.

'Nor is it only the British,' said Niko proudly, 'but the French also come, many French in caiques during the week. The girls are beautiful and half-naked and they dance the tveest on the rock below. Sometimes they drink too much. They also have lovely radios and make a great noise.' He sighed with rapturous pleasure at the thought. Kerkira said: 'It is a marvellous way of passing the time, for as you know nothing ever happens in Kalami. It is better than the cinema. The music is free. And they bring us trade.'

'How we bless your name,' said Athenaios with his gravely smiling eyes as he pressed my hand warmly with those toil-worn fingers.

'Thanks to you, Athenaios lives well,' said Niko. 'Perhaps you will write something about my house now?'

'Later we will start a hotel,' said Kerkira. 'And then they can stay here all the time with their radios. Already we have many who rent your room—remember where you used to work? She moved her fingers on an imaginary typewriter and went *pock pock pock* to illustrate just how I used to work.

My heart sank slightly, but I put a good face on it as I drained my wine. 'I am glad for you all.' Indeed I was, in a curious mixed-up sort of way. After all, why should I grudge them such a lucky windfall as a trade in itinerant celebrity hunters? Yet from another point of view, it was the twenty-year-old ghosts of the place which were threatened for me. Besides, how posthumous can one feel? I took a swift look at the silent nacreous sea outside the house with the trees growing in it upside down; the long swerving contours of the hill above Kouloura. There I had been once attacked by two eagles and had been forced to drive them off with a heavy club. I remembered with absolute clarity the shrill screaming and the soughing of their huge wings as they launched themselves at me from the steeper blue.

Athenaios stood beside me with an arm about my shoulder. 'You know,' he said, 'I was thinking that now you are back in Corfu you will come and stay with us again, won't you? It is not just or fair that we should enjoy all this glory and trade because of you, and that you should get nothing for it. It would shame us. No, you will live here. It will be very good for tourism, you will see. When the caiques come with the foreigners we will charge extra. They will pay to see the man himself. You will stand here upon the balcony and make a sign at them.'

He made a vague sketch of a demagogic gesture—like Mussolini addressing the faithful, or the Pope blessing the world. Yes, I would stand on the balcony (clad in some suitable uniform?) and confer a blessing on my admirers with their transistors. Afterward we would take the rowboat out to collect all the floating beer bottles and Ambre Solaire suntan-lotion flagons and rubber ware.

'You will sign their books,' Niko went on, 'and we will pass the time very agreeably together, you will see.'

'I shall reflect upon the matter,' I muttered vaguely. 'I don't know whether I can afford to leave my trees in France.'

'Pouf! You can go back for the harvest every year, and then return to us for the tourist season,' he assured me comfortably.

A lone green caique sputtered into view round the headland, carving the still, blue sea into curls as it crossed our line of vision. 'That will be Dimitri going to town to sell his fish.'

We finished our coffee and Niko led us down onto the white rock where his boat lay. It was a twenty-five-foot lateen-rig, sturdy but clumsy, and painted rust red. He had contrived a dashing but inappropriate housing for the front of it which gave the impression of half-decking. It was a tin form with a murky window. It would keep out the spray all right and provide some shelter in the sea, but being inappropriate to the type of boat would make her unmanoeuvrable when she was under sail.

'I know what you are thinking,' grinned Niko. 'It is very smart to look at but not very clever. We will take the cabin part off, I think.' The tin form was duly unbolted and dragged out upon the rock to make room for the three of us. We pushed off while the women of the family watched us with proud indulgence. 'Don't be too long,' cried Kerkira. Niko gave a display of sudden physical violence as he cranked the ancient engine until it fired asthmatically and sent us throbbing across the bay. It was a weird contraption, this ancient machine. Niko caught me eyeing it and said proudly: 'I know, my friend, it isn't a marine engine at all. It is really a water pump I found on an old well. I fitted the shaft and adapted it. It works well but it is very heavy.' It was indeed. If ever the boat overturned it would plummet to the bottom of the sea.

As we drew away I looked back at the familiar village and the diminishing figures of the women, who had returned to the high balcony over the water. Kerkira waved and we waved back. Here every twist of the headland, every rock and cove, was familiar. How often we had sat breathlessly for half the night gazing down into the dazzling pool of light cast by the carbide lamps, hunting for octopuses. Forgotten memories crowded in now, each one separate and vivid. One autumn night the bay was full of phosphorescence which turned our swimming bodies to fire; more than once after a winter storm we found the bay swarming with blue pipefish that could be gathered with a bucket. They behaved as though they were suffering from concussion. There on the big yellow rock by Agni, was Miller's private bathing place. He used to trot off across the headland with his towel and notebook every morning, to return only when the distant cry of 'Lunch' came to his ears across the olive groves.

Kalami disappeared now and we were in the throat of the open sea which stretched away across the calm carpet of water to where the Venetian town drowsed among its opalescent mists. Niko was talking to Atheniaos with animation. In the starvation period they had learned to eat the leaves of certain trees, which brought them out in boils. The gravedigger was too enfeebled by lack of food to pierce the rocky soil of the churchyard; the dead had begun to 'form queues' like the living, said Niko with grim humour. Nitsa dying had given a great cry and seen a vision of Greece free, once more. The smoke from the guns across the water had drifted about in the still winter air, unsubstantial as thistledown. 'Well', said Athenaios, 'we have seen many things come

[299]

to pass and yet, praise God, we are still among the living.' Niko grinned ironically and grunted. 'Not for long,' said he. 'At sixty-one it isn't for long. But so long as I can still eat and sail I don't care. Give me a few more years and I'll enjoy them.'

The sheep bells still tonked among the grassy glades above Agni; on the second headland there were fishermen at work. They were smashing up hermit crabs for bait, but they paused to wave. They were inevitably relatives of either Niko or Athenaios and by consequence were addressed in familiar fashion.

'Caught anything, you cuckolds?'

'Nothing. Where are you going, cuckolds?'

'To Saint Arsenius, cuckolds.'

'Is that the foreigner?'

'Yes.'

'Tell him welcome and wish him Godspeed.'

I thanked them and tipped a benign hat. We were heading down now for what we always regarded in the past as our own private beach. Elsewhere I have described the little shrine, the sentinel cypresses, the carved-out beach where we spent whole summers bathing naked. Once an ikon had been found floating in the sea and the faithful had taken this as a sign that Saint Arsenius was looking for a familiar place to settle. The shrine itself is hardly bigger than a large telephone booth, but the lamps are always in repair and the floor always dusted. How this is done is rather a puzzle, for the place cannot be approached by land, only by sea. Yet it has always been so. Once a year a priest comes by water with his acolytes and reads a service there.

It hadn't changed. We throttled down as we turned back the last headland like the page of a book and entered the little bay. But I am wrong; the profile of the rock has been altered somewhat by the explosion of an Italian land mine during the war. The shrine, however, had escaped unscathed. A few huge boulders had been scattered about the bathing beach, that was all. So still was the water that we did not bother to anchor. We snubbed the unfractious rock and climbed ashore, taking a line. Despite their age the two men climbed the rock as effortlessly as goats.

The door was lightly pinioned with wire, easy to undo. I entered the little chapel, after so long, with emotion. Battered by wind and sea the rotting ikon stared back at us in the musty gloom. The lamps were full but unlit. We crossed ourselves backwards, in the Orthodox way.

'Well, you old brute,' said Niko, addressing the squinting saint in terms of rough familiarity—tones one is permitted to adopt with close friends or relatives by marriage and which imply no irreverence. 'We have brought you back the foreigner at last.' I stood breathing lightly in the still, stale air of the shrine, and remembering. Athenaios grubbed about in the gloom behind the makeshift altar. He was hunting for a twist of wick. There is always a half-burned wick lying about in such places. I had found a small empty lamp among the branch of oil lamps hanging above the ikon. I unstoppered my phial of green oil and reverently tipped it into the glass bowl. 'Pour it all,' cried Niko with a sort of delighted voluptuousness, 'every drop.' The blunt fingers of Athenaios had found a small twist of wick. We set it afloat in the oil and waited for a moment to let it drink and settle. 'If it lights the first time,' Niko joked, 'it means that you are welcome and that he has no outstanding complaints against you.' I admit I felt somewhat anxious, for the saint has a beady and penetrating glare—indeed the stare of an elder Freud. And he might well have a complaint against me, for in the long years of my absence I had never sent him the smallest offering. But no. The wick flamed up and Athenaios clapped his hands softly. All of a sudden I saw the faces of my friends spring out of the gloom, touched by the yellow light; they had a chastened, ageless quality. I thought of the Byzantine faces which stare at one out of the ikons in Salonika, Athens, Ravenna—the dark eyes, the crisp curling hair, the long speculative noses. And behind this front rank, so to speak, the calm profiles of ancient Greek statues.

Niko's dark eyes twinkled with merriment. We crossed ourselves once more and embraced while Niko went on rallying the saint. 'Now you are drinking French,' he told the ikon. 'Drink then, drink deeply. Then tell us if the French oil is as good as ours.'

We stayed a while bemused, by the yellow flame of the wick as it burned on, unwavering in the still air. Outside the dark shrine with its little cone of vivid yellow light the sunlight beat down mercilessly on the rock and water. It was time to go blinking into daylight once more. Niko wound up the prayer session by calling for a blessing from Arsenius and, by his leave, for another covering blessing from his great senior, Saint Spyridon. Once more he used his ironic rallying tone, addressing them as wicked old brutes. But his eyes were grave and tender.

Suddenly I was reminded of the ancient shrines of Herakles which one could only approach backwards, uttering terrible curses. There had been one such in Lindos on Rhodes. A bit of bad language, a bit of familiarity, makes a saint feel at home with you when uttered in the right frame of mind. Standing once more upon that ragged rock face we grinned at each other and winked.

'Well, he's still there, as you see. Still on the job.'

So long as Arsenius is there the Greek world will remain right side up.

There was one more visit to be made—to the little underwater cave in which we used to hide whenever a passing boat hove in sight. In here, on the shallow slip of gravel beach, we used to leave our bathing suits so that we could put them on swiftly in any case where our nakedness might give offence to the peasants. I slipped overboard into the cool water and swam into the bay. Once we had made a clay statue of Pan and set it up in the cave and I was curious to see if anything remained. No. The winter sea had long since licked out the cave. There was no trace.

We dawdled for an hour in the little bay, reminiscing. Then I spread my wet body out in the boat and Niko started up his engine with many a cajoling oath. Slowly we drew away from the Saint once more, giving him a friendly wave as we passed round the headland out of his life once more, perhaps this time for ever.

It was later than we had imagined; indeed the sun was westering steeply when at last we tied up again at the white house. 'It is a great thing', said Niko sagely, 'to be a creator.' He used the ancient word 'demiurge' which is still current modern Greek. He seemed to have only the vaguest idea of what the concept stood for; and yet, perhaps not. After all, in the ancient world the gods walked about freely on earth and undertook many of men's duties. Why should not a 'demiurge' lend a hand with a little mild tourism and help a deserving cause? Zeus would not have blenched at the idea.

That evening the 'demiurge' held court, greeting all comers and meeting glass with lifted glass. Some were old friends, fishermen of the Forty Saints and Kassiopi; some were the grandchildren of old friends who came to press my hand and mutter warm greetings. Hands as horny as oaks, faces lined like druids, but with the fine manners of kings.

By the time we settled for supper, the moon was rising—a huge copper ball swinging up from behind the Albanian mountains, struggling free of the shimmering ground mists. It seemed to rise in one's very throat. Once more upon that silent balcony we sipped our last coffees and watched its wide shimmering path stretch across the straits. A liner slipped by with its thousand lights ablaze. But the moon outshone everything. There were stifled yawns now, for peasant folk sleep early, and I too was tired. My things had been laid out for me by Kerkira in the upper room, the old room. I dawdled a while to smoke a cigarette and watch the changing sea. A few old articles of furniture still remained—my old desk, for example, crudely painted and clumsy. The floor I had stained with my own hands once upon a time. The old fireplace which had cost us such diplomacy and anxiety had been bricked up, but I could still trace the lintel in the plaster of the wall.

I had decided that I would catch the dawn caique back to town, where other friends and other projects awaited me—alien from this small and perfectly composed world of the unsophisticated village. It was good, I thought too, to enjoy it so thoroughly without nostalgia, without false regrets. What had been lived had been thoroughly lived and thoroughly digested. Only the crumbs of old loyalties and loves remained, and they gave pleasure now, not pain. So bright was the moonlight that I could see the trees reflected in the water. A small fish broke surface under the house with the noise of a drawn cork. The flawless skin of the night sea settled again into its mirrored calm. I lay awake for a long time that night, thinking over the events of the day and watching the moonlight pouring onto the dark floor of the room. From time to time the sea gave a small sigh, like a child turning over in its sleep. Far up on the hillsides in the direction of Vigla a fox barked once and was silent. I slid slowly downhill into sleep, but so slowly that I could not discern the point at which one state superseded the other. They matched like silks.

France

'In Praise of Fanatics'

Published in Holiday. *Philadelphia. August 1962.*

The job of a provincial editor may not be a particularly enviable one in any country, but my friend Lejoie who guides the destinies of the largest of the country newspapers in Provence manages to make it sound full of variety and interest. He weaves his way with skill and tact among the diplomatic and political quicksands of the post—always gay, always tireless, always good-humoured. Also, being a Frenchman, he has a keen eye for the downright ridiculous, and provincial life is full of it—to the brim.

Nevertheless it is not easy to mediate effectively between all the different factions which assail the provincial daily and its chief—to poultice (for example) the wounds of a village mayor whose name has been spelt wrong twice running, to represent a strongly felt case for an augmentation of salaries without falling foul of government policy, to criticize an art show as honestly as possible within the limits of fair comment . . . ('Sir: I feel I must protest strongly on behalf of the village of Plages (200 souls) against the gross calumnies levelled against our artist-mayor in your columns.')

Perhaps it is the very intricacy of the job which has made Lejoie into a 'spare-time student of fanaticism'—as he says; I did not exactly know how he qualified the word until one day he cited, among the great number of French eccentrics who have left works of art behind them, the name of the Postman Horse—Le Facteur Cheval. He was delighted to find that I had never heard of this estimable man, or of the Ideal Palace which he built in response to a vision. 'As a spare-time work it is certainly unique,' said Lejoie wistfully. 'The man was a village postman in the Drôme whose duties involved him in a thirty kilometre tramp every day. On his return at night he would surrender himself to the intoxication of his vision and set about building this extraordinary monument which, if it had not been built in such an out-of-the-way place as his native village, Hauterives, might well have earned him a reputation similar to that other naïf Douanier Rousseau.'

'You think so?'

'I certainly do; and you will agree. I'll tell you more of him and unearth some pictures which will give you an idea. He's a sort of Gaudi—only touched with French fanaticism.'

'You mean a monomaniac?'

'No. Just a Frenchman. I'll find the pictures.'

He was as good as his word and on a subsequent visit he tumbled out onto the table between us a number of postcard views of this strange monument.

'Why, it's a sort of private Albert Hall,' I said.

'Except that it's got every style mixed into it. It isn't consistent to a single style or influence. It's got the whole blasted world of assorted architectures all rolled into one cake mix.'

The Ideal Palace of the Facteur Cheval was begun in 1879 and only finished in 1912, single-handed. The pictures which Lejoie showed me depicted one of the weirdest monuments which it has ever been my good fortune to gaze upon—a sort of giant wedding-cake of styles and moods all welded together into a building which was twenty-six metres long by fourteen broad; it was about twelve metres high—the height of a modern two-storied villa.

Only an inspired lunatic would have hoped to juxtapose and marry up all these different styles in one work—or at least that is what one feels as one looks at the pictures. To this proposition Lejoie replied: 'Yes, but there is something else which these pictures don't quite capture; they emphasize only its apparent eccentricity. There's more than that in it. It really deserves to be seen. As a matter of fact the thing is in my own village in the Drôme, and as a child I spent my holidays playing in the ideal Palace of the old Postman—his private Xanadu, you might say. It left the strangest impression on me. As a matter of fact I am distantly connected to the postman's family—hence the fine streak of fanaticism in my own make-up. Would you care to come north for a week-end and have a look at it? I could promise you other things of interest. My mother lives there and she is married to Chabert, the great chef. They run a tiny hotel to which they admit only friends who care about . . .'

'Don't tell me; let me guess. Food!'

'Sometimes for an Anglo-Saxon you are quite discerning. Yes, in a word, food. Such food!'

'I am your man,' I said solemnly.

When he left that evening he allowed me to keep the strange pictures, and also a small autobiographical fragment written by the Postman in his old age—a document almost as strange as the pictures.

It was written in simple schoolboy French which gave it an oracular ring, both touching and authoritative. It was a sort of artistic credo—but it smelt strangely of the direct vision of somebody like Blake. I read it over slowly and with growing admiration.

'The son of peasant folk [it began], and myself therefore a peasant, I would like to live and die in such a manner as to prove that even in my own order of life men of genius and energy can be born, can exist. I've been a village postman for twenty-nine years now. Work has been my only glory, honour my only well-being. Up to today, then, here is my strange history. Once in a dream I conceived and built a place, a château in which there were grottoes. . . . I don't know how to explain it . . . but so ravishing, so picturesque, that for ten years the whole thing stayed engraved in my memory. I could not get rid of it. Of course I took myself for a fool, a maniac. I was no mason, to start with; I had never touched a trowel. As for sculpture I'd never touched a chisel. As for architecture—leave it right out of the picture—I know nothing of it. I did not dare to breathe a word about my dream to a soul for fear of being laughed at in the village. To be truthful, I laughed at myself a bit. Fifteen years later, when I had almost forgotten this remote dream, a chance slip of the foot jogged my memory. I tripped and fell over an object. It was a stone of a form so bizarre that I slipped it into my pocket, in order to study it at leisure. The next day I went back to the same spot and found others, even more beautiful. The stone was of a softish kind, deeply worked by river-water and finally hardened by time into something as tough as possible; but the shapes—they represented a sort of sculpture so bizarre that I doubted if any man could imitate it. It was full of different species of animal, human caricatures. I said to myself then: "Well, if nature can sculp so easily I am sure I can master masonry and architecture." Here then was my dream at last. "To work," I said to myself!'

From that moment the Facteur Cheval was fully awakened to his real mission in life. A dream was trying to get born, to get transformed into a reality. He began to keep a sharp lookout on his thirty kilometre tramp for rare and curious stones—the raw material for the Ideal Palace. His vision was sharpened, his appetite whetted. Soon these lovely objects of *virtu* began to invade his heavy post-bag as he tramped along. It should be remembered that the Facteur in France does not only deliver letters. He has several other onerous duties as well—to pay pensions, for example, and to collect receipts. It is not an easy job, particularly when in addition to your mail-bag you load yourself up with stones. He also began to extend his range in his search for new beauties. Dry river-beds yielded him beautifully polished gems, the lush flanks of the rolling Drôme hillsides other treasures. A Japanese artist would have understood immediately what had happened to the Facteur Cheval, but in his own village they began to whisper that he was showing signs of incipient insanity. No matter. He was in the grip of the curious insatiable fever which only the artist knows and recognizes. Sometimes the stones grew so many that he was forced to leave them in piles by the roadside, strategically stacked for loading. At night when he got home he would take his old wheelbarrow and walk back to get them by moonlight, tireless, grim—absorbed in the first aesthetic pleasure he had ever known. Sometimes he was up until two or three in the morning ferrying stones for the Ideal Palace. One begins to see what the good Lejoie means when he uses the word 'fanaticism'. . . .

But you cannot please everybody—not even by trying to build a Xanadu. The Facteur's wife began to complain bitterly that his clothes were getting worn to rags by his exertions, and by the stones he carried. His pockets were all shot to hell and his trousers covered in mud. Sometimes just the *corner* of a beautiful stone caught his eye and he simply had to dig it out. Grimly he persevered, turning a deaf ear to family scolding and village gossip alike. But it wasn't only the stones; his poor wife, who watched the Ideal Palace growing in the rambling garden by the river, began to complain of the expense. Every spare sou was spent on bags of cement and lime. How could all this be done on a postman's pay? One can understand that from her point of view the whole thing was a grotesque folly, a monomania. In the final analysis the Dream Palace was to cost them 3,500 sacks of cement, and to represent 1,000 cubic metres of masonry; and on the Eastern Façade the old Postman was to engrave the legend:

'1879–1912

10,000 days

93,000 hours

33 years of hardship

If there is anyone more obstinate than I, let him fall to work.'

It was a splendid credo, and in the course of time the Postman's dream justified all these heroic efforts. But phew! It made my back ache just to think of the plain man-hauling involved for the project, let alone the task of building.

'It is not really a building,' said Lejoie patiently; 'nor is it quite a sculpture. It's a work which creates its own crazy idiom. Now in our age it is easy to recognize the force and charm of the naïve, we are trained to it. But this strange lump, chunk, object was completed in the year of Picasso's first cubist experiments. That is what is so odd about it. Anyway, wait till you see. By the way, all the arrangements are made. We set off tomorrow.'

We did. It was a Saturday. He was carefree. The great Chef Chabert had deigned to allow us to stay at his hotel, after many careful questions as to whether I merited the sort of cuisine in which he specialized. We could take an easy trip north, visit the Ideal Palace, and return to Tain which was only half an hour's drive from Hauterives. The first stop was to be somewhere near Perols where a meal had been planned which would serve, I gathered, as a sort of spiritual launching pad towards our objective.

So we followed the left bank of the Rhône which was relatively unencumbered by northbound holiday traffic, and once we crossed the border into Ardèche my friend, as if to signify a formal throwing off of responsibility towards his station in life, removed his coat and tie and donned a comfortable wind-breaker and scarf. He was no longer the grave and responsible editor of an important southern daily, but a holidaymaker like everyone else. It was only in his home department of the Gard that he risked being stoned to death by outraged painters, or torn to ribbons by ministers without portfolio, quizzed by communes, or caught with his pants down (metaphorically) by regional officials. That little sign by the roadside 'Vous êtes dans l'Ardèche' allowed him to feel, all at once, quite unbuttoned, uncorked, and set by the chimneypiece to breathe, like a good bottle of wine.

We sang a few songs, but not loudly enough to disturb the nightingales which had responded to a few light showers the day before and decided upon a snap daylight appearance. No, our music, which perhaps was not good of its kind, was at least without prejudice to man or beast. Here and there, too, we made a pretence of needing petrol and turned into inviting routiers' inns where, in a sunny garden, we took the measure of the country by addressing a local wine with gravity and aplomb.

If Lejoie had, so to speak, cast off the editor, I for my part was quite ready to cast off the writer and thinker. A touch of the scholar-gipsy was what the situation seemed to warrant, and I felt I had just that. This week-end, I told myself, I should be free to devote myself to higher living and lower thinking. Why not?

But once or twice I did seem to catch the reproachful voice of the Postman Horse whispering in my ear that laziness was all very well, but that nothing really gets done without brutish labour. I had brought his little autobiography along in my pocket, and we had been discussing it. 'I can't go into all the details,' writes the old Postman, 'nor describe the troubles and miseries that I had to endure; it would be wearying. Nor indeed does my limited education permit me to express it all. But quite simply I carried everything on my back, working night and day for twenty-six years, without a halt, without mercy. The visitors who come now from other countries—and in increasing numbers—have difficulty in believing the evidence of their own eyes; they have to be reassured by the testimony of the local inhabitants before believing that a single man, all alone, could possibly muster the courage and will-power to build such a masterpiece. They marvel, and keep saying: "No, it's not possible." "No, it's unbelievable." '

It sounds a little immoral I know, but the thought of all that back-breaking labour added a certain vicarious luxury to these moments of sunny ease and relaxation—the two of us sitting before a wineglass in a sunny arbour by the ancient Rhône. 'But then,' said Lejoie, spreading his hands in a self-excusing gesture, 'any gourmet will tell you that to eat and drink creatively is also a labour.'

'Yes, but rather a pleasant one.'

'Besides,' he added, 'one carries the raw material for that sort of work inside one, and not on one's back.'

'Thank God.'

But he had something there and I told him so. We faced up to the invisible spectre of the Postman's reproaches and ordered another glass before rolling on northward in the direction of Tournon, towards that beckoning table which stood under a lime-tree in an orchard, dappled with sunlight. For my part I was somewhat suspicious of the lunch, fearing first of all that if I overdid it my sensibility would be too blunted to take in the Ideal Palace; and secondly that I might find myself unable to do justice to Chabert's creations that evening. It would be horrible to be expelled from the hotel as a godless and unworthy guest, thus bringing discredit on my friend and sponsor. But Lejoie clicked his tongue reproachfully at me when I voiced these sentiments. 'Fear nothing,' he said, 'I have ordered a light meal which is calculated to sharpen the sensibility without wearing out your lining or overtaxing the liver. We will proceed according to a carefully graduated scale I have worked out.'

'In calories?'

'No. In tastes and smells.'

He was as good as his word and when finally we settled down at that sunny table, neatly spread with its check cloth, my doubts began to fade; after all it had been a long drive, full of intellectual conversation which takes it out of a man. Moreover the faint whiffs of cooking which curled out of the kitchen on to the tideless air of that vernal afternoon were curiously stimulating. A splendid bosomy matron had been charged to attend to us; rosy-cheeked and blue-eyed, she gave off waves of motherly confidence. A mother-figure, a repository for confidences—that is how one felt as one watched her roll across the lawn with a basket of bread. No. No harm could come to us here; we were among people who could be trusted not to send us reeling out into the main road with purple faces, with gorged, starting eyeballs. Well, we lunched according to the severely graduated scale of my friend, on a *tarte aux morilles,* a splendid sort of mushroom tart, and a *truite aux amandes.* At least these were the two main features of an excellent lunch. If there was any fear that the trout, dappled in the browned almonds, might prove a somewhat cumbersome dish for aesthetes, it was easily dispelled; we managed a couple each with the greatest ease, the most effortless sang-froid. The wine which my friend unearthed for the occasion was a delightful little Chante-Alouette (a 'Sing-Lark') calculated to put even the tone-deaf into a good mood. So we lingered, gossiping our way through cheese and fruit, and finally sat replete to watch the blue smoke of a good cigar hang above us in the sunlight, mixing its exotic flavour with that of the limes and the wet flower-beds.

We had broken the back of our journey; it was only about half an hour's drive to the Xanadu of the Facteur Cheval. The sun was well past meridian when we crossed the river and rolled eastward, cutting directly across the two great northbound arteries with their rushing traffic, and nosing out towards the greener country in which the village of Hauterives nestled in its green seclusion.

The landscape changed softly as we headed towards Hauterives, becoming gradually greener and more densely wooded. The clear limestone formations talked of subterranean rivers, of chalk, and of rich soil; the little hills wore dense green topknots out of which peeped the eaves of old châteaux; the roads began to turn and twist, to rise and fall like a conductor's baton. It was another of those empty corners of France, rich with farms but sparsely populated, where the jerry-builder and the money-mad industrialist have as yet seen nothing they could exploit, nothing they could rape. We ran down an inclined plane into the village and drew up in the market-place, surprised to find that the noise of the engine was replaced only by the cooing of doves and the drone of bees. There was not a soul about. 'From here,' said Lejoie, 'we walk a few hundred yards to Xanadu.'

It was late afternoon. There were few people stirring in the village of the Postman Horse. Once or twice we heard the clank of pots or the sound of someone stoking a furnace, but the only people we actually met were a few children eating sweets and talking in low voices.

Here and there some of the plaster had fallen from the wall of a house and I was interested to notice that it had been built entirely of rounded river-stones cemented by mortar; stones the size of ostrich eggs. There was a man trimming fruit trees in a desultory fashion. The sound of the sécateurs fractured the silence. Finally we skirted a long high wall and knocked at an iron gate. It was opened by a dark pleasant-looking girl to whom Lejoie said a word; she was at once all smiles, drying her hands in her apron. But I had already caught sight of the Ideal Palace, of which she was the custodian. It stood there, imposing yet modest in an ineffaceable sort of way, neither inviting nor repelling scrutiny. The gardens surrounding it were full of tall trees. It smelt of peace and repose and verdure.

[314]

We entered the little office to buy our tickets and I saw, with something bordering on irritation, that this girl—an ordinary peasant girl, talking with a marked provincial accent—was reading a book about abstract painting. It was lying face down, where she had left it in order to answer our knock. Really the French drive you mad with anxiety and frustration! Wherever you go, whoever you meet, you find them engaged in some intellectual pursuit, reading recondite books, painting, cooking, playing the harp or writing sonnets. Damn them, it is unfair that the whole country is creative, or trying to be; the whole blasted population, regardless of education or breeding, is obsessed by the maniacal desire to manufacture a work of art. Finally it gets you absolutely mad with envy when you think of your own damn nation, loafing about in a brutish daze, a sort of Philistine dementia. What ails these big-arsed cart horses at home that they cannot enjoy drinking from the source of all the fun in the world?

In a sort of way the Facteur Cheval, whose monument stood outside waiting to be examined, increased my feeling of self-reproach. We approached Xanadu in silence and Lejoie, with the typical tact of his kind, turned aside into one of the corners in order to let me take the thing in slowly, in the round. Well, it is not really large, of course. It is not the size of the Parthenon; indeed I should say that it is about the size of the Theseum. But there is a mystery about it, which has nothing to do with the strangeness of the subject matter. It is—and here I am weighing my words—one of the most *unexpected* of works. It is very much more than a folly: and I realized with shame that, despite Lejoie's warning, I had come prepared to be touched and amused by a folly. How British! I had really come to Hauterives to Betjemanize! And all of a sudden I was face to face with the fiery Blakeian vision of of an uneducated postman, but something brimming with a queer kind of authenticity of its own. Where did it lie?

Before I answer this question I must, so to speak, subtract the fantasy—this extraordinary monument, crawling like a Hindu temple, with a thousand different things: heads of martyrs, soldiers, monkeys, palm-trees, peacocks, apes, palm-trees, Crusaders, Romans, Greeks, Druids, Persians . . . but this is not all; almost every type of known architecture was represented here from Stonehenge to Altamira, from Rome and Greece to Babylon, from the White House to a Swiss chalet! There was a cascade, a labyrinth, a Saracen tomb, a menhir, a mosque, a Norman belfry, a labyrinth, a . . . but the thing was a sort of dictionary of every known style. I understood now why the Surrealists had claimed the Facteur Cheval as one of them (at least Breton did on their behalf) :the juxtaposition of styles and modes was fantastic and gave one the requisite Surrealist shock.

But this was not all; there was something else, something troubling and exciting about the whole work, which was not due to this eccentric mix-up of dissimilar styles and objects. I caught Lejoie as he was climbing the twisted turret staircase to the first floor, so to speak, and expressed my excitement by saying, as I pressed his arm: 'But the whole bloody thing has congruence.' He sighed as if with relief, but said nothing. Smiling we mounted the spiral staircase, bringing a whole new set of frescoes into sunny relief. The gargoyles of Notre Dame stuck out their tongues at Apes from Barbary; two Crusaders confronted an effigy from a sarcophagus of the age of Semiramis.

Then, all of a sudden, I understood why this whole piece of work enjoyed a kind of completeness of its own, the kind of completeness which only true works of art enjoy. The Facteur had been neither a madman nor somebody trying to show off. He had responded to the sacred vision honestly, that was all; he had actually copied his dream accurately, trusting it implicitly to carry him where it would, faithful only to it. There was, so to speak, not a dishonest thought, a *factice* element in the whole of this grotesque monument. In fact one might characterize it as a 'naturalistic' work—for where your naturalistic painter reproduces nature as fairly as he sees it, so did the Facteur Cheval. . . . If he had been a Surrealist, a gimmick-artist, a Dali, something would have smelt wrong about the whole work.

As it was, it had an extraordinary perfection, a repose. The Ideal Palace is indeed ideal—it is the palace of the world's childhood, admirably and deftly captured. I wished bitterly that my own children were with me to see it; it would have given them a strange aftertaste of their own daydreams. They would have recognized it inside themselves as something far more truthful than any Disney fantasy. A *real* childhood accords full reality only to visions, and respects them. Here was the Postman's vision in stone.

Here and there dotted about the old Postman carved up aphorisms in order to encourage himself, to freshen up his flagging forces, no doubt. Some are mere cracker mottoes, some little verses, some quotations from Holy Writ: some are free verse poems. It is like riffling the artist's notebook, or looking over his shoulder as he works.

> Sous la garde des géants
> J'ai placé l'épopée des humbles
> Courbé sur le sillon

> La vie est un océan de tempêtes
> Entre l'enfant qui vient de naître
> Et le veillard qui va disparaître

Finally, when the whole work was complete down to the last inscription he even built a tomb for the faithful wheelbarrow which had been his constant companion for so many years. More than that, he permitted the wheelbarrow (which appears also to have been endowed with an aphoristic turn of mind) to write its own verses, its own funeral inscriptions. This is how the barrow expresses itself:

> Je suis fidèle compagne
> Du travailleur intelligent
> Qui chaque jour dans la campagne
> Cherchait son petit contingent.

> Maintenant son oeuvre est finie
> Il jouit en paix de son labeur,
> Et chez lui, moi, son humble amie,
> J'occupe la place d'honneur.

Together with the wheelbarrow in its quiet niche lie the tools with which the Ideal Palace was constructed.

But the path of genius never runs smooth; at the completion of his grand work the Postman Horse announced that he proposed to be buried in it; he had prepared his own tomb. Here he ran into opposition from the Church which has always been against permitting people to get themselves buried in their back gardens—I have never understood why. . . . A long argument ensued, but finally the Church won. The Postman Horse must, like everyone else, be buried in the village cemetery. Whatever his feelings he accepted this fiat at last and bought himself the requisite site. But here his artistic feelings overcame him. The indomitable old man set about building himself a tomb which is like a small annexe to the Ideal Palace, identical in style and inspiration. It took him ten years to complete it, but complete it he did; and that is where he lies today, under a simple inscription which might well have been carved over a Greek tomb containing the bones of a Heraclitus or an Epicurus.

Le tombeau du silence et du repos sans fin.

We motored slowly out of the beautiful village of Hauterives, across the bridge which spanned the rushing trout-stream, in a pleasant silence—the only sort of tribute one can pay to artistic experience. Along these leafy green lanes I seemed to see the little postman tramping along, wheeling his choice stones back to the quiet house, talking quietly to himself as he walked. A plump pheasant walked across the road and Lejoie said: 'We shall reach Chabert's in twenty-five minutes.'

It was only, after all, a switch from one art-form to another, for Chabert we found to be almost as much of a visionary as the old postman. His little hotel stands in the main street of Tain l'Hermitage which has the air of being a little market-town running to urbanization. Like nearly all good eating places in France the exterior is unprepossessing. It is simply a pleasant old-world bar attached to a restaurant. The Hotel is a private one, a mere diversion you might say, for there are only seven guest rooms. You can only stay there if the master invites you, and he only invites a special race of men—*les gens qui vraiment aiment manger*. I could see him anxiously scan my face to see if really I merited his hospitality.

The great Chabert was a small compact man with greyish hair and finely cut features; he gave off a feeling of unhurried calm, of gentleness. He was obviously someone who could watch a pot boil without getting rattled; every movement of the hands was eloquent. They were the hands of a musician, of someone who was sure of his effects.

Of course there was a good deal of hubbub, introductions, explanations, when first we arrived. Lejoie's mother was delighted to see him; it was nearly six months since his last visit. He had brought characteristic presents for them both in the form of a rare cheese from Gascony and a bottle of liqueur. Our luggage was unloaded while we had a stirrup-cup. Chabert popped in and out of his kitchen where half a dozen white-capped young men juggled with the pots and pans under his watchful direction. The promised dinner was already on the slips. It would be ready within the hour. But first, said Chabert, he would like to convey some general information about the wines of the district and to this end we could profitably kill an hour or two before dining, combining information with pleasure. Chapoutier? Where had I heard the name?

As a matter of fact it is written in letters a mile high right across the hillside behind Tain l'Hermitage; you can read it four miles off. It signals the ownership of the best vineyards of the region. As we set off down the darkening street Lejoie refreshed my memory on this point. It was only two streets away from Chabert.

Chapoutier himself was seated before his desk in the imposing central office of the firm, waiting for us; before him stood a magnum of champagne. From time to time he touched it and turned it in its bucket with the air of a doctor taking its pulse. He was a young man, gay and spirited as became a wine-specialist. The keys to the great cellars lay before him.

Lejoie was an old friend, of course, which got conversation away to a merry start. Pouring out the champagne Chapoutier said deprecatingly that it should not be taken seriously; it was a mere *rince-bouche*, a mouthwash, in order to clear the palate before we tasted the wines in the cellar. I tried to regard it in this light, purely as a medicament, but I could not help enjoying it just a little. It had an exquisite flavour. In fact I could have gone on rinsing my palate all night with this admirable stuff.

But at last the bottle was finished, and deeming us all suitably clean-palated, Chapoutier pressed a tall goose-necked wineglass into each hand, and taking up his keys and his pipette he led us out into the dark street and across to the great cellars.

The night was clear and fine; the cellars deep and immense and secret. As the lights were switched on here and there they showed bins and barrels and *tonneaux* stretching away on all sides, into the darkness, around us, symmetrically ruling away perspectives into infinity. Keen-eyed, clean-palated, we followed our host slowly from bin to bin, accepting a squirt of each of the vintages from his hospitable pipette, and sitting down to savour it on the nearest cask. There is no need to go into the details of all we tasted. Chapoutier's wine is too well known and has been the subject of numberless essays and studies. It is, however, important to record that his conversation sparkles every bit as excitingly as his most sparkling wine. But then the object of good wine is, and always has been, good conversation. The eleventh commandment has always been, 'Drink well to talk well.'

In those cavernous cellars, their walls covered with a deep lichen-coloured fungus—the bloom you get on an over-ripe peach—in the semi-darkness, voices muffled by the thick medieval walls, we found conversation take wing. By the time we had broached the twelfth white bin and the fourth red we had discussed as well as toasted Rabelais, Mallarmé and Stendhal; we had sent Marxists about their business, decried religious bigotry, deplored the French Revolution, denounced the Bourbons and the Jesuits, flung defiance at nuclear physics, vaunted Byron, Poe and Rimbaud, rapped Henry James over the knuckles, and sung a few staves of Georges Brassens. Intellectually speaking we left no glass unturned.

By the time we staggered out into the night, somewhat dishevelled but still keen-eyed and burning with intellectual zeal, I felt as if I were moving on castors.

The night air was cool and soothing to our fevered heads, however, and while our tongues had been loosened by these excellent snecks of wine they were still attached to our brains. At any rate that is how it felt. Under a street lamp we all embraced ferociously like French generals conferring decorations upon each other, and swore undying blood-brotherhood. 'Come again,' cried Chapoutier with warmth. 'Any time at all. It is a pleasure to have some good conversation.'

By the time we reached Chabert's the cozy table had been laid in a private corner of the restaurant, and the master watched us enter with a quizzical eye. 'Ah, you are just in the right mood,' he said approvingly. 'Often people are knocked silly by a visit to the cellars and run the risk of not appreciating their dinners. Then I have to let them wait an extra half-hour—and of course I risk the quality of the dinner.' Everything is very finely calculated in France—according to a graduated scale.

Now began one of those famous Chabert dinners, gathering its way slowly like a Bach fugue, moving through scale after scale, figure after figure, its massive counterpoint swelling and gathering. And yet without any pomp whatsoever; quietly, deprecatingly the great Chef himself attended to the dishes, getting up from the table to make some minor arrangement with his own hands, and sitting down again to reminisce quietly over his early life in the French navy. He had started as a sea-cook when he was thirteen; slowly he had worked his way up

the scale into what he had now become, a master-chef, an artist. His
wife smiled as she listened, chin in hand, to these early adventures, and
then she in her turn spoke about the Facteur Cheval whom she had
seen when she was a little girl. 'An irascible quick-tempered little
man,' she said, nodding her dark Mediterranean head and smiling. 'He
was very much on the defensive because everyone said he was a fool.
He defended his own genius to the death.'

'He was right,' said Chabert approvingly.

'He was right,' said Lejoie.

'He was right,' said I.

Meanwhile this memorable dinner was slowly gathering form and
momentum before us. Later that night on my way up to bed I asked
Chabert to write it all down for me in his own hand. I wanted an auto-
graph as well as the Menu. It is perfectly useless to describe good food.
The thing escapes words, as poetry does, and indeed all good art. Here,
then, is what Chabert wrote down in his fine nervous hand.

> Les Quenelles de brochet à ma façon
> Le vin St. Joseph Rouge
>   Côtes Rôties 1952
> Pâté de Canard truffé avec des petits
> oignons à la Grecque et à la mode de chez-moi
>
> Pintadeaux nouveaux aux bananes
> (Sauces avec Madère, Porto, Crème, Glace de
> Viande etc.)
>   Petits Chèvres de Chantemerle
>   Coupe de Fraises Melba

The reader will notice the phrases 'à ma façon' and 'à la mode de
chez-moi', and imagine that like all great chefs Chabert is keeping his
trade secrets to himself. This is not the case; it is simply his modesty
which prevents him from adding his own name to the dish, as he would
have every right to do—as every great inventive chef does in France.
He deplores this habit and says that it smacks of pretentiousness. For
his part he believes that a great chef should do everything well and a
few things of his own choice superbly.

'You see? He is another fanatic,' said Lejoie as he listened smiling.
We were all sitting together over a glass of fine brandy listening to the
clock chime midnight. Soon I would be comfortably tucked up in bed,

my drowsy brain packed with dazzling impressions of this visit, trying in vain to sort them out. 'I hope you'll write something about it,' said Lejoie suddenly, as we were all saying good-night. 'I would feel the visit had been worthwhile.'

We lagged upon the staircase, slowly talking our way up into the darkness of the first floor.

'If I did what would I call it?' I said.

' "In Praise of Fanatics", of course,' said Lejoie.

So I have.

The River Rhône

Published in Holiday. *Philadelphia. January 1960.*

Every great river gradually grows its own history, its own temperament, its own quite distinguishable personality. It becomes an image of a nation or a capital city, a word with echoes. To the philosopher it has always suggested the notion of time, perhaps because it never flows backwards (except in mythology or poetry). To the map-maker it suggests a living artery in the body of a country. But to the historians it is always a road—a highway along which the peoples of the world have always undertaken their slow pilgrimages to distant shrines of worship; or more prosaically and more recently their business trips in search of customers for their wares.

Among these echoing river-names of Europe that of the Rhône has always been among the first. On the green map of France the rivers curve outwards like the veins on a tobacco-leaf, each with its private history and character, its climate, its particular morphology. Of the four great river-kingdoms of France that of the Rhône is the most various to study and perhaps the most delightful to explore, for in its relatively short course (it is the shortest of the four) it cuts across the two hemispheres which together make up the temperament of France itself: the cold dark north and the sun-dazzled Mediterranean. In a manner of speaking it *is* France, and if you journey along it you can study it as a sort of summation of the French character and of French history. Long before the Roman roads came into existence Bronze Age man thought of it as 'the amber road' towards the south; in the Middle Ages it was perhaps the pilgrim's chief hazard on the road to Rome. Every Roman army advancing on Gaul had to take it into account. Its bold rushing waters all but defeated the impetuous Hannibal's first attempt to cross it, washing away his army, terrifying his elephants, and forcing him to make a long detour north in search of a negotiable ford. . . . These were only a few of its early victories, but they were enough to establish it as a fickle, undependable river—a river which did not allow anyone to take chances with it.

Like the Rhine it is an intruder into France, for it is glacier-born, its head-springs start at 1,875 metres in the St. Gotthard massif, that 'château d'eau de l'Europe'. Perhaps the relative closeness of the two sources, of Rhine and Rhône, has given them a common parentage in Swiss folklore, for we are told that both rivers were invented by an idle and playful dwarf called Rollin. To this day he is supposed to sing a little song describing just how he did so. It goes like this.

> One fine emerald is in my yellow sand
> One pure sapphire is in my little jewel case.
> My emerald melts and becomes the Rhine
> My sapphire dissolves to become the Rhône.

Perhaps Victor Hugo was unconsciously thinking of the dwarf Rollin when he wrote: 'Each of the great Alpine rivers on leaving the mountains has the colour of the sea towards which it is flowing. The Rhône on leaving Geneva is as blue as the Mediterranean. While the Rhine on leaving Lake Constance is as green as the Ocean.'

One would hardly agree with him, however, if one picked up the southerly reaches of the Rhône, once it has crossed the divide into southern France; for there in the bright glare of the Midi it has turned olive-green, perhaps from the immense quantity of alluvial mud it ferries down into the lowlands with it—over three million tons a year. And what a journey! For in its lower straight course of some 230 miles between Lyons and the Mediterranean it separates the Lyonnais and Languedoc (on the westerly bank) from Dauphiné and Provence. Today of course both roads and railways hug it closely; yet most of the important towns lie on the eastern bank. Here its classical character is firmly established: you will not be able to miss the willow-clad islands, the ancient fortresses which line its banks, rich with the historic associations of the past. Its northern history is a mere record—its southern is a poetic evocation that includes the whole Mediterranean!

It does not really grow up before it reaches Lyons; it does not become the river which the Provençal poets described as wilder than a charging bull, more fickle than a women. Perhaps as the valleys open away southward, becoming more spacious and flat, the mere impression of its speed increases. Between Lyons and Arles, for example, its mean level drops by 156 metres as it covers the 282 kilometres between the two famous towns. But by now it is naturalized, has become a thoroughly French river: has forced its way into history and legend, so that it turns up even in such unexpected places as the Letters of Madame de Sévigné. 'Ce diantre Rhône', she calls it, after a journey full of hazards. 'This devil of a Rhône!' For by now the piercing irregular winds like the mistral have taken a hand. The mountains and tributaries on either side of it contribute sudden rushes of water after the spring and autumn rains which swell it and cause severe yearly floods. Yes, even today, when science has effectively bridged it, and even harnessed it for power in places—even today it remains capricious and unpredictable, capable of anything. There is no warning usually. The flood rises at an incredible speed. In last year's floods, the waters rose at the rate of a metre in ten minutes.

Its childhood, like that of so many great personalities, is relatively uninteresting. It is hardly the same Rhône which so peaceably crosses the canton of Valais between banks which are green and rich: Alpine, glacier-fed vegetation. But after two hundred and ninety kilometres it swerves out of Switzerland and comes up against the granite hefts of the Jura Range. A narrow gorge allows it to burst its way through into France at last, where it weaves west by south, curling round towards Lyons. Its only tributary here is the Ain which propels it onward with ever-gathering momentum.

The landscapes of the river's northern course have a particular splendour and variety, for though the mountains still etch themselves like drypoints upon the cool sky nevertheless the valleys begin to roll and curve, to open more spaciously towards the west and south. The long curving rides of the forests rise and fall with them, and the villages bury themselves in their folds like secrets. It is one of the richest corners of France as far as productivity is concerned for there are many rivers which traverse it in the same general direction. It enjoys all the abundance of a landscape rich in water; a fruitful soil that can be worked, moulded and patterned by the husbandman. It goes without saying that the cuisine is famous for it draws its raw materials from several counties, but the chief characteristic is perhaps the fact that butter and cream are used very liberally in the more famous dishes. Here the determined traveller should screw his courage to the sticking point and try *grenouilles à la crème*, or *escargots*. The trivial inhibitions of the foreign stomach will be swept away at once. As for the severely orthodox who cannot look upon such fare without blenching, they should remember the peculiar excellence of the fish from these mountain rivers and hidden lakes and stick to trout or *brochet*—or at least sample the famous *poulardes rôties* from the nearby county of Bresse. Famous experiences such as these may be enjoyed on the very banks of the Rhône at points like Seyssel or Bellegarde, where the river flows smoothly, serenely, and gives no hint of its future caprices.

Nor is this talk of food out of place—for the serious trencherman will not be able to traverse this country without emotion: without whispering to himself the magical name of *Brillat-Savarin,* the patron saint of gourmets. He came from these parts, and indeed there is hardly a little restaurant where you will not come upon someone bearing a marked resemblance to the great man, full of face and high of colour, with a flowing napkin tucked into his collar. ('L'abdomen est un peu majestueux', to quote the words of the Master himself.) This is the landscape in which to read slowly, lingeringly, those flowing periods in *La Physiologie du Goût* which have transformed the mere act of eating into a philosophy. What a country, and what a man! Brillat-Savarin came from fabulous, immortal stock. The reader must remember that his great-aunt died at the age of ninety-three while drinking a glass of *vieux Virieu;* while one of his sisters, two months before her hundredth birthday, uttered her last words—words which are graven in the heart of every true *gastronome*. They were 'Vite, apportez moi le dessert, je sens que je vais passer'. (Quick, bring in the dessert, I feel I'm going.)

But it is at Lyons that the Rhône comes of age, so to speak: has its first real love-affair with the quiet-flowing Saône, a river almost as wide but only half as swift. The point where they join hands below the town was always considered sacred in ancient times. But the two rivers at their junction are really responsible for the character of this great industrial city. Lyons has always been the hinge between the two climates and the two cultures of France, and while the ebb and flow of history has changed the disposition and architecture of the town over and over again, nothing has ever managed to alter its influence as a catalyst, a transformer between the hot-blooded southern Frenchman and his more reserved northern brother. Even in Roman times, as today, Lyons was the natural axis of the European road-system which

Agrippa planned—in an age when it took one thirty days to traverse Gaul from the Pas de Calais to Marseilles. Today the axis still holds good for the modern road and rail system which nets eastern France. All roads lead to Lyons, and no wise traveller will complain for this great city is also the axis of good eating—the very midriff of *haute cuisine*, as it were. Opinions have always differed about the climate of Lyons, yes; even among Frenchmen. But . . . you will not find a *gourmet* in France who has not made the sacred pilgrimage called the *Circuit du Beaujolais*, for the wine-country of that famous name lies just north of Lyons, and is easily visited by the ardent wine-prover. No traveller of taste can afford to ignore the experience, and if follow the Rhône we must . . . why, it will not be without many a tender glance over the shoulder at this incomparable mulberry landscape with its verdant rolling valleys and uninhibited wines.

As for Lyons itself, the second city of France, despite the splendour of its historic monuments, its great picture gallery, its magnificent squares and bridges, there is something not very inspiriting about its atmosphere. This is perhaps due to the river-mist which so often seems to hang over it, hazing up its sharp outlines. Despite the excellence of its *cuisine*. Myself I have always remembered the description of Daudet and found it not inapt. 'Strange town!' he writes. 'I remember a low-hanging sky the colour of soot, a perpetual mist rising from the two rivers. It never seems to actually rain. It mists over; and in the flatness of this wet atmosphere the walls weep, the pavements sweat, the balustrades of the staircases stick to one's fingers. The people, too, in their way seem to reflect this grey humidity; yellowish in colouring, with sleepy eyes, and with lazy dawdling accents which draw out the long syllables of words. . . .' No traveller will repeat these words to a Lyonnais without provoking the passionate cry: 'Unjust! Daudet was a blasted southerner. How could he appreciate our city?'

But there is much to reconcile one apart from the food, and the industrious and inventive people of Lyons are right not to pay too much attention to sun-drunk southerners. The history of the town has laid its mark upon so many arts and industries—from fine printing to silk—that really it should be exonerated for its sad climate. Here, after all, in some little bookshop you might actually stumble upon a bundle of medieval almanacs which provided Rabelais with an immortal pattern for his book! Or better still, if by hazard you find yourself on the banks of the Saône at dusk, hunt out the little marionette theatre (30 du Quai Saint Antoine) and spend an evening watching the exquisite *Théâtre Guignol* at work! This famous local Punch and Judy show dates from 1808. Yes, Lyons has its charms. It has in fact always been a favoured town owing to its unique location. The Romans were perhaps the first to fully recognize the fact—if we are to judge by the fantastic engineering feats they performed to bring water to it: struggles which resulted in a flow of a hundred thousand cubic metres a day!

Until comparatively recent times the Rhône currents presented a unique problem for the heavy haulage traffic (horse-drawn) which plied between Lyons and Arles. Who will say that the Lyonnais are not inventive as well as industrious? The first conquest of the Rhône currents by a steamboat was here, and the first steam-powered boat was Lyonnais in conception and design. De Jouffroy of Lyons built it and after several trials made his triumphal attack on the harsh cross currents of the river in the sight of ten thousand cheering spectators who lined the banks. He christened the animal 'the pyroscaphe' but even in the old pictures of this memorable exploit it is recognizably the grandfather of the Mississippi steam-boat (though it is only forty-six metres in length, and of 120 tons burthen). Nor is this a mere metaphor. This proud day in Lyons indeed determined the future of river-traffic in America for de Jouffroy's triumph reached the ears of the brilliant American inventor Fulton who was in France, and actually working along the same lines of thought. Following rapidly upon de Jouffroy he had several models built for him and tested them on the Seine in 1803. By 1806 he was satisfied with his tests and returned to America with his successful prototype, an eighteen horse-power river boat which was to inaugurate the first regular service between Albany and New York! No Lyonnais can listen to the strains of 'Ol' Man River' today without a thrill of fraternal pride. Unfortunately, however, this great invention was more easily exploitable in the new world than in the French Midi, though for a short while the old-fashioned river traffic was superseded by it on the lower reaches of the Rhône. Yet the final death blow to the old river-teams with their strings of thirty and forty horses was in fact the steam-engine. The railway was not far off.

So much for history. The traveller down the Rhône will certainly have more than his share of it, for the great river seems to traverse the richest corners of European history in its arrow-flight to the south. The fine roads leading south from Lyons echo its sweeps and curves, and this is a corner in which to linger for you are still in a relatively northern landscape with its verdant valleys and fine woodlands. It is only at Valence that suddenly, like a verse of Theocritus spoken in the mind, the olive-trees begin—the ageless grey silver trees of Pallas Athene. No, here you are still in sunny mulberry country. For some reason or other it does not seem much frequented. Yet Vienne, with its astonishing warren of medieval streets, its weird castle, and the lovely Corinthian temple, is worth lingering over, for it is really the cradle of Christianity in the West. It should be of interest, too, to diplomats for it was to Vienne that Pontius Pilate, the patron saint of the order, was exiled after his term of service in Judaea! At evening it is particularly entrancing when the blueness of the shadows, the round-tiled over-hanging roofs, and the many-pronged mulberries planted to feed the silk manufactories of Lyons, the dusty plains around it—everything conspires to remind one that one is moving southwards towards the heat of the Midi.

Le Chemin du Soleil, as it is known to travellers, rolls south from Vienne, through the rich plains around Ampuis towards Condrieu, along the willow-fringed banks of the river, through vineyards whose crops bear the proud names of vintages known the world over. From Vienne to Condrieu is only twelve kilometres but it is one of the most delightful and unfrequented stretches of the river for the landscape here hangs breathlessly suspended between the two worlds; it is a temperate zone so to speak between the white dusty heat of Provence and the misty verdant richness of a more northerly clime. It is a country, not only of vines, but also of cherries and apricots and pears— their frail blooms in the early spring turn every corner of it into Japanese water-colours of breathless distinction. Alas! how brief the flowering is, lasting for perhaps a fortnight at most, at the end of February, but how unforgettable.

Condrieu has few monuments of interest but it is a name which has a distinct echo for Frenchmen, for it used to be the headquarters of those bands of whiskered fishermen who manned the great barges on the Rhône. It is called *la patrie des nautes*, and Mistral's great poem of the Rhône has left us an unforgettable picture of the river-life as it was lived before steam ousted the horse. His poem, indeed, is the traveller's source-book for the ancient life of the river, and his central character Maître Apian is a character of Chaucerian dimensions. His is the most famous of the river haulage-teams, and Mistral simply transcribes the old river-sailor's memoirs in unforgettable verse. Maître Apian worked a team of forty horses, of great massive Charolais stock, and each of his convoys ferried about four hundred tons of goods up and down river. In summer, when the river was relatively low, such a convoy took twenty days to reach Lyons from Arles; in winter when the Rhône 'swelled like a muscle' it took thirty-five to forty days. These were old-fashioned barges with flared poops where the hammocks of the crew swung to the slow rhythm of the tugging currents. In the days of Apian, conditions on the river had changed little since the Middle Ages. His barges, for example, visited the famous Fair of Beaucaire, carrying 'the magnificent silks of Lyons, worked leather-ware, and bales of hemp'. On his return journey northward he loaded 'the fine-eared wheat of Toulouse, the wines of the Languedoc and sea-salt of the Camargue, the famous soaps of Marseilles, and Provençal olive-oil'. The going upstream was hard enough, but coming down again was harder because more dangerous. The swift river carried them down from Lyons to Arles in only three days. Frequently they ran aground on the shifting sandbanks, while the bridges constituted serious hazards. To cross Pont St. Esprit was like shooting the rapids when there was a strong mistral blowing. It was a rugged tradition to which Maître Apian belonged, and it died hard in the thirties of the last century. But Condrieu has not forgotten, and one of the proud boasts of the town is that it was the rivermen of Condrieu who first followed Louis to the Crusades. Maître Apian was simply the last heir of a great tradition which de Jouffroy of Lyons killed with his 'pyroscaphe'.

These, then, are the appropriate thoughts with which to pass a quiet hour on the banks of the Rhône at Condrieu drinking a glass of the famous local wine to the memory of Maître Apian.

Tournon, Valence, Montelimar and you are now in a new country, the kingdom of the olive and the cypress. Here the Mediterranean begins with its characteristic cuisine based on garlic and olive-oil, its concentration on herbs—saffron, thyme, fennel, sage, black pepper. Here, too, the apéritif changes to *pastis*—an aniseed drink which is a mild second-cousin to the brain-storming northern Pernod. This, too, is the territory in which to make your first tentative exploration of the little rosé wines which are (with the famous exceptions like Tavel) hardly known abroad. Under the dusty glare of the Provençal sunlight this new diet seems supremely appropriate; appropriate too that the accents begin to change from chicken and mutton to fish—which comes to its apotheosis in the great *bouillabaisse* cauldrons of the port of Marseilles! Even the most unobservant of travellers will have noticed already the steep low pitch of the roofs, the warm rose of Marseilles tiles, the ever-present black beret which characterizes the south; and more than one will stop in the shade of a plane-tree to watch the obsessional game of *boules* which gives idleness in Provence a very special flavour of timelessness. Provence! This new world is a pre-Christian one, with its mouldering monuments of the Roman occupation, its sculptured reliefs and shattered columns; even the bullfights you will see in the ancient arenas of Arles and Nîmes will remind you that the parentage of this ancient ritual goes back to Crete and is pictured on the Minoan vases. Long before Christian martyrs were thrown to the wild animals in these stately arenas, the god Mithras was worshipped or perhaps propitiated by the ceremonial bull-slaying of his devotees.

But of course the heart of it all is Avignon with its honey-coloured, rose-faded walls and machicolated towers rising steeply from a country dusted silver with olives, and—more likely than not—swept by the roaring mistral. An old distich alleges that it is the mistral which keeps the town healthy.

Avenio ventosa
Cum vento fastidiosa
Sine vente venenosa.

All I know of the matter is that when the wind is blowing at full force one must grip tightly to the balustrades of the bridge when trying to cross it on foot. Avignon belongs to the Popes as Venice belongs to the Doges. (Seven popes and two anti-popes succeeded in Avignon during the 'second captivity of Babylon', when, in the words of Petrarch, 'they kept the church of Jesus Christ in a shameful exile.') Nevertheless their relics have made of Avignon one of the most beautiful and romantic towns on earth. Even travellers like Dickens, who were fundamentally unsympathetic to the sunny south, were moved to admiration. Of Avignon he says: 'All the city lies baking in the sun, yet with an underdone piecrust, battlemented wall, that will never be brown though it bake for centuries.' He is right, for the tones of these marvellous palaces combine a dozen soft shades from the brown of dried tobacco or coffee to the violets and pearl-pinks of cooling lava—shades of nacre and bistre and honey according to the stoop of the sun. There is so much to see that the traveller almost succumbs, realizing that the town truly needs a residence of some weeks to be fully appreciated. As for the travel-writer—what can he do but feel abashed? So very much has been written of the place by so many writers of the front rank! Rabelais christened it '*Isle sonnante*' from the perpetual tolling of the convent bells which in the Middle Ages was the most characteristic thing about the approach to the city by water. That Laura should have been buried here seems appropriate; but why John Stuart Mill, why Bishop Colenso? History has a sense of humour perhaps? But if your time in Avignon is limited, try at least to visit the Church of St. Pierre which is reached by a strange rock-hewn street among the giant buttresses of the palace. From the clock tower you will get one of the finest panoramic views of the city.

The ruined bridge of St. Benezet somehow contrives to be the centrepiece of every good view in Avignon, and with justice, for it has made the city world-famous through the little *ronde* that has become a nursery rhyme for children everywhere. Severe textual critics, however, maintain that our children have got it slightly wrong. The bridge was never wide enough for dancing they tell us, and the correct wording of the little song should be:

> *Sur le Pont d'Avignon*
> *Tout le monde y passe.*

This criticism, however, has always fallen on deaf ears. The dancers are too lovely an image to sacrifice, and the little song (like 'London Bridge is falling down') will last for ever in its current form, whatever the grim professors tell us. (Besides, the correct version doesn't scan.)

The two most magnificent bridges over the Rhône were those of St. Benezet and the still intact Pont St. Esprit—a miracle bridge indeed; and magnificent both as works of science and as aesthetic monuments. It is true that Trajan managed to bridge the Rhône with a narrow stone bridge, but it did not last and for centuries heavy traffic had to be entrusted to wherries, or pick a suitable low-water season in which to try and ford the river. There is hardly a chronicle which does not mention the hazards of this crossing. The first real bridges were not attempted before the end of the twelfth century when St. Benezet, who was then a shepherd boy of twelve years old, had his famous vision in which Jesus commanded him to bridge the Rhône at Avignon. Infecting the good friars of the town with his message he actually put this fantastic project into execution. It took twelve years to build it, and when it was complete the river was safely spanned by twenty-three graceful arches and Avignon found itself on the main highway of the western world. But, as any traveller will see with a pang of regret, the Rhône had the last word. Of the ancient bridges only that of Pont St. Esprit is still standing with its brave span of twenty arches. For the rest, the steel hanging bridges have managed to do the job at last, but one cannot deny that they are less beautiful.

As the *route nationale* rolls south from Avignon the echo of the name prolongs itself; we are reaching the end of our journey, and the other 'children of the Rhône'—Beaucaire, Tarascon and Arles—strike a somewhat obituary note. So much has vanished from this sun-kissed world. The great Fair of Beaucaire was one of the famous sights of Europe. Three of our hundred thousand visitors flocked there every year, Maître Apian among them, to trade as well as to enjoy the carnival spirit which turned this great *entrepôt* into a brilliant city of lights and banners. Alas! today the monuments of Beaucaire are all that are left to enjoy. It stands proudly fronting Tarascon across the broad Rhône. But both are relatively dead. The great festival of the dragon (the Tarasque) was Tarascon's contribution to the yearly festivities which were fathered by the river. Attempts have been made at reviving them, but I doubt if the past is so easily recapturable. After all, the Tarasque belonged to the age of dragons; indeed it is one of the more famous of the legendary inhabitants of the river. From time to time it would emerge from the Rhône and carry off the villagers until the doughty Saint Martha heard of its depredations and marched up in the dust from the Saintes Maries to quell it. In honour of this notable victory the gallant poet-king René decreed a twice yearly procession in which this notable feat was re-enacted with a mock-dragon made of plaited osiers and reeds. But this, too, died with the river-trade of Maître Apian and his fellow-sailors, with the great fair of Beaucaire.

'Silence and monuments,' says a French traveller, 'echoes and elucidations of ancient history. Arles is the Mecca of the archaeologist; but its life, so severe and aristocratic, belongs to the past rather than the present.' I think the chief regret is that the Provençal costumes have disappeared—though they are proudly revived whenever there is a bullfight. The arenas of Arles are among the most famous in Provence for bullfighting of both the Spanish and Provençal kind. Before every fight the young girls and boys dress themselves up in the magnificent costumes of a hundred years ago and walk through the town in procession to be pelted with sweets and flowers. Only the life of the present-day Camargue still preserves some of its old flavour, and the hawk-featured *gardiens* with their bull-tridents at the ready, and their lovely wives in the saddle behind them, make the most impressive and most authentic picture of old Provence during these parades. Their life has not yet been changed, nor their costumes—and presumably will not as long as there are bulls to herd and horses to ride in those desolate green estuaries of the Delta.

After Arles the Rhône 'weary', says Mistral 'after so much journeying, slows like a pulse'. It has reached the sand-buffer of the Camargue Delta where it divides into two rivers, losing momentum and rapidity, losing its colour too as it fades into the dunes.

The two branches—*les Rhônes morts*—now cross the Camargue, that strange and rather desolate sand-delta, which is today a great zoological preserve. Of the two Rhônes the eastern is the only one worth following to the sea for it leads to the little Church of the Two Marys on the seacoast, the spiritual headquarters of the Gipsies of all Christendom. The long straight roads run between low dykes overgrown with white ranunculus, across plain covered with corn and vines. Here and there you pass a large *mas* or farm, often with the remains of a defensive tower still standing. Salt marshes stretch away on either side with their grey blighted vegetation; here in these grey expanses among the salt pans and swamps roam the herds of half-wild cattle and the *manades* of bulls destined to fight in the arenas of all the surrounding towns and villages. This is the breeding ground for the Camargue bull, smaller and more ferocious than his lumbering Spanish cousin. He is not destined to be done to death; he carries the red cockade which must be snatched from between his sharp and curving horns. They say that this little breed is a direct descendant of the bull of Apis, the unevolved child (it has six lumbar vertebrae) of one of the prehistoric bulls. It is not as unlikely as it sounds, for the Camargue has always been a desolate spot, left very much to itself because of the swarms of mosquitoes which even today are not under control despite large-scale efforts made to stamp them out. Successful efforts are being made now to grow rice and the ripe green paddy-fields break up the grey monotony of this salty estuary. But the real beauty of Camargue is inseparable from its most characteristic inhabitant—the small white horses, swift and mettlesome, which are of a Saracen strain and without which the ardours of bull-herding would be greater than they are.

This, then, is the end of the Rhône, no longer swift and unpredictable, but slow-flowing to the sea. There is little to see at the Stes. Maries save the beautiful and melancholy church where the gipsies come in May every year to worship St. Sara, their patron saint. But driving back across the delta the traveller will think he is in the Nile Delta, with its flights of pink flamingoes, of wild geese. At the half-way stop there is a small zoo which illustrates the wild life which exists, even today, in the Camargue. Foxes and wild boars abound; eagles and pelicans and buzzards patrol the white beaches. Beavers build their strange dams among the dykes. It is a natural paradise for wild birds, and a not inappropriate monument to the last part of the Rhône's long journey from the glaciers to the blue Mediterranean.

Laura, A Portrait of Avignon

Published in Holiday. *Philadelphia. February 1961.*
Republished in Woman's Own. *London. October 1962.*

The psycho-analyst incautious enough to ask me to associate freely on the word Avignon, or indeed to riffle through my travel diary, would not I think be too surprised by the word Laura as an opening gambit. Literary men are supposed to be literary. But what would he make of the other entries. I wonder? They run like this. (I always use the laws of free association in my diaries. It saves time and keeps them fresh.)

> Bringing Laura!! back.
> Plumber, water-tap, Gargantua.
> Edgar Allan Poe.
> 'If her ragoût is good. . . .'

Mysterious enough to baffle an analyst I think, but really quite simple. The truth of the matter is this, that I went to Avignon with a plumber called Raoul to find a water tap and bring back a bride called 'Laura'. There is nothing more Petrarchian than a girl called Laura, living in Avignon, who advertises in the Marriage section of *Midi Libre* saying, 'Lasse d'être seule, je veux me marier.'

But let me begin with the plumber called Raoul. He was, as plumbers go, one of the most careless and destructive men I have ever known. He had one hand rather bigger than the other, which may explain it. I don't know. But the fact is that if he tried to take a pipe out of a wall the whole wall came; whatever he tried to bend broke off short. He would stand with an air of dribbling amazement looking at the smashed object, blushing. He didn't know his own strength and seldom looked where he was going. When he fell down the earth shook. He had a high foolish neighing laugh which he used continuously. I imagine the damned in hell laugh in just this way. In fact I cannot think why I ever liked him. I think I was curious. He was so like an infant Gargantua, so typically Provençal, that I listened to his accounts of what he ate and drank like a man in a dream. Barrels of oysters, drums of red wine, whole oxen fresh from the spit. Often he ate so much that he was indisposed and this affected his work. His clients never knew at such times what might not come out of the kitchen tap. It was safer not to turn it on.

Now this absolute fool of a man had a mate, a silent morose little man who looked like Schopenhauer, whose job was to trot behind him and pick up the remains. He never spoke, the mate. It was hardly necessary. He wore a soiled beret and had a cigarette stuck to his bottom lip. When Raoul got playful he often threw pieces of pig iron about, and I think the mate kept all his energies for side-stepping. Anyway between them they broke the garden tap, a rather fancy one with a sort of key-shaped handle which could be removed in order to foil marauders. (In the summer a good deal of water-pinching from the neighbour's well is quite fashionable. You wait till your neighbour goes out and then swiftly water your geraniums.) The tap itself came from Paris, and it wasn't replaceable (so Raoul said) unless he went to the wholesaler in Avignon. This meant a journey of about seventy miles. 'Why', he said, 'don't you come for the ride?' The idea didn't seem a bad one. Raoul added suddenly, blushing to the roots of his mane—he grew his hair half-way down his back—'I have got to go there anyway soon to arrange for my marriage.' Then he showed me the advertisement in the paper. He had been in touch with the girl and she sounded rather promising. They had agreed to meet. Then he added hoarsely, 'Her name is Laura.'

Laura! I thought of the honeyed sonnets of Petrarch, of the long years of his agony (was it contrived?). I thought of the splendid simplicity of the old anonymous Abbé J. T. who described the meeting in his smoothly turned French. I have an old biography of Petrarch which I picked up on the banks of the Seine. 'Le lundi de la Semaine-Sainte, à six heures du matin, Pétrarque vit à Avignon, dans l'Eglise des Religieuses de Saint-Claire, une jeune femme dont la robe verte était parsemée de violettes. Sa beauté le frappa: c'était Laura.' It was as simple as that. Love at first sight! And now Raoul was going to get his. He looked quite dazed at having confided in me. For my part I had a sudden feeling of apprehensive sympathy for the poor girl.

With such an infant Gargantua for a husband anything might happen. She would have to be as stoutly built as a camel-backed locomotive, I thought, not to run the risk of being overlaid or hit by the odd piece of pig-iron.

I said I would go.

I have always been a rash, foolish, intemperate and hasty man. Raoul was delighted. 'In that case,' he said, 'I will drive you, and you will pay for the petrol.'

I said I would. Raoul appeared one afternoon in the strange old covered wagon which he drove round the countryside full of twisted taps and pig-iron. His mate sat behind nursing a large demijohn of a wine he called Picpoul. As we snarled among the white roads he decanted it precariously into a blue mug which was passed around, each taking a ceremonial sip. It was rather fortifying, though it did not loosen the little man's tongue. Raoul, on the contrary, was extremely talkative and was pleased to expound some of his philosophy of life to me. 'Now I would never have gone for a girl from one of those agencies,' he said confidentially. 'You never know what you get from an agency. But a girl who bothers to pay for her own advertisement is clearly serious. They cost a good deal, those private ads. I let hers run for over a week before I answered. It must have cost her a pretty penny. Of course one can easily be mistaken, though I must say she sounds all right from her specifications.' He sounded as if he were thinking of buying a barge. 'First of all,' he said, clearing his throat, 'she is religious and of good family; her father was a well-digger and she has a vineyard. She is strong and capable of a child or two, which would be fine. Lastly she is a Cordon Bleu. This is the only point on which one has to be a bit careful. Sometimes one passes these cooking exams through a bit of *piston*. So I'm going slowly until I know. We'll try her out on a *ragoût* first. It is my favourite dish. If her *ragoût* is good. . . .' Involuntarily we all licked our lips and passed the blue can of wine. It seemed to me such a healthy, such a practical attitude.

'Mind you,' added Raoul, 'one can easily make a mistake. It comes from lack of detail in the advertisements. It is so costly that you have to abbreviate everything. And nobody confesses to the sort of faults which make or mar a marriage. For example in a woman one would expect to find a list of the dishes she really does well, and whether she nags. But what woman would confess to nagging? Similarly in a man a woman should know if he snores, is bad-tempered in the morning, and if he leaves a razor and brush unwashed after using. Such small questions sometimes make or mar a marriage. And you cannot put them all into a two line advertisement. A friend of mine who was unwise enough to get his wife from an agency only found out too late that she liked the music of Chopin. All day long she was glued to the radio. She would not play bowls, and she hated the smell of drink on his breath. Naturally they are divorced. Now as for Laura, she confesses that she is often melancholy and lonely, but I think it is due to being alone. Her parents are dead. She works part-time in a mercer's shop. All this will have to be gone into very carefully before I decide any-thing. Also she says she does not dance very well, which makes me doubtful, for I love a good dance. However we shall see.'

Surprisingly his mate opened his mouth in the back to say, in tones of melancholy resignation, 'Ah she is probably a whore.' Raoul shook his head sadly; as one who deplores such a lack of faith in one's fellow man. 'You', he said softly, 'never believe anyone. Pass the wine.'

We passed the wine, and I watched the slow Provençal roads un-winding among the foothills to right and left of us. Raoul's car stank horribly of burning rubber and hot steel, but it seemed to go quite well.

'Will you bring Laura back?' I asked and Raoul shrugged an elephant-ine shoulder as he replied. 'First we must settle this matter of the cooking. Then I have to show her my papers, all duly certified by the notary so that she can see how much property I have. A girl has to be cautious too.'

'And if she is ugly?' I asked. The thought surprised him. He had clearly not taken into account any question of personal attraction in the matter of marriage. 'Well she looks all right from her photograph,' he said. 'Not beautiful but nice.'

The little pessimist behind us said: 'You can tell nothing from photographs. Do photographs show wooden legs? She may be a hunch-back for all you know.'

'In that case I shall withdraw from the deal.' said Raoul with simple dignity. 'I do not want a wife that one unscrews and hangs up from a nail each night. Naturally we shall have to examine every possibility.'

The little man belched.

With the warm sunlight and the pleasant though slightly tainted breeze that came in through the side-windows I fell into a comfortable daze. Northward glittered the Cévennes foothills. We were running down on the long straggling net of roads which leads to Uzès and the Pont du Gard. Raoul was in talkative mood and was discoursing on the life beautiful, with all modern conveniences naturally. 'Avignon', he said, 'is so old and so ugly. I could never think of living in such an old barrack of a place. Now give me a town like Alès.' I did not say anything, for there was nothing one could say. Alès is a hideous little mining town full of concrete brick modernities. The plumber's dream —every plumber's dream. 'In Avignon I should go mad,' said Raoul 'though I must admit', he added, 'that the state of the plumbing is so bad that I should have work for life. But those old buildings are so ugly.'

I thought of the crumbling violet palaces of the vanished Popes, of the Rhône's green swirling current around the smashed bridge of St. Benezet, and sighed. 'I can't think what they see in them. I myself would have the whole lot down and some decent modern apartment flats put up. Do you know that part of the town is still built on piles, and lots of the old houses have a trap-door in the basement which gives directly onto the river? It's weird. That is why such a lot of murders are committed. You just push the body through the trap and it's found later right downriver. It's easy. No, I shouldn't care to live there. It's unhealthy.' He talked as if the river were choked with corpses.

'And the tourism?' said the little man in the back, 'what of the tourism? Foreigners come for the ancient things. They have their own apartments at home. They come to see the monuments. In this way Avignon gets rich.' Raoul admitted that he hadn't thought of that. 'One must live,' he admitted, though rather doubtfully.

After Uzès he surprised me by suggesting a detour by the Pont du Gard. 'But I thought you hated old monuments,' I said. Raoul looked at me scornfully. 'That is science!' he said coldly. 'It is not art but science, sir. It is a Roman triumph of the plumber's science. I always take my apprentices out there. It is their first lesson in plumbing. Now the Pont du Gard I love and know well.'

'But it is beautiful, no?'

'It is practical, sir,' said Raoul firmly.

I was surprised that this unromantic soul was capable of such intellectual distinctions. I was even more surprised to find that he was not boasting, for as we entered the magnificent defile, which is so reminiscent of the gorges of Syria, he slowed down in order to drink in once more the beauty of this fantastic ruin. 'What do you tell your apprentices?' I said absently, letting my eye span the gorge to follow the harsh but sweet lines of the noble aqueduct. From whichever angle one comes upon it, at whatever time of day, that Pont du Gard is lovely. Raoul was talking. 'I always stop the car here and make them descend. I say to them quite simply: "This is the noblest Roman monument in the world, built by Agrippa to carry the waters of Eure and Airam to Nîmes. Note it well, my children. It has three tiers of arches. At the bottom there are three, in the second tier eleven of equal span, and in the last thirty-five. Though of such gigantic size it exactly reproduces the side of a Romanesque cathedral—so I have read. It supports a canal five feet high and two wide. At the top its length is no less that 873 feet." ' He broke off proudly. His erudition floored me.

'And what do they say?'

'Usually they are silent. After a moment I take them up like this onto the bridge to see its reflection in the Gardon. Is it not wonderful?'

'It is very beautiful.'

'But that is because it is useful.'

We did not pursue the argument. Besides in such a place aesthetics should be left to look after themselves. We idled about for twenty minutes or so among the great bronze arches, chatting in desultory fashion, awed by the spirit of place. Then once more we took the curling road into Remoulins, and so outward across the plain to where, beyond the shallow range of blue hills, the old town of Avignon lay waiting with its modern Laura.

'What will you do while I am busy?' asked Raoul a trifle anxiously for he did not wish to appear as failing in hospitality. 'I could find you a nice café. It won't take me long.'

'Don't worry about me. I have an introduction to someone. I'll go along and see if they are at home.'

'But we must have a point of rendezvous,' said Raoul. 'I will put you down at the Grand Café in the Place de la République. It is perfect. You will see all the actresses.' He licked his lips. I did not quite know the importance of this remark about actresses.

We were now rumbling through Villeneuve-les-Avignon on the right bank of the Rhône, the road climbing and curving into the sky, to descend headlong to the bridge which spans the river. At the last corner before you take the plunge you can see, misty across the long flat expanse of the smooth-flowing river, the conglomeration of towers and belfries which has made Avignon one of the most beautiful of the southern French towns. Beautiful and yet somehow barbaric (I was thinking of Raoul's emphasis on utility) Avignon is a colossal fortress, with its long crenellated ramparts (now burning rosy and honey-gold in the afternoon light) built for defence. For a hundred years it was a Rome in exile, and the proud Popes who inhabited it saw to the matter of defence with practical thoroughness that left nothing to chance. Less formally perfect than Venice, less symmetrical in organization than Carcassonne, it is nevertheless quite as magnificent with its muddle of towers and steeples and belfries as it rides, like a galleon in full sail, across the mistral-scourged plain. Today the sky was blue, with no wind. When the mistral gets up the blue skies of Provence turn white as a scar. 'Well', said Raoul. 'There she is. And the famous Pont d'Avignon. It looks silly all broken off like a tooth. I would have it down and build something nice with a railway across it.'

The big bridge which spans the island is an ugly one. In fact most of the architecture being executed in the south of France today conforms to type. We are destroying our monuments piecemeal in England, too. Nevertheless Raoul liked it. It was a step in the right direction, he thought. I reflected sadly that while each town has a Committee of Beaux Arts which is supposed to (and effectively does) protect the ancient monuments it has no powers over new buildings. Avignon is sliding down into urbanism like all the rest of the medieval towns. In fact Raoul gave a cry of delight at the sight of a giant crane poking up from behind the machicolated walls, and the glimpse of a new apartment block. 'Good,' he cried, 'there is something modern.' I wondered if in five hundred years from now these modern blocks would attract sentimental and wondering pilgrims as do the old palaces and churches today. Perhaps we are wrong and Raoul is right. But at any rate it was pleasing to see that urbanism was being strongly resisted in the vacant lots around the walls, for here were several large gipsy encampments, and all the apparatus of a great country fair—the stalls set up along the outer ramparts, buzzing with insanitary but effervescent life. We swerved into the shadow of the great walls and found ourselves inside the town with its cramped medieval streets. Here all traffic is slowed to the pace of a bullock-cart. Abuse, bad language and gesticulation reign supreme. The policemen give the impression of having surrendered completely. They shrug and smile and playfully wave you down streets hopelessly blocked by drays and handbarrows and lorries. Everything (this is part of the policeman's private sense of fun) everything is marked ONE WAY. If one were foolish enough to observe these signs one would go round and round forever. Raoul knew this. He ignored the traffic signs and wherever he saw a NO ENTRY sign he took it. Even so it was slow work, though from his point of view spiritually uplifting. The arguments! The oaths! The invocations to Our Lord! We literally swore our way across the town to what he thought was the Place de la République but which turned out in fact to be the Place Clemenceau. Here I got down at last, somewhat shaken but glad to feel terra firma under my feet again. It was a good place of rendezvous. A beautiful square with a shady café just by the theatre, outside which brooded the statues of Voltaire (to judge by the foxy look) and Molière: both much weather-eroded and pigeon-bespattered. 'Now', said Raoul, 'let us meet here. If I don't come, you keep coming back to it, say every hour. If you don't appear by midnight I shall assume that you have gone off with a girl and return home. You can come on by train tomorrow. I promise to remember the tap.' The tap! I had forgotten it myself by now.

I walked about a bit down the twisted streets in the violet shadow of the Palace of the Popes. I had an introduction from a man I had known in Paris to a Count who lived in Avignon. It took me a little time to find the Count's lodgings. I had despatched a telegram the day before asking if I might pay him a visit. Unfortunately he was away. His housekeeper however had a letter from him in which he apologized for his absence on business and then, with characteristic southern hospitality, added: 'However I will not fail you entirely, for I have asked the Provençal poet Robert Allan to keep you company for the few hours you are here. You probably know his work. Curiously enough he is a descendant of Edgar Allan Poe.' Curiously enough! It is, appropriately, the most popular of phrases in the French Midi, and justly so. Everything that happens is curious, unexpected, out of the way.

The rendezvous arranged by the Count was happily the café which I had just left, and I returned towards it at a leisurely pace, deliberately taking a turning or two out of my way in order to enjoy the sinuous windings of the little streets. Now, at twilight, the little square was humming with life. Waiters were setting out supplementary tables and all the bon ton of the town converged upon them; the lights had begun to go up, outlining the leafy trees and throwing into greater relief the violet sky against which the huge architectural lumber of the palaces loomed with an air of solitary abandon. Avignon at evening is like a rook's nest. The Grand Café was bursting with life, its mirrors were swimming with colour. This was partly due (here come the actresses!) to the fact that it was a stage pub, situated hard by the stage door of the theatre. Consequently (stage people being the same all over the world) it was crowded with actors waiting for their cue, and actresses waiting for the call boy—and all in full make-up. At a glance it was clear that the piece was a Provençal epic, perhaps *Mireille,* for the mirrors threw back from a dozen corners of the room the costumed figures of Old Provence—figures which must have been familiar to Van Gogh and Gauguin during their ill-fated stay at Arles. High-coiffed Arlésiennes with their coloured bodices, and leather jacketed and booted *gardiens.* In the midst of all this swimming colour a youngish, dark man rose and came towards me with outstretched hand. It was the poet. In fact it was a rook's nest of poets. As he murmured an introduction to verify my identity he said: 'We are entertaining a poet from Spain. Please join us for a drink. Afterwards if there is anything you wish to see. . . .' His resemblance to the author of 'The Raven' was striking.

To most tourists Provençal is an obscure dead language of the past, something once used by the troubadours and now forgotten. Quite the contrary is the case. There are more people who read and speak Provençal today than there are who speak the Portuguese language. Geographically it is distributed over the whole of southern France, though it varies slightly with the district. The language found its Burns in the poet Mistral who used it for his great epic poems, and who indeed founded the poetry of Provence. It stemmed from a small group of poets in Avignon who called themselves 'The Félibres'. No one knows what the title means today, but the poets have maintained their distinctive look. They wear a narrow tie of coloured wool. Young Allan was typical of them with his hair grown rather long at the back and his pronounced sidewhiskers. He wore a shirt of cowboy check. Of course he was a youngster. In later life he would doubtless graduate to

rather long Victorian coats with a tail and a sombrero. The modern
Félibres are as proud as the Scots of their tradition, and while they are
all Frenchmen who could as easily write in French they prefer to keep
the native tongue of the Midi alive. As Allan said: 'The proof of a
language's existence is its poetry. So long as a language is "worked"
by poets it never dies.' He used the word 'travailler' which is a happy
one, for it is used also for tilling the earth. I was introduced in rapid
succession to three other poets. (I began to have a sneaking feeling that
everyone in Avignon was a poet.) Two were mildly bearded. One was
extremely self-assertive and flamboyant and wore a sort of long-
brimmed Homburg. I think he had had a drop or two for he was de-
claiming something with gestures, and casting hot side glances at a
bevy of Arlésiennes who were waiting for the call boy in their pallid
make-up. They at least were drinking coffee. Women are so rational.
We poets were well away on some kind of local fire water. The assertive
one in the hat was, I was told, the best bullfighting poet of the age.
His only theme was the bullfight, and at every Easter *corrida* his ode
usually won the prize.

It is perhaps foolish to imagine that a group of people around a café
table can give you any sort of insight to a place, and yet it is true. Just
as you can smell the whole of London in one pub, or the whole of Paris
on the crowded *terrasse* of a little student-quarter café, so Avignon
became much more real to me as I talked to this little group of soberly
dressed people. It was not their present conviviality either which suggested to me that the keynote of the place was gaiety. It was something
about the smell of it all—the evening sinking behind the squat buttresses, drenching the plain and the long green curve of the Rhône
with its successive washes of colour. And inside these walls, which one
day enclosed the hopes and fears of all Christendom, lay this brilliantly
lighted little square with all its colour, movement, and animation. I
asked Allan if Avignon was gay. His eyes sparkled and he nodded. 'It
is strange isn't it? I mean that we have a wretched climate. It is cold
in winter and the river makes the air humid. And then the blasted
mistral when it comes plays havoc. I think the town is probably the
most exposed to it in the whole south. Talk about dancing on the
bridge! Why, when the mistral gets up they have to stretch ropes
along it for people to hold on to as they cross. Without the ropes you'd
have to crawl on all fours. Yet, in spite of these apparent drawbacks,

it is gay. Yes. You know that it is really the second town of France for the intellectuals. It is to Paris intellectually what Lyons is industrially. The visiting theatre companies adore playing here and the big festival is quite something to attend. There are quite a crowd of painters and writers living here. And then the gipsies. They can't get rid of them. They camp outside the walls. And then of course all the gangsters and white slavers from Marseilles come here for week-ends to cool their minds. It's quite cosmopolitan though it's so small.'

'I suppose you could say that of Aix.'

'No. Aix is essentially a town for artists and tourists. But Avignon is like a small capital of a province. All the young painters in Aix want to get to Paris. Nobody ever wants to leave Avignon, and very few people do. As for the gangsters, if they do go to Aix it is with the intention of robbing some rich foreigner. But they come to Avignon to relax. Some of them are very stimulating indeed. There are one or two intellectuals among them. Last week I met one who owns a chain of bawdy houses and he turned out to be a book-collector. He has the finest collection of fourteenth-century books in the whole of France.'

So we spent the time in pleasantly convivial chatter while I waited for Raoul. A cool river-breeze had begun to shiver the awnings of the lighted shops and a young moon was struggling into the sky. The cast of *Mireille* came and went about their business, responsive to the sharp cry of the call boy, plunging into the darkness like divers into a pool. I was wondering whether to propose dinner to my host when the plumber materialized suddenly at my shoulder. He wore a vast smile of complaisance which hovered as if suspended by his pink flapping ears. 'Eh alors,' he cried jovially. 'She is all I thought and better. We have been talking before a notary. And I have your tap.' He flourished it as he spoke.

'Is she coming back with you?'

Raoul shook his head. 'She will come day after tomorrow by train. She had some things to attend to. But first, before we leave we must visit her family house and have a drink. She promised that to her father's memory. You will come won't you? She is outside in the car.'

Reluctantly I took my leave of Edgar Allan Poe, promising him to return one day with more time at my disposal. The poets bade me goodbye with the delightful civility of the south, removing hats and berets before shaking hands, while the convivial ones added a thump on the back for good measure. I made a feeble attempt to pay for the drinks I had had, and was shouted down and all but pushed out into the street. Raoul was waiting in the shadow waving his tap. He had parked his wagon down a side-street. Laura was sitting in the front seat and Raoul introduced us with a sort of shambling nervousness which he tried to offset by giving his nerve-shattering laugh. Laura was all that I hoped she might be, tall and strongly built, with great peasant hands. A sculptor would have caught his breath to see the way her square head was set on her spine, thick and true. She had the kind of beauty which comes from being perfectly designed for a traditional purpose— like a spade, say; she was the perfect peasant in a state of nature. She had very good grey eyes well set in her face, a short rather beautifully shaped nose, and high cheek-bones. Her hair was done in a bun. It was thick and lustrous in its darkness. Good teeth. Raoul really was in luck. I climbed into the back beside his mate and sat down on a box. The little man appeared to be half asleep. We started to negotiate the rabbit warren of streets, edging towards the river, and Laura politely apologized for detaining us. 'I promised my father that if I married I would offer my intended a drink in our house on the first day of the meeting.' she explained seriously. Raoul chuckled. 'And I want to see the house.'

Laura settled her shawl round her shoulders and said: 'The house is not very much to see. It is on the island, and the garden is always flooded in autumn and spring. Nevertheless we lived there.'

The lights of the gipsy fairground twinkled like fireflies against the piecrust gold of the old wall. The moon picked up its own misty reflections in the swift flowing river. By night the hideous modern bridge did not look so ugly after all. We swooped across it like a swallow, to turn right and roll steeply down to the low flat Isle de la Berthelasse with its shady ribbons of tall willows and planes and poplars. On the other side of the river the beautiful fortress of Philippe le Bel rose clear and incisive from the shadowy ramble of buildings which marked Villeneuve-les-Avignon. The little island which divides the great river is low lying and always half shrouded in river-mist. Despite the fact that it is so frequently flooded when the Rhône is in flood, the peasants still keep their tenacious grip on it, for the soil is the richest hereabouts. Indeed as you roll down its narrow willow-fringed roads you have the sudden illusion of being in Normandy rather than in Provence. Cows graze peacefully in green fields. Yes, it is a landscape by Corot. This effect was much emphasized by the weak moonlight which hazed in every perspective. Across the river the strange crocketed steeples and fortresses had receded into dark anonymity, their outlines along the ceinture of medieval wall being marked only by the lighted booths of the gipsies. We turned at last into a dim gateway. Laura's house was a modest one built on the typical Provençal pattern over a magazine where one might store barrels of wine or other produce. It consisted of one large room approached by a flight of steep steps. She led the way and after a struggle opened the door for us. We stood outside on the porch while she busied herself in the dark interior to find a lamp and matches. 'This is all,' she said at last, holding up the yellow lamp to let us see the forlorn and deserted room, unceilinged and apparently undusted for long months. 'It is dirty now. I live in the town and only come here for my free Sundays. Afterwards, however, you may get a good price for it,' she added, turning to Raoul who stood on one leg picking his teeth. 'There is a little land, and on the island land fetches a good price.'

She busied herself once more to make preparations for the ceremonial drink. Raoul and his mate started poking around down below, peering into the barn. Finally they settled themselves on a fallen tree-trunk. Laura came softly deftly down the stairs with some tall-stemmed glasses on a tray with a bottle of spirits. She trod carefully holding the lamp in her left hand. In the strange mixed light—half pale moon and half butter-yellow lamplight—she looked more than ever a fitting mate for an infant Gargantua. I thought suddenly of one of those large-bosomed Pomonas of Maillol which seem to express all the fruitfulness and happy sensuality of the Mediterranean. How he would have loved to sculp this young peasant girl with her strong hands and shapely arms. We took our glasses and she filled each one with a dose of the Vieux Marc of the region. It is raw and powerful and catches one by the throat. We stood and Raoul raised his glass, saying: 'To the memory of your father.' Laura herself did not drink, but stood there quietly smiling. 'I promised him,' she said simply. With the ceremony completed everyone relaxed and a second dose of Marc was gratefully accepted. Raoul jogged my arm. 'Look at the boat,' he chuckled. 'That is in case of flood.'

It was a small wooden coracle such as fishermen use on shallow lakes, and it lay on its side in a corner of the yard. I was intrigued to notice that the long iron chain which was attached to the prow was fastened to a staple in the house-wall outside the first-floor window. Laura noticed the direction of my glance and smilingly explained: 'Sometimes the flood comes so suddenly that you don't notice it. You awake and find that it has reached the bedroom window. But when you have a boat attached high like that it floats up and so you step into it from the first floor.'

'Clever,' said Raoul, giving his foolish neigh of laughter. We had one more drink and it seemed time to depart. We planned to stop somewhere on the road to Béziers and have a bite of supper—Raoul knew a little place patronized by the routiers. So, locking up the house, we ran Laura back over the bridge and dropped her at the ancient gate. She shook hands with us all and with her new fiancé with a grave and pleasant composure. 'Then day after tomorrow,' she said and Raoul nodded. 'I shall be waiting for you at the station.'

'Everything will be as arranged.'

'Everything will be as arranged.'

She turned quietly on her heel and was gone through the great stone portals. Raoul sighed as we climbed back into the covered wagon and edged our way out through Villeneuve towards the dark hills. The little man in the back was definitely asleep now, I could hear an occasional snore. Raoul yawned luxuriously and lit a cigarette. 'What did you think of her, eh? Isn't she fine? Just what I needed.' I agreed, and indeed wholeheartedly. It was a great stroke of luck for him; there wasn't much romance about the modern Laura, perhaps, but perhaps this was just as well from Raoul's point of view. Instead of spending twenty years writing passionate sonnets he could get on with the work of the world and raise himself a brood of children shaped like spades, with red knees, huge hands, and grey eyes. . . .

'You look surprised,' he was saying, 'but actually as I told you it is all a matter of scientific judgement. The golden rule is never to trust an agency in a matter of real importance.'

I told him I never would.

[349]

Across Secret Provence

Published, as Ripe Living in Provence, *in* Holiday. *Philadelphia. November 1959.*

The image evoked by the word is of course a map, but not the conventional map such as tourists obtain from a travel agent. No, it is a highly selective personal map, rich in pictorial data, and the skilful needles of an Algerian tattooist have pricked it out nobly, grandiloquently, like a musical score, upon the chest and abdomen of my friend Pepe. This map enables him, when overcome by national patriotism or simply by the desire to discourse on some elementary point of local geography, to make the gesture of a Napoleon returned from Elba—throwing open his shirt in order to growl: 'This is the true Provence! I have it all engraved upon my breast!' Then he gives a bray of laughter. But of course you have to be an intimate of his first, to have shown yourself worthy of the secret country which the map depicts—Pepe's private Provence.

A series of lucky accidents admitted me to the great man's company on a blazing June afternoon when the red dust was rising like smoke under the hooves of the bulls in the bull-rings of Orange. He admitted afterwards that he was intrigued in the first place by the dog-eared copy of Mistral's poems which was sticking out of my knapsack. (Would not an American be touched to see a copy of *Leaves of Grass* sticking out of a hobo's pack?) But sitting jam-packed in that thirsty throng on such an afternoon was something of an ordeal for a mere foreigner; and clearly I was a person of some discrimination—for had I not come to cheer the exploits of 'Gandar', the greatest cockade-carrying bull of the age? Our hoarse cheers mingled in the dusty air as those famous black hooves rumbled on the arena floors, as if on the vellum body of some mighty drum. Two of the seven *razeteurs*, as they are called, had already been disposed of—one being carried out on a

[350]

stretcher, and the other helped limping from the outer ring by the gendarmes. Twice in the bull's honour the loud-speakers had grated out the triumphal march from *Carmen* which is the formal accolade granted, not as an honour to human bravery, but to the power and tenacity of a champion bull successfully defending the red cockade which nestles between his curved horns and may be plucked out only by the white-clad fighter with courage enough to run across him as he charges. This peculiar form of bull-dusting is, according to Pepe, the heart and marrow of Provence. ('Provence is where the cooking is based on garlic and olive-oil, and where the *course libre* flourishes.') I do not think he is wrong about this, despite the greater publicity given to the Spanish form of bull-fighting in the newspapers. That is, at best, he says, a picturesque form of ritualized murder; but the *course libre* is an exciting and extremely dangerous game, a test of strong nerves and speed. And the bull is the darling, the hero of the crowd, never the man. . . . Some of these facts he growled at me during that first blue afternoon while the little knot of sweating bullfighters in their white clothes and coloured sashes edged softly and circumspectly around the ring, hoping for the vital half-second of distraction on the part of the bull which would enable one of them to make his temeritous curving run in under the horns to snatch at the coveted cockade with his short metal comb (*lo razet*). The prizes mount with the danger, and 'Gandar's' cockade and horn-strings (which must also be snatched) have seldom been worth less than fifteen thousand francs. It is dangerous a way of earning a livelihood—for as you turn to snatch the cockade your feet must have got up enough speed to carry you like a swallow over the barricade to safety: beyond the reach of those slashing horns. Moreover it is only at the very moment when the bull lowers his crest for the toss that you can snatch at the cockade he wears! One false step here, a miscalculation in your timing. . . . Four or five *razeteurs* are killed every year, and more hurt; yet the tradition lives on.

Yes, the odd thing about it is that the official hero of the *course libre* is the bull. His is the name traditionally printed in scarlet poster-type on the placards, and his the applause when a *razeteur* is sent sprawling over the barrier with a broken rib or tossed in a crumpled heap against the stockades. 'And that is how it should be,' says Pepe roundly. 'In Provence the bull is king! And that is how you will see it depicted on the Cretan vases from which our game derives.'

[351]

I have mentioned the copy of Mistral's classic poems in the Provençal tongue. This Pepe certainly eyed with guarded approval; but his old eyes really kindled when I confessed that I had come down the Rhône to Avignon in the traditional old-fashioned way (forgotten today by the rushing tourist)—by river-barge. Yes, I had woken at dawn under those rosy battlements to watch the pearly mist lifting and to hear the lazy jackdaws calling from the abandoned Palace of the Popes; I had tasted the river-winds with their eddies of honeysuckle and rosemary bruised by the hooves of riverside cattle, and had drifted in a labyrinth of trembling stars in which, sights and sounds all mixing, I heard the background of nightingale-song interrupting the hoarse distant singing of boatmen and the heart-tugging moan of barges up-river. . . . This in a sort of way proved I was 'genuine'. His wrinkled old face wore a smile of unwilling admiration. 'She must have been a beautiful girl,' he said at last in his growling voice. I understood the allusion. In the old days Provence was the recognized cure for northerners with broken-hearts—just as the more taciturn British went off to East Africa to shoot big game! But here alas! I could only disappoint him, for my visit was of no such romantic provenance. I was simply hoping to unstick a novel which refused to get itself written, by taking a brief holiday; sometimes it is the only way. So I had idled my way south by bus and train, stopping off here and there to buy a child's *cahier* in a village stationery-shop, and to sit for a while on some shady *terrasse* by a meandering Roman river, pen in hand, 'just to see' if that missing chapter would come. . . .

I told him some of this, but not all. He shook his head slowly and understandingly and then grabbed my arm in the grip of the Ancient Mariner himself. 'We will be friends,' he said. 'For I can tell you many things.' I smiled at the resolute brown figure with its square hands. He wiped his flowing moustache with a silk handkerchief and nodded sharply. 'You will see,' he said. And then we both dutifully rose to add to the storm of clapping and cheering which greeted 'Gandar's' return to the pen. The bull's sweat starred the red dust like raindrops.

Pepe wore, if I remember rightly, a brown hat with a very wide brim, and more than a touch of toreador about its design, which I was afterwards to recognize as the Stetson of the Camargue (a miniature Wild West, devoted to horse-breeding and bull-raising, which extends across the shallow alluvial delta where the Rhône reaches the sea). He wore this with a distinct tilt and an air to match it. Then a leather waistcoat with beautifully stitched pockets over a ferociously checked shirt with sleeves fastened by expensive-looking cuff-links. His tie was a narrow black ribbon. His gaberdine trousers were strictly tapered into a shape which suggested riding-breeches, and their ends fitted snugly into an ancient pair of soft-leather jack-boots. His appearance was flamboyant in a reserved sort of way, though not eccentric. His head was magnificent, and his smile somewhat costly—for many of his teeth were gold. His voice was pure gravel, and every enunciation of his was a challenge. One felt that he was prepared to strip and fight for the least of his opinions—even those in which he did not believe. . . . What else? Yes, he snuffed instead of smoking—snuffed vigorously with great inhalations and magistral explosions into a green silk handkerchief which he wore in his sleeve and waved about a good deal to illustrate his observations on bulls and human nature in general. Oddly enough, for one so elegant, he carried no snuff-box but a twist of brown paper filled with what looked to me suspiciously like unrefined sulphur. He offered this about liberally to all and sundry, confident perhaps that nobody but himself snuffed in the whole of Provence. He regarded my packet of *Gauloises Bleues* with a commiserating air. Perhaps he had heard of lung cancer? I did not ask.

His opinion of 'Gandar' was high on that sultry afternoon, I remember, but his opinion of human nature low. 'They call themselves *razeteurs*,' he growled. 'Why, in my day a bull like Gandar would have been stripped of his prizes—*dépouillé*—in under a minute.'

As I was no specialist in the matter it was not my business to contest his view; I contented myself only by murmuring that already that afternoon two of the fighters had been carried off, one with a rent in his thigh and the other with a broken rib, if nothing worse. Pepe snorted: 'Pouf! That is nothing for Provence.'

Our friendship survived this small disagreement, and indeed gained further ground when he found me drinking *pastis* at the refreshment booth—the aniseed drink so beloved of Provençals, which turns white with the addition of water. 'Good!' he cried. '*Moi aussi.*' We seated ourselves on a fragment of Roman column under a tree, and it was now that he gave me to understand that he regarded my intentions as honourable—that I was henceforward to consider myself his familiar. 'You wish to see Provence!' he said, as he slowly unbuttoned his dramatic shirt. I was to be vouchsafed a first view of his private map. I confess I thought for a moment he was taking off his shirt in order to challenge me to mortal combat, and was relieved when the proud gesture revealed only this splendid piece of *art nouveau*. 'It is all here,' he said simply, proudly. I gazed rapturously at this copyright map printed on his body by a devoted Algerian artist. 'I was homesick,' explained Pepe. 'I bade him make me a map of the true Provence.'

Roughly speaking it was diamond-shaped, pinpointed in the north by Montélimar and in the south by Marseilles, and it followed the whole romantic valley of the Rhône with its fantastic gallery of historic names. In the West it stretched beyond Nîmes, in the East as far as Apt.

'*Tiens*,' I said, 'it's a beauty,' and Pepe glowed modestly. Montélimar started high on the chest, while Marseilles was all but lost in the folds of the abdomen, unless Pepe held his breath, which he was doing now in order to let me feast my eyes on this treasure. 'I had to stay tight as a drum while he did it,' he explained hoarsely. 'And it was painful. But I was young. I stayed drunk on *arak* while he worked.' It was true that with the spread of middle age and the growth of a comfortable bow-window the southern ends of the map had begun to spread a bit. The *Etang de Berre* waxed and waned in size with his breathing. But when all was said and done it was a most original production, though of little use perhaps to motorists. He gazed triumphantly at me. I gazed at his stomach. I had realized at once that the map illustrated his main contention about Provence, for it covered roughly the area he had already described—the garlic and cockade belt, so to speak; I had also recognized by now from his appearance that Pepe had a particular intimate connection with bulls and horses—he was a mixture of Spanish landed gentleman, Southern Colonel, and the 'Horsey Gent from Newmarket' beloved of Surtees. But he was quite unmistakably representative of a tradition which was original, was none of these things. 'Do you notice the bullet-holes?' he said, after a pause, with an air of opulent complacence. 'I had him paint in a few bullet-holes in order to charm the ladies. Women love a man of action. I have always tried to please, though in fact I have never been in action.' They were extremely cunning bullet-holes, most vividly executed, and I said so with conviction. He winked and grunted. 'Then you will notice something else. My home-town is the belly-button. Centre of the world for me. Centre of the Universe. *Gaussargues*! I bet you have heard of it.' I had not. He frowned as he rebuttoned his shirt. His face wore a disapproving look. '*Gaussargues*', he said in his deep voice, 'is the greatest little village on earth.'

These words, I realized, were in a way an adoption formula. So long as I stayed in Provence, he added, in a voice which made it sound as much a threat as a promise, I was to be his guest. I would learn to imagine as well as to see this hallowed ground through his eyes. Indeed, could anything have been luckier? For I had tumbled upon an initiate both knowledgeable and completely drunk on his native country. The old platitude about not being able to appreciate a place in a short time is far from true; everything depends on the company you keep. All told I was only a few weeks in Provence, yet thanks to Pepe I know it better than many other places where I actually lived—in some cases for years.

I think the secret of the matter is one of attitude; for Pepe it was only the 'sights'—the mouldering copper and violet ruins of Roman amphitheatres in places like Nîmes, Orange and Arles; or the parched buttresses and crenellations of medieval palaces snoozing away the centuries under that ripe old sun; these set-pieces we visited to be sure—but always *en route* for some contemporary gala, be it a bull fight, or a battle of flowers, or a cattle-branding, or a carnival. Who else can have seen Daudet's windmill through a glass of *Tavel rosé*—that magnificent topaz-coloured wine which shares with *Châteauneuf* a comfortable dominion over the southern vineyards? And if we paid passing homage to the Nîmes arena (which Panurge built in three hours!) it was while we were hunting for a particular Provençal dish—*brandade*—which must be tasted if my initiation was to be completed. Indeed, to be truthful, the wines and cheeses of this region have worked their way into the landscape, so that my memories of it are shot through with the prismatic glitter of them. They are, so to speak, the living score upon which the reality of the place is written, and they gave colour to those romantic names of the region's heroes—from Rabelais, Nostradamus, and Van Gogh up to Paul Valéry. (At Aigues-Mortes, Van Gogh's coloured boats still idle up and down the green canals among the dragonflies; it seems less than a moment since the painter folded up his easel and left.) Tarascon, Beaucaire, and the Stes. Maries (the headquarters of all the Gipsies in Christendom). . . . And where Petrarch mourned his beloved Laura, we had an obstinate but lucky puncture which enabled us to pledge the lovers in a decisive little Blanquette which Pepe had provisionally decided not to open till the following day. But the heat and effort made him recant. ('By God,' he said reverently, 'what a wine. And nameless yet! They should call it Laura's Tears.') Neither of us could remember a line of Petrarch to recite in memory of that virtuous and star-crossed shade; but we felt a sense of kinship with her as we drank to her in that memorable defile, by the cold clear water. ('I once loved a girl from Avignon called Laura,' said Pepe. 'But she was far from virtuous like her namesake. As a matter of fact I prefer them that way—though I yield to none in my admiration of Petrarch's lady-love.')

For a whole week we wove backwards and forwards thus across Provence, like spring-intoxicated dragonflies; and yet this for Pepe was a business trip, for several of the bulls he owned were fighting. There were long shady confabulations in taverns, under trees, in stifling offices. There was money to collect and staff-work to be done before we could return to the navel of the world which (he promised me) would cap everything. Meanwhile . . . the familiar prospects of vines, olives, cypresses; one comes to believe that they are Platonic abstractions rooted in the imagination of man. Symbols of the Mediterranean, they are always here to welcome one—either trussed back by the winter gales in glittering silver-green bundles, or softly powdered by the gold dust of the summers, blown from the threshing floors by the freshets of sea-wind. Yes, the great wines of the south sleep softly on in the French earth like a pledge that the enchanted landscapes of the European heart will always exist, will never fade against this taut wind-haunted blue sky where the mistral rumbles and screams all winter long. Yes, even if there were no history here, no monuments, no recognizable sense of a past to indulge our twentieth-century sense of self-pity, the place would still be the magnet it is. These Emperor cheeses, these magnificent unworldly wines still attest to the full belly and the rugged physical contents upon which Rabelais built his view of the ideal world of laughter. They are the enemies of literary nostalgia. The existence of Laura, of Tartarin, of Cézanne—the continuity of the world of the imagination—they are simply the proofs, so to speak, that some spots on earth are the natural cradles of genius. Provence is one. So long as the wines and the cheeses hold their place, such immortal company for the imaginations of men will never fail us. . . . Idle thoughts, drifting through the mind as we sit on a shady *terrasse* near Arles drinking *Côtes du Rhône Gigondas* with a prime St. Gorton cheese and fresh bread (Pepe winking derisively at a Coca-Cola sign on the wall opposite!). So we worked our way south to where at last the Rhône slows down like a mighty pulse to push its massive way across the flat Camargue to the sea, and after a final sunset-cup under the little church of the Saintes Maries we turned back to cross the plains and foothills to *Gaussargues*, the navel of Provence, the belly button of the world, Pepe's personal omphalos. . . .

Here again he was right—or was it simply the deceptive sense of repletion and content in that green-rayed dusk, travelling along the dense plumed avenues of planes as if under a green tent of coolness? No, the little Roman town with its graceful bridge and ambling trout-stream was certainly somewhere to linger. It figures in no guide-book—its time-saturated antiquities are considered unimportant beside those of its neighbours. But it is a jewel with its tiny medieval town and clock-tower; its rabbit warren streets and carved doorways with their battered scutcheons and mason's *graffiti*. Rooks calling too, from the old fort, their cries mingled with the hoarse chatter rising from the cafés under the planes. *Gaussargues!*.

And here Pepe somehow came into his own—on the shady water-front café before the tavern-hotel called 'The Knights' where I was lodged, and where the affairs of the world were debated to the music of river-water and the hushing of the plane-fronds above us. Yes, if it was not entirely a new Pepe it was an extension of the old flamboyant figure in new terms—for here he was at home, among his friends, these dark-eyed, keen-visaged gentry wearing black berets and coloured shirts and belts. Their conversation, the whole humour and bias of their lives revolved about bulls and the cockades they carried, about football matches against the hated northern departments and the celestial fouls perpetrated during them; and more concretely about fishing and vines and olive-trees. Here too one entered the mainstream of meridional hospitality where a drink refused was an insult given—and where travellers find their livers insensibly turning into pigskin suitcases within them. Such laughter, such sunburned faces, and such copious potations are not, I think, to be found anywhere else outside the pages of Gargantua. At times the rose-bronze moon came up with an air of positive alarm to shine down upon tables covered with a harvest of empty glasses and bottles, or to gleam upon the weaker members of the company extended like skittles in the green grass of the river-bank, their dreams presumably armouring them against the onslaughts of the mosquitoes. Those of us who by this time were not too confused with wine and bewitched by folklore to stand upright and utter a prayer to Diana, managed to help each other tenderly, luxuriously to bed. . . .

Murier the dentist, Thoma the notary, Carpe the mason, Rickard the postmaster, Blum the mayor, and Gradon the chief policeman: such an assembly of moustaches and expressions as would delight a Happy Families addict. Massively, like old-fashioned mahogany furniture, they sat away their lives under the planes—village characters belonging to the same over-elaborated myth which created Panurge. They were terrific and they knew it! And such vaunting, such boasting, such tremendous feats of arms: as when Pepe fought a duel with the dentist. I forget how it all began—doubtless over some trifling disagreement about who should stand who what to drink. But the challenge was given and taken up at once. Followed a grave choice of seconds and an even graver choice of weapons: which in the end proved to be open umbrellas. The duellers faced each other with a full wine-glass in the left hand, umbrella in the right. 'On guard,' cried Murier hoarsely, and the battle was joined. It was clearly to be a fight to the death, with no quarter given or asked.

I wish I could say that thrust and riposte flashed back and forth as quickly as sheet-lightning. It would not be true, for both contestants were somewhat unsteady and attacked each other with the sort of unhealthy expression that one sees on the faces of chess players. In this stately but relentless fashion they moved up and down the main street until a balcony window opened and an old lady in curl-papers menaced them with a loaded chamber-pot if they did not desist; this had the effect of causing a momentary diversion when, taking advantage of Murier's lowered guard (he was under the balcony), Pepe drove his umbrella home to the hilt, upsetting his enemy's wine all over his trousers. Prolonged applause, and a return to the *terrasse* where Gradon moodily suggested arresting the whole lot of us and putting us in irons.

These were good, informative days, for during them I saw Provence standing at ease, as it were; saw it from the narrow aperture of ordinary village life which does not blind one to defects but shows everything in its true proportion. I understand, too, why it has remained so fresh and unspoiled to this day, for its comforts are few and its hardships rugged ones—such as the almost total absence of main drainage and bathrooms in the hotels, which would be enough to discourage the tourist even if the word 'mistral' did not exist.

Mistral! There is something of Olympian Zeus about the way it roars and rages down from Mount Ventoux, always unexpectedly and always at full force, rolling boulders and dust ahead of it and whistling down the river-valleys like a herd of mad bulls. In the dusty plain of the Crau the trees are all hooked into weird shapes, twisted and bent by its force. It is upon you at a moment's notice, cramming the words back into your throat, sending the dust-devils spinning and whirling like so many dervishes among the vineyards. But it belongs faithfully to the landscape, and matches it as the dragon matches the fairy-tale; your Provençal treats it with a boisterous contempt despite the feverish headaches and general malaise it brings with it—due probably to the tremendous drop in temperature which accompanies its appearance. 'Somehow one would not be without it,' says the Count de C.-J. as we watch it racing across the plain towards the château. 'Every rose must have its thorn.'

The Count, who is one of France's best essayists, lives virtually the life of a recluse among his magnificent vineyards. He is a good-looking and somewhat reserved man in his middle forties, with a withered arm. Quiet of voice and seldom smiling except with his expressive dark eyes, he dispenses a less boisterous but equally warm hospitality beside his own quiet lily pond, seated under a shady pergola of vine and plumbago.

Once, they say, he was a great figure in Parisian society, but some early tragedy led him to abandon *la vie mondaine* and retire to a life of unbroken seclusion upon the family estates. Exactly what the tragedy was no one would tell me—though everyone seemed to know. Was it too painful for the village to mention—or was this simply an example of supreme tact? I shall never know. But I can guess why he was so admired: for though he was every inch a *seigneur*, and though he never set foot outside the grounds of the château except to labour in his fields, he was somehow still part of the active robust life of the community. Fishermen caught poaching or families in distress knew that Pepe had only to carry their story to him for help to be forthcoming. Nor was there a café-reveller who thought twice about invading the château after dark for a 'stirrup-cup'. In this, I suppose, Pepe was himself the worst offender by far, and several times he led me scrambling and blundering up the dark paths at midnight to ring the bell on the great oak door. He was always sure of his welcome, and always with the same unsmiling politeness the Count would appear, often pyjama-clad, to light a lantern and (if the hour was late and his housekeeper in bed) to hunt out drinks for us from his vast cellars. I think he shared some of my own amused admiration for the flamboyant Pepe; at any rate they addressed each other comfortably in the singular like old intimates. 'Ah! the devil,' he would say as Pepe recounted some dark triumph of skill or business acumen. 'Ah! what a trick to play on a fellow creature'—with his smiling affectionate eye upon the face of his friend glowing rosy in the lantern's light. Blundering homewards down the dark path after such an evening, Pepe would explain. 'He himself leads the life of a blasted nun, but he enjoys visitors up there. But he has never set foot in the town and never will.'

So the days lengthened quietly into sunburnt weeks, and gradually those missing chapters (the quest for which had first led me south into Provence) began to take shape in my mind. A curious process like pack-ice breaking up. I did not dare to ascribe it only to the wine! But one fine morning I found my child's *cahier* had begun to fill up and I realized with a pang that it was time to make tracks, to get back to Paris and my dusty typewriter. My decision, so firmly announced over *pastis* on the *terrasse* of 'The Knights', was greeted with a chorus of disapproval. I had as yet seen and heard nothing, they said. I knew nothing as yet of Provence—as if this immortal hangover were not experience enough! Pepe himself was almost in tears. But I stuck to my guns. I had to leave, and in order to nail my resolution to the sticking-point, I actually chose a date of departure. A long and pregnant silence fell over those vintage characters as they sat before their drinks. Softly the river ran, softly the dark fronds of the planes hushed above us.

'It is the day', said Pepe sorrowfully, 'of the *Anciens Combattants*. We have a memorial dinner every year for the class of '34. We had planned to make you an honorary *combattant* for the evening. Wait till you see the menu—it is pure trigonometry, *mon vieux*. You will feel quite faint.

No, put it off, this rash decision. Put it off a week or two, my dear friend.' It would have been easy to put it off perhaps for ever; but I remained adamant. The silence of perplexity fell once more. Murier suddenly sat up and said: 'But the last train does not leave until midnight. There would still be time to dine with us and catch it. It would be some sort of a send-off for you. Otherwise we would be wounded in our *amour-propre* for in *Gaussargues* we always try to do the right thing by our visitors.'

As it turned out it was one of the most memorable send-offs I have ever had, thanks to two factors whose importance I could not then foresee. The evening in question turned out also to be the duty evening of the Voluntary Fire Brigade, whose relief commandant was Pepe. But this little fact only dawned on him as we actually sat down to dinner by glossy candlelight in the medieval cellars of 'The Knights', our tables flanked appropriately by barrels, bottles, butts and bins of wine against which we could lean if overcome by the fumes of the . . . but no, I will not give the Menu. I will always keep it a secret, locked in the recesses of my heart. I will not even give the wine list. . . . We were regaled by the music of a Spanish guitar played by Porot, the hawk-featured sacristan of the church, and served by two twinkling dark Provençal girls whose ears (though tanned) flushed increasingly as they listened to the highly robust quatrains which poured from the good Porot's lips. It was in the middle of the first toast that Murier turned pale and cried: '*Pardi*, there are six relief *pompiers* here tonight— and it is the Voluntary's duty evening. If the widow Chauvet should become lonely. . . .'

Here I should explain the immediate roar of laughter which went up, and the rueful growling annoyance of Pepe who was obviously the target for it, to judge by his grin and the way he slapped his thigh and said 'Damn the widow!' More laughter.

Now the good widow Chauvet was a delightful old lady in her late seventies who lived a life of studious eccentricity in a tiny villa on the hill. In appearance stately and decorous she was nevertheless rather a flamboyant character too, in her own quiet way. Her hair for example. . . . It was as good as a firework display. It was clear that some local illusionist posing as a hairdresser had subjected her to the worst indignities. Yet she was proud of it, and proud that it was her own. In parts her coiffure resembled a Maclaren tartan, fading away around the sides to verdigris, kelp and bistre. In other parts it spanned the whole spectrum from high violet to a brilliant, ringing gold which suggested that at some time she had been subjected to electrolysis. Twice a week her advertisement appeared in the personal column of the *Courrier du Sud*. It read as follows:

> Charming gifted widow, 45, with furniture worth nine million and small annunity, seeks distinguished Catholic husband who will appreciate and share august but dignified country life. Agents please abstain.

Whether she ever received any replies to this appeal nobody knew; but for years now she had been quite determined to find another husband to replace number three ('parce qu'il faut faire une vie quand même'). This was all very well, and indeed she was rather admired for refusing to give in to old age, but the trouble was that latterly her choice tended always to centre on poor Pepe, who certainly had other fish to fry. It had become a joke: one of those long-winded village jokes which make life so delightful in places where the atom bomb as a subject for discussion has not been heard of. Yes, she was a *brave fille*, this widow Chauvet. But sometimes, on a duty evening, she would deliberately set her chimney on fire, overcome by what was described as a *faiblesse* (due to the Tavel *rosé* she took with her meals?), and in this way secure a certain modicum of male company in the form of the gallant brigade of *pompiers* led by Pepe, who would rush up the hill to the rescue in their fire engine. It was rumoured that such was her love for Pepe that she kept a duty roster of voluntary *pompiers* pinned to her kitchen wall, so that she would know exactly when to set the chimney alight. At any rate she had never done this on an evening when the gallant Pepe was not himself in charge. The inference was clear.

This interruption, then, was very much to be feared; and for a moment the knowledge that the widow might strike cast a gloom over the company. But the food was so delicious, the candlelight so charming, the songs of Porot so clearly demoralizing to the two young serving-girls, the wine flowing so strongly . . . that everyone settled down at last to this memorable banquet in good earnest. I kept an apprehensive eye on a wrist watch and wondered whether I should have to be taken aboard the train on a stretcher.

It was a quarter to twelve when the siren went; just after the thirteenth recitation and the fourteenth comic song. Murier had stood on his hands 'just to prove' something or other; Thoma the notary had sung a selection from an unidentifiable opera; Gradon had done the can-can and sung a little song which had for chorus the refrain: '*Merde Merde Merde au flic*'. It was clear that he was due for a court martial if he went on like this. I was just about to recite (on request) the speech 'from *Hamlet* by Laurence Olivier' (sic) when the first haunting moans filled the air.

'The siren! It must be the widow,' cries Pepe tearing his hair and gazing wildly around him as if hunting for his sense of duty. Clearly I had just time to get to the station. The telephone began to ring slowly, painfully in the little vestibule of 'The Knights' where my rucksack already lay, its straps adjusted against my departure. One of the duty *pompiers* clattered up to answer the call, and clattered down again grinning. He did not need to utter the words, for they were taken out of his mouth by the company which intoned fervently: 'The widow Chauvet is on fire again,' before breaking into croaking guffaws like so many bull-frogs on a lily-pad.

But they were also racked with an apologetic sense of hospitality steadily floundering in that slow insistent wail. Pepe, like the captain on the bridge of a sinking ship, cried: 'Fetch the machine and the *casques*,' and four of the guests left at the double.

'Listen,' says Pepe to me with anguished deliberation. 'Fear nothing. All is in order. We will drop you at the station on the way to the widow's house.'

That is how I came to find myself perched on the *Gaussargues* fire engine, surrounded by grim-faced gentlemen in formidable *casques* of gleaming brass, while Murier piloted us down the main street at what seemed to me to be the speed of sound itself. Sound! The horn of the machine honked dolefully like a series of dying swans as we swerved across the esplanade and over the bridge, and out along the road to the railway station.

'Fear nothing,' said Pepe, himself by now accoutred in huge rubber boots and an axe. 'All will be well. You will see.'

The functionaries of the railway were clearly under the impression that I was pretty important as visitors go—perhaps an atomic scientist or mad oinologist. I was rushed on to the platform by a posse of gentlemen in tremendous brass *casques* with such impetus that the stationmaster bowed from the waist. It was not a moment too soon; our watches must have been bedevilled by the town clock—a not uncommon thing in *Gaussargues*. Doors were shutting and flags were being waved. A dozen brown hands were flung out to clasp mine. 'Goodbye,' I cried inadequately. 'You had better hurry.' Up there on the hill there seemed quite a fire; it looked as though the widow had done it properly this time for the roof itself was alight. Pepe drew a deep breath as we shook hands: 'You will come back?' he asked. I nodded. 'As yet you know nothing of Provence, nothing.' I admitted it. The train jerked once, twice, and began to slide. 'Good luck,' I said, 'and good weather in *Gaussargues*.' Pepe waved his *casque* in stately fashion; through his shirt I caught a glimpse of his tattooed hide— Montélimar to Avignon, unless I am mistaken. 'We'll always have a place for you at the *Anciens Combattants*,' he yelled suddenly as the distance widened, and then we turned a corner and he vanished.

It is some months since I left *Gaussargues*. I am writing these words in Paris. I have seen and heard nothing of Pepe since I left, and though I occasionally scan the meridional press for news of my friends in the Midi, *Gaussargues* itself is never mentioned. It is a pity. It would be nice to round off the story in some way, perhaps even by being able to report Pepe's marriage to the widow Chauvet; but I think he is not very much interested in furniture worth nine millions.

Old Mathieu

Published in Time and Tide. *London. 6 December 1958.*

He must be in his early sixties, yet though his hair is white and his face as wrinkled as that of a tortoise he is still sprightly of step. He swings up the hill to his holding of vine and olive with the air of conqueror and is prodigal of good-mornings. His greeting sails over the garden wall like a thrown flower. On his way back at dusk he occasionally stops for a gossip. Yet somehow this year he has become less cheerful, less confident—and indeed his concern is understandable, for it matches that of his fellow *vignerons*. The failure of the '57 harvest was a blow whose full effects are only now beginning to be felt with the appearance of imported Spanish table wine and the hushed incredulous talk of wine-rationing by next August. In France! 'Yes, the Spanish wine has come,' he admits with an air almost of self-reproach. He is not critical of its quality—everyone admits that some is even superior to the local *gros rouge*. No. He utters the words with the hangdog air of a cricketer who might say: 'We have been forced to invite three American baseball players to join the Test team!'

Wine for Old Mathieu is neither a cult nor simply a business; rather is it something between a livelihood and a vocation. Talking of it he sounds rather like old Wilfred Rhodes discussing famous spin-bowlers of the past. The little soiled and folded copy of the trade paper peeps out of his pocket—*Le Vigneron*. Sitting down on a stone he unfolds it slowly and reads out the report of the last harvest with the wounded and shrinking air of a soldier studying a casualty list. 'C'est bien grave, monsieur.' And indeed it is. On his lips the famous names sound full of the regional poetry of old county regiments or county cricket teams decimated in a year of bitter crisis. 'Bordelais. N'a que la moitié d'une récolte normale. Nettement inférieure à '52, '53, '55, sauf quelques rares crues. Bourgogne. 1957 ne représente guère plus que la moitié d'une récolte normale.' Here and there, however, there are frail gleams of hope to mitigate this terrible casualty list, and over these few items he lingers. In the Bourgogne report, for example, satisfactory production was signalled from several points on the battlefront, notably in the Côte de Nuits—at Gevrey-Chambertin, Morey, Chambolle-Musigny, Nuits St. Georges; but 'très faible' production on the Côte de Beaune, notably Le Mâconnais and Le Beaujolais. Nevertheless on the Beaujolais front (his voice picks up) there are *bonnes cuvées* to be signalled from Fleurie, Moulin à Vent, Côte de Brouilly, Morgon and in the Beaujolais villages. 'Mais le Beaujolais '57 est bien loin d'être un grand millésime.' Sighing he turns a page, first carefully picking his finger and peering short-sightedly at the small newsprint. 'Vous voyez? C'est bien grave, monsieur.' The news of Champagne is nothing less than calamitous— 160,000 hectolitres against a normal production of 350,000—and this only of 'qualité moyenne'. The news from the Alsace and the Jura is equally sad with production tumbled down to below half and all the qualities indifferent. The production in the Loire region down to six-tenths of its normal size with some total failures to be recorded after the bitter spring frosts of last year. 'Récolte presque nulle à Pouilly sur Loire, très faible à Sancerre, Vouvray, Savennières. Mais . . .' and once more the old voice rises hopefully as he records, 'une bonne qualité dans les Côtes de la Loire'. But it is quality against quantity. On the home front, so to speak, things are not quite so bad. The Côtes du Rhône and Provence production was up to three-quarters of normal with some superior wines to be signalled, notably from Châteauneuf-du-Pape. Also the Vins Doux Naturels show a silver lining with production standing at well over half the normal and quality relatively high all round. But in the South-west once more the tale of disaster is repeated, with production whittled away to under half—vine-regiments decimated by the frost. How marvellous their names are! Montbazillac, Rosette, Pecharmant, Montravel, Bergerac. Côtes de Duras. Jurançon, Madiran, Pacherenc, Du Vic Bilh. 'Le vignoble de Monbazillac fût particulièrement éprouvé par les gelées. Qualité moyenne.' An epitaph for a famous vineyard.

He folds up the little magazine and tucks it carefully back in his pocket. 'The Vines!' he says reflectively, shaking his head as if over their beloved incorrigibility. Indeed in this anxious year they have become presences standing out there in the rain. And the weather reports for April and May have deepened the gloom everywhere with their talk of snap-frosts and rainy spells to come. Are the vines to fail again this year? I am beginning to see them through the eyes of Old Mathieu. They are planted from end to end of the wintry horizon in regular symmetrical lines, as if on a chessboard. In the landscape foreground they look like small pagan headstones in some huge cemetery; and as they fade back into the hills in diminishing lines they dot the fields of tobacco-coloured earth like cloves.

And the plants themselves . . . hairy as the thigh of a village Pan they writhe out of the dark ground, ash-dark and swollen with the promise of leaf and fruit, but nude now; and everywhere by March there are men in blue blouses bending over them as if over street casualties, binding a limb, setting a splint, tending them. All the silences in these white villages are full of the snap of sécateurs, and carts trudge round in the mud collecting the dead vines—or those which for one reason or another have failed to bear. Spades dig them coarsely up—extirpating them like rotten molars and tossing them into the carts which soon brim over with these little brown statuettes, arms raised on high, primitive woodcarvings of Dionysus himself; each a small figure with raised arms, knotted, tumescent, as if from the pressures of the soil itself—a strength cut back, contained, muzzled by the surgeon's sécateurs. The April rain hisses down among them, condensing in great glistening beads on their shaggy skins, like sweat —sweat and tears from the drawn-out agony of growth.

Each elbow of vine is left with two points, two dry points of contact with the sky like terminals. Each shaggy little statue raises two arms, each arm has two fingers. And then, as the slow spring advances, a leaf appears on each of the fingers—a frail yellow pilot-light. It questions the air delicately, timidly, like the horns of a snail. Another follows and another. So the great hairy thigh of Dionysus blossoms in yellow leaves which advance with a downward-pressing movement, wriggling along between earth and sky as if uncertain which to seek; a curious snake-like downward movement.

But by the time June comes the whole valley will be in leaf, plum-dark, transformed. The dry brickdust and tobacco-veined earth will have become smothered by the new heraldic green of the vines, manufacturing the shade in which the fruit is to ripen.

It is Old Mathieu himself who taught me how to trim the vines in the neglected and abandoned vineyard in which this old house stands and which we will soon be leaving for good. In a single year of neglect the vine can throw out a four yard withe which sprouts upon it like those long and silky antennae upon the heads of certain nocturnal beetles. These must all be trimmed back to 'make the vine push', in the words of Old Mathieu. He brings up his sécateurs on two successive Sundays and patiently shows me how the operation must be conducted. It is not unlike a spell at the nets under an exacting yet patient coach. Holding the long-shanked cutters you straddle the vine, cutting downwards, having first chosen your trimmings. Gravely he instructs you: press down and keep the sharp side of the cutters against the body of the vine. 'Il faut tourner doucement avec la souche.' (I am reminded of a difficult shot to cover-point—or of a glide through the slips.) 'Tourner,' he cries softly. 'Il faut tourner, Monsieur.' It has its own rhythm, this downward cut with the sécateurs, but it is not too difficult to learn. Together we work slowly through the orchard in front of the house. 'The one at the back you shall do by yourself,' he says with a smile. 'And when I pass up the hill in the morning I shall see if it is properly done or not.'

One can trim about sixty or seventy vines in a day, and it is absorbing work. First the choice of the shoots to be cut away, the cleaning and barbering of the trunk, and then the operation which will leave two fingers upon each branch, and not more than six upon each single vine. 'Il faut de la patience. Il faut bien le juger.'

Working with the invisible presence of Old Mathieu at my elbow I complete the job. Anxiously as a student I await his early morning passing. Presently I hear his cheery good-morning on the road below. I find him standing with his critical and friendly eye upon the vineyard. 'C'est pas mal,' he says. For an amateur *vigneron* this is an accolade indeed.

Women of the Mediterranean

Published in Réalités. *Paris and New York. June 1961.*

A suggestive title, a phrase full of echoes and associations—although at first it is a little difficult to say why. Perhaps it is due to the qualifying of a mysterious noun by an even more mysterious adjective. . . . Are they really any different from other women in other places, and if so, how? Certainly you could not alter the adjective without damaging the rich mental image conjured up by the phrase. (Try to say 'British Women' or 'Swiss Women'—and all at once you feel that you are talking about a different genus.)

The Mediterrannean woman has never subconsciously forgotten that, by origin, she is descended from her foam-born prototype Aphrodite. If the Nordics ever had a type-goddess of the same epoch she must have been a goddess of fertility, of marriage, of domesticity, and not one who raised woman's independence into a cult which combined freedom and sensuality in equal parts. As for the actual historic specimens of Mediterranean womanhood, a poet could get drunk simply by making a rosary of the great names they have bequeathed us. ('When Mausolus died, his wife Artemisia pounded his bones in wine and drank the potion that she might get his skill in battle. . . .') Metanira, Cleopatra, Hypatia, Theodora, Beatrice, Laura, Catherine Cornaro, Sappho, Agrippina, Lucrezia Borgia, Clytemnestra, Thaïs, Penelope, Bouboulina . . . the list could be prolonged almost indefinitely. They are all children of this mysterious sea, occupying its landscapes in human forms which seem as unvaryingly eternal as the olive, the asphodel, the cypress, the laurel, and above all the sacred vine.

I would be right, I think, in suggesting that the word 'Mediterranean' should be applied to all the wine-drinking countries around the basin; and that the character of their women emerges as distinctly as the odour of thyme bruised by the hoofs of the sheep on these sun-drunk hills and dales. I must remind the reader that the vine was first discovered in Egypt.

In this context, then, as a creature of a landscape one sees her very clearly. She is to be distinguished from other women by the violent coherence of a character which is composed of fierce extremes. The poetry and the vehemence of her feelings are both proverbial; but they combine happily with a certain innocence, a purity of mind. You will easily see what I mean if you reflect upon the Nordic version of her—if you think of Catherine the Great or Queen Elizabeth. The contrast is instructive, for in the North something had had to be sacrificed in order that these women might become as great as they undoubtedly were. The something is *femininity*. In order to perform their great deeds they had to become, in a sense, mannish women. What characterizes the southerner is that she can do just as great deeds without once sacrificing the female side of her character. (Theodora, Semiramis, Cleopatra.) There is a constant in the character which does not change however various different women were. This difference of character seems all the more marked when we reflect upon the long battle which women in the North have fought for equal rights. In the South, no such battle has been necessary, for women do not envy men at all. Why should they ask for equality with the feebler sex—man? They know that nothing is stronger than the mother and the cult of the mother—and they have been content with their role as procreators, the handers-on of the man-children.

She is as various as the history of the Mediterranean itself, the Mediterranean woman, whether she is skirting the dark labyrinths of Crete, whether she walks knife in hand along the blood-soaked corridors of Tiryns or Mycenae, whether she poisons with a Renaissance smile or accepts with beating heart the blood-spattered trophy from the toreador's crimson hand. But we dare not imagine that she has no weaknesses—for her overpowering sensuality and single-heartedness, the pride and naivety of her feelings have more than once driven great poets to open their veins, or great soldiers to start unjust wars in her name like Helen did. Yet we would not wish her otherwise than she is. Even the Moslems who say that women have no souls are unable to imagine a Paradise which is not perfected by her presence: their after-world is peopled by the fluttering shapes of the 'hanoumi', brilliant and soulless as fireflies on an autumn night.

[370]

Her struggle, it seems to me, has always been the same one: to break through the pattern of sexual greed and self-indulgence in order to discover herself, to find a magical identification with the earth-rhythms whose slow pulses beat in her blood. (I am thinking of the abstracted faces of Greek women as they join in the age-old dances and beat up the red dust with their bare soles. Faces purged of everything except the sensual concentration on the music's throb and swing. They burn inwardly like altar candles. I am thinking of the Spanish dancers with their proud-shrill parrot-voices and the maddening rataplan of their castanets upon the watchers' heartstrings. I am thinking of the peasant dancers in Italy who pause as the first flights of fireworks stain the dark velvet sky in honour of a patron saint (as in Ischia), only once more to resume the grave poignant measures which have been handed down to them through the generations and which were first intended, perhaps, to copy the motions of the stars.)

But the Mediterranean is older than history and stronger than religion; one of the reasons why we love it so much is this unfailing sense of continuity with which it invests the present. If you go to an Easter service in a Catholic church at Marseilles, Naples or Madrid, you feel very certainly that the Christian mysteries were evolved out of the Eleusinian mysteries and that invisibly the worshippers are linking hands with their ancestors through the communion of the saints. This feeling is even stronger in an Orthodox church, because the Greek language of the service vibrates like the wind in the Aeolian harp of the mind. What do these faces tell one except that nothing Mediterranean can change for it is landscape-dominated; its people are simply the landscape-wishes of the earth sharing their particularities with the wine and the food, the sunlight and the sea.

And the woman of this landscape? At certain times she has been better-loved and understood than at others; though she has always been feared. I think the Greeks got nearest to treating her as such a rare animal deserves to be treated. Pythagoras included her among his pupils as did Apollonius. Epicurus built up a philosophy to share with her which is perhaps the most perfect ever made—a philosophy of poetry which excluded her from nothing. She was granted the importance and the affection which today she finds only in Paris. Indeed, it is not simply a whim to see that France, even today, is as near as modern man has got to Ancient Greece.

[371]

The two worlds, northern and southern, have maintained a curious dialogue in art and culture. They hate much about each other, but they envy more. Perhaps, unconsciously, they feel that each is complementary to the other. But the axis (the spiritual axis) which passes through them crosses the centre of France, from Alsace to Provence, from beer to wine, from Gothic to Romance. It passes, like white light, through the brilliant, discordantly radiant prism of Paris which will always remain the mediatrix between these two aspects of European temperament. What gives the French temperament its balance and form is precisely the uneasy polarity between these two influences. What gives France the enormous range and span and force of its art is, quite literally, that the French artist has the best of both worlds. He can choose, so to speak, the mixture he needs for his work. The spark of French genius leaps between the two poles, northern and southern, Puritan and Pagan. Where else can you span the two worlds so effectively—that of Rabelais and Pascal, that of Stendhal and Chateaubriand, that of Camus and Genet? It was through France that the Mediterranean woman projected her power and influence northward to inflame the imagination of the slow and ox-like northerners. In the time of Shakespeare, the Elizabethan heroine was really a Mediterranean. Stendhal, who discovered Shakespeare in middle age, was delighted to find that his heroines shared many of the qualities of energy and passion that he admired among his beloved Italians. 'How he *Italianizes!*' he writes with delight. In the Elizabethan age, the power of the Italian tradition in feeling was a marked one on the stage— and it alarmed the Puritans who were always attacking this southern infatuation.

> The Englishman Italianate
> Is the Devil incarnate.

With the political and religious broils which severed the British from Europe and inflicted on them the deep psychic wound which has not healed today, this vein of feeling became exhausted. Nowadays, the British artist is still vainly trying to join the Common Market in arts and letters.

Here an anecdote comes to mind which will perhaps describe the Mediterranean woman better than a dozen historical generalizations which the reader might find arguable. During the last war an Italian lady of Alexandria who sympathized with the Allies gave a weekly tea-party for the troops stationed in town. To this little party she always invited a dozen or so of the prettiest and most eligible Italian ladies of the town thinking that their beauty and their conversation would be some compensation to the allied soldiers and sailors for the harsh life of danger which was theirs. On one of these occasions a young American was present, very shy, extremely polite, and undoubtedly inhibited by the beauty of the ladies and the magnificence of the house in which he found himself. A young lady approached him and began to converse. In order to show himself anxious to make a good impression, the young man, after racking his brains for a subject, took out his fountain-pen (a very modern one) and demonstrated some of its gadgets to her. They discussed it. The subject once exhausted, he showed her some even more modern gadgets on his expensive wrist-watch and chronometer combined. They discussed it. Finally he passed to his cigarette-lighter which was also a marvel. The young woman put up with this for some time, but finally she leaned forward, touched his wrist gently with her forefinger, and smiling beatifically at the Anglo-Saxon said: 'Yes—but *what do you feel?*' at the same time placing one hand upon her heart. There was no answer to this artless question. Stendhal would have been ravished, but the youth choked on his tea and took himself off as fast as he could.

It is the sacredness of emotion, the uncritical enjoyment of feeling for its own sake, that is one of the keys to the Mediterranean woman's character.

'In Italy,' writes Stendhal, 'a country totally devoid of the vanity of France and England, every man laughs at his neighbour and even despises and detests him. His judgement of the arts is founded solely upon his own feelings. The Italians . . . form a total contrast, it is clear, to the inhabitants of France and England who are better off politically, but who have been deprived of all individual character by their ambition to become, in every sense of the terms, a fashionable and well-bred copy of a certain conventional pattern. Unlike the Englishman and the Frenchman, the Italian listens only to the promptings of his own heart, employing all the energy of his character to give predominance to his own peculiar mode of feeling.' Our author, who divined the Italian character so clearly, remains in my opinion somewhat unfair to his own country. (The symbol of Marianne is still quite

[373]

recognizably Mediterranean, but not that of Boadicea.) Stendhal, who came of what we might call puritan inheritance, simply longed to free himself from it and espouse the pagan side of the national character. He never quite succeeded. He hated all that was cold, vain and calculating and loved everything that was energetic, passionate, simple and generous. The mystery to me is why his sojourn in Marseilles did not teach him that the spirit he so admired was the very lifeblood of the French Midi.

But if this direct abandonment to her feelings is one of the great strengths of the Mediterranean woman, it is also one of her signal weaknesses. It has given her great powers but it has also enfeebled her political and social position. Men have not been slow to take advantage of this factor; she is extremely male-dominated in the countries of the Mediterranean where cheerful use is made of her as a beast of burden and a money-raiser. In Greece, in Egypt, it is she who does the rough work, carrying and fetching, while the male is content to sit under a tree and fan himself or talk politics. He seems to be quite content with his role—why should he not be? He has the pleasure of begetting the children, she the trouble of bringing them up. Indeed, perhaps her bondage is a willing and self-created one. Who else is responsible for all the truly Mediterranean fetishes which have grown up about the idea of a male child? We confidently assert that Anglo-Saxon males are mother-fixated, but whoever had watched the way Mediterranean mothers bring up their male offspring would hesitate to be so dogmatic. Before her son can walk or talk, the Mediterranean mother has crowned him the king of her life. He can do no wrong, and his sisters soon learn an appropriate female attitude of inferiority before this young god whose word is law. In some ways the bondage of the Mediterranean female may be said to begin in the nursery; she can thereafter only recover her independence by the creation of a male child of her own. Her self-respect as a woman is deeply bound up with the question of whether she can bear sons or not. This mother-son link seems to me every bit as strong as that described by the psychologists in the North, and in some ways even such a great novel of the Oedipus complex as *Sons and Lovers* could be translated into Mediterranean terms and remain true to its thesis. (I have noticed over and over again that sea-sick Greeks and Italians and Spaniards are apt to call upon their mothers when *in extremis*—often in the accents of five-year-old children.)

[374]

But if the Mediterranean woman spoils her male child the balance is often restored by the pattern and rhythm of her family life which is unvarying in its respect for certain basic values. The importance of the family as a tribe is perhaps the most important aspect of the matter. The family holds together as a living unit and provides a frame inside which there is room for every generation. Granny, for example, whether you find her in Naples or Madrid, in Marseilles or Piraeus, is the dominating member of the Latin household. She is not only loved and admired but also deeply respected; more important than this, she keeps on working right to the end. In England today, when a couple marries the old people are relegated to the scrap-heap, so to speak; to the furnished hotel on the South Coast. They are no longer useful or productive. In the North, the idea of a family (look at our advertisements) has come to mean only mother, father and the children. In the Mediterranean it is a whole tribe, shading away on all sides to the most remote corners of cousinship or aunthood. So complicated does this cobweb become that some nations (I am thinking especially of the Greeks) have a full vocabulary to express the fine distinctions of relationship. I once heard a man say to another: 'Please go to the hotel in Athens and give this letter to my brother's second cousin's aunt Loula—the one by marriage and not the divorced one.' It is possible that this notion of family pattern has been helped and engendered by Catholicism as some people have said; but I think this explanation does not go far enough, for it exists in Orthodox countries as well. It existed among the ancient Greeks.

The Mediterranean woman, then, while from many points of view she may seem enslaved, is nevertheless the queen bee of the family hive. She is the beloved tyrant of her grandchildren.

Is she herself religious? Not in the strictest meaning of the word. An anthropologist would say that she was more superstitious than religious. This is because in her passion she is wholly uncritical. She loves her church as she loves her man or her son—with a completely unrationalized self-surrender. She refuses to make a theology out of her passions. Moral questions, questions of principle or judgement, do not sway her. Her life has no critical apparatus so to speak. She has never bothered to worry herself with all the paradoxes of existence. Life for her is as simple as a glass of wine—and she drinks her wine without water. This is what makes me suspect that all the changes of politics

and history are, from her point of view, illusory; she has always remained a pagan, devoutly and unconsciously pagan. This is so apparent
to anyone who watches her at prayer in a church of Marseilles or
Naples! Even if you go further south and watch her Orthodox counter-
part praying at the miracle-working shrine of the Virgin on the island
of Tinos on the 15th of August every year. See how she attacks the
shrine with her prayers, as if she would wrench, by the irresistible
force of her prayer, the required miracle from it. No, she does not
'pray', for the very word smacks of self-conscious intercessions with
forces which she fears; she besieges her God as she does her lover. She
is importuning an earth-force, something elemental which existed long
before the Gods were condensed into conceptual forms.

Fundamentally she enjoys everything, even her own despair, with a
vibrating innocence. . . . If you like, we could consider this a sort of
passionate blindness—a limitation. Yet, if it is one, it effectively blinds
her to many things which bedevil us northerners, and which we would
gladly shed. I recall that in many years of lecturing about literature to
boys and girls I never succeeded in making Mediterranean students
fully grasp the literary notions which have grown up about two northern concepts: namely 'Spleen' and 'Ennui'. As for 'Angst' I did not
even dare to try.

This portrait, I know, lacks much fine detail: it is too black and
white. Nevertheless, it is the best that one can do in words. Luckier
men have pictured her in other media more successfully, more truth-
fully. In the Pomona of Maillol, for example, you see the young earth
Goddess that she is, fruitful and heavy-breasted. She is a spirit of place
and not simply 'a woman'. She defeats words, as all true goddesses
must.

Finally, let us talk a little about her as a lover. I do not use the word
'wife' for that to her is a duty she performs perfectly and unself-
consciously. She is destined to be a wife and she knows it and accepts.
She is *born* to be a lover. And when she is in love she shows her
Mediterranean character at its highest potential. We know the phrase
of Shakespeare about Cleopatra: 'Age shall not wither her nor custom
stale her infinite variety.' This phrase which echoes in the European
subconscious and which may be thought by some to be only a piece of
poetic licence is in fact a factual statement, and as true as a stock report.
The infinite variety comes out of her innocence. Whether she wears a

pistol and chooses her own lovers by force (as Bouboulina of the Greek Independence days) or whether she will have no lovers because she is in love with someone whom she cannot have—the pattern is the same: a totality. She can die for love as easily as a bird leaves a branch. In the North we have not begun to live for it. She can let her sensuality overturn a whole world if it is given free rein, but on the other hand she can become an anchorite because no other men (except the one she loves) seem worth loving. It is this comprehensiveness of her passion which can inspire great poets, can inspire men to become eunuchs for her sake. (That is why she is dangerous to the ordinary run of men.) In fact, she was born to sire poets, and she will continue to try to do so as long as olive-trees and asphodels exist, and as long as the blue waves of the Mediterranean roll upon these deserted beaches. Who would want her otherwise?

Three Roses of Grenoble

Published as 'The Wordly University of Grenoble', in Holiday. *Philadelphia. January 1959.*

'I may tell the reader', writes Stendhal, 'that the Dauphiné has its own way of feeling, lively, stubborn and analytical, which I have met with in no other country. To the seeing eye music, landscape and the novel should all change with each shift of three degrees of latitude. For instance at Valence, on the Rhône, the Provençal nature ends. . . .'

These observations are not the less exact for being over a hundred years old, and you become conscious of their truth as you take the great motor highway which branches off north-eastward from Valence, describing a long slow ellipse towards Grenoble. Feature by feature Provence flickers out with the hard blue accentuation of its sunlight. The olives are the first to desert you, and next the salty twang of the southern accent; later still the queer-pitched roofs of Provence give place to the high awkward style of building which betrays its concern not so much for wind and heat alone as for snow and rain. The meadows are damp. Everything begins to go up on stilts to keep dry. Only the warm rosy Marseilles tiles cross the border with you to bring a fugitive light to the lichen-encrusted roofs of barns, and to blend softly with the grey of slate or the lacklustre of lead. . . . And as you move in towards the old university town of Grenoble the Alps begin to rise, tier on tier, with their cold fuming peaks buried in the shifting mists. Hereabouts it is becoming apple country, hazy with mists, where the roads hover in and out of sleeping valleys and dense woodlands. Suddenly the romantic landscapes of Claude, of Poussin, become quite real to the traveller. Those islands half buried in mists, those old fortresses carved upon the green density of glittering foliage, those limitless prospects of woodland and lake—they are all real! Yet one always believed them to be the inventions of romantic fancy. No, in Dauphiné you suddenly realize that the romantic painters were simply copyists of nature after all.

Yet though the predominant feeling of the landscape is Alpine you notice fields and fields of tobacco—the Régie plantations they must be (government monopoly)—which argue summers hardly less burning and intense than those of Provence. These valleys, then, are suntraps lending themselves to easy exploitation by the industrious Dauphinois. And the red roses which decorate the arms of modern Grenoble are no imaginary emblems either, for the highroad runs between huge nurseries packed with them, gleaming magnificently in the autumn air.

The leaves had already begun to fall when I reached Grenoble, and the air was spicy with the first sharp hints of the turning year. It was perhaps the best moment to pay it a visit for it was relatively empty, the university not yet in session, and there was an opportunity to visit and assess its faculties and to talk to professors who were then preparing for the approaching academic year, and who would later be too burdened with work perhaps to turn a patient ear to the enquiries of visiting journalists. The town, too, with its spacious leafy squares and avenues showed to its best advantage in the softening light of early autumn. Its site is truly magnificent, pitched in the lee of towering hills and thrown across the confluence point of two swift rivers, the Drac and the Isère. The Alps nudge the sky at the end of every street. Grenoble is dominated by the old fortress in which Laclos wrote perhaps the cruellest book on human love—*Les Liaisons Dangereuses*. ('It is *not* cruel!' said Martine puffing at her Gauloise. 'But simply exact and unsentimental. Some of the dryness of the professional artilleryman comes through the style. Target-practice.')

But here I should explain: apart from the official introductions with which I had armed myself, I had also taken the precaution of bringing a visiting card for a student—in the form of a twelve livre *bonbonne* of wine. The old sea-captain had lurched down the hill with this wicker-covered trophy saying: 'If you are going to Grenoble look up my daughter Martine, and take her this wine.' It was a lucky stroke of fortune, for it was through Martine that I was able to make contact with life at the student level, without which this article would be simply an assembly of cold facts, thrown down one against the other. ('And don't drive too fast,' the old man had added. 'It is bad for the wine. And not on bumpy roads either. It is also bad for the wine. And tell Martine to let it rest and breathe after its journey. And ask her why she insists on staying up there in the summer. We have a right to know. She mustn't work too hard.')

Of Grenoble itself I knew relatively little. I had visited it many years before, but fleetingly, as a tourist. I did know, however, that its most illustrious son had loathed it, and had painted its portrait with a savagery that seemed to me now (walking the streets with Martine in her blue jeans and duffle coat) somewhat unmerited. 'Grenoble is to me like the memory of an abominable attack of indigestion; there is nothing dangerous in it but it is utterly disgusting!' So writes Stendhal; but I think that if he could have heard his words quoted with affectionate laughter by the young woman of twenty he might have been tempted to modify them.

The University of Grenoble occupies an enviable position in the academic esteem of Frenchmen, and is among the first three universities of France, sharing its honours with Paris and Strasbourg. But it is also peculiar to itself, for of all the centres of learning in France it is the most international in outlook. Perhaps geography has something to do with its cosmopolitanism, its Swiss and Italian orientation; or perhaps it is simply the excellence of its summer courses for foreigners, and the fact that some two thousand students a year from other countries spend the summer here. Since the inception of these *Cours de Vacances* in 1896 over 80,000 foreigners of 45 nationalities have studied here; and of course this figure does not include those foreigners who (summer courses aside) become fully fledged undergraduates of the University and complete their studies here. ('You don't want a lot of dull figures,' said Martine. 'Yes I do.' She sighed. 'All right. I'll go to the Rectorate where they will give me the answers to any questions you have.')

Figures, dull as they are, can often be illuminating, though Martine herself wore a distinctly contemptuous air as she rode up to the hotel on her Vespa with her bundle of jottings sticking out of the pocket of her duffle coat. '*Voilà*', she said, and added, 'Though I don't know who you are going to interest with this sort of thing.'

Nevertheless, she sat patiently, if somewhat quizzically, in the lobby of the Three Dauphins (where Napoleon is supposed to have lodged during his lightning advance northward on Paris during the Hundred Days); and she even accepted a glass of *rosé* while I tried to sort out the skeletal structure of the university from the neatly tabulated lists of *chiffres.* It did not take long to sift the relevant detail: though when I shut my notebook and slipped the official papers back into their green envelopes she still looked rather unconvinced. 'What have you found?'

I had, in fact, found one or two things of great interest. The student body of Grenoble is about 5,500 strong, though the registrations for the new department of Theoretical Physics and Nuclear Fission (just opened) is expected to add another five hundred pupils to the list this year. Of this number some six hundred students are foreigners, and in the academic year '56–'57 Britain, the United States and Germany provided the greatest numbers—in that order. Of course the foreign students are nearly all grouped in the faculty of letters—understandably enough; countries which are technologically advanced would have centres of learning at least as specialized for them to attend at home. There would be less incentive for Americans, British, Germans and Swiss to take scientific degrees here. Hence they throng the Faculty of Letters. But the more backward nations which are still grappling with a shortage of technicians do send their students to Grenoble— Syria and Greece are both well represented. The spacious dining-hall of the Maison des Etudiants at lunch-time has the air of being a miniature United Nations. Martine and I lunched in a group consisting of a Chinese, a Japanese, a Pakistani and an American (Sidney Simon of Brooklyn College, studying French). The Japanese had been four years in Grenoble studying letters, and had a good deal to say in praise of its excellence both as an academy and a ski-centre. It was queer to listen to his lucid and faultless French to which he had added the use of typical gestures of the hand and head. He was a chemist. 'All the emphasis today is on science. More and more people are enrolling for science and technology courses. It is understandable. Grenoble is the best of the universities for a scientific training—as Cambridge is in England.' It is not merely that the University is expanding its technological faculties faster than any other—it is also that Grenoble as a town is growing fast towards the position of a small capital, with new industries and plants springing up everywhere. Here (and this is unique in France) the industrialist works in with the university authorities to help accentuate the studies of technicians, often subsidizing their studies or putting forward incentives such as the guarantee of a reserved job. 'Once', said the American, 'a university was regarded as a mind-trainer. But today it is becoming a meal-ticket. Science is a hungry monster and needs more and more hands and brains.'

Here I was able to throw down a question which has been exercising the Anglo-Saxon mind of late. 'Is there a tug-of-war between science and the Humanities here, as there seems to be in England and America? Is there a disquiet about technical education, and a clear division of aims and ends?'

There was a long moment of silence. 'Yes,' said the Japanese, but thoughtfully, reflectively. 'There are more girls taking letters, more men taking science, these days.' It was not quite the answer I was hoping for and I waited. Finally it was the spidery French student from the end of the table who provided it; he had been listening in silence with his chin on his hand. 'I don't agree,' he said. 'And I think that French educational attitudes would prevent such a *décalage*. I understand your question and have read a number of articles in the English press about the matter. Apparently you woke up the other day and found that the Russians were producing more scientists than England and America put together; some sort of panic followed. But if you don't mind my saying so it seemed to me to be based on a fundamental misunderstanding as to what science really is. It is not simply the multiplication of amenities, the practical and applied end of things. Applied science is based upon something far more profound, namely the abstractions of pure mathematics. Ideas are everything to science. It isn't based on reasoning, but imaginative *daring*; the amenities like bombs and penicillin are simply by-products. But the supply of these would soon dry up if it were not sustained by the purely abstract work of the mathematicians. (After all, the whole science of hydraulics is based on an idea of Leonardo.) Now in France we consider that scientists are really poets too, poets of ideas. You can't read Poincaré's account of how his imagination works when he is thinking mathematically without admitting that it is the same order of phenomenon as what happens to Valéry when he drafts a poem. In other words the key to both crafts is intuition; and the function of a Humanist education is not simply to supply a training in moral or ethical values, but to nourish the intuition. I think this is the French spirit which animates our education, and this is what has distinguished the French student from the Anglo-Saxon one. At any rate visit our medical and technology faculties and see how many people are painting and writing as well as studying these subjects. I don't believe there is another country which has this attitude; and I hope France will never lose it.'

'He's right,' said Martine. 'But. . . .'

'But what?'

'Will it outlast this generation?'

This of course was not a question that any of us could answer. But the spidery French student nodded firmly and precisely. 'If science itself is to go on it will have to.'

'Things have changed so much.'

But here our deliberations were interrupted by the chimes of a clock and the students began to bustle off to their lecture halls. Martine, too, had a lecture to attend, and this left me free to wander along the quays by the swift-flowing icy Isère for an hour, listening to the lazy sounds of life from the Place Grenette, and trying to reconstruct from my memories of Stendhal what it all must have been like to this awkward fat boy of sixteen, standing at an upper floor window to watch the Lyons coach rumble into the square at dusk. ('Here are my memories,' he writes. 'The sound of the bells of St. Andrés when they were rung for the elections; the sound of the water-pump when the maidservants at night used to pump with the great iron bar; last the sound of a flute played by some merchant's clerk on a fourth story of the Place Grenette.')

It was in search of that vanished flute that my steps led me to where St. André now stands in its twilit corner by the river, shabby, beautiful and with that air of indestructibility which only good works of art have. I sat for a few moments by the yellow stone slab under which lie the mortal remains of Bayard—the Chevalier Sans Peur and Sans Reproche—reflecting on the fact that it was France which invented chivalry, and so nourished the historic imagination of Europe for centuries afterwards. And now? The stained-glass windows filtered their jewels into the dark church. I could hear the river flowing. Also the clicky click of the small wooden sabots—some children were playing hopscotch outside the great doors, their heels clicking on the paving stones. 'Un deux, trois . . .' the small voices pierced the gloom, so touching and so clear. Then suddenly the darkness was shivered into pieces by the vibrations of a bell and I reluctantly rose to complete the interviews for which I had been sent on what for me was (but the editor must never know) a sentimental pilgrimage to the shrine of my favourite novelist.

Up in the sky! The *téléférique* or cable-car is one of the most delightful features of Grenoble. It spans the outer bastions of the fort and the further bank of the Isère, lifting you with a cradle-soft smoothness up into the night, swinging over the glittering river water until drop by drop the whole city is spread out before you, a dazzling criss-cross of coloured lights, diamonds, lozenges, and harsh single spots of emerald or scarlet. The whole valley brims with the soft furry pollen of light filtered through mist. And behind it the snows rise, majestic, unruffled, stretching away north and south. The view from the bastions of the fort with its great green T-shaped lighthouse is magnificent. The three of us hung there for a while over the city, speechless with pleasure, like the gargoyles over Notre-Dame. Somewhere around us in the darkness I could hear voices, and the faint strumming of guitar strings. The night was deeply pine-scented. 'They are up there,' said Martine and led me upwards along the dark paths.

Somewhere up above us a voice was softly singing a verse from one of those traditional student songs replete with all the healthy bawdry of adolescence.

> *Dans son boudoir*
> *La petite Charlotte*
> *S'donnait d'la joie*
> *Avec une passoire.*

Martine giggled. 'I hope you are blushing,' I said severely, though it was too dark to see. Nils said: 'That is Pierre. As for blushes poor Martine was initiated last year and blushes no more. Here, give me your hand.'

'Do you still have the famous initiation ceremonies they used to call *bizutage*?' I asked.

'Yes. Student folklore is dying out, but we medicals and the long haired Beaux Arts boys still keep them up.'

'It's horrible,' said Martine. 'I found a cadaver's thumb in my soup. And afterwards they sang a very dirty song.'

'Comparatively mild stuff,' said Nils. 'There are more serious ceremonies, and somewhere, in the lab there is a witch doctor's outfit made of bones, and a necklace of human vertebrae, and . . . other items. The girls got off lightly.'

There was a camp fire burning—in the sky it seemed, so intense was the darkness. A group of faces surrounded a simmering pot from which came the delicious odours of *fondue*. We were introduced to each other, and Pierre sang a small and highly questionable song in my honour which met with general acclamation. I offered suitable thanks and took my place in this congenial circle of light carved out of blackness. Dimly one could feel the shoulders of mountain running up into the sky behind us. The toast was piping hot and wrapped in a white napkin. 'The cold air makes you hungry,' said Pierre. 'Dip, my children.' We sat there talking and dipping. Martine's *bonbonne* of wine was produced. It was obviously thoroughly 'rested', and tasted magnificently rich. Below us, on the floor of the world glittered the jewelled city.

So we sat and talked in that cold and disembodied Alpine air, and drank the good wine, and utterly banished from our minds the problems of the world and its future.

It was late when we reached the town again and set off to walk through the gardens where the fallen leaves were being whirled and scratched along the walks by the night wind.

Martine always crossed the little garden in order to have a glimpse of the little terrace of Stendhal's grandfather with its thick trellis of vine. It is over a hundred years old, and is today exactly as the good Poncet (the amiable drunk carpenter) built it for the old man. Yet you can only peep at it over a high wall with an iron door in it. 'I've always wanted to walk on it,' said Martine. 'But in some mysterious fashion it has been cut off from everything. I've tried to reach it through the grounds of the school, but you just can't; it is too high, perched on the Roman wall. And none of the houses appear to give on to it.'

'The entrance must be in the Grande Rue,' I said.

'The Grande Rue is all shopfronts with no courtyards. I have asked in every shop on the façade. There seems to be no way to reach it. And yet once I saw a silver-haired old lady dressed in an old-fashioned way standing up there under the vine. It gave me a start; I wondered if it were the ghost of Séraphie, the dreadful aunt who tormented him so when he was a small boy.'

We gazed through the flickering street-lamps' light at the little terrace, and sighing turned back towards the Place Grenette where the brilliantly lighted Café du Commerce was serving its last black coffees to its clientele of students. I thought no more of the little trellis. It was late and everyone was sleepy.

It was the next afternoon that the adventure befell me; I had packed my things, and was taking a last walk round the town. Martine and Nils were to meet me at my hotel to say goodbye. I wanted to drive to Valence and spend the night there on my way home. Dusk had fallen, and the whole façade of the Grande Rue was ablaze with lights—shops crammed with Alpine sports-wear, souvenirs, toys, and huge boxes of walnut *pralines*. Instinct must have led my steps, for I was not thinking of anything in particular, and certainly not of Stendhal—though it is true that I had just bought a copy of *De l'Amour* to give to Martine as a parting present.

There was a tiny aperture between two shopfronts—a sort of dark tunnel at the end of which I could see a dim patch of shadowy light, as in an aquarium. I walked warily down it to see where it led. In a gloomy courtyard there was a little old man repairing fuses in a fuse-box. Suddenly I saw that there was a staircase leading upwards. I paused. The old man turned the face of a benevolent earwig to me. 'Are you looking for someone?' he asked. I hesitated and said: 'No. I had an *envie* to walk under the trellis of Stendhal.' (One can say this sort of thing in French without looking foolish). 'But there is no way, is there?'

He thought for perhaps half a minute. I could hear the traffic in the Grande Rue and children's voices crying. 'There is,' he said at last. 'It belongs to a private apartment. An old lady lives there. Three flights up.'

I walked up the stairs of the Gagnon house with a beating heart and rang the bell, beset by an absurd sense of familiarity. An old lady with silver hair opened the door and asked my business. She was dress-ed in a dress of some silvery material which gave her an air of great and completely unemphatic distinction. A low melodious voice. Falter-ing rather—and feeling like some annoying intruder—I told her that I was an *ami de Stendhal* and that I was overcome by an absurd *envie* to walk upon the terrace where he had spent such a great part of his childhood.

'But of course,' she said warmly and impulsively, and stood aside to

[386]

let me enter. I followed her across the tall severe rooms and found myself standing on the parapet under the vine, under the trellis at which Martine and Nils gazed so lovingly the night before. The old lady was smiling but silent. The terrace looked out across the dark foliage of the park. 'This is the place; it is completely unchanged. At least if you can remember the drawings he made of it in *Henri Brulard* you can follow his life here, *room by room*; here is the little study with the natural history collection—do you remember?' I did. She took fire at once, leading me from room to room while we recalled to memory those trivial childhood events of the great man. At last she folded her hands and said: 'Would you care to pluck a leaf or two from the old vine?' It was still there, hairy and twisted with age, but as thick as the thigh of Pan himself; I plucked three of the broad green leaves and thanked her.

'People say', said the old lady ,'that he was hard on Grenoble in his writings, but it is so clear to me that his memories were poisoned by the death of his mother here. Do you remember where he says "She perished in the full flower of her beauty" and then adds the quick phrase "*Là commence ma vie morale*"?' She paused for a moment, and stood in the sunlight staring thoughtfully at the old vine. Somewhere a church bell started to ring, full of the leisurely sleepiness that comes from deep valleys full of drowsing cattle, and high mountains. She said: 'And do you remember where he writes about the Church where she was buried? I can quote it: "The very sound of the cathedral bells produced in me in 1828 when I returned to Grenoble a dull and arid grief, without any stirring of the feelings, a grief akin to rage." ' She sighed.

Together we walked in silence across the terrace, through the little study and the tall severe rooms. 'And yet', she added with a smile, 'he also says that he detested Paris at first because it had no mountains and woods! In other words he detested it because it wasn't Grenoble! Such are the paradoxes of the feelings.'

At the front door I thanked her and kissed her slender hand. 'I am happy about your visit,' she said. 'But I must ask you a favour. Please don't tell other people how you came to find this place. There are not enough leaves on Dr. Gagnon's vine to give to Stendhal's admirers; and, then, one has one's own life to live. Will you promise?'

I promised. I did not realize how late it was until I once more reached

the Place Grenette; it was in fact time for me to take the highroad back
to Valence. But I slipped two of the vine-leaves into the little copy of
De l'Amour. Martine and Nils were standing in the vestibule with
Pierre and two other companions of the night before. It was good of
them to come and see me off. The car was already loaded up with
baggage. 'Here,' I said, not without a certain complacence I suppose.
'Here is a present for you both. Somewhere in it you will find two
leaves from Stendhal's vine, just as green as his prose is.'

They were aghast and rather disposed to disbelieve me I think.
'How did you find the trellis, how did you actually get in?' cried Martine
aghast with surprise, and flushed with pleasure.

'I have promised not to tell,' I said.

I started the car amid warm goodbyes and pushed her out across
the handsome bridges which span the loops of the Drac and Isère. It
was getting late. But it was only when I reached the first big turning
south that I noticed something on the back seat and realized that the
students had also thought up a parting present for me: a little wicker
basket full of roses, the famous roses of Grenoble.

The Gascon Touch

Published in Holiday. *Philadelphia. January 1963.*

Gascony (my friend Monsieur Prosper never tires of repeating it) is geographically a figment. 'But', he adds impressively, laying one large hand palm downward upon the map of France and the other upon his heart, 'it is a poetic fact. It is the name of an idea, a temperament, a way of looking at the world.' Ever since Caesar civilized the nine peoples in Novempopulana, as it was first christened, the geographical boundaries of the place have constantly fluctuated, following out the rhythmic rise and fall of the great houses. Even its name has changed, from time to time first to Aquitania, then to Vasconia (Basqueland). Very roughly this figment comprises all the land which lies between the left bank of the Garonne, the Atlantic and the Pyrenees.

'It's a patchwork quilt of races and customs,' adds my friend, 'all of them extremely touchy and proud. The Béarnais, the Bigourdians, the Armagnacs, the Landais. . . . They each think they are the real Gascons.'

'This is all very well, Monsieur Prosper, but Gascony, if it exists at all, *what* is it? Where does one go to hear its heart beat?'

Prosper closes one eye and puts his head on one side. 'When I next go you shall come with me. You will be in good hands, travelling with a Knight of the Road.' He drinks a small toast to himself in red wine—a toast which includes all those members of his profession—and indeed manages to invest it with a distinct glamour for me. He is a commercial traveller in 'Savegoose' and Gascony is one of his assignments. As a matter of fact, I don't think that anywhere in the world you could find a body of men so generally cultivated and so wide-awake, as the commercial travellers of France. They may not be book-learned in the ordinary sense, but their native curiosity does duty for any education they may have missed, by keeping them on their toes intellectually.

[389]

It is not merely that they are adepts of the food and drink through which they must fight their way, but they are also very consciously a race of *amateurs* in the French sense of the word.

When finally we did set out on our journey the fact was brought home to me very vividly, for all the way along we kept passing Monsieur Prosper's professional acquaintances—other Knights of the Road —beating up or down the hills in their dusty station-wagons. A wave, a shout, and they vanished; but Monsieur Prosper would say: 'There goes Poincaré. He travels in silk. He's written a play which they are going to put on in Lyons.' Or else, 'Ah! that rogue Dupont! He's quite a painter. His last show in Toulouse was a great success.' And so on. Like migratory birds they hum about along the great Nationales to pollinate the retailers of France, if you like to think of it like that. The only real mystery to me is how they never seem to die of over-eating, for they have that highly developed nose for good fare which comes of a lifetime's experience. Perhaps they become stoic philosphers, though to judge by Monsieur Prosper, I should doubt it.

'Long periods at the wheel', explains my friend, 'turn one into a Reflective one. It is the ideal life for an artist. Ah! if only I had talent like Dupont, if I could write or paint, or even collect Roman coins like Dubarry. . . . Alas! I am simply one who lives the good life.' Can you be French and not be a natural Epicurean?

Yet, of course, even the good life has its penalties. Monsieur Prosper pushes his floppy beret back in order to scratch his forehead with his little fingernail. 'I overdo it,' he admits with a touch of sadness. 'I grossly over-eat. Indeed I suffer from a rare liver-condition which must sometimes give me the look of the geese whose Saviour I am. But what is to be done? I do not chase women, cannot stand the cinema. My vices are those of my profession. I read a good deal, and I eat more than I read.'

He sighs. 'Thrice I have been given up for lost and been given the Last Sacraments. Each time I have rallied. I have felt a sudden surge of Faith. I have sat up in bed and called for a bouillon made with a glass of white wine (if possible, Blanc de Blanc!). Miraculously my liver has responded. Within two days I was back on the road. But I admit the Gascony run is a taxing one. Yes, it taxes every nerve. Ah, wait till I take you—take you to the "real Gascony", for I and I alone know where that it.' With a spatulate finger he stabs the Nationale 117 and draws it along the borders of Spain, slowly moving northwards in a slow arc.

We were on our third glass of red wine, I remember, in a restaurant at Sète. He had just come down from Gascony after a successful goose-saving journey and would not be returning that way until the autumn, when he proposed to allow me to accompany him. 'The best time to see it,' he said, 'if the weather holds out. Ah Gascony!' holding his glass of wine up to study its brilliant garnet topaz colour.

'Two winds contend for the Gascon's soul,' he went on with a fine flourish of rhetoric, and in a tone which left me in some doubt as to whether he was quoting or improvising. 'The two winds they call Cers and Autan—both of them fully fledged devils. Yes, it's hard country. Cers is a bitch-wind which brings the cold as it comes rolling up from the Atlantic. Country people say it stirs the sap and quickens the fruit trees. How should I know? It brings the coastal fogs as well. But Autan is even worse—a real *casse-jambe*, a break-your-leg wind which nobody has a good word for. Oui, mon cher, Autan alanguit les sens, brise les nerfs. Combien de fillettes séduites qui, sans lui, n'eussent jamais fait le moindre manquement! (Yes, Autan softens up the senses, cracks the nerves. How many young girls have been seduced who, had it not been for him, would never have been guilty of the slightest lapse.)'

Prosper sighs heavily. 'Yes, Autan is a brute, and they treat him as such. The countryfolk call him *porc* and even *puto de Marseille*. So they fight it out all winter, these two winds, a long bitter battle which lasts until Easter. Ah! then comes the turn of the season, usually about Holy Week. For a few days you have the taste of snow mixed with the scent of the early flowers. A yellow rain falls. The spring begins. And Re Artus goes away—did you know, by the way, that faint folk-memories of King Arthur still remain in Gascony under that name? On windy nights they say that Re Artus is hunting among the clouds, driving them before him. It is a fitting memory to remain, for the Gascon soul is nourished in a warlike tradition, a tradition of chivalry.'

'You mean D'Artagnan, too?'

'Of course. And I will reveal his secret to you.'

And so the promise of this autumn journey was made though Monsieur Prosper left it so long that I wondered whether it would be wise to accompany him when at long last he reappeared. Even in the so-called radiant Midi of France late November is a questionable time at which to start a journey northward. In fact I felt somewhat disposed to chide him as he rolled up in his battered old Aronde, an ancient battle-wagon at least ten years old. But his smile disarmed me as he climbed out grunting to shake my hand, removing his beret first with the punctilio of a great Chevalier. He stilled my doubts by pointing to the distinctly grey sky overhead and saying: 'A little rain will warm things up for us; then we shall have blue weather for at least a week.' Reflecting that he had had years of experience in these matters I allowed myself to be disarmed and packed a suitcase which I flung into the back of the car—which was stacked with life-saving packets of 'Save-goose' and somewhat minatory posters.

I should explain that in goose-country, where the practice of force-feeding geese (*gavage*) is in operation, there are always a goodly number of casualties. Geese suffer from rare liver-conditions as much as the gourmets who finally eat them—that is the whole point, after all. Now the wonderful, the sovereign power of 'Savegoose' is that it helps the costive digestions of the geese, makes liver-trouble easier, and so helps to limit casualties in this lucrative trade. It may seem somewhat ironic that a man with a rare liver-condition should himself be chosen for the onerous task of peddling this nostrum, but then life is like that. I asked Monsieur Prosper whether, when he himself was *in extremis*, the idea had never come to him to try a teaspoonful of his own magical 'Save-goose'. 'Strange you should say that,' he said. 'Indeed it often has. But as the composition of the stuff is a trade secret that the makers won't reveal, I don't feel I should dare. Who knows—it may contain Cali-fornian syrup of figs—then where should I be? Or liquorice? I might blow myself up.'

The posters, however, with their wonderful pictures of extremely thoughtful looking glassy-eyed geese lying on their sides, or flapping their wings and glowing with health after a dose of 'Savegoose', were quite unequivocal. 'For every liver-condition,' they insisted. Prosper nodded and agreed. 'Surely,' I said, 'there is a fifty-fifty chance that it works on men, too? Think, you might have found the one specific for which all good gourmets are hunting. "Savegoose" might be the answer to adult prayers as well.'

Monsieur Prosper pursed his lips and considered the matter thought-fully, but he did not comment further. I think he was perhaps a little bit hurt that I should treat his healer's role with levity. 'It is certainly miraculous stuff,' he said after a long silence. 'You should see how the geese get sometimes.' He made an extraordinary face for a second to show me, and then switched it off like a light. 'But after a single dose. . . .' He made another equally extraordinary face—a face glowing with health, positively candent with joy of recovery. He practically flapped his wings.

At Montpellier we were hit by such a thunderspout and such a torrential shower, that my heart sank. 'Here goes Gascony,' I thought. We should spend our time dragging the car out of mud, or skidding along iced-up roads like a pebble on the surface of a pond. Or else we would be marooned for three days out of reach of help and have to exist on this blasted 'Savegoose' in the back of the car. Our bodies would be found later with faces contorted by the last dreadful spasms and our livers swollen up like footballs. (Would they stuff them and mount them on velvet and put them in the Musée de l'Homme as a warning to all men?) But no. Monsieur Prosper was not downcast, on the contrary he seemed elated. 'Just as I said,' he cried. 'One touch of the wind and the sky will be clear as a bell.'

And to my annoyed amazement so it proved; by the time we reached the borders of Roussillon the sun was out, the sky had been peeled back to blue, and a wind like a hacksaw was tearing at the long undulating plains. The wind! I have known many unpleasant winds—there is one in each country usually which has a dreadful effect upon one: Italian sirocco, or the winter 'koshava' in Belgrade which turns the milk; but the mistral is a match for any of them. It sends temperatures toppling below zero in a matter of hours. The sky may be blue but . . . one's extremities become polar. As Monsieur Prosper explained when I lay exhausted on a hotel-bed in Narbonne protesting that I would not live to see Gascony, 'You should not eat so heavily when there is a mistral because all the blood is drawn away to the stomach by the digestion and you risk getting frostbite.'

But the wind explains at least two serious lapses of a tourist kind on my part, for instead of lingering in Pézenas, Bouzigues and Béziers, as I had intended to do, we made Narbonne in one jump like a scalded cat, the old car humming and trembling with fatigue in every shock absorber. I had particularly wanted to taste the little sweet mutton pies of Pézenas which are its 'specialty', partly for gastronomic but also for patriotic reasons, for they are of Anglo-Indian provenance. No less a mogul than Clive of India, who once spent a long holiday in Pézenas, attended by a retinue of colourful Indians, is the grandfather of the Pézenas pie. His Indian cooks imported it, and the local inhabitants adopted it. But Pézenas was dancing with dust devils and autumn leaves and when I opened the window to look at it the force of the wind blew Monsieur Prosper's beret into the back of the car.

I fared no better at Bouzigues with its famous lagoon full of oyster-beds where, in good weather, one can dangle one's feet in the water and eat oysters to one's heart's content. The water was slashed and gouged by this mistral with such ferocity that I feared for the morals of the oysters slumbering in its depths. We whirled into Narbonne only just under control. The wind had invaded the town sweeping showers of brown autumn leaves before it. They rose in clouds, blinding us.

We pulled in and found lodgings for the night at the little Lion d'Or; one of the really important factors of travel with a Knight of the Road is that they always lodge very modestly, but they always know where to find a small hotel with first-class food. The Lion d'Or, for all its smallness, was comfortable, wonderfully heated and spotlessly clean. The little dining-room which was also a public restaurant and bar was staffed by people who knew their jobs. The food was excellent.

This, by the way, is not always the case in the Midi of France. Contemptuous northerners will always tell you that *cuisine* in the true sense stops short at Valence, and that the *gens du Midi* eat primitively. The truth of the matter is that they eat Mediterranean fashion, and have fewer elaborate dishes; but those few are first class. So good, in fact, that after dinner I felt simply dreadful; it seemed clear to me that I was either developing polio or else a cerebral meningitis. Refusing an offer to play cards with Monsieur Prosper, I tottered to my bed and spent a very bad night listening to the screech of the wind outside the windows.

In the morning I felt too ill to get up and confessed to Monsieur Prosper that this was the case. He shook his head impatiently. 'It is only the mistral,' he said. I knew it was . . . and had I been at home I would have fought it off with a glass of *vieux marc*. My feet were cold, my nose blue, my courage at low ebb, my pulse slow, my stomach in disarray. No, I would never make Gascony. Monsieur Prosper stared at me thoughtfully for a second and then said, 'I will have you on your feet in ten minutes'.

Retiring to the bar he returned with a glass and a long green bottle. 'Drink this,' he said. I drained the colourless liquid obediently and immediately began to struggle for air, reaching out blindly before me with one hand and clutching my throat with the other. The stuff ran through me with the power and fury of a forest fire in brushwood.

'What is it?' I gasped as soon as I could get my breath.

Then Monsieur Prosper uttered the magic name of this life-giving draught—a word which is now burned into my memory and will probably be inscribed on my tombstone. 'It is simply Arquebuse,' he said gently, almost modestly.

'This is the most terrific firewater in the world,' I said reaching for the bottle; but only to examine the label for another glass of the stuff would have blown me out like a candle. 'Arquebuse' it was called all right, and the label showed it to be a 50 degree drink; but its mysterious title and descriptive matter were almost as intriguing as its obvious powers to heal every ill of the flesh. This was what Ponce de León hunted for—the Elixir of Eternal Youth! I knew that I should never suffer from a day's illness from now on. Monsieur Prosper beamed. 'I told you so,' he said. 'It is purely medicinal, this stuff. It is for those whose digestions are seriously disordered by too much food and drink.' The remorselessness of French logic, the subtle twinings of the Cartesian mind! So one took a 50 degree shot of this Lion's milk in order to cure the effects of overdoing things with 12 degree wines or a 40 degree Pernod! What could be simpler? Who but the French could have thought it up? I leaped out of bed like a tiger, and while dressing examined the holy bottle (was *this* what Rabelais really meant?) with a clearer eye.

I pass on my information to all travellers in mistral country. Arquebuse for example is not described as a drink at all but as 'Eau vulnéraire'. It is made by the good fathers of St. Genis Laval, and is composed of the purest alcohol into which they insinuate a secret mixture of carefully gathered herbs and simples which they macerate. The label is somewhat conservative. Arquebuse, it says, derives its name from a mixture which was originally invented to cure the terrible wounds made by the weapon of this name after it was invented in Europe. It does not explain how the change from external dressing to internal cure came about, and it would be idle to quibble.

Clearly one day a thirsty archer who was having his wounds dressed took a swig from the bottle while the doctor's back was turned. So magical was the effect that from then on the thing has been issued to the general public as a sort of supernatural stand-by in times of stress. And yet, on the bottle you will find the good monks insisting drily that it is 'neither a liqueur, nor any kind of alcoholic drink, nor is it really a medicament of any kind—it can most accurately be described as A VULNERARY.' A magnificent word, and a marvellous example of diplomatic exactitude. Besides, having once tasted it, I was in no mood for dialectical quibbles. I did not want those quiet monks to give over their steady, subtle maceration of herbs in order to argue with me. Nor did I want production of this marvellous tissue—enlivening liquid to fall off because of a few barren arguments about the nature of medieval archery. No. Monsieur Prosper was delighted by my enthusiasm for his little vulnerary which clearly was one of the trade secrets of the Knights of the Road. I was dressed in a flash and ready for anything; my soul wore boots and spurs. Taking up the magic bottle I slipped it into my haversack. As we swept out of Narbonne the wind howled no less wildly but now I did not care; indeed I opened the window and laughed tauntingly at it. I know that Arquebuse would see me through.

Desolate salt pans, the reeds stiff with rime, and a wind-shocked hinterland leading gradually away down to the Spanish border, with Perpignan as our last point of reference before we picked up N.117. And the red earth of Roussillon—the colour of topaz, of ox-blood, of terra-cotta, of raw beef, of beetroot according to the slant of the sun. How desolate the landscape becomes and how beautiful in tone and rhythm. It is the first great orchestration of Spain, of course, for Catalonia is really Spain—and Spain is simply red ground, a blood-soaked and sun-soaked emptiness. Somewhere here, I recollected, disappeared from living memory France's great gallows' bird of a poet Villon. The dust devils whirled and snarled across the fields. Little dusty forts crowned the shallow valleys. The country is baked and cracked like terra-cotta It conveys the intensely archaic feeling of the Spanish temper with all its colours—its nobilities and absurdities and prides; its contempt for the easy life; its Mithraic pulse. Yes, for the sun here goes down like a stricken bull.

We had now turned our backs on the sea and were buzzing northwards towards the foothills, forcing a passage in the eye of the wind.

The Catalonian landscape did not last long. Yet its sunburnt rock and dusty chalk undulations were an admirable preparation for what was to come, making the change so surprising. Estagel, Latour-de-France, Axat rolled away under our wheels, and then quite suddenly the road penetrates the long narrow throat of the Aude and begins to climb and dip along narrow ravines whose banks are clothed with rich fern and spruce; ravines so narrow that they must see the sun only for a few hours every day. Safely cradled in its stony bed the Aude flows like an arrow. There are nightingales singing and the splash of trout. Taking these long sinuous curves which follow the meandering of the river we came upon little groups of attentive trout-fishers like statuary, intent on the chase. The wind had gone. Brilliant sunlight poured down. The sky was blue—not, to be sure, the brilliant Attic blue of Provence or Languedoc but the deeper, more violet blue which you find over the verdant inland places. After the harshness and poverty of the Catalan plain the change was astonishing. As we left the river and grumbled up the hills towards Quillan everything told of richness—rich mud, rich marls, verdant hillsides with thick grass.

Monsieur Prosper pointed out the characteristics of the place with a kindly sparkle of good humour. 'Geese, you see.' The farmhouses were gabled and built with deep lofts for winter fodder. For the first time we saw the ox cart drawn by these characteristic curly horned oxen. We saw too everywhere great bins of corn cobs gleaming butter yellow in the sunlight. 'That is for the geese and fowls,' said Monsieur Prosper, adding that as far as he could tell the poultry of this region was far richer and far more succulent than the more famous products of Bresse. He promised me a chance to judge for myself. And he also discoursed knowledgeably on other matters, such as *le Vert Galant*, who left behind him a tradition for the manufacture of Gascons which is alive to this day among the peasants. The secret is this: if you have a male child rub his tongue with garlic and give him a sip of the fine wine of Jurançon. This cannot fail to make him both witty and wise. To illustrate the sort of wit (*narquois* is a completely untranslatable word) Monsieur Prosper gave me an example. The Gascon La Hire, the companion of Joan of Arc, patented the following prayer to God to be used in time of peril. 'O God,' he prayed. 'In this hour of peril try and act towards La Hire as La Hire would act towards you, if he were God and you were La Hire.' Subtle and appealing logic!

And while we were talking he suddenly put out his hand dramatically and shouted 'Look.' We had climbed fairly high now and with
dramatic suddenness the Pyrenees had come swimming up on our left,
their flashing snow caps ranged like fangs across the horizon, leading
away in diminishing graduation towards the Pic du Midi. They were
all the more theatrical in their beauty by being cut off from us by a
violet-black line of foothills which framed them as a proscenium frames
a stage. The roads grew straighter now; we had passed the shallow
range of hills where Quillan and Foix stand, tucked like an envelope,
into the side of the hills.

We lodged that night at St. Girons at another excellent small hotel
where Monsieur Prosper began to take an interest in the bill of fare in
order not to spare me any of the local specialties. I must say our dinner
would have made a goose feel faint, but as the only other diners were
a couple of Dominicans who were eating even more heartily I somehow
felt that we would be absolved. After all, food is a serious matter in
France. This, then, is what Monsieur Prosper urged upon me. A *pâté
de foie gras maison*, to begin with. (This should normally be spurned by
the discriminating unless one is in poultry-country where no self-
respecting cook would serve *tinned* foie gras.) On this occasion Monsieur Prosper, whom I trusted implicitly, ordered it for both of us
without consulting me. God bless him—it was the best I have ever
eaten. As we were still under the spell of that magical, tumbling trout
river, the Aude, we also agreed upon a fish course that was quite perfect: fat white trout in a *sauce meunière* enhanced by the addition of a
little goose-fat to the sweet butter.

Monsieur Prosper had frowned over the wine list and had then said
firmly to the pretty waitress: 'A Blanc de Blanc to accompany the *pâté*
and the fish, and then a Grenache . . . let me see . . . yes, a Paziols.'
I protested vigorously: 'Grenache is a sweet wine, Monsieur Prosper—
I am sorry but I will not drink a sweet wine with a meal!' He crowed
with joy at my mutinous behaviour, and said, 'You will see.' And, of
course, he was right—the Grenache was not a sweet one, but a marvellous dry and fruity wine, and the second bottle was ordered within
minutes. It brought out the best in my young roasted pigeon on
toast—the tender meat of which bore witness to the excellence of a
sweetcorn diet. Monsieur Prosper chose preserved goose (clearly an
obsessive choice) and pressed me to taste it: it was delicious, but

terribly rich! The dessert was a specialty of the house for which we had to wait a little and which was well worth waiting for: an Armagnac soufflé which made Monsieur Prosper wink at me and say: 'It is better than a *pouding*, *hein*?'

After dinner, much enlivened by a glass of Armagnac and a cigar, my friend fell in with two other Knights of the Road, and, leaving me to brood upon life for a while, enjoyed the mild dissipation of a game of pontoon which seemed to lead to a good deal of cheating and endless argument. So to bed.

Next morning dawned fine and cloudless and we were early in the saddle, and eager to attack some of the specialties of Tarbes, of which I had heard a good deal. The white peaks kept us company, bobbing along the skyline as we rolled along. There was the hint of ice in the air, but the sky was blue and serene. The landscape was studded with magnificent trees and green curves of downland criss-crossed with rivers; one might have thought one was on the Loire had it not been for those mountain tops glittering like snowdrops on our left. 'First,' said Monsieur Prosper, 'first I shall disappoint and disgust you by taking you *into* Tarbes, then I will give you an aesthetic thrill by looking back on it.' This sounded somewhat cryptic, and I only understood what he meant when we reached the town—which by the way is a perfectly ordinary French provincial town.

It is not Tarbes itself that is unduly depressing, it is the almost permanent mist which enshrouds it. It is set in a deep depression, surrounded by hills and carved out by rivers. And while it is famous for food and drink it has the somewhat moist and depressing atmosphere of Lyons. We pottered about in it for half an hour while Monsieur Prosper made a phone call, and then set off westward again. Eignt kilos outside Tarbes the road starts to climb into the sky. On the very top of this hill lies the little inn much beloved by all true Knights of the Road which has been most appropriately christened the Beau Site. The view is simply magnificent, and here at least Monsieur Prosper's boast about an aesthetic thrill was justified, for the whole valley swam below us in a cinnamon-coloured mist which shifted and slid about in parcels and blocks. Tarbes itself looked most beautiful as it emerged and receded into definition, printing now a cathedral spire or an office block on the mist, and then letting them dissolve again. Here and there a river bed sucked at the corners of the cloud, engulfed suddenly (like suds down a sink) a whole line of metal pylons stuck like ninepins in the ground, or perhaps a long diagonal line of poplars. Suddenly an airfield would emerge and release a couple of silver planes, only to blow itself out again. Apparently the valley of Tarbes is always thus, mist enshrouded. Beyond looms the great white snag of the Pic du Midi, the highest of the chain, with its tiny white observatory nudging the clouds.

It was splendid to sit in full sunlight on the terrace of the Beau Site and watch this ever changing spectacle. As for the food, Monsieur Prosper paid close attention to it, muttering that we had a long march ahead of us and should stoke the fires while we could. It was in the course of this memorable meal too that he first revealed to me the boundaries of his Gascony—the only true one. Making his fingers into compasses he laid one upon the town of Auch and turned it through an arc which roughly demarcated the Department of Gers. 'This,' he said (not without a glance over his shoulder lest some benighted Bigourdian or Landais should overhear him), 'This is it.'

'But Auch is the ancient capital of Gascony.'

'It still is for me.'

'Then Gascony is slightly larger than Armagnac.'

In his opinion the area was comfortable, bounded by the great main roads which set out from Toulouse, one running northward to Agen, the other traversing the southern end through Tarbes to Dax. 'It is definitively the true Gascony—only don't say it too loud in the taverns. I don't want to prejudice my trade, you see.'

'I see.'

I began now to understand more clearly. We continued along the main road as far as Pau with its air of shabby opulent desuetude, its orange trees, and its permanent hotel population of old folk sitting out the sunlight on sunny terraces surrounded by potted palms, absorbed in ancient newspapers or games of rummy and patience. Like all such resorts it was both depressing and faintly romantic with its freight of vanished memories; an elephant's graveyard for the Royal House of the Old Europe. It is now what Baden-Baden must have been in the days of Edward VII. But here at long last we crossed into the imaginary Gascony of Monsieur Prosper's election, for leaving the main road we chose a network of small but excellent departmental tracks leading us back towards Auch by Morlaas and Vic le Bigorre. It was bosomy rolling country, and its steep wooded roads skimmed up and down the

hills with the trajectory of swallows. Once more the rich farms with
their deeply staggered roofs, their deep granaries: and gigantic cani-
sters of corn-cobs lying stacked up as poultry feed; huge slow-moving
cattle and oxen; and the unfamiliar wayside crosses which somehow
reminded one of Austria. And everywhere the somnolent lines of
turkeys and geese. It gives a great sense of peaceful loneliness, perhaps
because it is not densely populated. The farms are spacious and sparsely
distributed. You could travel for half a day and hardly encounter a
soul. Yet the very sense of solitude was itself welcoming.

Towards evening—we were heading for Mirande la Jolie—Monsieur
Prosper revealed to me gravely the secret of D'Artagnan. 'They say',
he said, 'that he was born at the Château de Castelmaure, which we
will visit. But in my opinion Dumas was in error. I will show you his
native village.' And sure enough up popped a road sign saying
'Artagnan', and with a chuckle Monsieur Prosper turned the car down
a network of country lanes to reach it. It is so small that it is not marked
on any of the ordinary motoring maps. It is really a hamlet rather than
a village—a cluster of peaceful farmhouses set in rolling country. We
reverently switched off the engine and let the quiet sounds of the
countryside invade our senses—the lowing of cattle, and the thin high
cry of a girl driving turkeys across a field. A man in waders squelched
across a muddy field practically pushing a cow before him. Its hooves
sank glibly into the deep black mulch of the farmyard. 'This is where
he was born,' said Monsieur Prosper firmly, with an air of academic
precision. 'I am sure of it.' By now both of us had forgotten that
D'Artagnan was a creature of fiction; he was extremely real, the patron
saint of Gascony. I half resolved to do a long and contentious literary
paper about this discovery of Monsieur Prosper's.

It was dusk before we rolled into Mirande la Jolie, which lived up
to its name, despite its rather straggly unwashed air, and its dilapidated streets; but this was to be our headquarters for ten days or so while
my companion worked the rich goose-country round about. We
celebrated our arrival that evening with a dinner made up of the
famous local delicacies and topped off with a smoky Armagnac. Quite
overcome by the sensation of having completed his journey and given
me the promised introduction to this magical place, Monsieur Prosper
actually broke into song, a song which paid tribute to it all. As far as I
remember, it went like this:

Dans les chênes des cours, lorsque tombait la nuit,
Des dindons imposants semblaient d'énormes fruits.
La fermière gorgeait les canards et les oies,
Afin d'en obtenir les plus onctueux foies.

It was, so to speak, the overture to the Gascon symphony—a symphony of food and wine which has almost blurred all perspectives.

For ten days we flitted about the region, as lightheartedly as fire-flies. Monsieur Prosper did his medicine-man act as swiftly and deftly as only a Frenchman could, and wherever it was unduly prolonged he would set me down at some antiquity to wait for him, or simply on a terrace over a river with a glass of some irreproachable wine before me. One could have made a rosary from the names of the villages alone— Bassoues, Peyrusse, Vicnau, Miélan, Masseube, Plaisance, Riscle, Gouts. Their names echo in memory like the motifs of a fugue. And of course whenever the flesh failed me under those cargoes of good food and wine I resorted to the one specific for all human ills—the good Arquebuse.

Nevertheless, Monsieur Prosper was right, it was distinctly taxing in the matter of diet. It could not be prolonged indefinitely. I began to feel I was walking like a pouter-pigeon. And on the tenth day I saw the high towers and walls of Auch rise up before us with a certain sense of relief. Monsieur Prosper was a master of the appropriate effect and it was in Auch that we austerely studied a Velazquez and went to Mass in the famous cathedral before seeking out a suitable lodging in the town in which to spend our last Gascon night—for tomorrow we were to head south once more, back to the frugal and dusty borders of Languedoc.

Nevertheless, as one last concession to Monsieur Prosper's expertise I faced up to one farewell meal chosen by my friend with all the old care and thoughtfulness.

'This time', he said, 'no fish. Plus ça change,' (and he giggled) 'et moins c'est la même chose.' He ordered snails, and I assured him I was an expert on them, having tasted them in every snail-proud region of France and even in Switzerland. 'Gascon snails will add to your collection,' he said serenely. They did indeed, and to my waistline, and I reflected that they were probably fed Armagnac and foie gras for months before cooking. Monsieur Prosper was sorry we should not have time to savour (he underlined the word audibly: *déguster*) a Castelnaudary *cassoulet*—as unique, he said, as the Pyramids—but instead we should have (I quailed at the words) goose-liver and raisins. But the fresh, whole, parboiled liver, served in a simple sauce of its own juice, thickened with maize-flour and bubbling raisins from the local vines, was a pure enchantment which I later exorcized with the help of the good monks of St. Genis.

Our conversation was slow and hushed as was proper in a temple of gastronomy, but Monsieur Prosper's gallic lightning flashed now and again, as when I enquired about the Jurançon we were drinking. 'You appreciate it? Everyone from the *Vert Galant* to Brillat-Savarin has extolled its charms. *And it does not affect the liver.*'

Seeing the doubt in my eyes he went on. 'As a Knight of the Road, and with my peculiar complaint, I *know*.' He ordered another bottle, and then said: 'My dear friend, companion of the table and of the road, I am only a Gascon by adoption, by love so to speak; but here, in this part of France, grow the largest grapes, the largest goose-livers, the largest appetites, and . . . the largest lies! Truth is so splendid in Gascony that one simply has to improve on it. . . .'

It is an appropriate time and place to say farewell to him, sitting there with his spectacles on the end of his nose, his napkin tucked joyously into his waistcoat, his sharp birdlike eye quizzically adjusted to a bill of fare with the intensity of an explorer studying a map.

Solange

Written in Paris about 1938, lengthened by about half and retouched 1967. Not previously published.

I

Solange Bequille b. 1915 supposedly
Far from Paris towards April sometime,
Familiar of the familiar XIV arrondissement

   four steps up
   four steps down
   two three four *five*
   where the sewers discharge
   by the turret of an urinal
   six seven eight
   steel ducts voiding
   in shade and out of the wind . . .

Relatively impossible despite so much practice
To word-parody the tantamount step, but easier
Copy for the lens a powder-blue raincoat, beret,
Cicada brooch, belted and bolted waist of wasp,
Dumb insolent regimental shoes, sheeny rings,
The whole of it amberstuck through twenty winters,
Carried round the globe in damp suitcases,
Some pedlar's pack of visionary ware like
Her rings of a vulgar water reflecting

   black testicles of buoys
   tugging at the Seine
   lovers in leaden coffins
   pelting the dead with crusts
   the prohibitions of loneliness
   being twenty-two with a war

[404]

hanging over them, its belly hard,
noting the orgasm of Hegel
defining all death as 'the
collapse into immediacy'.
Ah, dangerous salients of youth,
loving in a crucial month.

II

Over the bridges the meandering scholars
Deambulating flowed over the Pons Asinorum
Of the five arts between the capable white
Wide-flowing thighs of their seventh muse,
A sharpshooter by a steel turret
Waiting to smelt down whole faculties,
Captives of youthful salt with their elaborate tensions,
They passed and passed but always hesitated,
Leaving their satchels when they could not pay,
The score was kept on a matchboard wall.
A hundred a quick one, five the whole night,
Whole doctorates granted in prime embraces.
The arts of the capital being matured and focused.
Five for the collective wisdom of this great city!

> baisers O noirs essaims
> desires grown fair of dark
> the cross-roads of smiling eyes
> complexities of season, spring
> or winter's black water
> bridges of funereal soot
> working with pink tongue or tooth
> towards some mystical emphasis,
> a life without sanctions
> in the forever, so long ago,
> so far away from all this
> contemporary whimperdom
> > Solange
> sole angel of the seekers,
> their prop medal and recourse
> faces crisper than oak-leaves
> your burial service covered all
> the coward and the brave
> the perfectly solid fact as
> symbol of humanity's education
> less a woman with legs than
> something, say that oven into which

SOLANGE

Descartes locked himself in order
to enunciate the first principle
of his system; the oven Planck
consulted after all the
spectroscope's thrilling finery
to deduce the notion of quanta.
always the same oven, never any bread,
the XXth century loaf is an equation
                Solange
be like mirrors accumulating nothing.

III

The change from C major to A flat
Is always associated with summary thefts,
Certain women powdered by suns,
Street-lamps' fresh breath in cradles,
As simply as birds reacting to rain
We recover small fragments of the unknowable
To render back to nature her darkest intents
In allegorical bandages of old hotels
Receiving into their no-womb the anti-heroes,
Tang of the metro and rotting dustbins
Needles seeking the iron vein
Astrology's damp syringe

       a woman of good intent
       distributing the river winds,
       drawing with scarlet fingernail
       on foggy panes high above Paris,
       one glassed-in balcony
       with tubs for plants' green hives
       so apt for tall trees' dews
       days robbed and nights replaced
       whatever the single vision traced
       four steps up
       four steps down
       wherever the emphasis was placed
       whoever the woman's image finds
       dyed into living minds

By the dead butts of infernal cinemas
Or at the Medrano lulled by some old
Circus animal's tarnished roars,
See the heads discharged by guns in baskets falling
Smelling of new bread or blood. The muscles
Now hanging in Museums, the thoracic cage shaken
By typical sobs, the eyes of congers' spawn,
Then the plumage of soft shrieks in dark streets,
The running feet, silence, and something lying
In Paris on such April nights when stars
Crunch underfoot the Luxembourg's cool gravels,
Night poised like a lion's paw
Where her prowl crosses some angle of the abstract town.

        four steps up
        four steps down
        where the sewers discharge
        by the urinal's turret
        stairs too narrow for the coffin,
        minds too narrow for recognitions,
        hearts too severe for introspection,
        different categories of the same
        insolent vision marrying
        four steps up
        confederates of the darkness
        soon they must all die or
        go away, soon you will be left
        alone, writing wholly for yourself,
        struggling with the idea of a city
        a whore of the city's inward meaning,
        animal intents all bruising
        the wingpoint of other myths
        outmoded or outvoted gods
        the muffled censors of the time
        ripening in the latest ages
        beyond the scope of liveried men
        past the intentions of the wise
        towards a death promoted by the sages.

IV

Even then was he somehow able to undress his dolls' thoughts to sleep beside the sleeper, lay figures of the dreams which uncoiled among the mnemonic centres of the mind which thinks without knowing that it thinks, slips, punctures process with ideas. Faut-il enfin dépasser le point de tangence qui sépare l'art et la science, tout en les traitant comme les religions primitives en faillite? Oui mais comment? Even then, even then; but his snores might not awake the tiny amorous snores as of the congress of guinea-pigs in vivisectionists' cages, unaware of being watched, syringe in hand. Et le chaos même, dandy ou nègre? Faut-il éprouver la plénitude charnelle d'un acte spontané? In the cheap edition of 'Causality' she had given Leibniz a moustache and printed a lipstick kiss to hide the crucial figure, adding in the margin the proverbial merde. If only she could have delivered him from the vices of introspection, the verses in p'tit nègre, the torn paper tablecloths with their thorny sketches; but alas vers libre is like le ver solitaire. The head shows and the atlas of the stare; it can be broken off by the forceps, but there will always be more packed in the gut. Beware.

the communes raise their walls
around the dreamer's bed,
cold crusts of cults devoured
the science-mocking magics spread
like viruses distributed
by the redeemers' dreams
on altars sourly smoke
the witnesses disperse
among the smoke of thought
to share the ignoble joke
some medieval urinals
mingle the proffered wine
to pour from snouts of stone
the griffins far below
on the river's quays
famous star-waterways incline
turn water into wine,
the simple torturers go
when night undresses all the trees
unsleeping gargoyles tell you so.

V

Born of torpid country-folk versed in cumbrous ways and too hapha-
zard to chime with this spawn of factories with anvils and poisonous
oxygen, this decomposing fabric of stone, the sepia cards of churches
begging for disablement pensions; but kindly stubborn intractable
stock, she imported into the deadly estate of the town frail rural vir-
tues, rotted in a primeval humus. Gone this Solange or that, but the
mould remained unbroken revolving through worlds of dissimulation,
spheres, hatcheries of unique sensation, seen through the pinshead of a
tiny mind. Turning slightly towards the sun as winter flowers may do,
the bonfires and speeches and the eternal inquests within the frontiers
of the self, still the fated questions yawned as they do for all of us. And
what then of Pascal, the man she loved: sullen, morose and leaden when
not in the air flying from ring to ring with an acrobat's fury, the
webbed feet, sympelmous toes, O rabid specialist in a bird's beauty.
They exchanged wordless days, and doses, the sempiternal clap. In full
flight over the city he took her like a ring, swung over the edge of the
abyss. I studied their famous loves to reimburse myself. Once I saw the
expression on his face which must have settled her fate—in mid-air
swinging in an orgasm of fear and stress, but shriven too; this look had
impaled her mind. Then he went, without saying goodbye, perhaps on
tour, but never to return I believe; perhaps much later to dangle from
some whore's rafter or at the end of a silken parachute illustrating
some mysterious law. But his undertow haunted her body for a season,
celebrated in absinthe and funereal silences; many profited from this experience, many coupled through her with the wiry loins and loafing smile.

> statues on cubes of frost
> equestrian pigments of the snow
> somewhere the carrefour was crossed
> munching footsteps trail and slow
> stealthy gravels underfoot
> sectioned by the tawny bars
> street lamps fiction up the dusk
> world unending of past wars
> when will the exemplars come
> four steps up
> four steps down
> where the sewers discharge
> by the urinal's turret.

VI

The dreams of Solange confused no issues, solved no problems, for on the auto-screen among our faces appeared always and most often others like Papillon the tramp, a childhood scarecrow built of thorns. He turned the passive albums of her sleep with long fingers, one of them a steel hook. Papillon represented a confederacy of buried impulses which could resurrect among the tangled sheet, a world of obscure resentments, fine and brutal as lace, the wedding-lake lying under its elaborate pastry. His ancient visions sited in that crocodile-mask fired her. And such dreams as he recounted revived among her own—Paris as some huge penis sliced up and served around a whole restaurant by masked waiters. And the lovers murmuring 'I love you so much I could eat you'. She takes up knife and fork and begins to eat. The screams might awake her, bathed in sweat, to hear the real face of Marc the underwriter saying something like: 'All our ills come from incautious dreaming.' There were so many people in the world, how to count them all? Perhaps causality was a way of uniting god with laughter? Solange avec son œil luisant et avide, holding a handbag full of unposted cards.

Add to the faces the Japanese student whose halting English was full of felicities only one could notice; as when 'Lord Byron committed incense with his sister, and afterwards took refuse in the church'. He too for a season cast a spell. Then one day he recited a poem which met with her disfavour.

> She was eighteen but already god-avowed,
> She sought out the old philosopher
> Expressly to couple with him, so to be
> Bathed in the spray of his sperm
> The pheuma of his inner idea.
> Pleasure and instruction were hers,
> She corrected her course by his visions.
> But of all this a child was born,
> But in him, not in her, as a poem
> With as many legs as a spider
> In a web the size of a world.

Then Deutre, the latest of our company
Who believed all knowledge to be founded
Deep in the orgasm, rising into emphasis
As individual consciousness, the know-thyself,
Bit by bit, with checks and halts, but always
By successive amnesias dragged into conception,
A school of penuma for the inward eye
Reflecting rays which pass in deliberate tangence
To the ordinary waking sense, focuses the heart.
Patiently must Solange pan for male gold
White legs spread like geometer's compasses
Over her native city. The milk-teeth fall at last.
Gradually the fangs develop, breathing changes,
And out of the tapestry of monkey grimaces
Born of no diagrams no act of will
But simple subservience to a natural law, He comes,
He emerges, He is there. Who? I do not know.
Deutre presumably in the guise of Rilke's angel
Or Balzac's double mirrored androgyne.
Deutre makes up his lips at dusk,
His sputumn is tinged with venous blood.
Nevertheless a purity of intent is established
Simple as on its axis spins an earth.
It was his pleasure to recite
With an emphasis worthy of the Vedas
Passages from the Analysis Situs: as

> la géometrie à n dimensions
> a un objet réel, personne n'en
> doute aujourd'hui. Les Etres
> de l'hyperespace sont susceptibles
> de définitions précises comme ceux
> de l'espace ordinaire, et si nous
> ne pouvons les répresenter nous
> pouvons les concevoir et les étudier.

The third eye belongs to spatial consciousness
He seems to say; there is a way of growing.
It was he who persuaded me at Christmas to go away.
Far southwards to submit myself to other towns

To landscapes more infernal and less purifying.
He persuaded Solange to lend me the money and she
Was glad to repay what the acrobat had spent,
But she saw no point in it, 'Who can live outside
Paris, among barbarians, and to what end?
Besides all these places are full of bugs
And you can see them on the cinema without moving
For just a few francs, within reach of a café.
But if go you must I will see you off.'

Remoter than Aldebaran, Deutre smiled.
Only many years later was I able
To repay him with such words as:
'Throughout the living world as we know it
The genetic code is based on four letters,
The Pythagorean Quarternary, as you might say.'
He did not even smile, for he was dying.
Man's achievement of a bipedal gait has freed
His hands for tools, weapons and the embrace.

                         the days will be lengthening
                         into centuries, Solange
                         and neither witness will be there,
                         seek no comparisons among
                         dolls' houses of the rational mind
                         coevals don't compare
                         a gesture broken off by dusk
                         heartless as boredom is or hope
                         blood seeks the soil it has to soak
                         in the fulfilment of a scope
                         fibres of consciousness will grow
                         lavish as any coffin load
                         and every touching entity
                         the puritan grave will swallow up
                         the silences will atrophy.
So we came, riding through the soft lithograph
Of Paris in the rain, the spires
Empting their light, the mercury falling,
Streets draining into the sewers,

The yokel clockface of the Gare de Lyon
On a warehouse wall the word 'Imputrescible'
Then slowly night: but suddenly
The station was full of special trains,
Long hospital trains with red crosses
Drawn blinds, uniformed nurses, doctors.
Dimly as fish in tanks moved pyjama-clad figures
Severed from the world, one would have said
Fresh from catastrophe, a great battlefield.
'O well the war has come' she said with resignation.
But it was only the annual pilgrimage to Lourdes,
The crippled the lame the insane the halt
All heading southwards towards the hopeless miracle.
Each one felt himself the outside chance,
Thousands of sick outsiders.
A barrel organ played a rotting waltz.
The Government was determined to root out gambling.
My path was not this one; but it equally needed
A sense of goodbye. Firm handclasp of hard little paw,
The clasp of faithful business associates, and
'When you come back, you know where to find me.'

> four steps up
> four steps down
> the station ramp eludes
> the mangy town
> the temporary visa
> with the scarlet stamp
> flowers of soda
> shower the quays
> engines piss hot spume
> giants in labour
> drip and sweat like these
> slam the carriage door
> only this and nothing more.

I write these lines towards dusk
On the other side of the world,
A country with stranger inhabitants,

Chestnut candles, fevers, and white water.
Such small perplexities as vex the mind,
Solange, became for writers precious to growth,
But the fluttering sails disarm them,
Wet petals sticking to a sky born nude.
The magnitudes, insights, fears and proofs
Were your unconscious gift. They still weigh
With the weight of Paris forever hanging
White throat wearing icy gems,
A parody of stars as yet undiscovered.
Here they tell me I have come to terms.
But supposing I had chosen to march on you
Instead of on such a star—what then?
Instead of this incubus of infinite duration,
I mean to say, whose single glance
Brings loving to its knees?
Yes, wherever the ant-hills empty
Swarm the fecund associations, crossing
And recrossing the sky-pathways of sleep.
We labour only to be relatively
Sincere as ants perhaps are sincere.
Yet always the absolute vision must keep
The healthy lodestar of its stake in love.
You'll see somewhere always the crystal body
Transparent, held high against the light
Blaze like a diamond in the deep.
How can a love of life be ever indiscreet
For even in that far dispersing city today
Ants must turn over in their sleep.

Down the Styx

Published in Two Cities. *Paris. Spring 1961.*
Privately printed in an edition of 250 copies, with a translation into French by
F.-J. Temple. Montpellier. 1964.

Dear Auntie Prudence,

I am writing to reassure you about the journey. There is no cause
for alarm. It is very simply done and many facilities are available. If you
were one of the quick while living everything will be all right, as in the
case of Uncle Sam. They will bring you down to the water's edge with
the obol sewed into your mouth for safety, and leave you alone to wait
for Charon. There will be no sign of the black barge as yet, but do not
get impatient. Realize that there are not many services per day because the toll is not high enough for the old man to make a decent
turnover. Spend the time in rearranging your emotional luggage and
drawing on your long white gloves.

You are confronted, then, with what appears to be simply an enormous cave—until you notice that the floor is a floor of water. Notice
how slowly it moves; a heavy black thrust of water, glacier-slow,
protruding from the darkness like a naked limb. The interior appears
fathomless, mesmeric, labyrinthine. Make the ritual offering of rice
and, as if by magic, the enigmatic boat appears from the depths. Step
into it firmly, holding the cherry-wood crucifix. There is no cause for
alarm. Do not address the figure at the helm. Charon is a singular old
fellow to be sure, but his voice is unpleasant: the voice of a gnat. To
watch him open his mouth is like watching a prehistoric sandwich
being prized open; his rimless gums are laid in an appetizing manner,
like layers of crab or prawn between two lids of lip. Occupy yourself
with memories of Bournemouth, and prepare for the change, as you
enter the deep maw for the tunnel, propelled by no oar but simply by

the deep stagnant flux of water, an amniotic lustreless soup on whose elastic back you, my dear Aunt, are seated. As you enter the eclipsed interior you will be aware of having entered as it were, the ganglionic processes of some giant bug; it sounds hardly reasonable, I know, but the idea will become accustomed to you. Face it. You are sitting in a black boat sailing down the arteries of the Minotaur itself. The walls, you notice, are not made of rock but of some dark fungoid plasm which trembles ever so lightly and exudes the rich teeming scent of musk. Their range of colour exhausts the spectrum; from the gold speck in the eye of the strawberry to the pigeon-violet seams which trace themselves in granite or Maltese marble. The surface of the chambers resembles the moist, horny palpitating skin which you have seen perhaps on the backs of toads. Ammonite, shale, dolerite: carbuncles and facets which blind. You will not be amazed by this time to find your body become dimensionless—without substance as if projected on the screen of some giant cinema. You are seeing with the X-ray eye now, dear Aunt Prudence: the eye which strips the features and traces the zygomatic arch, bores the hollow temples and observes the mastoid processes ticking like a watch: the eye which dissects the flaps of the abdomen and finds destiny curled up beside the liver like a clock-spring. You are seeing now as the butterfly sees who is pure of heart. It is the cataclysmic second-sight given to the blind.

If you are thirsty remember that the water is nourishing; the Stygian flux is warm, very faintly saline, and palatable. It crusts on the mouth, suggesting a heavy albumen content. It varies, also, at each stage of the journey, in colour. When you reach, for example, the endocrine network of caves, you will observe it thickening to the consistency of lava, boiling and sheeting, coughing up splashes of lymph and clots of arterial blood on the walls. But you have some way to go before you reach that point. The scenery is temperate and clarid for several light-years as yet; in the carotid tunnel you will become aware of a persistent drubbing on the sides of the boat, as of small rubber bladders. Lean over and stare down. At this point the bottom is clear and the infiltration of light will show you, to your surprise, that the water is crowded with small foetuses, for all the world like coloured fish. They will approach the boat in great playfulness and without suspicion. In fact they are quite tame. Notice the rudimentary gills. They long to speak to you, to say something, but in the present state of development can-

not. Therefore they signal by banging themselves against the bottom
of the boat

smiling the foetal smile and flirting their limbs in the luminous fluid.
They are tremendously amusing little fellows. You will be quite sorry
to pass them and enter the long tunnel of calcium where the temperature becomes suddenly quite polar and the air vaporous. On each side
lies a thick bank of frozen marrow, whose edges are warmed to a
squashy, musky thaw by the waters of the Styx; on these you will see
the eternal and amusing bacilli playing their careless games. They are
all dressed alike, resembling penguins, and stand about to watch the
barge pass, in little groups, hands behind their back, like financiers.
On the metatarsal promontory you will doubtless observe some scarlet-
fanned flamingoes, fishing ravenously for eel in the little backwater
where the discharge from the marrow-bank precipitates a little pool of
pus. The odour is not pleasant, dear Aunt Prudence, but there is
nothing to be done. You will pass this tunnel and enter the cardiac
whirlpool which smells of oil and makes a curious inaudible but regular
roar. On the right hand, sculptured it seems, hangs a huge and
brilliantly coloured vulva, like a sea-anemone magnified a thousand
times, holding to the walls by a terrific act of suction. A thick piston of
gristle agitates the walls of the cardiac monster and communicates a
thumping noise to the shaky barge. As you pass under the vast sticky
arch of pink integument be sure of putting up your umbrella, because
you will find yourself moving in a soft rain of blood and ashes. The
water is studded with violet fish, turtles, sperm whales at anchor, and
all varieties of *religious experience*. The barge drives its long black
furrow through them. By this time you will be weary of wondering if
this journey has a destination: the face of Charon is sphingine. Do not
ask, but fall asleep.

When you are awakened you find yourself in clear water, between
open banks, falling away from the river to a vast tortured skyline hung
in rags of cloud. It is so silent that your breathing sounds enormous,
noisy as a blacksmith's bellows. The boat goes so infinitely slowly that
you will have time to get off and examine this territory which is
without doubt the most interesting you have yet seen. It is a section of
the Tibetan colon; the silence, the utter cessation of being here will
explain itself when you examine the plants and trees which stud the
banks. *It is a mineral world.* It is a world calcined, petrified, shrunk

down to its elemental carbon. Now do you understand why there is no sound? You can no longer hear the sap moving in the trees, no longer hear the pulse-beats stirring the throat of the bird. You cannot hear the mole tunnelling, the blind worm chewing his pinshead of mud. They are all there—trees, birds, fruit, worms: but *mineral* now. The iris of the blackbird's eye is shaken with a rich moving lustre for which there is no musical expression; the worm is withered down to the colour of the prune. So silent is it that the white grapes in the vineyard gleam crystalline, like pearls; and the tree of the Forbidden Apple is clustered with enormous shining globes of trite slag. Here, if you look, you will see that every apple is an El Greco, every whale a Cézanne. Do not miss the boat wandering here in this enchanted world, for there are penalties. You will find yourself affected slightly even after a few moments spent here: you cough up fragments of diamond-dust and horsehair into your handkerchief. But do not be alarmed. It is only your liver which has been turned to speckled granite. Had you stayed longer you would have suffered a seachange. The light is strangely unvarying here, also: it is the light given off by spores of copper ore or freckled litharge in the bowels of the earth; it is consistent, even, polar: and contributes a mineral falsity to the fields and trees as of a lighted stage.

Well, my dear Aunt Prudence, there are many stages on this interesting journey, but I have not time or memory to describe them all to you. You will pass some time, of course, in the territory of the impregnable amnion; outside its walls you will observe the spermatozoa being trained for the great assault. Quaint shock-troops in their uniform of cellophane, their long pigtails which they use like a giant fin, dorsal, caudal and pectoral all in one. They develop enormous speeds and are famous for their audacity. In the schoolrooms you will see whole classes of them sitting at desks and learning the theory of tactics. They chant in unison the only lesson which is aural, and compulsory to master. You will be drugged by their steady repetition of the words: 'Doctor Livingstone, I presume. Doctor Livingstone, I presume, Doctor Livingstone, I presume.'

There is nothing in all this to cause you a moment's anxiety. But like all great journeys this also has an end; unlike most journeys however, this turns out to be a beginning. You are sailing down, dear Aunt, towards the great beginning of nothing, which is the ending of everything. You will hear your memory falling away little by little.

He lay in bed with you for forty years but his name you cannot recall: a rose by any other name. In the vegetable garden you could see him with his great thumbs lined with soft rank soil. He treads in your womb towards the hour of eight when the village clock chimes and the rain hisses among the taciturn statues. He is everywhere. But now it is *you* who are nowhere. Neither the memory nor the photograph impinges. The scalpel in one movement severs the ganglionic cords and you are deaf. Sit there primly in your Sunday clothes while the great black barge noses down into the abyss of gestation. He was a bone from your side but the apple was rotten. You cannot read the brass tablet in the village church where his identity is insisted upon. Dear Aunt Prudence, his name is engraved on the brooch and written in the hymnbook. He was a bookmarker in your life. Where is he now, on which side of what ledger-debit or credit, anode or cathode, electron or neutron? To these questions I can give you no answer. To the rest of the journey I can give you no card, no compass, no latitude, longitude, rainfall, humidity, curious isobars. The boat tilts now and enters the outskirts of the falls. You are in for great changes; I can say no more than that. You have been formed up suddenly into a great watery ball of anguished blood. The smell of civet pervades everything. Charon's face is outlined in the sharp red flares. *You are being swallowed.* This is a placental nightmare in which you are being carried through a solid filter of lochia; giant hairs, bald scabs, detached ulcers, wedding-rings, knucklebones, sets of carious teeth. It is a vast suffocating whirlpool where all this human garbage is being assembled together; the walls contract and expand, scarlet, purple, suffocating, distended. The eyeballs of horses choked with blood. A biological dementia in which the barge ploughs through these dripping walls of red sponge, hung with rags of tissue, goitres, stalactites of calcium, calculi. Aunt Prudence, with the hair-pins in her hat and the hymnbook in her fingers; Aunt Prudence, with the sebaceous cysts and the spinal anomalies.

The centrum itself is built of steel, with ribs of colossal girth, watertight bulkheads and a periscope with a magnification of eight. It resembles an enormous grenade. The walls are bathed in blood and mucus and are too hot to touch. You will find by this time that both Charon and the barge have disappeared. The problem of gaining admittance remains. What is inside nobody knows except myself.

Courage, Prudence, in the sight of the Lord; this is the chamber where the sight of the usually sightless is unsealed. This is the womb of the Minotaur, the abyss, the dining-room where in the person of your foetal self you can break the bread and partake of the first supper.

You will enter. You, the ghost of Prudence will enter, clean and shining like a knife-blade; you will enter like a sacred wafer between the lips of Christ. The walls will admit you. Inside you will stumble upon the body of a young boy, lying in a pool of blood. Paralysing beauty and silence. The lips hang there like cherries. The eyes are silent, behind their beautiful stone lids. He is the first-born. There will be nothing to say. Simply sit down beside him for a short rest, and absently begin to count the spokes of your umbrella. The worst is over. Trust in your inner ghost and be upright. Let me kiss you on the forehead and wish you Bon Voyage in the black barge, my dear. It is all I can do.

Your affectionate nephew,
Lawrence

Reflections on Travel

Published in the Sunday Times. *London. December 27, 1959.*

Almost every year, usually towards the autumn, I receive at least one such card from a returning traveller; its expressed disappointment carries more than a plaintive hint of reproach. 'Couldn't you have warned us that we'd find St. Juan (or Bevalo, or Kalamas) so very hot and dusty and full of our compatriots?' it always runs. Reading it with a sigh I always find myself wondering why nobody has compiled a Handbook of Hazards which might offset the flowery verbiage of the travel bureaux. For the truth is that with so much excellent travel writing being published, and with so many inducements held out to visit foreign parts, there is nevertheless no compilation to which one can turn for the naked and unvarnished truth about the smaller hazards. How simple if there were! One envisages a set of small guides, each devoted to a single country, which could forewarn and forearm intending travellers against every possible disenchantment. Thus one might turn to the letter D and read, under the section entitled 'Drainage, Main and Otherwise' a brief but truthful account of the lavatories to be encountered (three stars) in out-of-the-way spots like Macedonia or the Pyrenees; or under the sub-title 'Drinks', be advised that *vieux marc* and *slivovitz* alike are the only specifics against winds like the Provençal *mistral* or the Yugoslav *koshava*. Within these pages one would find the only way to deal with the Mediterranean affliction of high summer known to us all as 'tummy' (Egyptian, Greek or Naples tummy). A single tube of magic Entero-vioform (make a note of it) will enable one to throw off all grim forebodings about melons and grapes, unwashed salads, or those magnificent *cassata* ices which spell death in Naples to small children with nordic stomachs. Similarly, one would be advised to take witch-hazel against hornet stings or infected mosquito bites—so much stronger than the useless arnica preparations which one finds. . . . These may be trivia but what a help it would be to have them recorded! Guides of such a nature would at least prevent the traveller from making the elementary mistakes which, to judge by the autumn mail, he is still making. ('Couldn't you have said that Athens is a steam-bath in August?'—'Just back from Sicily. Never again. *Why* didn't you warn us?')

One sympathizes deeply, but what is to be done with people who are still in the habit of deciding at Christmas to run down to Nice for a little sunlight? Nothing. Just let them try it. To sit shivering in a draughty hotel without central heating during the short but ferocious winter season of the Côte d'Azur . . . why, one might as well be in Bournemouth. The pines in the Garden of Fragrance moan not more ghoulishly than the swaying palms on the Promenade des Anglais. Now if only they would wait until mid-March it would be quite a different story, for by then the weather has really begun to stabilize. The weather, yes, *but not the sea*. Disappointment with Nice usually drives these same blithe people to set off from the Piraeus on a sea-cruise in mid-March. Now there is a patch of good weather usually in late March when, for ten days or so, one imagines one is in high summer; calm seas, warm nights, blue days. . . . It is very deceptive. The Greeks call this little patch The Little Summer of Saint Demetrius. It is followed usually by a longish bout of north wind, high seas, cloud, thunder, hail, rain and often snow. So very often one finds oneself sea-bound in Heraclion or Leros for a spell with nothing better to do than to address yet another insulting postcard to me. (If only someone had *said*. . . .)

But if on the one hand we need a large and frank dictionary devoted to the hazards of travel, we also need something like a Year Book which would list, under the months of the year, the places which are worth time and money to visit. Professional tourism has tended to encourage the belief that travel belongs to certain seasons of the year, whereas the truth is that there is always *somewhere* which will answer the traveller's need at whatever time of the year. Such a book might prevent his going to Nice but it would also suggest that (unless he is an alpinist) the only truly stable winter climate is that of the North African coast, from Alexandria to Casablanca. Here he will find brisk, radiantly sunny days and cold nights. I can think of only one place towards the opposite shore of the Mediterranean which seems blessed with the same sort of stable winter. (Ischia, Corsica, Cyprus, Corfu: *never* before April and May.) But the two winters I spent in Rhodes were of a totally different kind, sunny, cold and dry. It was particularly interesting to notice also that the sea was warm, autumnal warm, and that one could bathe in January without turning blue. This is certainly not possible in other islands where I have resided. Perhaps these two winters were exceptional? It is hard to say. The inhabitants claim that winter is always like that in Rhodes, and certainly Tiberius (a great connoisseur of wintering spots) chose it for seven years for this reason.

My own contribution to such a Year Book would suggest North Africa for the heart of winter; mind you, for those who like myself do not ski or climb and yet who love snow once in a while, I would add in the margin the name of Slovenia, that little-known country which joins Yugoslavia to Austria. The little lake of Bled, for example, is an enchanting place to spend a snowbound winter. Nor is it less delectable in summer. But for the spring and summer I should think there is nothing to equal the Mediterranean. One could go island-hopping from April to the end of June, starting in Ischia and touching Sicily, Crete and Cyprus. But though I share the ordinary northerner's passion for heat, I think Athens and Stamboul should be avoided (no less than Naples) in August. This is the month to spend on a small Greek island with its permanent cool sea breezes, or among the foothills of the Lebanon, or in the Cévennes. But, of course, everyone will have his own preference. The point of such a Year Book would be that it would be constructed on the lines of a great anthology. Its contributors would range far and wide over Europe and Asia, giving us the fruit of their experience, season by season. Each month would offer the reader a bewildering choice of projects, often by his favourite writers; Mr. Connolly would advise him how to eat well, and where. Mr. Quennell would infect him with his own enthusiasm for landscape and history. Mr. Patrick Leigh Fermor would put him onto the only village in Crete where travellers are knocked down if they try to pay for their lodging and entertainment. . . .

Indeed, all the valuable information brought back year by year by our literary wanderers, and which peters away in memorable conversations or private letters . . . it would all be gathered there within the pages of one gigantic tome which would be as ubiquitously available as a telephone directory. Here one would be able to draw courage and instruction from travellers as various as Freya Stark, Sir Harry Luke and Gavin Maxwell. . . .

But as I write I realize that the project, however magnificent, is impossible of realization. Where is the publisher with enough vision and money to embark upon it? Where is the editor who could harness such a team of brilliant dissimilars and prevent his contributors from coming to blows over the relative merits of Greece, Italy or Syria? All might end in confusion and acrimony and letters to *The Times*.

Finally, where is the traveller to merit such a project? It is possible, too, that the true traveller (who is not a tourist) might scorn such a work, and with justice? For he will have realized that part of the adventure of travel resides in those unexpected disappointments and hardships such a work would be helping him to avoid. Let the tourist be cushioned against misadventure; but your true traveller will not feel that he has had his money's worth unless he brings back a few scars like that hole in his trousers which comes from striking Italian matches towards instead of away from oneself. No, the mishaps and disappointments only lend relief to the splendours of the voyage. Things should be left as they are, despite those sad autumn postcards.

Index

All books not otherwise attributed are by Durrell. Details of his writings and Durrelliana are given in the Bibliography by Alan G. Thomas appended to *Lawrence Durrell: A Study* by G. S. Fraser.